STUDIES IN MEDIAEVAL HISTORY

Edited by GEOFFREY BARRACLOUGH

Vol. VIII

STUDIES IN THE AGRARIAN HISTORY OF ENGLAND IN THE THIRTEENTH CENTURY

STUDIES IN MEDIAEVAL HISTORY

It is hoped that this Series, intended in the first place for students in the Universities, may help to bridge the gap between the textbooks and the learned monographs in which English and continental scholars of the present day are re-writing the story of the Middle Ages. Its object is less to furnish an outline of facts, than to introduce the student to major problems of interpretation.

1-2. Mediaeval Germany. *Essays by German historians, translated with an introduction by* G. BARRACLOUGH. *2nd imp.*, 1949, 2 *Vols. Introduction.* 12s. 6d. *net, Essays,* 21s. *net.*

3. Church, State and Christian Society at the time of the Investiture Contest. *By* G. TELLENBACH. *Translated by* R. F. BENNETT. *2nd imp.*, 1949, 18s. *net.*

4. Kingship and Law in the Middle Ages. *By* F. KERN. *Translated by* S. B. CHRIMES. *2nd imp.*, 1949, 18s. *net.*

5. In preparation.

6. Crown, Community and Parliament in the later Middle Ages. *By* GAILLARD T. LAPSLEY, 1951. 30s. *net.*

7. An Introduction to the Administrative History of Mediaeval England. *By* S. B. CHRIMES, 1952. 27s. 6d.

8. Studies in the Agrarian History of England in the Thirteenth Century. *By* E. A. KOSMINSKY. *Edited by* R. H. HILTON. *Translated from the Russian by* RUTH KISCH, 1956. 37s. 6d. *net.*

STUDIES IN THE
AGRARIAN HISTORY
OF ENGLAND
IN THE THIRTEENTH CENTURY

By E. A. KOSMINSKY

Member of the Academy of Science of the U.S.S.R.

Edited by R. H. HILTON

Lecturer in History, University of Birmingham

Translated from the Russian by
RUTH KISCH

KELLEY & MILLMAN, INC.
NEW YORK

Printed in Great Britain

PREFACE

IN my *English Village in the Thirteenth Century*, published in 1935, I summed up the results of my research on English agrarian history, some of which had already appeared in Soviet historical journals. In 1947, this work, revised and supplemented as a result of fresh research, was republished with its present, more suitable title, and is now offered (in a somewhat abbreviated translation) to the English reader.

It has not been my aim to give anything like a complete picture of the agrarian structure of medieval England. All that I wished to do was to illuminate certain questions which seemed to me to be particularly important for the understanding of English agrarian development. I mean such questions as types of manorial structure; the part played by free tenures; the divisions among the English peasantry (in particular with regard to the size of their holdings); the various ways in which the labour force on the thirteenth-century manor was exploited. I was also particularly interested in the special features of the small estate as compared with the big manors of the great (especially ecclesiastical) feudal lords. For the prevailing ideas about the manorial régime were based largely on a study of the big estate. It seemed to me, therefore, that a study of the small estate would advance our understanding of English medieval social and economic development.

I have used quite a limited group of sources in these studies, the most important being the Hundred Rolls of 1279. This material has never been the object of special study, although Vinogradoff pointed out as early as 1883 how important it was for the study of English social history. The special characteristics of the Hundred Rolls, which I have analysed in these studies, are such that they are particularly suitable for tackling the problems I have mentioned. In particular, they are irreplaceable for the study of the small estate. Furthermore this material enables us to use the statistical method over a considerable area. It will be noticed, however, that I use these

statistics without trusting them overmuch. Yet the problems
on which they shed light are hardly soluble by other means.

I have supplemented the information derived from the
Hundred Rolls by using the Inquisitions *post Mortem*. This is a
very difficult source to use, as well as being very unreliable.
Here again, with proper care the inquisitions can be made to
yield important information. Other sources, such as extents,
manorial court rolls, and ministers' accounts have only been
used on occasion as a check on the main sources. Other
documents, too, had their use—Domesday Book, for instance,
allows one to extend the chronological framework of one's
investigations; the records of the royal courts illustrate the
forms which the conflict between classes assumed in the
thirteenth-century village.

My work has been written on the basis of Marxist-Leninist
method, and in it I use Marxist terminology. Work done in
England by such Marxist historians as M. H. Dobb, R. H. Hilton
and C. Hill has already to some extent familiarized the English
reader with this terminology. Even so, I feel I must say more
about the meaning of certain fundamental terms.

I deal here with a number of problems of English feudalism.
Now by 'feudalism' Marxists mean a definite 'mode of pro-
duction' which was predominant throughout medieval Europe.
Its distinctive features were:

1. A special type of landed property which was directly linked
   with the exercise of lordship over the basic producers of
   society, the peasants, though of course with considerable
   variation in the degree to which that lordship might be
   exercised.
2. A special type of class of basic producers with a special
   connection with the land—which remained, however, the
   property of the ruling class of feudal lords.

It must, of course, be understood that the predominance of
the feudal mode of production—as in the case of all other
modes of production—was never 'absolute'. And so in thirteenth-century England we still see some survivals of pre-feudal
relations, remnants of the old free peasant communities. We
can also see germs of new relationships, signs of the developing

changes within feudalism towards a new mode of production—the capitalist—and with it the characteristics of new 'relations of production'. We can see these new relations when the basic producers appear as hired labourers, deprived of their land and of all means of production.

Feudal property achieves its economic realization in feudal rent—dues (of whatever form) which the dependent peasant hands over for the benefit of the feudal landowner. In a broad sense, feudal rent includes everything which the proprietor gets from the peasant. However, in most cases the sources reveal only the basic part of the rent, that which the peasant pays over, more or less related to the size of his holding, in labour, kind, or money.

The traditional organization for the appropriation of feudal rent is the feudal estate—the manor. But the manor assumed great diversity of type according to the form of rent predominant, resulting from local economic, historical or geographical conditions.

The classics of English economic history have given us an analysis of the typical large manor, based on servile labour rent. In my work I have been mainly concerned with phenomena which might be called 'non-typical'—with manors whose structure departs from the typical, with free holdings and free rents, with money rent, with the small estate, with hired labour (in the limited sense in which it is found in the feudal manor). But it is precisely in these 'non-typical' phenomena that we may see the germs of the new relations of production.

Of the reviews which the second edition of my book received, the most thorough is that of the well-known economic historian, Professor M. M. Postan, published in the *Economic History Review* for 1950. I think that this review most completely sums up the objections which my book might provoke among non-Marxist English historians. Therefore the preface to the English edition of my book seems to me the right place for a reply to this criticism.

Professor Postan makes very large demands of my book. Whilst this is very flattering, it opens a very wide field to criticism. Therefore from the very outset I should emphasize again that I have never claimed to offer an exhaustive, much less a 'classic' study of the history of the English countryside in the thirteenth century. I intended only to subject to critical review some of the problems which seemed important and at the same time incorrectly or insufficiently treated by previous historians. Hence when Professor Postan indicates a series of problems which I have not touched in my book, I can only answer that I did not set myself such broad aims. I shall be satisfied if I have cast new light on those problems to which I have consciously limited myself, and which seem to me to be important. My book does not deal with problems of agricultural technique, with the influence of climate and soil on the character of the economy, or with the relations between cultivation and live stock breeding. It does not deal with problems of demography, with forms of settlement, internal colonization, land hunger, and the struggle for land; it does not treat of the character of the market, the influence of price fluctuations and the value of money.

This list of problems which are not dealt with at all, or are only incidentally touched upon, could be further enlarged, but for their solution it would be necessary to write a completely new work.

The problem of the manorial system lies at the centre of my work. Professor Postan thinks that this problem is not so significant as was formerly believed. He considers that 'the manor is an established convention of Marxist historiography'. Here Professor Postan is incorrect. The manor is rather an 'established convention' of the classical school of bourgeois economic historians of the nineteenth and early twentieth centuries. The manor interests the Marxist historian only as the concrete form in which the productive relations of the feudal period (feudal property and the forms of exploitation flowing from it) are usually embodied. We see the manor not as an 'established convention', but as a real fact, characteristic of the medieval countryside, provided, of course, that one does not attribute to it the narrow significance which the classical school headed by Seebohm and Vinogradoff did. My aim, in fact, has been to show that over-simplification in this regard is misleading, and to reveal the extreme complexity of the manorial pattern characteristic of feudal England. But even taking account of all the additional problems which Professor Postan has indicated, the problems of feudal property and exploitation, of their emergence, development and decay, and of the concrete forms which these foundations of feudalism adopted, remain, as before, a central question in the history of feudal society.

The study of agricultural technique, demography, the market, prices, and the like, must not be allowed to distract us from this central problem or be substituted for it. I hope that I have succeeded in bringing greater precision to our conception of the manorial system. However, I am far from claiming that I have discovered something new when I refer to money rents, the differentiation of peasant allotments, and cottars. The existence of these factors has long been known. But it seemed worth while to define more closely the problems they raise. In particular, the question of the dominant form of rent remains unsolved, and disagreements on this point still exist among historians.

Of all the criticisms made by Professor Postan the most substantial seems to be that of the absence or inadequacy of chronological perspective. This criticism has often been made in the U.S.S.R. as well. In fact, the main source which I have used, the Hundred Rolls, relates to a specific year, 1279, and the other sources I have used also relate to approximately the same time. I refer to an eleventh-century source (Domesday Book) only occasionally, in order to make certain comparisons. Why, then, did I think it possible to base my conclusions on the study of this type of material? I have tried to answer this question in my book. I think that any moment in history contains elements of both the past and the future, and that the study of any particular moment sheds some light on both preceding and subsequent developments. But here I am concerned with answering the charge that as a result of an incorrect historical perspective I am tied by the conception of 'continuous movement away from the pure forms of natural economy and manorialized agriculture towards the freer and more capitalistic forms of economic life'.

I hope that I have made it clear in my book, that I in no way share this conception. If this was in fact the fundamental line of development in the Middle Ages, that is not to say that it was

a 'continuous' line. In the first place I am far from holding
over-simplified notions about the correlation between natural
economy and the manorial system. In a number of cases the
development of the market leads to the temporary strengthening of the 'manorial system', that is, of labour rents and serfdom.
I have emphasized more than once that the strengthening of
the manorial system, of labour rents and the exploitation of
the serfs, was a response to the development of market relations
in the thirteenth century. I think that the manorial system
was more developed in the thirteenth century than in the
eleventh or twelfth, and that, in fact, it then reached its apogee
in England. This primarily relates to the large manors of
the lay and ecclesiastical lords.

The small manor, on the other hand, as is shown by its
structure and the nature of its rents, evidently never attained
full development as a feudal manor, and adapted itself to the
requirements of the market by other methods which were a
definite step towards 'more capitalistic forms of economic life'.
A special chapter is devoted to this problem.

In the transition to more capitalist forms an important role
was played by peasant and especially large-scale peasant
economy. But I did no more than draw attention to this side
of the matter, since the break-up of the large feudal manor
and of the manorial system as a whole took place as late as
the fourteenth and fifteenth centuries, and therefore lies outside
my period of study.

Professor Postan also ascribes to me the view that the 'size'
of manors was the determining factor in their structure. He
refers to the contradictions to which this conception leads when
taken in conjunction with the conception of 'continuous development'. But since I do not support either of these theories I am
unable to observe in my conclusions the contradictions to which
Professor Postan refers.

The diversity in the structure of manors does not, of course,
depend only on their size. I am quite well aware (and I refer
to this fact) that considerable variations can be observed in the
structure of both large and small manors, and that the structure
of the manor and the type of economy adopted in it are determined not only by its size, but also by a number of other
conditions. These include the historical origin of the particular

manor, the predominance of pastoral or arable farming, the conditions of the market, the distance from the centre of the estates of the particular lord (this applies to both small and large manors), and the internal struggle taking place in the manor.

I merely pointed out that the typical 'serf-labour rent manor' is to be observed in the thirteenth century chiefly among large manors; as regards small manors, they manifest some peculiarities of structure, both in the relative size of the demesne and in the social composition of the peasantry and the nature of rent.

Changes in the general character of feudal economy, whether they make for the strengthening or for the weakening of the manorial system, are not necessarily accompanied by changes in the quantitative relation of large and small manors or in their average size, and Professor Postan is wrong in drawing this conclusion from my work. The strengthening of the manorial system in the thirteenth century was the result of the strengthening of labour dues in the large manors. I see no contradiction in the fact that the proportion of large and small manors did not undergo substantial change and that the average size of the manor remained approximately as before.

There is no over-simplification in holding that the lay and ecclesiastical magnates owned large manors and the small feudal lords owned small manors. I have made a special examination of this problem and have reached the conclusion that large manors are in fact concentrated on the estates of the great lords and small manors on the estates of the small lords. But I am well aware of exceptions, including the peculiarities of the estates of the Templars and the Hospitallers; nor do I ignore the special features of ecclesiastical estates, whether of the old or the new religious houses. But if the student should not simplify and schematize his material, he should also not lose sight of the fundamental guiding lines because variants exist.

In conclusion, I should note that Professor Postan, in his criticism, several times attacks the Marxist conception of historical development. It seems to me that these remarks spring from an over-simplified conception of Marxism, and often miss the point. As I have already noted, he is wrong in seeing in the manor an 'established convention of Marxist historiography'.

The divergence between us and the historical school to which Professor Postan belongs is, I think, rooted not so much in the evaluation of the historical role of the manor as in the denial by this school of features specific to the feudal mode of production as a whole.

The Marxist conception of a 'natural economy' is seen by Professor Postan in an over-simplified fashion. He says: 'The notion of the Middle Ages as a period of natural economy may still linger in Marxian writings, but has very few adherents elsewhere'. This is said in connection with my conclusions on the predominance of money rent in thirteenth-century England. But a natural economy is in no way conceived by Marxist historians in an over-simplified way, i.e. as consisting merely in the absence of a market and of money-circulation, or of money rent.

The exaggerated contrast between a 'natural' and a 'monetary' economy is a source of considerable theoretical errors, and is characteristic, not of Marxist, but of the crudest nineteenth-century bourgeois historiography. It provided a basis for the equally crude counter-assertions of Dopsch and his school. The Marxist conception is opposed to over-simplified views of either type. Exchange and money, and with them elements, too, of money rent appear at extremely early stages of development, during the predominance of a natural economy, i.e. an economy in which the product is produced not for sale, but directly for consumption. But certain surpluses over consumption can go for sale and become commodities. According to Marxism the opposite of a natural economy is not a 'monetary', but a 'commodity' or a 'commodity-monetary' economy, in which the product is produced as a commodity. Urban production in the Middle Ages was, from the very beginning, primarily of a commodity type. Agricultural production, predominant in the Middle Ages, gradually became more and more commodity production, though long preserving the basic features of natural economy. At the end of the medieval period, the dominance of *simple* commodity-production, already a transitional stage to capitalist production, was characteristic. Capitalist production only begins when labour-power is also transformed into a commodity. It should at the same time be noted that capitalist relations are gradually generated *within* the feudal mode of production.

Furthermore, money rent, according to Marx, is not at all a 'non-feudal rent'; it is only the last stage of development of feudal rent. Elements of it can appear very early, but its predominance already signifies the breakdown of the feudal mode of production. Marx makes a definite distinction between feudal money rent and capitalist rent, which has completely different economic characteristics and can only arise in capitalist society.

Professor Postan thinks that the conception of continuous development which he finds in my book, is characteristic of Marxism. As I have already stated, I do not adhere to this conception, and it is certainly foreign to Marxism. The transition from a feudal (or 'manorial') economy to 'more capitalistic forms' does not represent a direct line of development, and the growth of the market can, in certain circumstances, be accompanied by an intensification of feudal exploitation, as Marx showed.[1] The development of the productive forces, also, does not appear in the shape of a continuous progress. Here, too, halts and setbacks due to varying conditions both of a natural and, more often, of a social character are possible, while, quite often, the strength and duration of natural retarding factors are determined by social conditions. Professor Postan is wrong in thinking that a fatalistic faith in the automatic progress of mankind is a feature of Marxism; a faith in continuous evolution is even less characteristic.

If I succeed in completing my plans, I shall try to link the analysis of the *relations* of production in feudal England, which I have given in my book, with an analysis of the productive *forces* and trace, in the conditions of medieval England, the operation of the economic law of the necessary correspondence of the relations of production with the character of the forces

[1] *Capital*, Vol. i, 'The Greed for Surplus Labour. Manufacturer and Boyard'. Engels speaks of the same thing, calling it 'second serfdom'. Many Soviet scholars refer to this, for example, B. D. Grekov in his *Peasants in Rus*.

of production.[1] But this is a new, large, and complex task. The present book only partly carries out this theme.

However, I hope that I have succeeded in posing in a new way a number of questions of fundamental significance for the history of medieval society.[2]

ACKNOWLEDGMENTS

I should like to add a note to express my gratitude to my former teachers, Academician D. Petrushevsky and Professor A. Savine, under whose guidance I began my work on English agrarian history. I owe my thanks as well to many English scholars, some of them unhappily no longer with us—Dr. Hubert Hall, Professor Eileen Power and Miss E. Levett.

I enjoyed the constant help of my fellow-workers whilst I was at that incomparable repository of archives, the Public Record Office, and Professor Postan's knowledge of the English historians was of especial assistance in my work.

Finally, I must extend sincere thanks to Professor Barraclough, General Editor of the series *Studies in Medieval History* in which my book appears, to Dr. Hilton, the editor of this English version of my book, and to Miss Ruth Kisch, the translator.

[1] As formulated by J. V. Stalin in his last work, *Economic Problems of Socialism in the U.S.S.R.*

[2] I am very grateful to Professor Postan for the detailed analysis of my book. But I should like to point out certain of his inaccuracies. I have never asserted that 'leases of demesne among peasants became frequent as early as the beginning of Edward III's reign'. I spoke, of course, of the reign of Edward I. The upper limit of arable in small manors I considered to be not 100 but 500 acres. On pp. 263 and 367 of my book (Russian edition; or pp. 205-6 and pp. 296-7 below), there are no such assertions as those to which Professor Postan makes reference. But these, of course, are details.

EDITOR'S INTRODUCTION

EVGENY ALEXEYEVICH KOSMINSKY'S name is well known to historians of medieval England as the author of three articles published in the *Economic History Review* in 1928, 1931 and 1933.[1] The first of these deals with a theme often taken up by Kosminsky—the traditional interest shown by Russian scholars in English history; while the second two deal with the problems of thirteenth-century English agrarian history which are more fully examined in this book.

Kosminsky stands in the tradition of Vinogradoff, Savine and Petrushevsky and like them has been closely linked with the teaching of medieval history in Moscow from the date of his graduation in 1915 in the Faculty of History and Philosophy at the University. His research and teaching at various historical institutes culminated in 1934 in his appointment as head of the department of medieval history at Moscow University, a post he held until 1949. At the same time (1936–52) he was head of the medieval section of the Institute of History of the Academy of Sciences of the U.S.S.R. He was also, for a period, in charge of a group in this Institute which was concerned with the promotion of Byzantine studies. In 1939 Kosminsky became a corresponding member, and in 1948 a full member of the Academy of Sciences of the U.S.S.R., the highest academic honour in the country. Much of his activity of late has been curtailed through ill-health, but it is characteristic that he should have been chosen in 1952 to be editor-in-chief of the journal *News*, devoted to a cause dear to his heart, the furthering of understanding between his own country and the English-speaking world.

In addition to making his own contribution to historical knowledge Kosminsky has been responsible for the formation of a younger generation of medievalists. The strong bent of these younger historians towards English history may be seen in the pages of the periodical *The Middle Ages*[2] and in the new

---

[1] *Economic History Review*, vols. i, iii and v.
[2] Issued by the Institute of History of the Academy of Sciences of the U.S.S.R. Four volumes have so far appeared.

History of the English Revolution, a work of collaboration between Kosminsky and some of his pupils.

If Kosminsky continues a great Russian historical tradition, he does not mark time in the footprints of his predecessors. Whilst appreciating their contribution he also criticizes their conclusions, not only because of the appearance of fresh evidence, but also from the theoretical standpoint. Kosminsky is a Marxist, while his predecessors were not.

It is not necessary either to be a Marxist or to have an extensive knowledge of the Marxist historical method to appreciate Kosminsky's work. However, the writings of Kosminsky and his school can be better understood if one has some acquaintance with its approach and terminology. The author, in his preface, has endeavoured to explain some of the terms he uses, and occasional editorial footnotes attempt further clarification. It may also be useful to indicate here some of the most important sources of Kosminsky's method, particularly some Marxist writings which are not widely known in this country.

* * *

The first volume of Marx's *Capital*, and especially its historical chapters, is clearly very important in the formation of the theoretical background of Marxist historians. It has been well known to English students for many years, as have a number of other expository works dating from what may be called the first period of the elaboration of Marxist theory.[1] On the other hand the third volume of *Capital*, edited by Frederick Engels and published posthumously, is much less well known outside Marxist circles though its importance in the development of the Marxist historical method is considerable. It contains two historical chapters of great interest. These are Chapter XX, entitled 'Historical Data Concerning Merchants' Capital', and Chapter XLVII, entitled 'Genesis of Capitalist Ground Rent.' Briefly their argument is as follows. In the first, Marx analyses the part played by merchant capital in historical development, with critical implications for the theory in vogue in his day, and since, that it was the develop-

---

[1] Such as the *Manifesto of the Communist Party* (1848) by Marx and Engels; Marx's *Introduction to the Critique of Political Economy* (1859); Engels' *Anti-Dühring* (1877) and *Ludwig Feuerbach* (1886); and other lesser Works.

ment of international trade and the accumulation of money
capital that brought about the disintegration of feudal, and
the rise of capitalist, society. The second contrasts what Marx
calls 'feudal rent' (whether in labour, in kind, or in money)
with capitalist ground rent. According to Marx, the level of
feudal rent is determined by the degree of non-economic
compulsion which the landlords, because of their ownership
of the land and their political power, can exercise against the
peasant producers. The level of capitalist ground rent, on
the other hand, depends only partly on the landlord's monopoly
and mostly on the general level of capitalist profit.

It is a fairly widely held misconception that Marx was little
interested in the peasantry. His earliest political battles had
been in defence of the common rights of the Rhenish peasantry,
and towards the end of his life he became very interested in
the revolutionary potentialities of the Russian peasants. Even
so, it was primarily the Russian Marxists who developed the
theoretical analysis (from the general Marxist standpoint) of
the peasantry as a class in feudal and capitalist society. It
was a practical political problem for them. Although they
opposed the peasant utopianism of the Populists (the Narod-
niki) in order to emphasize the importance of the small but
highly concentrated industrial proletariat, they could not
ignore the fact that Russia was primarily a peasant country.
It was essential for them to explore peasant society, and to
examine the social and economic tensions in the Russian
village which would make revolutionaries of some peasants
and reactionaries of others.

This was a problem which V. I. Lenin studied a great deal
in the early days of the Marxist movement in Russia. His two
chief works on the subject were 'The Development of Capitalism
in Russia' and 'The Agrarian Problem in Russia at the End
of the Nineteenth Century'.[1] Based on official statistical
material, his analysis owes much to the chapters in the third
volume of *Capital* already mentioned. Since conditions in the
Russian countryside, even after the liberation of the serfs,
were amazingly medieval in many ways, it is natural that
Soviet historians in approaching medieval English agrarian
history should have the history of their own peasantry in mind.

[1] Lenin, *Selected Works* (English Edition), i.

b

And in view of the great prestige of Lenin as a theoretician of Marxism, we must add these two books to our list of works which must be considered of importance in the formation of the historical school to which Kosminsky belongs. The reader will see for himself what analogies Kosminsky feels able to draw between the history of the Russian and of the English peasantry.

The foregoing remarks do not aim to be in any way comprehensive as a presentation of the theoretical bases of the Soviet historical school, but the English reader who wishes to understand a little more about the background of the Soviet medievalists would be well advised to consult the works mentioned.

*   *   *

The conclusions at which Kosminsky has arrived as a result of his detailed study of the Hundred Rolls of 1279 are already well known in outline to English historians from the articles already referred to. The importance of their contribution can be appreciated if one notes the references to them in most works dealing with the medieval English social structure that have appeared since their publication. The importance of this present book is, of course, partly in the extra material which it contains. But for the English reader it will have an additional interest. The author's method of inquiry is one which has been little used in medieval studies in this country; and the author fully explains the application of his method to the reader during the course of the inquiry.

The novelty of Kosminsky's method is neither in his use of statistics nor in the choice of questions which have been put to the material, but rather in a combination of the two. Such statistics as we find in most contemporary medieval agrarian studies are not in the same class as those used by Kosminsky, for the tables illustrating the growth of estate economy (the most characteristic subject of study to-day) are based on comparatively scanty data. However, we must note that it was one of our own greatest medievalists who stated the case for the use of what our author calls 'mass statistics'. Referring to Domesday Book, F. W. Maitland wrote: 'Far be it from us to say that microscopic labour spent

upon one county or one hundred is wasted; often it is of the
highest value; but such work is apt to engender theories which
break down the moment they are carried outside the district
in which they had their origin. Well would it be if the broad
features of Domesday Book could be set out before us in a
series of statistical tables.'[1]

Kosminsky has done precisely this, for the only source for
English agrarian history in the medieval period which can be
compared with Domesday Book. He has corrected impressions
derived from microscopic labour, spent not so much on one
county or one hundred as on the individual large estate. He
has shown that theories based on the most conscientious and
meticulous examination of the documents of the large baronial
or monastic estate can also break down the moment they are
carried, not to another country, but to other forms of property,
such as the small estates of rich peasants or small knights, in
the very same district. The statistical analysis of the manorial
structure, forms of rent and availability of labour on hundreds
of these small estates throughout the Midlands is one of Kosminsky's chief contributions to English economic and social
history.

Another important feature of Kosminsky's work, distinguishing it from many previous writings, is the treatment of the
problem of rent. The emphasis on rent is not simply due to a
more or less arbitrary selection for special attention of one
among a number of important topics. It results from the
conception that in the payment of rent are embodied the
essential features of the social relations between the two basic
classes of feudal society—landlords and peasants. We must
bear in mind that for our author, 'feudal rent' in the Middle
Ages is analogous to 'surplus value' in capitalist society. It
represents the maximum amount of their product, surplus to
the subsistence and reproduction (i.e. re-investment) needs
of the peasant household, which the landlord can extract from
the peasants at any given time.

'Feudal rent' is not necessarily everything that is left after

[1] *Domesday Book and Beyond*, 467. The reader will see that Kosminsky has studied
Maitland carefully. But he has, of course, other precedents in the use of the
statistical method in agrarian history, such as the works of Lenin mentioned above,
and the work of I. I. Granat, the Russian historian, critically discussed below,
pp. 208-11.

*b**

the peasant has fed and clothed himself and his family, and provided seed, stock and implements for the next cycle of production. Custom and peasant resistance can reduce the amount that the individual landlord, or the state representing the landlord class as a whole, can obtain. Furthermore all manner of circumstances can determine the form in which the rent is paid, whether in labour, produce, or money. Again, the position of different peasant groups *vis-à-vis* the landlord, may be strengthened or weakened in different degrees according to the form rather than the amount of rent. Hence, a commutation of labour services for money is to the advantage of the well-to-do peasant who wants to increase production for the market, but not to that of the middling peasant concerned only with subsistence. In Kosminsky's view, the period of the Hundred Rolls was one in which—in spite of the prevalence of money rent—the level of feudal rent in general was very high. But his conception of landlord-peasant relationships is not over-simplified. The book demonstrates the very great diversity in the level and the forms of rent at the time of the compilation of the Hundred Rolls; and were he to carry the story further he would show how considerably the level of rent was affected by the temporary tipping of the balance of social forces in favour of the peasants, especially after 1381.

The peasant rising of 1381 occupies a prominent position in Kosminsky's conclusion, in spite of the fact that it occurred a century after the period about which the book is mainly concerned. Since the author's conception of feudal rent necessarily includes a conception of social conflict, it is natural that he should project his examination of the rural class struggle forward to this formidable expression of it. But this is not the only aspect of his interest in the rising to which we should draw attention. There is also a more general feature of the interpretation of history to which Kosminsky subscribes which is worth noting, the refusal to separate the economic from the social and political sides of historical development. Thus, the successful increase of rents obtained by landlords in the thirteenth century was an aspect of the general increase in their political and social power. The fall in rents in the later Middle Ages was due to political and social action by the peasants in defence of their interests.[1] Kosminsky does not discount the more impersonal elements of economic development (such as the supply of and demand for the various factors of production), but lays much greater stress than do most contemporary economic historians on the human factor, in the sense of the more or less conscious pursuit of social aims by the principal contending classes. For this reason, the expression of aims in the Smithfield and Mile End programmes is seen as the crystallization of peasant ideas after two centuries of minor conflict over issues connected with attempts to increase feudal rent.

Finally, we must draw attention to the treatment in the book of the key problem of labour supply. Among the best sources for an exact estimate of the relative amounts of servile and wage labour in the thirteenth century are the annual accounts of manorial bailiffs. Kosminsky does not use this source to a great extent, although he employs the accounts of some of the Earl of Norfolk's manors as a check on his principal sources. But the estate accounts, in spite of their detail and precision, do not allow that wide comparison of labour problems on estates of different size and structure which the author aims to achieve. Hence his most important conclusions about the employment of wage labour on the properties of peasants and small landowners are drawn by inference from calculations from the Hundred Rolls concerning the inadequacy of labour services.

It will be noticed that Kosminsky introduces an element in his discussion of labour problems which is perhaps new to many English readers. This is the question of the extent to which medieval wage labour was subject to non-economic compulsion. If the growth of a body of propertyless wage labourers, free to sell their labour power in any market, is a necessary prerequisite for the development of the capitalist mode of production, the extent to which labourers *were* free to sell their labour power will be of considerable importance. The same non-economic compulsion that was used by the landlords in obtaining rent was exercised against wage-

---

[1] This fall in rents is not, as some historians seem to imagine, incompatible with vast accumulations of wealth by certain families. These efforts at concentration were probably caused by the *crise des fortunes seigneuriales*, which was not confined to England.

workers in so far as many of them were recruited from servile families and subject to the legal disabilities of villeinage. These features of pre-capitalist wage labour affect the mobility of labour, rates of wages, and so on, and Kosminsky naturally has to concern himself with these matters when discussing embryo capitalist forms on the estates of the small landowners.

*   *   *

In the Russian edition of this book, the author's introduction and the first chapter dealt with the bibliography of the subject and with some of the general problems of English agrarian history. Since it was necessary, for the English edition, to economize on space, it was decided with regret that these would be the most suitable parts of the book to omit, particularly since the argument was directed to the Soviet rather than to the English student.

R. H. H.

June 1955

CONTENTS

CHAPTER I

CHAPTER II

CHAPTER V

CHAPTER VI

MAIN ABBREVIATIONS USED

Br. Ac.	British Academy, *Records of the Social and Economic History of England and Wales.*
C. Glouc.	*Historia et Cartularium monasterii Sancti Petri Gloucestriae,* Rolls Series, 3 vols. (1867).
C. Ram.	*Cartularium monasterii de Rameseia,* Rolls Series, 3 vols. (1884).
D.B.	*Domesday Book,* Record Commission, 4 vols. (1783–1816).
Ec. H. R.	Economic History Review.
E.H.R.	English Historical Review.
I.P.M.	Inquisitiones post Mortem (in Public Record Office).
M.A.	Ministers' Accounts (in Public Record Office).
N.B.	*Bracton's Note Book,* ed. F. W. Maitland, 3 vols., London (1887).
O.S.S.L.H.	*Oxford Studies in Social and Legal History,* ed. P. Vinogradoff.
Pl. Abbr.	*Placitorum Abbreviatio, Rich. I–Edw. II,* Record Commission (1811).
Pollock and Maitland	Pollock and Maitland, *History of English Law,* I and II, 2nd edition (1898).
P.Q.W.	*Placita de quo warranto,* Record Commission, 4 vols. (1818).
P.R.O.	Public Record Office.
R.H.	*Rotuli Hundredorum,* Record Commission, 2 vols. (1812–1818).
R.H. (War.)	P.R.O. Miscellaneous Books, Exchequer K.R., Series I, No. 15 [Warwickshire Hundred Rolls].
Rot. Parl.	*Rotuli Parliamentorum,* Record Commission I–III, (1767).
S.S.	Publications of the Selden Society.
Stats.	*Statutes of the Realm,* I, II, Record Commission (1810, 1816).
T.E.	*Taxatio Ecclesiastica Angliae et Walliae auctoritate papae Nicholai IV,* Record Commission (1811).
T.R.H.S.	Transactions of the Royal Historical Society.
V.E.	*Valor Ecclesiasticus,* Record Commission (1810–1834).

STUDIES IN THE AGRARIAN HISTORY OF ENGLAND IN THE THIRTEENTH CENTURY

CHAPTER I

REVIEW OF THE SOURCES

NO other country can compare with England in its fund of sources for the study of agrarian history, both printed and unprinted. Of these sources, we shall choose those which are most suitable for our purpose—mass statistical calculations covering large areas.

I

MANORIAL RECORDS

Manorial documents are the most important for the agrarian history of the thirteenth century, and of these we must first mention the manorial surveys or extents, and the records of the manor courts.

Manorial surveys, usually based on the depositions of the most respected, that is, the most prosperous peasants, give a detailed catalogue of free and servile holdings on the manor, with all their dues. The demesne land is often described as well. Although the term 'extent' (*extenta, extentum*) presupposes that tenants' dues and income from demesne are given in money,[1] the term is commonly applied to all surveys of this type, whether or not they include monetary assessments of revenue and dues.

Court rolls contain short accounts of all cases heard in manor courts, some indication of fines and amercements paid to the lord, the decisions of manorial juries, and the occasional record of rulings under manorial custom. They abundantly illustrate the inner life of the manor, its customs, and many aspects of

[1] Cf. R. V. Lennard, 'What is a manorial extent?', *E.H.R.*, xliv (1929).

everyday existence.   They are a unique source of information
about the never-ending class struggle which filled the daily
life of the manor's inhabitants.

These two types of document formed the main material for
the description of life on the classical manor, as found in the
works of Seebohm, Vinogradoff and Petrushevsky.   But from
the end of the nineteenth century specialists more and more
concentrated on a third source—ministers' accounts.   These
include the annual accounts rendered by reeves and bailiffs of
all manorial income and expenditure, in both money and
produce.   They also include a statement of all labour services
owed, whether rendered as such or replaced by money payments.   An analysis of these accounts gives particularly valuable
results when there is not one separate account, but a whole
series covering a number of years.[1]   No other source can illustrate in such detail the links between the demesne and the
market, the commutation of labour services for money, or the
expenditure in the maintenance of the demesne economy.   But
these accounts must be used carefully.   Separate items both of
income and expenditure often combine different elements
without apparent reason, demanding careful analysis.   For
example, fixed payments made by free and villein tenants are
usually confused under the single heading *Redditus Assisae*.

Another important source of manorial origin is contained in
the instructions to reeves and bailiffs regarding demesne
administration and the keeping of accounts.   Such instructions
often shed light on a problem about which other sources are
vague—the life of the lord's household and the part played in it
by the unfree house and farm servants.

The sources so far mentioned have one common feature: they
are all of manorial origin and depict the life of the manor
from the standpoint of the demesne economy and manorial
administration.   This determines both their strong and their
weak points.   Sources of this kind only exist in sufficient
abundance for the large church estates and to a lesser degree
for lay estates, mostly in the south and east of England.
Complex and accurate accounts and court rolls only existed,
generally speaking, in the establishments of large estate

[1] Important studies based on analyses of series of accounts include A. E.
Levett, 'Black Death on the Estates of the See of Winchester', *O.S.S.L.H.*, v,
(1916); F. Davenport, *Economic Development of a Norfolk Manor* (1906).

owners—or of such as had adopted forms of monetary accountancy. These sources, in fact, show us how things worked in the large feudal, and especially in the church estates, of southern and eastern England. They shaped the older studies upon which current conceptions of the 'classical' manor are based.

DEEDS

A very rich and by no means fully utilized source consists of deeds, some in the original, others collected in cartularies. They deal with gifts, land sales, divisions of property, bequests, and court decisions on land ownership, among other topics. They contain valuable information about the composition of estates, about rents, tenures, and forms of alienation, as well as agrarian conditions. They are especially valuable since they are not confined to any one type of landed property, as in the case of documents of manorial origin. The studies of Gray, Stenton, and Douglas, based principally on this type of material have yielded important results in the study of local agrarian conditions.[1]

GOVERNMENT RECORDS

Next, we must consider materials of government origin: surveys, court cases, legal treatises, legislation, and so on. Their abundance illustrates the large part—by comparison with continental Europe—played by the state in feudal England, and the Domesday survey of 1086 is but an early example of such documents. The activity of royal commissions and itinerant justices increased under the Angevin kings, and financial and legal inquiries served to create a class of records of great importance for agrarian history. Among these, pride of place goes to the Hundred Rolls, especially those of 1279. These form a cadastral survey far superior to Domesday Book in detail and accuracy. Surveys for taxation assessment are also of great significance, in particular for the evidence they provide of social stratification within the villages. The group also includes surveys for special purposes, such as those made

[1] H. L. Gray, *English Field Systems* (1915); F. M. Stenton, 'Types of Manorial Structure in the Northern Danelaw', *O.S.S.L.H.*, ii (1910); D. C. Douglas, 'The Social Structure of Medieval East Anglia', *ibid.*, ix (1927). Deeds are, of course, the basic source for the pre-Conquest period, but this is not under consideration here.

when estates fell into the king's hands on confiscation or because of the death of a tenant-in-chief (*inquisitiones post mortem*). We should mention here the accounts rendered by the crown officials in charge of such estates. A group of surveys also worthy of mention is that of church estates and church revenues made several times during the thirteenth century, the most important being the *Taxatio Ecclesiastica* of Pope Nicholas IV (1291).[1]

Legal records are an abundant source for the history of agrarian relations in the thirteenth century, of which a good sample are the *Placita de Quo Warranto*.[2] To these legal records we should also add the records of court cases made by practising lawyers, known as the Year Books. Court cases reveal many aspects of the class struggle, particularly the struggle between lords and peasants. This source is, of course, very important for the study of Wat Tyler's rising, but has also been used by E. F. Jacob in his picture of the class struggle at the time of the Barons' Wars, and by R. H. Hilton in his study of the class struggle in the English village in the thirteenth and fourteenth centuries.[3]

Legal treatises based on court practice express the point of view of authoritative jurists of the period on a number of problems concerned with agrarian relations.[4] Historians have long used these works, and their use has raised a number of complicated problems concerning the relation between legal theory and reality. Agricultural treatises, too, are of great interest, especially the best known of them, that of Walter of Henley.[5]

To finish this cursory sketch of the main sources for English agrarian history in the Middle Ages we must mention legislative enactments and literary sources. Of the former, the Statutes of Merton, Westminster II, *De Viris Religiosis*, and *Quia Emptores* are most significant for the thirteenth century; and enactments

---

[1] *Record Commission* (1802).   [2] *ibid.* (1818).
[3] E. F. Jacob, 'Studies in the Period of Baronial Reform and Rebellion', *O.S.S.L.H.*, viii (1925); R. H. Hilton, 'Peasant Movements in England before 1381', *Ec.H.R.*, 2nd ser., ii, 2 (1949). *Bracton's Note Book* (ed. F. W. Maitland, 1887) is an important source of the type under discussion.
[4] E.g. Glanville, *De Legibus et consuetudinibus regni Angliae*, ed. G. E. Woodbine (1932); Bracton, *De Legibus et consuetudinibus Angliae*, ed. T. Twiss (1878–83); *Fleta seu commentarius Juris Anglicani*, ed. J. Selden, 2nd edition (1685); 'The Mirror of Justices', *S.S.*, vii (1893).
[5] *Walter of Henley's Husbandry*, ed. E. Lamond (1890).

such as those connected with the regulation of labour become abundant in the fourteenth century. Of the latter, chronicles, literary works and political tracts provide information on agrarian matters and especially details of everyday life which cannot be found in other sources.

EVALUATION OF SOURCES

Our choice of sources is determined by the tasks we have set ourselves. For their accomplishment we require information on a massive scale which will enable us to extend our knowledge beyond the limits of the large (usually ecclesiastical) manor. Although manorial extents are concrete and detailed, and although court rolls and bailiffs' accounts are rich in information about everyday matters, they are limited and one-sided. Hence, to begin with, we must turn to the more summary government surveys, which cover a wider field and are of large-scale application. Among these we must assign first place to the Hundred Rolls of 1279. This was the source which troubled Seebohm because of its complications and confusion; drew Vinogradoff's attention to the importance of the free tenants of the manor; and provided Maitland with the basis for his attack on the 'classical' conception of the manor.

As early as 1883 Vinogradoff drew attention to the first-rate importance of the Hundred Rolls of 1279 for the social history of England, setting them on a level with Domesday Book.[1] Yet, although Domesday Book already has a whole literature of its own, no one has dealt specifically with the Hundred Rolls of 1279, although their thoroughness and detail, and the possibility of checking and supplementing them from other contemporary sources, promise much more precise and valuable results than those extracted with such difficulty from the famous eleventh-century record. The reason for this neglect lies, without doubt, in the fact that, whereas Domesday Book towers high above the other scanty sources for the eleventh century, the Hundred Rolls are overshadowed by a quantity of more 'live', detailed and concrete material, the bias or one-sidedness of which is not at first sight apparent. Furthermore, the 1279 Hundred Rolls cannot compare with Domesday Book in territorial scope. They are only a fragment; but the fragment

[1] *Athenaeum*, 1883.

is a very large one, taking in more than 700 centres of habitation in an almost unbroken band from Suffolk to Oxfordshire.

An investigation based upon such a source will not, of course, give an exhaustive answer to the problems of the structure of the English village in the thirteenth century, but it will lay a solid foundation for such an answer. Precisely because it is a large-scale survey executed at one time and composed on a uniform plan, it affords a number of advantages which are practically never present when work is done on scattered sources emanating from different places and different periods. It provides a guarantee against the one-sidedness which commonly results from deliberate selectivity. The Hundred Rolls describe, cheek by jowl, church and lay estates, large and small estates, typical manors, and agrarian structures such as can scarcely be called manors at all. For very many estates they are the only source of information. Furthermore, all parts of the survey were carried out at the same time, which is a safeguard against the inclusion in one picture of features peculiar to different phases or periods. The very nature of the survey, its division into hundreds and counties, stresses local peculiarities and guards against their obliteration. Lastly, and most important of all, a survey of this kind permits the employment of statistical methods.

The region covered by the Hundred Rolls of 1279 is very well defined. It is the area of the Upper Thames, the Ouse and the Avon—one of the most fertile areas of England, with a good system of waterways, a predominantly arable region. The localities described by that part of the survey that chance has preserved for us are thus similar in character, and we must be careful not to apply observations and conclusions drawn from this material to areas or places with different characteristics. This is the region of arable farming, of serfdom, of the stubborn survival of labour dues. Here were entirely favourable conditions for a full development of the manorial system.

In order to extend my study beyond the area covered by the 1279 Hundred Rolls, I have drawn upon one further source—a source already used by Gray for the study of the vicissitudes of feudal rent in England. I refer to the *Inquisitiones post Mortem*, which provide a vast series of surveys of the estates of lay vassals of the king beginning in the thirties of the thirteenth

century. These allow us to carry our observations a little
further back in time and to broaden them to cover practically
the whole of England. I have studied more than four hundred
manorial surveys appended to the inquisitions of Henry III's
time and of the early part of Edward I's reign. They are one
of the most difficult sources, and to approach them without
due criticism is dangerous. But it does permit us to lay bare
a number of features which cannot be described by any other
means. It will help us to place the conclusions we reach on
the basis of a study of the Hundred Rolls in their proper setting
within a wider and more generalized picture.

2

The Hundred Rolls

Under the general name of Hundred Rolls, *Rotuli Hundredorum*, there are preserved in the Public Record Office a number
of sources close to one another in both time and content.[1]
The most important of these are: (i) the inquiries by itinerant
justices in the thirty-ninth year of Henry III's reign, into the
feudal rights of the crown, and of private individuals and into
the state of the royal forests; these have been preserved, in
fragmentary form, for five counties; (ii) the investigations
by the special commissions of the second and third years of
Edward I's reign (1274–75) into the feudal rights of the
crown, their usurpation by private individuals, the feudal
rights of the great lords, and, in particular, into abuses of
power by the king's officials; these have been preserved *in toto*,
or in later extracts, for almost all counties; (iii) the inquiries
which interest us, that is, the inquests of 1279 (7–8 Ed. I.).

The *Rotuli Hundredorum* were published by the Record Commission in two volumes (1812 and 1818), but their edition
cannot be treated as final. For the 1279 survey it gives, in
whole or in part, the descriptions of the hundreds of Willey
and Stodden in Bedfordshire; Mursley, Banstow, Stodfold
and Mucha, and the borough of Marlow, in Buckinghamshire;
almost the whole of southern Cambridgeshire (the Isle of Ely
is missing), viz., the town of Cambridge, the 'suburb' of

[1] See H. M. Cam, *The Hundred and the Hundred Rolls* (1931); and the same
author's 'Studies in the Hundred Rolls', *O.S.S.L.H.*, vi (1921).

Barnwell, the hundreds of Chesterton, Chilford, Flendish, Northstow, Papworth, Staine, Staploe, Longstow, Thriplow, Wetherley and Whittlesford (the hundreds of Cheveley and Radfield in the east, and Armingford in the south-west are missing). The survey of practically the whole of Huntingdon-shire is extant (the hundreds of Hirstingstone, Leightonstone, Normancross and Toseland, and the town of Godmanchester), and almost the whole of Oxfordshire—the hundreds of Bampton, Banbury, Bullington, Chadlington, Dorchester, Ewelme, Langtree, Lewknor, fragments of the survey of the town of Oxford, the hundreds of Pirton, Thame, Ploughley, Wootton, and the royal demesne of Woodstock; the hundreds of Bloxham in the north and Binfield in the south are missing.[1] Altogether the surveys of about 640 centres of habitation have been published in whole or in part. Among the Miscel-laneous Books of the Exchequer in the Public Record Office there is a volume of 120 pages, discovered by Vinogradoff, which contains a copy of the survey for the two Warwickshire hundreds of Stoneleigh and Kineton, bringing in about 110 more inhabited places. In the Cambridge Public Library and in the British Museum, in two old registers which belonged to the abbey of Bury St. Edmunds, Powell discovered copies of the survey dealing with eight Suffolk hundreds. Although these copies are headed *De itinere Salomonis Roffensis et sociorum suorum anno regni regis Edwardi filii Henrici III incipiente XV* (i.e. 1286–87), Powell succeeded by means of a comparison with the inquisitions *post Mortem*, in establishing beyond doubt that the actual date is about 1280, and that we therefore probably have here a copy of the 1279 survey. The copies in this case are not full; only those parts of the survey are given which the monastery saw fit to record for its own purposes. In some cases, however, places are included which have nothing to do with the abbey's estates. There are also omissions

---

[1] Giuseppi in his *Guide to the Public Records*, 1, 340–42, points out that not all the Oxfordshire and Cambridgeshire surveys have been printed. He refers also to two unpublished documents which contain a survey of Middlesex. But these documents, in fact, have nothing to do with the 1279 survey. For Oxfordshire, there is a short survey of the borough of Banbury which has not been published. For Cambridgeshire, a small fragment of the survey of the hundred of Northstow (it can hardly be deciphered), and the survey of the village of Dullingham in the hundred of Radfield, remain unpublished.

and abbreviations.[1] In any case we do not have more than one-tenth of the whole survey. There also exists a copy of a shortened survey of the Leicestershire hundreds of Guthlaxton and Gartree, made by the early seventeenth-century antiquary, William Burton. This shortened version was probably made at the Exchequer from the 1279 survey.[2]

BACKGROUND OF THE 1279 SURVEY

The 1279 investigation belongs to the period of intensified royal activity, after the end of the troubles of the latter years of Henry III's reign and following the accession of his son. In October 1274 a number of commissions were appointed to investigate the loss and destruction of royal rights owing to the troubles of the preceding reign and the dislocation of local government.

Surveys of this sort were nothing new in English practice. The crown made wide use of inquests by juries, and the same method was used by feudal lords for their own purposes; and it is possible, as Brunner, Maitland, H. M. Cam and others have argued, that the practice may have derived from that of the Frankish kings. Domesday Book is a monumental example of such a survey; but it is not an isolated one, and should be set alongside a multitude of other inquests, stretching in unbroken succession from the time of the Norman Conquest. As the functions of the monarchy, especially the administration of justice and of finance, became wider and more involved, they gave a further impulse to the development of such investigations. The royal revenues, and the rights connected therewith, are their principal subject. Landed property and the payments made by vassals, and above all the question of franchises, are the things which interest the king, matters which, in the past had been investigated both by special commissioners and justices on eyre.

In Bracton we find a catalogue of the *Capitula Itineris*, that is, of the questions committed for investigation to the justices

---

[1] Part of this document was published by E. Powell, *A Suffolk Hundred in 1283* (1910). It is printed in full in *The Pinchbeck Register*, ed. Lord Francis Hervey, ii, 30–282 (1925). See also D. C. Douglas, 'Feudal Documents from the Abbey of Bury St. Edmunds', *Br.Ac.*, viii (1932).

[2] See R. H. Hilton's essay in *Studies in Leicestershire Agrarian History*, ed. W. G. Hoskins (1949).

on eyre. Bracton notes that these questions vary according to circumstances, and are sometimes more and sometimes less numerous.[1] As this practice is developed, however, the list of questions tends in general to become longer and longer. Among them three main groups may be distinguished: (i) questions concerning the king's rights of ownership, escheats, wardships, etc.; these investigations did not lead to punishment or legal proceedings, but simply produced information which might later be used in a number of ways; (ii) questions concerning the usurpation or abuse of franchises; here, too, as a rule, only information was called for; it was the business of the Exchequer to decide whether a case of *quo warranto* should be brought; (iii) a very important group of questions concerning the activities of sheriffs, coroners and bailiffs.[2]

The 1274–75 investigation was entrusted not to the itinerant justices on their usual circuits but to a specially appointed commission. Some new questions were introduced and some of the old ones dealt with in more detail. In general this inquest was intended to be more thorough than its predecessors; its purpose was to liquidate the abuses perpetrated by feudal lords and officials during the period of unrest under Henry III. The investigation covered the following questions: which royal manors were in the king's hands and which had been alienated? What fiefs were held from the king in chief and which of these had been alienated? Questions were put on the alienation of lands from the ancient demesne of the crown, on the alienation of lands in favour of the church, on the farms of hundreds and towns, on hundreds in the hands of the king and others which had been alienated, on services due to the king which had passed to other persons, on franchises and their abuse, on chases and parks newly established or enlarged, on the failure of lords or their agents to carry out royal commands, on knights' fees and other lands which had passed into the hands of the church or of other persons to the detriment of the king's right. At the end came a long list of questions concerning the malpractices of royal officials. In all those cases where the rights of the crown had passed into other hands the inquest

[1] Bracton, ii, 182 sqq.; *Statutes of the Realm*, i, 233; *Munimenta Gildhallae Londoniensis*, i, 79, and ii, 347.
[2] Pollock and Maitland, ii, 521; cf. Cam, *O.S.S.L.H.*, vi, 9–113.

was to determine from what date and by virtue of what authorization (*quo warranto*) the transfer had been effected. From this time forward all these questions, under the name of *nova capitula*, were included in the usual *capitula itineris* of the itinerant justices.

The result of the 1274–75 investigations was the records which historians refer to as the *Rotuli Hundredorum*, although in fact they form only one part, though the principal part, of the rolls.[1] They give a very clear picture of feudal England at that date, and their value is enhanced by the fact that the records have been preserved, either in entirety or in abbreviated versions, for the majority of counties. There is a connection between this investigation and some heads of the First Statute of Westminster (April 1275) which are directed against the malpractices of the king's officers; there is also a connection with the Statute of the Exchequer which regulated the sequestration of property (October 1275) and with the Statute *de Judiciis Assignatis* (*de Ragemannis*). The inquest of 1274–75 was also without doubt the starting-point for the Statute of Gloucester (August 1278), which laid down that those who claimed any franchise must appear before the justices on eyre or before the king and prove their rights.[2]

In 1278–79 eyres of justices itinerant were ordered to take place, in the course of which the judges initiated a long series of suits *quo warranto* on the basis of the 1274–75 investigation. Many of the commissioners who had made the previous inquiries were now appointed to go on circuit as judges. But in the same year, 1279, other commissions were appointed to carry out a new survey on a different and very sweeping programme. The headings of the questions to be answered by this survey have not been preserved separately; but they are frequently repeated in the actual text of the answers, sometimes in shortened and sometimes in more detailed form. By comparing different sections of the record it is possible to reconstruct with fair accuracy a long list of these questions;

[1] In Stubbs, (*Constitutional History of England*), in the *Political History of England* (ed. Hunt and Poole), and in Oman (*History of England*) and in a number of general works on political history, 'the Hundred Rolls' means the record of the 1274–75 investigation.

[2] *Stats.* i, 26, 197, 44, 45.

each is formulated in great detail, sometimes even with considerable verbosity.[1]

Some questions repeat the *capitula* of 1274-75. These concern the king's manors and their alienation; holdings in chief and their alienation; the alienation of lands of the ancient demesne; hundreds in the king's hands and those which had been alienated; services due to the king but lost by him; franchises; lands which had passed into the hands of the church or of other persons to the detriment of the king's rights; and other infringements of the rights of the crown. A number of heads are reminiscent of the investigation of 1255 or of the *Capitula Itineris* in Bracton: those on wardship, marriage, escheats, garrison service, and church patronage. The questions on malpractices by the king's servants were not included in the headings for the new investigation. On the other hand, there are a number of entirely new questions, the answers to which did in fact form the main content of the new Hundred Rolls.

The commissions were charged to make investigation into the following matters: what holdings were held by each archbishop, bishop, abbot, prior, earl, baron, knight, freeman or townsman in the cities, boroughs, townships and villages; what castles they had, what knight's fees, land-holdings, demesnes, woods, meadows, parks, pastures (common and private), preserves for hunting, fairs, markets; what were their revenues from rents, from villein holdings, from cottars, from labour services done by serfs; from waters, common and private fisheries, rivers, fish-ponds, mills, gardens, heaths, marshes, peat-beds, alder-groves, etc. Inquiry is to be made as to who holds his estates in fee and who by fee-farm, who for life or for a term of years, who holds of the king in chief and who of other lords, and in the latter case which lords and for what services or payments. Further, the inquiry is to discover what demesnes, freeholders, villeins, serfs, cottars and other tenants each of the aforementioned parties possesses, and whether they hold immediately of their lords or through mesne tenants; it is to establish also the size of the holding of each free man, villein, serf or cottar, and its terms, that is from whom held

---

[1] The heads of the questionnaire are given in the greatest detail in the survey of the Cambridgeshire village of Kingston (*R.H.*, ii, 514-17).

and against what services or dues; and to find out which fees and other holdings should pay scutage and how much, who holds these fees, on what conditions and from what date.

This programme completely altered the character of the inquiry, pushing into the background the questions which had provided the main content of previous surveys and deliberately setting before the commissions the monumental task of a general cadastral survey of all England—and one, moreover, incomparably fuller and more detailed than that carried out by the Conqueror.

The instruction to the commissioners stated the motives that prompted the government to undertake so complicated a survey.[1] In view of the usurpations that have taken place of other men's rights, in particular those of the king, it is essential to establish with exactitude the limits of the rights both of the king and of other feudal lords, 'so that we may know for future time what belongs and should belong to us, and others may know what belongs and should belong to them'.[2] It was in this light that the commissioners understood their task, and their survey is almost entirely devoted to cadastral questions.

The survey of 1279 must be considered against the background of the Barons' Wars of 1258–67, the 'tempus guerrae', when the estates of the rival factions among the barons so often changed hands, resulting in a long series of court cases, and eventually the return of most of the confiscated lands to their previous owners. The struggle within the feudal class, modified as a result of the intervention of the knights—the 'communitas bacheleriae Angliae'—and the burgesses, ended with a compromise. The feudal class banded together around the crown, and to whatever extent the social struggle had extended beyond their ranks in the period of the rebellion, the great feudal lords remained the dominant social and political force in the kingdom. In any case they had never pursued separatist policies, rather attempting the transformation of the monarchy into a submissive organ of baronial

[1] The commission is printed in the preface to the Record Commission's edition, vol. ii. See also H. Hall, *A Formula Book of English Official Historical Documents*, ii (1908–9), 141–42.
[2] Cf. the definition of the purposes aimed at by the compilation of Domesday Book as given in the *Dialogus de Scaccario*: 'ut videlicet quilibet iure suo contentus alienum non usurpet impune.' (ed. Charles Johnson (1950), p. 63).

government. With the political compromise went, in effect, a delimitation of the respective rights of the king and the lords to feudal rent; the rights of each party, so frequently infringed, were exactly defined so as to ensure the regular, perhaps even the increased, flow of rent. The Hundred Rolls of 1279, then, were to provide a complete account and definition of feudal rent with an indication of the rights by which each lord laid claim to his share. The crown naturally wished to recover its full share, and formulated strict rules for the proof of franchise rights, but in practice it was ready to find an acceptable compromise. It was the investigation of 1274-75, however, which was most concerned with franchise rights; while that of 1279 was to provide the completest possible picture of the division of rent and the tangle of feudal relationships. It was to provide a reliable source of information for administrative, judicial and financial purposes.

COMPILATION

For carrying out the survey special commissions were appointed, usually of three men each, each commission (so far as one can judge from the fragments remaining) apparently dealing with two counties. In the Hundred Rolls the commissioners are denominated *Justicie domini Regis* or *Inquisitores domini Regis*. In the commission for Cambridgeshire and Huntingdonshire William Muschet, Nicholas of Bassingbourne and Geoffrey of Sandacre participated.[1] In Oxfordshire the survey was executed by Sampson Foliot, and Fulk of Ruycote *cum sociis*.[2] In Warwickshire and Leicestershire those responsible were Henry of Notyngem, Henry of Seldon and John Arundel.[3] With reference to the 1274-75 commissioners Miss Cam notes that in some cases at least an attempt was made to choose persons well acquainted with the counties to which they were sent. This is applicable to the 1279 commissioners as well. W. Muschet owned lands in Cambridgeshire, and in the same county there were many lands belonging to the Bassingbourne family, while Sampson Foliot had estates in Oxfordshire. Three of the 1279 commissioners had taken part

[1] R.H., ii, 402.   [2] R.H., ii, 688.
[3] R.H. (War.). In the preface to the Record Commission's edition other names are given.

in the 1274–75 investigation, and some of them had served as justices on eyre.[1] In any case, they were experienced and knowledgeable men, belonging to the upper ranks of the royal bureaucracy.

How, then, was the actual survey carried out?

Some information of this can be found in the royal instructions; much material is yielded by the text of the survey itself; some questions which are not clear can be elucidated by analogy with the practice of the itinerant justices as given by Bracton, and with that of other government inquiries—particularly the inquests for the assessment of movables for the levy of the fifths, eighths, and fifteenths, which were no less complicated than the work of the 1279 commissions.

The royal writ instructs the commissioners to visit in person all places in the counties allotted to them, to take evidence from juries, and to question each man conscientiously on his fiefs and holdings. In case of necessity they are enjoined to make a second investigation.

The sheriffs of the counties are given orders to call together on a given day and at a given place as many knights and other 'good and legal men' as may be necessary for carrying out the survey. The whole population of the counties concerned is required to give the commissioners every assistance in the execution of their task. The names of all the vills, hamlets and holdings were to be distinctly copied into special books which must then be handed over to the king. The commissioners had to take an oath to carry out the commission entrusted to them without fear or favour,[2] and not to fail in their duty through gifts or promises, or to accept church benefices, pensions or any other offering without the king's permission. The oath was not out of place; we know that monasteries practised bribery on a wide scale in such cases.[3]

The king's orders give only fragmentary and vague instructions on the execution of the survey. Indeed, there was apparently no need for detailed instructions, since here the commissioners followed the established practice of the itinerant

---

[1] Cf. Cam, *O.S.S.L.H.*, vi, 126–27.

[2] 'Ne pur bienfet, doun, ne premesse de nulle que fet vos seit ou vos purra estre fet.' The text is given in the foreword to the Record Commission's edition, vol. ii, and in H. Hall's *Formula Book*, ii, 142.

[3] See, for example, *Liber Memorandorum Ecclesie de Bernewelle* (1907), 171.

justices, which Bracton describes as follows. Against the arrival of the judges the sheriff, who receives specific orders from the king to that effect, must call together a full assembly of the county court. Then the bailiffs of the hundreds must choose four knights from each hundred; these in their turn must choose twelve knights, or, if knights cannot be found, plain freemen, who are capable of carrying out the king's business in a proper manner. The lists of these men are handed over to the justices. The twelve men chosen must take an oath, the form of which is given in Bracton. After they are sworn in, they have read out to them in order all the heads of the questions to which they must reply before the judges. One must assume that they were given copies of the question headings, especially in the case of such complicated investigations as those we have cited. Then a day was appointed on which the jurors must appear with the answers. The jurors carried out their investigations, each jury for its own hundred, and appeared before the judges on the appointed day. Each jury in turn passed before the judges and gave its answers to all the questions in the *capitula itineris*.

The 1279 survey must have been carried out on many points according to the practice of the itinerant justices. If we turn to the Hundred Rolls themselves, we see that their information emanates from jurors, whose names are often given; there are almost always twelve of them for each hundred. How did the jurors collect their information? The king's orders and the commissioners' oath assume the active participation of the commissioners in the compilation of the survey. They are enjoined to go round in person to the various places in the counties and to cross-examine individuals on their fiefs and holdings; and the population at large is ordered to give them all the necessary information. The wording of the oath assumes direct contact between the commissioners and the persons whose estates were being surveyed. But in Bracton the judges play only a passive part; they make known the question headings to the jurors, and then examine them according to those headings. All the work of collecting information falls upon the jurors, and no indication is given of how the latter discharged their difficult task. But one quite simple method was possible. The surveys given by the Hundred Rolls are very close in character to the manorial surveys, the extents. In the compilation of manorial surveys all the evidence was provided by jurors selected from members of the manorial court; the complicated and detailed Ramsey surveys of the mid-thirteenth century were compiled on the basis of information given by small juries of three to five men. It seems probable that the hundred jurors in making their investigations followed the practice used in preparing private surveys and made use of the same machinery. The organization of the manor and manor courts may have been used in carying out the survey. Sometimes we find in the Hundred Rolls such expressions as *Veredictum villatae de Curtligton*,[1] and headings such as *Halymot de Lewes, Halimot de Clanefeud*.[2] In these one may see indications of village assemblies. The survey was made according to vills. But the use of manorial organization also can be perceived. Within the limits of the different vills the material is arranged according to the manors (when the manor and the vill do not coincide); sometimes the manorial arrangement even infringes the prescribed order.[3] It would, however, be a mistake to assume that the whole survey could be carried out with the help of manorial assemblies and manorial juries. In many vills there are separate holdings or groups of holdings which do not come within any manorial organization or which are connected with manors lying in far distant vills. These holdings may have been surveyed by means of the personal cross-examination of their tenants. In some cases we have direct evidence of such personal examination; the survey of the hundred of Mursley (Bucks.), for example, ends up with a list of persons who had refused to answer the jurors.[4]

One may reach the following conclusion: the hundred jurors were left to acquire the information demanded of them as they saw fit. Probably they made use of manorial organization and of the machinery of the manor for their survey where these were forthcoming. In other cases they had recourse to personal examination of the people concerned.

It is hard to decide to what degree the jurors made use of manorial documents, first and foremost of the extents. A

---

[1] *R.H.*, ii, 822.   [2] *R.H.*, ii, 690–91.
[3] See, for example, the survey of the vill of Bampton (*R.H.*, ii, 688 and foll.) or of Little Odell (*R.H.*, ii, 328 and 331) and many others.
[4] They are listed by name; *R.H.*, ii, 338.

B

comparison of the text of the Hundred Rolls with the existing Ramsey extents[1] shows clearly that the jurors did not make direct use of the latter and certainly did not repeat them. But this does not preclude the possibility of their having used other surveys which have not come down to us, especially if such had been made not long before the government investigation. It is also possible that jurors made use of material contained in official inquiries concerning single manors or groups of manors, the inquisitions *post Mortem* in particular. In the Cartulary of Ramsey Abbey there is a copy of the inquisition dealing with the abbey's manor of Elton (Aylingtone),[2] which is also surveyed in the Hundred Rolls.[3] The Ramsey cartulary dates the document from the third year of Henry III (1218–19), but incorrectly; a more likely date is the fifty-second year of Henry III (1267–68).[4] Comparison leaves no doubt that the corresponding section of the Hundred Rolls is in part copied word for word from the 1267–68 inquisition, and in part is a close paraphrase of it. Evidently the authorities of the manor of Elton placed before the hundred jurors the comparatively recent survey, which gave them all the information they might require. This satisfied the jurors who probably made out a new copy for themselves, at the same time making corrections, which were at times of a very imperfect nature. Thus, in cases where a tenant named in the escheator's survey had died (or otherwise ceased to be a tenant) they substituted 'held' (*tenuit*) for 'holds', which did not, however, prevent them from referring to him later in the present or even the future tense. Nothing is stated as to the fate of the holdings after the disappearance of these tenants, or by whom they were held in 1279.

The end of the escheator's survey was not included in the Ramsey Cartulary, and for this reason it is impossible to assert categorically that the jurors, instead of making their own investigation, simply copied out a survey which was not, after all, quite up-to-date, making only a few superficial corrections. In any case, it is clear that one source of the jurors' information, in addition to the examination of the inhabitants of the village

---

[1] See below, p. 28 ff.   [2] *C. Ram.*, i, 490.   [3] *R.H.*, ii, 656.
[4] The mistake in the date may be attributed to the resemblance between the figures iii and lii.

or representatives of the manorial lords, was found in manorial records.

The Elton survey is in its style little distinguishable from many other Huntingdonshire surveys, and other surveys outside Huntingdonshire also. Evidently the jurors set about their investigation by putting the same questions as the escheators, and the inquisition *post Mortem* could serve at times as a source or at any rate as a close precedent for the Hundred Rolls. However, this case is unique. A comparison of the text of the Hundred Rolls with that of other inquisitions of near dates does not reveal any direct connection between these sources.

On the other hand, a comparison with the extents brings out very clearly the dependence of the Hundred Rolls upon the 'daily round' of manorial affairs from which the extents themselves sprang.[1] In the Hundred Rolls a whole series of manorial customs are given which were more or less immaterial from the point of view of the survey. Evidently the questionnaire was filled in by the local manorial officers. At times there are even details of manorial life not included in the extents themselves. We hear the voice of the guardians of manorial custom who compiled the extents, and see a repetition of the same familiar items of information, even the same familiar words and turns of phrase.

A comparison of the Hundred Rolls with the Eynsham Cartulary and the *Liber Memorandorum Ecclesie de Bernewelle* leads to the same conclusions.

The jurors of the hundreds were given a wide measure of freedom in the interpretation of the questions presented to them, which were put in a very generalized form and left considerable room for different interpretations of detail. Was it necessary to give the size of the demesne only, or also its value? Should the villeins be listed one by one, or only the total number, or was it sufficient to indicate the area of villein land? Should a detailed description of labour-services be given, or merely an overall assessment of their value? Every jury answered these questions in its own way, and the result is variations in the record which make its statistical analysis very difficult. We find some very detailed surveys closely

---

[1] Among the Ramsey documents, the survey of the manor of King's Ripton is particularly interesting from this point of view.

approaching the style of manorial extents, others which are
dry, short and systematized. Sometimes the jurors introduced
supplementary questions, which were apparently not among
those supplied by the commissioners. Evidently people also
seized the opportunity to air their complaints, which led to the
inclusion in the survey of some information unforeseen by the
official plan.[1] Sometimes the supplementary information is
reminiscent of some previous survey.[2] But in some cases
supplementary questions were put by the commissioners
themselves.[3]

Undoubtedly the jurors took down a detailed record as they
made their investigations. These records were then apparently
dictated by them to the commissioners' clerks, and in this
form they became the actual rolls which have come down to us.

What part was played by the commissioners themselves?
Were they merely intermediaries between the Exchequer
and the jurors, or did they carry out the king's instructions
and take an active part in the work of investigation?

We are left with the impression that the commissioners' part
consisted only in instructing the jurors, hearing their answers
and, possibly, taking special measures in cases where information was refused. The actual work of collecting information
was left entirely to the jurors.

The question of the class sympathies and connections of the
jurors was considered by Vinogradoff, who concluded that the
jurors' findings reflected the interests of the landowning class.
In his opinion the 1279 survey helped to bring about an
extension of the rights of landowners. It was not, he said, false
as a whole, but it was apt to throw different things into the
same mould, and to do it in the interest of landed proprietors.[4]
Hence it is imperative to determine as precisely as possible the
social composition of the juries. The survey preserves twenty
lists of jurymen, of which I have examined eighteen representing rural areas and comprising about a hundred and eighty

[1] For instance, *R.H.*, ii, 685.
[2] *R.H.*, ii, 689—extortion under pretext of distraint of knighthood.
[3] E.g., at the end of the survey of an Oxfordshire hundred, we read: 'De
inquisitionibus libertatis extra capitulis iniunctis per preceptum domini Samp-
sonis de Foliot de dominicis forestis et boscis domini Regis, et de his qui debent
esse milites per preceptum domini Regis, et de his qui manucaptores inde inveniunt'.
R.H., ii, 725.
[4] Vinogradoff, *Villainage*, 155.

jurors. This is a sufficient basis from which to judge their social composition,[1] which varied greatly from one district to another. We can speak of a predominance of 'the land-owning class' only in Oxfordshire (and there not for all hundreds) and Huntingdonshire. In Cambridgeshire (with the exception of a single hundred) and in Buckinghamshire the landlord class is either quite unrepresented on the juries or very scantily represented. Here the free peasantry of middle rank predominates, and there is even a percentage of near-landless jurors. It is, however, possible that our information on the possessions of these persons is incomplete; it is also possible that their property status was based on other considerations than land.

Even where 'the land-owing class' predominates, its representatives are mainly small knights who by no means always owned serfs, and who in a majority of cases possessed only few. Great lords, particularly great serf-owners, occur only exceptionally, and those that do appear are 'great' only comparatively. The middle to the lower strata of the knights, and the free peasantry form the basic element in the juries, and one would hardly attribute to them any tendency to defend the interests of the serf-owners. At times they note abuses committed by the great landowners and record the peasants' complaints against the increase in dues, the decline of their social position, and the seizure of common rights.

But while the commissioners did not take a personal part in collecting material, they undoubtedly exerted a certain influence over the jurors' work, both by the way in which they briefed them at the start and by the way in which they examined them and recorded their findings. In each county, in spite of all variations from hundred to hundred, we find certain characteristic traits. The summary and systematic surveys of Bedfordshire and Buckinghamshire are sharply distinguished from the detailed accounts of Oxfordshire and Cambridgeshire. A number of recurring formulae, of which each county has its own characteristic assortment, reflect the way in which the jurors were examined and the way in which the surveys were finally given shape. It depended on the commissioners whether this or that piece of information should

[1] A more detailed analysis of the composition of the juries is given in chapter v.

or should not be included in the rolls, whether this or that formulation should be employed.

As to the thoroughness and conscientiousness with which the survey was executed, it is important to determine the length of time which was taken to complete it. The commission appointed for Huntingdon and Cambridge completed its survey of the former county in the seventh year of Edward I, that is between March 12, 1279 and November 20 of the same year; the survey of Cambridgeshire was completed after November 20, 1279, as was that of Buckingham; in the Warwickshire hundred of Stoneleigh the jurors handed their information over to the commissioners on December 14, 1279. We may assume that the whole survey was completed by the end of 1279. The earliest date mentioned is that for the Oxfordshire hundred of Lewknor; here the jurors were examined by the commissioners at Oxford on April 10, 1279. Probably about this time the whole survey of Oxfordshire was completed. This means that within twenty-nine days the sheriff had received the king's instructions, had summoned to Oxford from the different hundreds the men from among whom the jurors were to be chosen; the commissioners had arrived in Oxford, the juries had been formed and given the appropriate instructions; they had carried out their investigation, and had returned to Oxford with their material prepared. If the date of April 10 is correct (and we have no grounds for questioning it), the survey was carried out very quickly. However, such speed is nothing exceptional for official inquiries in mediaeval England. According to Miss Cam, in the 1274–75 survey the whole procedure took no more than a week in each county; but she considers it possible that the heads for questioning had been sent on to the sheriffs in advance.[1] Even so, the jurors would scarcely have had enough time to pay close attention to the information received or to check dubious points. But it was at any rate not easy to deceive them, since they were local people well acquainted with the narrow circle of their own hundred. The whole procedure of inquests was familiar and commonplace for the population concerned.

[1] In Shropshire the investigation was carried out in six days; in Wiltshire, where it was done from four different centres, less than two weeks were needed to complete it. In Norfolk the jurors complained that they could not collect all the information *propter brevitatem temporis.* Cf. *O.S.S.L.H.,* vi, 125.

Nevertheless, incompleteness and omissions were still possible *propter brevitatem temporis*.

USE OF THE ROLLS

The material for the Hundred Rolls, then, was collected with great speed, without hitch or hindrance, by means of an already existing and tried-and-tested machinery from a population accustomed to all manner of manorial and official investigations. It is impossible to say what use the government afterwards made of the extensive and complicated record that had been executed at its command. It is possible that the findings of the 1279 survey were used as a basis for bringing suits of *quo warranto*; but the close resemblance between the 1274–75 and the 1279 surveys makes it impossible to distinguish with certainty cases for which it was so used. An interest was shown in the survey; copies from it were taken; as we have seen, a copy of part of the survey for Suffolk was included in the Bury St. Edmunds Cartulary, and there is another, which, judging by the script, belongs to the late thirteenth century, containing a survey of two Warwickshire hundreds. Annotations in the margin of the latter indicate that users were mainly interested in those franchises on which the jurors had reported: *nesciunt quo warranto*. It is possible that this copy was made for the legal commissions which were to initiate pleas of *quo warranto* in Warwickshire, although it is not clear why for this purpose it was necessary to transcribe the full text. We have already mentioned also the abbreviated copies of the 1279 Hundred Rolls which were made at the Exchequer, of which one, relating to two Leicestershire hundreds, was copied by the Leicestershire antiquary, Burton. In the Public Record Office there is another manuscript dating from the first half of the sixteenth century[1] which contains the beginning of the survey of the Ramsey manors as given in the 1279 Hundred Rolls, and which possibly was in some way connected with the dissolution of the monasteries. But in general I am not clear what was the practical application of the 1279 survey, nor whether it was completed for all the counties of England, and why, if so, the greater part of it has been lost.

[1] P.R.O., *Rentals and Surveys* 8/56.

We have before us fragments—impressive fragments, it is true—of this survey. But how far can we trust the results of the work of the king's commissions and the jurors of 1279? How are we to understand their sometimes laconic and cryptic formulae? What questions can we put to them, and what degree of accuracy can we expect in the answers?

Structure of the Rolls

We must start with an analysis of the construction of the rolls. The material is arranged according to counties and hundreds; the survey for each hundred represents a record of the findings of a separate jury of that hundred. As we have already indicated, in the work of every commission and in that of every jury certain individual peculiarities can be remarked. Peculiarities of the same sort can sometimes be found even in the surveys of particular villages and manors within the same hundred. Because of these variations statistical treatment is very difficult.

It has already been indicated that the survey was made on the same lines as the manorial extents. The main point of difference is that in the Hundred Rolls the unit of the survey is not the manor but the village, the vill. Where the manor coincided with either a vill or a number of vills, or when a vill divides exactly into several manors, with nothing over, this difference does not matter. But in cases where a vill includes non-manorial elements or parts of manors—sometimes distant manors—the plan of the survey naturally departs from the usual manorial scheme. But the principle of division according to vills is not maintained strictly and is often replaced by division into manors.

For each manor our source usually gives us the following information:

1. The name of the lord, the name of the manor, the number of knights' fees, the chain of lordship up to the king, a list of franchises.

2. A survey of the demesne: (a) the arable land in carucates, hides or acres; (b) meadow land; (c) pastures (enclosed); (d) woods or parkland; (e) fishing grounds; (f) (rarely) yard and garden; (g) mills, often with an indication of their revenue.

The surveys of some hundreds (e.g. Chadlington), give over and above this, an assessment of the revenue from the demesne. But the surveys of demesnes are usually shorter than this, and for some hundreds are totally absent.

3. A survey of the villein land. Here considerable variations are found. In the most detailed surveys a list of all the villeins by name is given, with an indication of the size of their holdings and with a detailed list of all their dues, money, produce and labour included, plus an assessment for each variety of labour-service. But more often we are faced with summary surveys that give no assessments of labour-services. In some cases we are given only general assessments without qualification of different kinds of services, and sometimes money payments are insufficiently distinguished from labour dues, only general assessments of the villeins' dues being given, without indication of the different forms of rent (as in Bedfordshire and Buckinghamshire).

4. A description of the free holdings. Here, too, considerable variations occur. Usually a list of the freeholders by name is given with the size of their holdings and the amount of their dues indicated. Where necessary the names of the intermediary or mesne lord are given.

5. Occasionally descriptions are given of common rights, especially in forests.

Comparing the Hundred Rolls with the extents, we are bound to note the brevity and summary character of the former. The list of dues is sometimes incomplete. Sometimes a number of small customary rents are omitted. Rarely are payments such as tallage or aid mentioned. Feudal and 'forinsec' service, the payment of scutage, the sheriff's aid, hidage, etc., are often omitted.

Like the extents, the Hundred Rolls ignore or give only passing mention to many rents which were not chargeable in fixed sums but which played an important part in the manorial revenue, as may be seen from other sources, ministers' accounts in particular. Thus the revenues of the manor courts (although there are occasional references to merchet, pannage, and revenue from monopoly rights) remain outside the field of vision. Among the obligations of freeholders, that of attendance at the manor court is often mentioned, but reference to it is by no means regular, and its absence does not necessarily imply that it was not exacted.

Not infrequently the Hundred Rolls use abbreviated descriptions which make calculations more difficult. Thus a very common omission is that of details about sub-tenants, who are written off in the formula: 'N. cum suis tenentibus ... cum suis parvis tenentibus, cotenentibus, parcenariis,' etc. In some cases—more than once in the Oxfordshire surveys—we have grounds for supposing smallholders to have been omitted altogether. Some hundreds in Oxfordshire are distinguished by the large size of their free holdings, and by the small number of small-holdings (e.g. Dorchester). But behind these large holdings small sub-tenants may be hidden.[1] We find even villeins of substance (holding one hide, four virgates, three virgates) having sub-tenants, who are not mentioned separately, but of whose existence we learn from the list of dues.[2] Further, there is always the danger of confusing free tenants of villein land with villeins. The fact that a holding is for life, or for a term of years, or at the lord's will, is not always mentioned, and it is easy to mistake these for hereditary tenements.[3]

ACCURACY OF THE RECORD

Mistakes made by the jurors or by the clerks who took down their findings are by no means infrequent.[4] Many are simply slips of the pen.[5] In some cases we find a repetition of informa-

---

[1] *R.H.*, ii, 752, 754 and many others.

[2] *R.H.*, ii, 748.

[3] This peculiarity is common to the Hundred Rolls and the extents. Cf. Vinogradoff, *Villainage*, 330: 'Manorial extents are sparing in the notices of leases, because their object is to picture the distribution of ownership, and temporary agreements are beyond their range'. Some of the holdings referred to in the Hundred Rolls as hereditary, turn out to have been for life, if we refer to the Quo Warranto proceedings; cf. *R.H.*, ii, 329, and *P.Q.W.*, 5; *R.H.*, ii, 330 and *P.Q.W.*, 11, on tenants in the villages of Harrold and Wilmington.

[4] Cf. Stenton, *Br. Ac.*, v (1920), cxi, on 'The mistakes continually being made by the hurried clerks of the travelling justices'.

[5] Such slips of the pen are very frequent in the matter of proper names and of figures. E.g. 'Jossel' instead of 'Johannes Russel' (*R.H.*, ii, 473); 'Walterus f. Rogeri' is on the same line referred to as 'Willelmus f. Rogeri' (*R.H.*, ii, 724); and many more. Often we find xi instead of vi; vi instead of iv and vice versa; and omissions of an x (xvii instead of xxvii—*R.H.*, ii, 348). Mistakes occurred especially often when reckonings were made by scores. Thus, on p. 421 the holding of Elis. Banbury is given as 20,000 acres instead of 240 (mxx instead of xii^{xx}).

tion already given, sometimes with certain discrepancies.[1] In
other places we meet with the mistakes in addition which are
so common in medieval accounts.[2] Omissions are a very
common phenomenon. Apart from sometimes very considerable gaps due to the loss of individual membranes, the jurors
not infrequently made omissions in the surveys of individual
holdings and lists of dues. Sometimes blank spaces are left
where there should be the number of acres or the sum of an
assessment. Apparently they had not succeeded in obtaining
the appropriate information. Remarks are common to the
effect that the jurors could not get an answer to this or that
question, or that they are giving an approximate or hypothetical
answer. Of common occurrence are such expressions as
'nescitur quid nec quantum', 'non possunt inquirere quantum',
'nescimus nec inquiri potest', 'de residuo non potest amplius
inquiri', 'ut credunt', 'ut intelligunt'.

In addition to the mistakes made by the clerks of 1279, we
should also mention the mistakes of the editors of the nineteenth century. The Record Commission's edition was an
achievement in its time, but it does not satisfy modern standards. Material is incorrectly arranged;[3] there are passages
which have been incorrectly read,[4] and inaccuracies in proper
names.[5] But upon the whole, comparison with the original
manuscripts reveals only a comparatively small number of
editorial mistakes, and generally speaking the Record Commission's edition is still serviceable. We have already mentioned

[1] The Abbot of Dereham's holding of 18 acres is repeated on p. 589 from
p. 588; Galfr. de Lewknore's holding of 10 virgates is mentioned twice on p. 749;
so is the holding of Juliana Beche on p. 472. Inaccurate repetitions—on p. 735
Thom. Laungel's holding is given as 6 acres and on p. 739 as 4 acres; the holding
of the heirs of Walt. Godard is described on p. 335 twice, and incorrectly the
second time. See also the descriptions of J. de Lomeri's manor on pp. 341 and
342.
[2] Thus the revenue from Ric. Williamscot's manor is given as £10, but the parts
of it reckoned up come to £14 4s. (R.H., ii, 728–29). Cf. Sombart, Der moderne
Kapitalismus, iv (1921), 296 sq.
[3] E.g., the survey of the vill of Wickam in the hundred of Chilford appears for
some reason between the surveys of the hundreds of Wetherley and Whittlesford
(on p. 568 instead of on p. 429 of the Record Commission's edition).
[4] R.H., ii, 554: 'faciet duo averagia sine messe fuerit'—which should, of course,
be 'si necesse'; R.H. ii, 528: 'latinos' instead of 'libere tenentes'; R.H., ii, 487:
'facini' instead of 'nativi'; R.H. ii, 322: 'continentibus' instead of 'cotenentibus'.
[5] E.g. Beine and Reine, Boceswith and Rokeswith, Bollenhuth and Rillehitch,
Lynham instead of Kingham, Collendriht instead of Rollwright.

the fact that it is not quite complete. It is, perhaps, time for
the question of a new and full critical edition to be considered.

The problem of the accuracy of the information conveyed
in the 1279 survey can be answered best by comparison with
other analogous sources, about whose accuracy there are no
reasonable doubts. Since the Hundred Rolls approximate
more closely to the manorial surveys than to anything else,
they should first of all be compared with the extents. The
greatest abundance of material for comparison is provided
by the famous Ramsey cartulary, in which the majority of
dated extents relate to the years 1251–52, and are thus separated
from the Hundred Rolls by twenty-eight years. The others
refer to an even earlier period. This makes comparison somewhat difficult, and raises the further question, how changeable
conditions within a manor were, and how fast and in what
ways they may have changed. We shall make our comparisons
mostly with the dated extents of Ramsey abbey, so as not to
introduce yet a third unknown quantity.

Parallel surveys are available in the Eynsham cartulary
as well, which provides extents of Oxfordshire manors dating
from 1269 and therefore only ten years earlier than the
Hundred Rolls.[1] Further material for comparison dating this
time from 1295 is provided by the *Liber Memorandorum Ecclesie
de Bernewelle*. Altogether we can make comparisons covering
twenty-six church manors. In addition, a number of extracts
(more than fifty) from the inquisitions *post Mortem* can be used
to serve as parallel material; and finally there are the Hundred
Rolls of 1274–75, closely related in origin, and the *Placita de
quo warranto*.

Comparison with the extents of the Ramsey manors, which
show little variation so far as dimensions and manorial
structure are concerned, leaves a general impression of the
accuracy and reliability of the information in the Hundred
Rolls. There are no vital mistakes or discrepancies. If there
are mistakes, they can in the majority of cases be traced to
copying errors.[2] But the Hundred Rolls are shorter and more

---

[1] *The Cartulary of the Abbey of Eynsham*, i, ed. H. E. Salter (1907), pp. 9–11.
[2] *R.H.*, ii, 602, gives 18 virgaters' holdings on the manor of Wistow: *C. Ram.*
i, 356–63, gives 28; at Holywell-Needingworth *R.H.* ii, 603, gives 26 holdings of
one virgate; *C. Ram.* gives 16. In other cases we have the common clerk's error of
writing xviii instead of xxviii, xxvi instead of xvi.

summary. They make much more use than do the extents
of conventional and fiscal measures and figures. This comes out
most clearly in the description of demesne arable land. In a
number of cases the manorial surveys do not state how many
acres or other units of land there are on the demesne, and confine themselves to listing the places where the different parts
of the demesne are situated, sometimes stating that the exact
measurements in acres are not known. In order to define
the total area of arable land they indicate the number of
ploughs needed for its cultivation. But the Hundred Rolls
state precisely the number of demesne 'carucates'. In this
instance the term 'carucate' represents a conventional unit
which it is not easy to translate into terms of real land measurements. The clear, short and simple statement called for in the
government survey compelled those who provided its information to over-simplify their reply to a question to which they
did not know the precise answer.

Meadow land is described very carefully in the Ramsey
extents, but usually without indication of its total area, though
sometimes the areas of some parts of it are given. On the other
hand all the places where the meadows lay are listed and named,
the customs governing the use of the meadows are defined,
and so are the special rights of particular individuals, if such
there be. Probably if the tenants who gave evidence about
the meadows had been asked 'quot acrae?' they would, to
satisfy their consciences, have answered 'nescitur quantae
acrae in eisdem continentur', as they sometimes answered in
the case of the demesne arable.[1] But for the government
survey they have ready round figures (forty acres, twenty acres,
fifteen acres, ten acres),[2] evidently reckoned 'by eye'. Where,
however, we are in a position to compare particular points,
we find the data given in the Hundred Rolls to be correct.

What has been said about meadow land might be repeated
in the case of pasture and woodland. Here, too, the extents
give a painstaking list of locations, and define conditions of
use, but omit total area. The Hundred Rolls, on the other
hand, usually give the areas in round figures, defining the
length and breadth of woods and pastures in leagues or parts
of leagues. In this instance they are following the practice

[1] *C. Ram.* i, 294.   [2] *R.H.* ii, 603, 602, 601, 600.

of Domesday Book, and sometimes the figures given agree with those of Domesday Book. Mills are mentioned more frequently in the Hundred Rolls than in the extents. Possibly these were new mills that had been put up in recent years.

When we pass to tenants' land, and, first of all to villein land, two questions arise: (i) how correctly do the Hundred Rolls define the total areas of villein land and the numbers and dimensions of separate villein holdings? (ii) how accurately do they specify the total amounts and varieties of payments and labour-services required from villein holdings?

Comparison between villein holdings as given in the Ramsey extents and as given in the Hundred Rolls, indicates that in twenty-eight years no considerable changes in the area of villein land or in the dues and services owed by villeins had taken place. Almost all the discrepancies in the sources are to be attributed to mistakes of copying. Inaccuracies appear mainly in small matters: sometimes a number of the very smallest holdings are ignored,[1] or the fact that the tenants of large holdings often hold small supplementary holdings as well, is overlooked.[2] At times some discrepancy, though usually inconsiderable, is noticeable in the definition of the size of a virgate,[3] but the virgate was, of course, not a constant measurement and varied even within the same manor, 'aliquando maior, aliquando minor'.[4] In sum, so long as we do not bother about the odd acre or rood, the Hundred Rolls should provide us with accurate information about the extent of villein land.

As to villein dues, the Hundred Rolls provide a wealth of descriptive material, sometimes detailed, sometimes only summary. How reliable is it? Comparison between the Hundred Rolls and the Ramsey Cartulary shows that, although the former is very summary, its description of dues and services is sufficiently accurate. In describing the different sorts of labour dues, the compilers of the Hundred Rolls were interested mainly in total estimates, for which purpose dues were very reasonably divided into three basic groups: *opera*,

---

[1] At Holywell-Needingworth the *R.H.* omit 11 or 12 villein crofts which are shown in the *C. Ram.*

[2] At Wistow, Ripton Abbots, Warboys-Caldecot, Broughton.

[3] At Woodhurst the *R.H.* define a virgate as 15 acres, the *C. Ram.* giving it as 16 acres; at Oldhurst the *R.H.* give 30 acres, the *C. Ram.* 16; at Holywell-Needingworth the *R.H.* puts 16 acres to the virgate, the *C. Ram.* 18 and over.

[4] *C. Ram.* i, 370.

araturae, and *averagia*, together with *precariae*. The basis of this division is simply convenience in reckoning, and in fact so far as system and clarity are concerned, the Hundred Rolls are considerably superior to the extents; but in attaining this clarity, they over-simplify the complications attending the allocation of labour dues, and commit inaccuracies in totalling them up. The labour dues of small holdings, as well as various small and occasional payments made from villein holdings, are sometimes carelessly described. Finally, and most important, the Hundred Rolls make no mention of the practice of the commutation of services. If we did not possess the manorial surveys—and for the majority of estates described in the Hundred Rolls we do not possess them—we should regard the majority of the manors of Ramsey Abbey, which we have discussed, as examples of the 'classical' type of manor worked by servile labour. The extents, on the other hand, make clear that on some manors at least the lord had the right to demand money payments instead of labour services (*opera*), and that even those labour dues which were included in the category of '*opera*' were assessed in terms of money, in case the lord wished to commute them.

In respect of free holdings comparison with the Ramsey Cartulary does not yield much useful material. The only serious discrepancy is in the case of Wistow, where we must assume that there is an omission in the Hundred Rolls. In general, the surveys in the Hundred Rolls and in the Ramsey Cartulary give closely similar figures, but since it is very rare that the details can be compared, a final judgment is difficult. The Hundred Rolls describe individual holdings more concretely than the Ramsey Cartulary, usually giving the area of land on the farm, its meadow land, and a list of sub-tenants and their dues. But their description of the dues owed to the abbot is more summary, and many details are lost in their account. A vital omission from our point of view is that of mention of the small labour services, particularly ploughing, which were demanded of very many free holdings. We cannot here assume commutation, because the disappearance of the services is not accompanied by any increase in money rents. In this respect great interest attaches to Ballard's observations, based upon a comparison of the Hundred Rolls with the Pipe

Rolls of the bishopric of Winchester, for 1277 and 1278.[1] Ballard notes that the Hundred Rolls put the amounts of money rent considerably lower than do the Pipe Rolls. The latter give a total of £41 17s. 10½d.,—£17 5s. 2d. more than the Hundred Rolls; the Pipe Rolls give the money payments made by a virgater as 5s., while the Hundred Rolls give 3s. 9d.[2] Ballard has noted a similar tendency in the case of the manor of Woodstock.[3] Nevertheless, according to Ballard's own reckoning, the Hundred Rolls give a very accurate assessment of the labour dues of a virgater, perhaps even putting them a little too high: 10s. 10d. instead of 10s. 7d. The Hundred Rolls give a slightly different figure for villein virgates from that of the Pipe Rolls—sixty-three instead of sixty-two—but the sources are not exactly contemporaneous (there is a year between them) and the mistake is trifling.

A comparison of the Hundred Rolls with parallel material in the *Liber Memorandorum Ecclesie de Bernewelle* reveals major omissions in the Hundred Rolls, which may, in part, be explained by the loss of individual membranes. Thus in the survey of the manor of Bourn the Hundred Rolls omit practically all the freehold and all the rents of the freeholders.[4] But there are also omissions which cannot be explained in this way; thus, in the survey of the manor of Bourn some of the labour dues of the villeins are omitted, and so are some of their money rents. In the description of the villeins' holdings the small enclosed plots (*clausa*), which they hold at the lord's will, are not indicated. It is possible, however, that these were added after 1279. Comparison with the Eynsham Cartulary is made difficult by the fact that the latter gives very summary and, apparently, incomplete information. There is one major mistake, which cannot be explained except

---

[1] For the manor of Witney, see *R.H.* ii, 703.

[2] *O.S.S.L.H.*, v, 186.

[3] A. Ballard, 'Woodstock Manor in the thirteenth century', *Vierteljahrschrift für Sozial-und Wirtschaftsgeschichte*, 1908.

[4] *R.H.* ii, 524–25, and *Lib. Mem.*, 294–98. There is a similar omission in the surveys of the manors of Comberton and Madingley (*R.H.* ii, 555 and 446–7, *Lib. Mem.*, 299 and 307–310). In all these cases the omission can easily be explained by a loss of part of the enrolment; the survey breaks off at the end of a membrane, and we may assume that the succeeding membrane, containing the continuation, has been lost. Omissions of whole vills or manors, owing to the loss of single rolls, are not uncommon in general in the Hundred Rolls.

as the result of negligence.[1] The Eynsham Cartulary shows a considerable area of freehold ($9\frac{1}{2}$ virgates, with rent of £7 1s. 8d) in the manor of Weld,[2] where, according to the Hundred Rolls, the abbey possessed no estates at all. In the same way the Hundred Rolls mention no estates of the abbey at Filkins, where the cartulary shows a rent of 6s. and a mill with a revenue of 14s.[3]

We have already said something of the difficulties involved in checking the Hundred Rolls against the evidence of the inquisitions *post Mortem*. The most serious is the difficulty of finding really contemporary sources, for if the sources are not contemporary there is always the possibility of changes in the composition of different estates. There are a number of inquisitions which show very close coincidence, but there are also a large number which reveal marked discrepancies. Nevertheless the inquisitions are useful. They confirm our impression of considerable gaps in the Hundred Rolls and indubitable mistakes come to light: thus at Camps the demesne is given as 9 acres,[4] but an inquisition of 1263–64 gives 740 acres. The second figure is very plausible, as the labour dues of villeins shown on this manor are very considerable. Important also is the fact that in some cases where the Hundred Rolls mention only labour rents, an inquisition speaks of their being commuted into money.[5] An example is at Catworth, Hunts., where the Hundred Rolls speak only of labour dues and the inquisition only of money rent from the villeins.[6] Here the inquisition comes only one year before the Hundred Rolls. This observation confirms the conclusion already drawn from a comparison of the Hundred Rolls with the Ramsey extents.

The Hundred Rolls in the majority of cases give one-sided and incomplete information on the extent of the possessions of individuals. The majority of estates are described only in terms of arable land. The areas of meadow, wood and pasture

---

[1] The Hundred Rolls give only 16 villein virgates at Charlbury instead of 32 (*R.H.* ii, 709; *Eynsham Cartulary* i, 9); but the dues of a virgater are assessed almost identically.

[2] *Eynsham Cartulary*, 11.   [3] *ibid.*, 11.   [4] *R.H.* ii, 424.

[5] Especially Hamerton, Hunts., I.P.M. Ed. I, File 4-16, and *R.H.* ii, 624–26; in this case the I.P.M. precedes the *R.H.* in time, being from the second year of Edward I.

[6] I.P.M., Ed. I, File 22-8, and *R.H.* ii, 624–26.

C

land are sometimes mentioned in the descriptions of demesne, but this is not by any means the rule. As a rule only those parts of meadow, wood and pasture are mentioned which are in the separate use and possession of individuals. Common lands escape us. True, the overall area of these for the whole village is sometimes given, but not always, and when it is done the areas are given very roughly, briefly and vaguely (usually merely the length and breadth in leagues and quarters). Thus the basis for our assessment of the scale of this or that individual holding is, as a rule, the area of arable land alone. We can only guess, from various details, at the part played by the exploitation of pasture or woodland, and our basis of calculation is here very shaky. It is true that the territory covered by the Hundred Rolls is predominantly one of arable farming, but it is not wholly so; yet very rarely do we find mention of industries and crafts. Only mills, it would seem, are noted more or less accurately. Blacksmiths' forges are not usually noted, even in cases where the tenant's appellation (*faber*) and his dues give us every reason to assume their existence. More generally, such appellations are often an indication that the main occupation of the person concerned was not agriculture. However, the Hundred Rolls do not confine themselves to arable land alone, but often mention land attached to the homestead, vegetable plots. But it was necessary to have a homestead, at least a vegetable patch or to be mentioned specifically; only householders with their own establishment were comprised in the survey. If, for instance, there were in a village labourers who had no roof and no farm of their own (and such men are indirectly mentioned in the rolls), we shall learn nothing of them.

Lenin has pointed out that data on the area of arable land are an insufficient basis on which to form a judgment of the character of a holding. 'The grouping of farms according to area introduces undue simplification and crudeness into the conception of the development of agriculture in general and of the development of capitalism in agriculture in particular.'[1] This, of course, applies with less force to pre-capitalist conditions, but here, too, we undoubtedly see undue simplification

---

[1] V. I. Lenin, *Selected Works* (English Edition), xii, 235.

and crudeness. Particularly regrettable is the lack of information on the use of pasture land, so important in medieval
farming.

Unit of Measurement

Our estimate, nevertheless, of the extent of any individual
economy must in the circumstances be based on its arable
area. Our chief statistical work consists of calculations concerning arable land. But an essential prerequisite for precise
statistics is a common unit of land measurement. How do
matters stand here in the Hundred Rolls? We must note first
of all that sometimes the size of holdings is given in the most
indefinite terms. For instance, in some hundreds of Cambridgeshire the overall areas of different manors are given only in
fiscal units (hides, or, more often, knight's fees and parts
thereof). The fiscal hide, and still more the knight's fee, are
extremely indefinite quantities. But in the majority of cases
arable land is given in definite agrarian units of measurement—
hides, carucates, virgates, acres, roods. It is not necessary to
discuss the well-known problem of variations in the number of
acres in a virgate and of virgates in a hide.[1] As we know, the
size of a virgate can vary even within one and the same vill;
and since the larger units are not always translated into acres,
variations in the size of hides and virgates often remain hidden
from us. Moreover, can we be sure that the acre represents a
fixed quantity?[2]

For practical purposes we are obliged to treat the acre as a
constant and, failing more precise indications, to assume an
average virgate of thirty acres.[3] But we must never lose sight
of the rough and imperfect nature of these units of measurement. Even when an exact translation of hides, carucates or
virgates into acres is given, we cannot feel any very firm ground
under our feet, since all such equations seem to be only
approximate. As we have already seen, there are discrepancies

---

[1] Cf. F. Seebohm, *Village Community*, 37; N. Neilson, *Economic Conditions on the Manors of Ramsey Abbey* (1898), 14.
[2] Maitland, *Domesday Book*, 373-75, 379 sqq.; Vinogradoff, *Villainage*, 240-41. From Levett's observations one 'measured acre' sometimes equalled two to four 'customary' or 'field' acres. (*O.S.S.L.H.*, v, 50).
[3] Calculations from Hundred Rolls material give an average virgate very close to 30 acres.

between the Hundred Rolls and the Ramsey extents regarding the number of acres in a virgate; probably the equation used in the enrolments should have been modified by the word 'more or less' (*plus vel minus*).

The carucate also, the usual unit of measurement of demesne land, gives rise to a number of problems; but here some illumination may be gained by a comparison of the Hundred Rolls with the corresponding Ramsey extents.

Comparison with a number of other sources, particularly the Ramsey and Gloucester Cartularies, Domesday Book and the Taxation of Pope Nicholas IV, leads to the conclusion that the carucate of the Hundred Rolls did not always mean the same thing. Sometimes it denoted a piece of land of a definite number of acres (most frequently 100 or 120), but in a number of instances manorial officials apparently did not know how many acres there were on the demesne, and instead of answering the question *quot carucatae?* they substituted the answer to an easier question: *quot carucae arantes in dominico?* And we also find in some cases a repetition of traditional figures going back to Domesday Book. This may be evidence of the unchanging size of demesnes between the eleventh and the thirteenth centuries (the material refers in this case to old-established Benedictine monasteries), but it may also be evidence of the extremely unreal nature of the term 'carucate' in government surveys. In taking, for purposes of calculation, the carucate of the Hundred Rolls as equivalent to a definite average number of acres, we are, undoubtedly, risking a considerable degree of inaccuracy.

A great many difficulties arise in reckoning the extent of holdings such as cottages, messuages, crofts and tofts. Their area is by no means always given, yet they were not always insignificant in size. While in Cambridgeshire a cotter's holding is very small (on the average about one acre), it is much larger in Oxfordshire and Warwickshire, and we sometimes find cottages with ten, twelve and eighteen acres, cotlands of twenty-four or even thirty-four acres.[1] Sometimes the dimensions of assarts are given, and these also are not small; sometimes they are thirty acres or more.

[1] *R.H.* ii, 721, 630.

FRAGMENTARY RECORDS

A number of difficulties arise from the fact that we have to deal with what are only fragments of a large survey. Apart from the point that these fragments do not comprise the whole of many vills and manors, so that in making calculations from the parts which are extant one may get a certain disproportion in the results, the fragmentary nature of the enrolments gives rise to yet another danger. For example, in the case of manors extending into a number of vills, the extant parts of the survey may only comprise a few portions of the manor; and if the section of the survey covering the main manorial centre happens to be lost, we may easily take the separate parts of such manors to be independent units. Again, owing to the complicated character of free holding, whereby often a holding may consist of several parts scattered over various manors and vills, it might easily happen that a man treated as a cotter in one vill would turn out to be a large-scale landholder, if we knew of his holdings in vills the survey of which is lost.

We must also take into account the fact that the fragments extant for different counties are not all on the same scale. A comparatively small piece of the Bedfordshire survey has been preserved, and that for Buckinghamshire is not much bigger. Best represented are Oxfordshire and Huntingdonshire. In assessing our statistical material we must bear in mind this unevenness, and not let a chance factor such as the better state of preservation of certain parts of the survey, with all the local peculiarities of those parts, influence our conclusions.

An important feature of the surviving fragments of the Hundred Rolls is that they cover an economically homogeneous area, which was not, however, representative of the whole country. This area was fertile, well provided with means of communication by land and water, and (especially Cambridgeshire and Huntingdonshire) distinguished by a high level of commodity production.[1] The Upper Thames area had easy access by river to the London market, and the eastern areas had an outlet through one of the largest centres of the medieval corn trade—King's Lynn. It was in this area, dominated, as we have mentioned, by arable farming, that typical manorial

[1] See N. S. B. Gras, *Evolution of the English Corn Market* (1915).

forms reached their highest development. Material for this area, therefore, is the most suitable basis from which to check the assertions of the 'classical' manorial theory.

While noting the economic homogeneity of the area covered by the Hundred Rolls we must not, however, forget that it can be divided into two historically differentiated parts: an eastern region (Cambridgeshire, Huntingdonshire, Bedfordshire, the northern hundreds of Buckinghamshire) and a western region (the southern hundreds of Buckinghamshire, Oxfordshire and Warwickshire). The first of these came within the southern Danelaw and was connected with East Anglia; the second came within English Mercia. We shall have to take into account not only peculiarities created by economic conditions, but the legacy of the historical past as well.

FACTORS IGNORED IN THE HUNDRED ROLLS

We must also bear in mind that the compilers of the Hundred Rolls—the Exchequer officials, the king's commissioners and the jurors of the hundreds—were not interested in the same things as economic historians to-day. The purpose of the Hundred Rolls was to investigate not economic relationships, but first and foremost tenurial relationships; they therefore give an over-simplified and inaccurate picture of the relations between individual holdings. As in the extents, 'temporary agreements are beyond their range'.[1] They rarely give any indication of existing leases, yet the practice of leasing was already making considerable headway in the thirteenth century.

We know quite well that the economic exploitation of the demesne might be in the hands of a lessee, a *firmarius*, or in the hands of the village community, or it might be leased out in parts to different individuals. The enrolments rarely inform us of such cases. In the same way, the villein tenements did not function in the ordered symmetry which we see in the descriptions in the Hundred Rolls and in the manorial extents. The records of the manor courts show that the peasants gave and took leases of villein land, and there are grounds for believing that not all 'deals' of this sort were recorded as they should have been. Leasing must have been widely practised

[1] Vinogradoff, *Villainage*, p. 330.

among the free holdings also. The symmetry is further spoilt by the fact that free men often held villein land, and villeins free land, which is a thing our sources record very rarely indeed. Therefore the picture of tenurial relations given by the Hundred Rolls may be at variance with the actual distribution of land between the economies of the lord, the villeins and the freeholders. But how greatly at variance? We may believe, and the sources generally speaking confirm this, that in the second half of the thirteenth century the land of the demesne was as a rule exploited by the lord, and that the liquidation of the lord's economy and the leasing out of the demesne was a process which only later began to take place on a large scale. In considering the peasants' holdings we must bear in mind that the differentiation between them was, in fact, greater than is shown by the Hundred Rolls. But it is essential to note that for free holdings the Hundred Rolls themselves show very arresting evidence of integrations and disintegrations which cut across the tenurial relationships.

By ignoring 'temporary agreements' and recording primarily the more permanent forms of tenure, the Hundred Rolls also over-simplify the distribution of feudal rent and its incidence on the different peasant economies. As R. H. Hilton has re-marked,[1] the Hundred Rolls 'are almost unique, so that we may, through the intensity of our interest in them, be misled into assuming too great a permanency for the social and tenurial structure which they mirror'. But this danger will not, perhaps, be so great if we realize it and take it into account. If we con-sider the English thirteenth-century village not as a perfected system in a state of equilibrium, ignoring its past and its future, as Homans does, but rather follow Lenin's admonition and ' . . . examine every question from the standpoint of how the given phenomenon arose in history and what principal stages this phenomenon passed through in its development',[2] then we shall scarcely exaggerate the permanency of the relations re-flected in our source. It is a fundamental requirement of historical method that a subject should be studied as a unity, and yet at the same time in all its complications and contra-dictions, a ceaseless process of movement and change (which is not, of course, always of a progressive nature). Naturally,

[1] *Op. cit.*, p. 19.   [2] Lenin, *S.W.*, xi, 642.

a source which concentrates our attention on a particular date, and emphasizes chiefly the more stable elements while taking insufficient account of the fluidity of relations in real life, calls for a cautious approach. But the eye of the historian will discern, in the facts 'frozen' in the record, both survivals from past relationships and the embryonic forms of future developments, and will discover movement and development in apparent stability and immobility.

THE RELIABILITY OF THE HUNDRED ROLLS

Here we are faced with the question whether the material contained by the Hundred Rolls is suitable for statistical purposes at all. Do not their incompleteness and patchiness, the presence of gaps and mistakes, the vague and unreal nature of many of the figures and terms of measurement, all render hopeless any attempt to obtain an accurate answer? Doubts such as these almost invariably arise in dealing with any medieval source on so wide a scale, and their solution is of importance, not only for the Hundred Rolls themselves but also more generally as a matter of historical method. The historian must discover the real import of the figures in the enrolments; he must have a precise knowledge of all its gaps—and traps; he must accustom himself to its variations and irregularity, changing his methods of calculation accordingly. At the same time he must abandon any idea of getting precise arithmetical answers to the questions raised. He must remember that all his answers will be merely approximate, probabilities and not certainties; but he will be satisfied if the path he has chosen makes possible results which are un-attainable by other methods of investigation.[1]

The preceding analysis has shown that the Hundred Rolls sometimes give quite precise surveys, little inferior to the extents, but that at times we come up against gross errors, large omissions, incomplete surveys. If it were our purpose to

---

[1] I recall the words of Savine whose work on the *Valor Ecclesiasticus* has served as my model. Having noted the urge to narrow specialization among contemporary historians, their concentration on criticism of sources and 'wearisome calculations', he remarks: 'Even those who concern themselves with wearisome calculations are aiming merely at probable, approximate conclusions, at laying bare the dominant tendency, but they know no shorter or more reliable way to reach their goal than by laborious calculation'.

describe one single manor on the basis of this source, we might well get a completely distorted picture. But matters are different if our aim is simply to reveal 'dominant tendencies', based not on individual figures but on a mass of material. With overall calculations the mistakes and omissions—I refer in the first place to mistakes and omissions of an accidental nature—in the source are evened out and eliminated. In the same way, mass statistics iron out the variations in the size of the virgate, coming close to an average figure of thirty acres. It is different with inaccuracies of a non-accidental nature, which recur continually and are due to the peculiarities of the source itself. In that case we must try to detect such peculiarities, and to make approximate corrections in estimating the results of our calculations. It must be emphasized once more, that in using statistical methods we do not wish to create a false impression of the exactitude of our conclusions, that we are not aiming at precise figures, and that we shall be satisfied if we can, with a greater or lesser degree of probability, reveal 'dominant tendencies'.

We have many more accurate types of source—extents, accounts rendered by reeves and stewards, rolls of manor courts. But how accurate are the answers they yield to the general questions which interest us most of all? Quite apart from the fact that even here there is much that is open to doubt,[1] these sources provide, as we have seen, only a fragmentary and one-sided picture. In the Hundred Rolls, we have a much more summary and more dubious source, but nevertheless a source on a massive scale, which includes materials not found elsewhere. Although it contains a number of mistakes and distortions, we have no grounds for thinking that the general picture it draws is false. The basic difference lies in the fact that the extents and ministers' accounts give exact figures for individual manors and extremely shaky ones for the country-side as a whole, whereas the answers derived from the Hundred Rolls increase in accuracy as one passes from the particular to the general. We have before us a source in a class by itself, which calls for a special approach; but the risk involved in its

[1] Even ministers' accounts with all their thoroughness, do not make it possible to define the areas of the demesne and the holdings, or to separate the areas of the demesne and the holdings, or to separate the money rent of freeholders from the money rent of villeins, etc.

use is no greater than that which always arises when we cease to be satisfied with limited answers to particular questions and seek to solve a general problem as a whole.

METHOD OF PROCEDURE

In working on statistical material derived from medieval surveys there are certain general rules by which we must be guided. These I would define as follows:

(i) In the majority of cases the figures obtained give only an inexact and conditional answer. This is due both to the inexactitude of the figures themselves and, most important of all, to the difference between our aims and the aims of those who made the surveys. Therefore all figures are in the nature of approximate guiding lines only.

(ii) It is essential to determine what each figure in the source really represents. In addition we must decide what factors cause the figures to vary in such a way that the answers to the problems we might wish to solve are imprecise. It is essential to correct one's calculations in accordance with these factors.

(iii) The inaccuracy and incompleteness of the source makes it necessary to avoid conclusions based on individual figures, unless it is possible to check them. One can operate only with large numbers drawn from a sufficient number of instances. The conclusions in which we can put most faith are those based on relative, not on absolute figures.

(iv) One must abstain from precise conclusions and detailed distinctions, since conclusions can only be drawn in a very general form, and then only on the basis of statistical evidence which retains its validity even if major corrections are made one way or the other.

(v) In those cases where our calculations do not provide sufficiently clear results, and where the averages are based on an insufficient number of cases, conclusions can only be conditional and require checking and confirmation from other material.

Summarizing our analysis of the Hundred Rolls, we may now note the questions which this source may reasonably be expected to answer, the methods by which they can be answered, and the dangers to be guarded against in the employment of these methods:

(i) The very structure of the rolls, which make the village, not the manor the basis of the survey, permits us to raise the question—which remains vague in the majority of manorial records—of the relations of village and manor. The fact that manors of all types—large and small, church and lay— are included indiscriminately, provides us with material for an examination of types of manorial structure. Especially important is the elucidation of the peculiarities of the small manor, which has been little studied by previous workers.

(ii) We can, by comparing the scale of villein and free land, determine the role of the latter. However much units of land-measurement may vary, in mass calculations the hide, the virgate, and the acre approach their average connotation. Again, when mass calculations are made, the omissions noted above, which, if individual cases are taken, give a false proportion between the areas of villein land and of freehold, are ironed out. These omissions are not frequent and there is no ground for supposing them to occur systematically in respect of any one variety of holding, although from our observations it appears that omissions are more frequent in the description of free than of villein land.

(iii) We can, in a number of hundreds and manors, define at least the approximate area of the demesne. But its area is not always given, and when it is, it is often in very unreal and approximate terms. Here, therefore, our statistics are least reliable; but we can nevertheless obtain certain guiding lines.

(iv) In a number of hundreds (not everywhere) we can count up the number of villein holdings and their size; these figures give a somewhat over-simplified and schematic idea of the actual distribution of villein land, since there are grounds for assuming a greater degree of differentiation and a lesser degree of symmetry among villein holdings than is shown in the source. Here we shall have to emphasize the evidence of social stratification among the unfree peasantry which the rolls themselves clearly reveal.

(v) There are considerable difficulties involved in a similar analysis of free holdings, which, as indicated above, are scattered over various estates, manors and even vills. Nevertheless these difficulties are not sufficient to compel us to abandon these involved calculations, though owing to their difficult nature it was only possible to carry them out for particular hundreds and villages.

(vi) In many cases we can calculate both the overall amount and the composition of villein rents. The lists of villeins' dues, which vary considerably from one hundred to another and even from one manor to another in the Hundred Rolls, allow us in a number of cases to define the relative parts played by labour rents, money rents and produce rents. The role of the last item is insignificant, although we should, perhaps, considerably increase its amount in view of the lords' monopoly of mills, ovens and the like, on which our source is silent. A comparison of the amounts of labour and money rents can be made on the basis of the cash assessments of labour services, or of the sum total of a villein's dues, which we often find in our source. In cases where such cash assessments are not given, but a list of services is included, average assessments can be employed. In some individual cases we find omissions and simplifications in the description of labour services, but on the whole there is little danger of our obtaining very exaggerated figures. The danger here lies in the fact that the Hundred Rolls, like the manorial surveys, commonly ignore the practice, which figures prominently in ministers' accounts, of yearly commutation (*venditio operum*); for in the thirteenth century this practice was in extensive use. We can assume that part of the dues which are shown in the source as labour services were levied each year in money form. We are far more in danger of exaggerating the role of labour rents in comparison with money rents, than of the reverse. Furthermore, in a considerable majority of cases the Hundred Rolls give only an incomplete list of money rents. Such major items as court revenues, aids, pannage, not to mention small customary rents, often escape notice in the surveys. Without doubt, we should assign considerably more importance to the villeins' money rent than we find attributed to it in the Hundred Rolls; when comparing the labour rents and the money rents of villeins the ratio should be substantially revised in favour of the latter.

(vii) The Hundred Rolls yield exceptionally abundant material for the study of free rents. Although simplifications frequently occur in their descriptions of these rents (e.g. the omission of minor labour dues), on the whole the many-sided variety of the rents of free tenants is fairly accurately reflected. Analysis of free rent in many cases enables us to reveal its origin either as a survival of the pre-feudal order or as a product of feudal disintegration. We shall obtain material for judging how far the so-called 'free' peasantry in England was subjected to feudal rent and how far small-scale property was developing.

(viii) In spite of difficulties in calculation, a comparison of the area of the demesne arable with the amounts of labour dues on the same manors will yield some figures that can be used for considering how far the demesne economy was adequately provided with unfree working hands. This, of course, does not in itself indicate the type of demesne economy in any individual case, but it does to a certain extent allow us to form an idea of the part played by wage labour even as early as the thirteenth century. The role of the latter is also brought out when we reckon up the numbers of small and very small holdings, both villein and free.

(ix) Although a study of the Hundred Rolls gives, generally speaking, a static picture of the English village as it was in 1279, we can nevertheless perceive some indications of the changes taking place in agrarian life. Such phenomena as the increasing mobility of land, the differentiation of holdings, the 'engrossing of farms', the seizure of the commons, the commutation of labour dues, the intensification of the pressure brought to bear on the peasantry by the landowners—all these are reflected in our source, although far from abundantly. To trace in detail the development of the English village we should have to compare the surveys in the Hundred Rolls with other earlier and later surveys of the same villages. This, however, is a complicated problem, which I cannot now undertake. Comparisons with earlier sources (mainly with Domesday Book) and later sources have only occasionally been made, for the elucidation of specific questions which seemed to me of special importance.

(x) Although the Hundred Rolls cover only a comparatively small portion of England, and that a part more or less homogeneous in its social and economic characteristics, the material in them does nevertheless make it possible to note certain local peculiarities. The difference between the east and the west comes out clearly. But in order to extend our observations to cover a wider ground, we must use other sources. For this purpose I have turned to other official surveys, namely the inquisitions *post Mortem* which yield abundant material for the thirteenth century.

3

INQUISITIONS POST MORTEM

The use of the inquisitions *post Mortem* on a wide scale for investigating problems of agrarian history has been discussed by H. L. Gray.[1] Gray, however, did not examine this type of material critically enough, and consequently used it with too much confidence. Since we, too, propose to use the inquisitions, a critical examination is necessary.

The procedure of investigation by royal officials[2] into the lands of tenants-in-chief on the death of the tenant was elaborated in Henry III's reign. The results of the inquiry were sent to the Chancery by the escheators, with a copy to the Exchequer, to which the escheators had to account during their period of custody of the lands—that is, until the succession of the heir. The inquisitions should have been made in great detail, for according to the instructions of 1259[3] the most thorough survey of the economy of demesne and tenant land was to be made. But the jurors of the hundred, who bore the burden of these as of many other investigations, often returned very summary information, sometimes merely a general estimate of manorial revenues. Generally the investigating officials returned much too low a valuation to Chancery and Exchequer, and orders for another inquiry were common, the subsequent inquisitions often showing a considerable rise in the figures of revenue. Undoubtedly the escheators had good reasons for returning as low a valuation as possible, since they had to render accounts to the Exchequer, which would be checked against the figures given in the inquisitions.

---

[1] 'The Commutation of villein services before the Black Death', *E.H.R.*, xxix (1914).
[2] Originally made by the sheriffs, then by the escheators (cf. Lodge and Thornton, *English Constitutional Documents 1307–1485*, pp. 356–8; H. Hall, *Formula Book*, ii, 70-2).
[3] Hall, *op. cit.*, ii, 70.

In addition to these escheators' accounts, there is in the Public Record Office a vast series of files, beginning in 1236, in which are collected the writs of *diem clausit extremum* ordering the inquisition, and the escheators' returns, including more or less detailed manorial extents. For the purpose of this study, I have confined myself in the main to the inquisitions of the reign of Henry III and the first years of the reign of Edward I, but with the additional examination of a few fourteenth-century inquisitions.[1]

The great advantage of the inquisitions as a source lies in the fact that they provide material relating to practically all the counties of England. And while general works on English agrarian history in the Middle Ages have mostly been based on ecclesiastical material, the inquisitions, with some few exceptions, give surveys of the estates of lay lords. They therefore represent a valuable corrective to established views.

DESCRIPTION OF THE INQUISITIONS

The inquisitions provide us with figures which at first sight seem precise and simple. But before we can use them for our purposes, it is essential to decide what is their import. Allowing for variations, they usually give the following heads of information:

VALUATION OF DEMESNE

1. Estimated value of homestead, court, garden, vineyard,[2] dovecote, etc.
2. Area of arable land, and its estimated value.
3. Area of meadow land in acres, and estimated value.
4. Area of pasture land, and estimated value.
5. Area of woodland and its estimated value, often with an indication of the different items of revenue from this source.
6. List of mills, and their estimated annual revenue.
7. Secondary sources of income: salt-pans, peat, fisheries, ovens, breweries, etc.

[1] The Record Commission's printed *Calendarium Inquisitionum post Mortem* (4 vols. 1806–28) is inaccurate. The Calendars published since 1904 by the Stationery Office have mainly been used by genealogists and detailed extents are not printed, though their existence is indicated.
[2] Or fishpond; *vinarium* is sometimes misread for *vivarium*.

Valuation of Holdings

1. The money rent (*redditus assisae*) of free holdings.
2. The money rent of villein holdings.
3. The labour dues of villeins and their equivalent in money (often only a money assessment of these dues is given).
4. Produce rent, sometimes valued in money terms.
5. Revenues of the manor court (*placita et perquisita*).
6. Estimate of revenue from view of frank-pledge, market, trading dues, the hundred-court.

Often not all of these items are given; sometimes several of them may be added together. The main item is the estimates of the money value of different items of income. How were they arrived at? In some cases it was a very simple matter. It was not difficult to determine the sum total of the tenants' money payments. The practice of commutation of labour services made it possible to give a monetary estimate of labour rent. It was much more complicated in cases where an average rate of net revenue had to be given, as in the estimate of the arable, and of other items of demesne revenue. In order to obtain figures for net revenue various deductions were made from gross revenue.[1] But the usual method of estimating average net revenue from any source was to reckon up what annual rent could be obtained by leasing out.[2] Generally speaking, estimates of this sort were made by rule of thumb, and give a figure which is quite unreal. Sometimes, when they had no other data available for estimating the value of the demesne land, the jurors used the value of the tenants' land, based on the tenants' rent, as a guide.[3]

Home Farm

The home farm is usually not highly rated. Sometimes we find a very detailed description of all the buildings showing the state of repair of each. The main part of the revenue from the home farm is made up of the sums brought in by the garden, farmyard, kitchen garden and dovecot. These are not usually

[1] E.g. for payments to manorial administration, for the repair of buildings and equipment.

[2] About a mill: *Si non fuisset in manu domini possit tradi ad firmam pro 1 mk.*

[3] C. Hen. III, File 25/12 ... *sunt in dominico et villenagio 62 bovate terre unde quelibet bovata valet per annum 6s. 8d. et est summa 20 libre 13s.*

large figures. Yalding (Kent), where the garden was seven acres in size and the *fructus cum herbagio* was valued at £1 6s. 8d., is an exception.[1] Often the revenue from the homestead is not given at all, or is included in the revenue from the demesne.

DEMESNE ARABLE

The arable land is the main source of demesne revenue on most manors. Usually we are given the number of arable acres, more rarely the number of carucates or bovates, still more rarely of virgates, and the estimated value of one acre of arable (or of one carucate, bovate, etc.). The land is frequently divided into several categories, according to the quality, and the areas and values are given separately for each category. The principle followed in arriving at the number of acres is not always the same. Usually the whole area of the fields is given, but sometimes only the parts sown to corn are counted, land lying fallow being left out. In those cases where there is an indication that only the sown acreage has been counted, the calculation of the total arable area is made more difficult by the fact that it is not always clear which system of agriculture is being followed. The number of acres is usually reckoned on the basis of the 'short' hundred of one hundred acres, but sometimes on that of the 'long' hundred of one hundred and twenty. It is usually possible to tell which of these methods has been followed, but a fair number of cases remain doubtful. Great caution is thus called for before one accepts even figures giving what seem to be very precise acreages of demesne arable. In any case, the average figures for acres of demesne arable given by the inquisitions are as a rule lower than the actual ones, and the extent of the demesne arable is sometimes indicated in extremely vague terms. Often it is given in bovates or carucates, the exact size of which was not known even to the local inhabitants.[2] Even 'acres' can have the vague meaning of 'field strips'.[3]

The assessments of arable land vary greatly, from 1d. or 2d. to 2s. 6d. per acre.[4] The use of marl raises the estimated

---

[1] C. Hen. III, File 27/5.
[2] *Quia terra illa nunquam acrata fuit*, C. Ed. I, File 14/2. *Carucate non per acras estimate*, C. Hen. III, File 28/17; and many others.
[3] *Non per perticas sed sicut iacent*; C. Hen. III, File 21/12.
[4] Fleet, Kent, C. Hen. III, File 31/1.

D

value.[1] A higher valuation is given to land which can be sown to wheat and barley than for land which can only grow oats.[2] The value represented by the pasturing of cattle on the stubble is usually included in the assessment of the demesne arable, but is sometimes reckoned up separately. The revenue from the straw is also sometimes accounted for separately.

At times we find very summary valuations of the arable, and sometimes the assessments for the meadow land, the pasture and even the homestead are included with it. The bovates of the demesne are often counted *cum pertinenciis*—i.e. the meadows and pastures attached to them are reckoned in with them. Usually the demesne was in the lord's hands. Cases of its being leased out to tenants are very rare. At Chillaton (Devon) it is rented in this way by villeins.[3]

MEADOWS

Meadow land is usually counted in acres (rarely in bovates). Its estimated value is always higher than that of the arable: the highest estimates I have encountered were 3s. 1d. per acre at Radcliffe (Notts.) and 4s. at Tadcaster (Yorks.). Sometimes the quality of the meadow is indicated: *debile, debilior, non falcabile, pessimum*, etc.,—evidently to explain low assessment. In addition to the number of acres of meadow land given in the actual estimate, one may assume the existence of other small portions of meadow in the form of appurtenances to the arable. The valuation of meadow land usually includes the pasturing of cattle after the hay has been cut, but this item of revenue is sometimes given separately.

PASTURE

A great many difficulties arise in regard to revenue from pasture land. The first question is whether the inquisitions give only the enclosed pasture belonging to the lord, his *pastura separabilis*, or whether there is also an estimate for his share in the common pasture, as the royal instructions directed. In some cases where the number of acres is given it is clear that it refers only to separate pasture. Sometimes there is no estimate

---

[1] On some manors in Sussex and Kent *terra marlerata* is given a higher valuation.
[2] Hamsey, Sussex, C. Hen. III, File 42/6.
[3] C. Hen. III, File 14/13.

of the area of pasture land in terms of acres, probably because the precise area in acres was unknown. Sometimes there is a note to the effect that a valuation refers either to separate or to common pasture. In cases where the extent of the pasture is measured only in terms of the head of cattle on it, or is not given at all (only an assessment in money being shown), it is difficult to judge whether it is separate or common pasture that is in question. Sometimes the valuation of rights of pasture on land appurtenant to the demesne arable may be included in the valuation of the arable itself. But we have every ground for supposing that common pasture was often not included in the valuation of pasture revenue. This is especially clear in surveys of northern manors, where we know that stock-breeding was highly developed, yet where there is often no mention at all of revenue from pasture—but in some few cases we find mention of many hundreds of sheep and horned cattle and of revenues from pasture land exceeding all other items of manorial income.[1] This makes the figures given for revenue from pasture quite valueless; they can only give us some idea of the extent of the separate pasture of the demesne—not always even that.[2]

WOODLAND

Revenue from woodland was of a complex nature. It included sale of timber and particularly of brushwood and of deadwood, heybot and housebot, herbage and pannage and income from nuts. These items for the main part were not revenue from operations of the demesne economy, so much as levies on the tenants for the right to make use of the demesne woods. Pannage, housebot and heybot in particular were of this nature. The 'sale' of wood and brushwood does not mean sale in open market, but a payment by manorial tenants for their right to take and use the same.[3] The valuation of herbage was made up partly of an estimated value for the use of the pasture by the lord's cattle,[4] and partly, again, of payments

---

[1] At Harbottle (Northumbr.), C. Hen. III, File 9/1—pasture for 1,140 sheep, 1,400 cows and an unspecified number of horses, estimated at £41 18s. 4d.
[2] Part of the revenue from pastures might consist of income from the leasing out to tenants of portions of pasture; see Eastbourne (Sussex), C. Hen. III, File 2/7, *pastura quam pastores tenent*.
[3] Somborne (Hants.), C. Hen. III, File 21/12, and Weston (Hants.), (*ibid.*).
[4] Laxton (Notts.), C. Hen. III, File 13/10.

for the grazing of the tenants' cattle. Sometimes we find very
large sums as revenue from woodland, apparently connected
with extensive felling; but commonly the revenue from woodland is reckoned *sine wasto*. Brushwood was usually cut in
sections: every year a quarter, a fifth or a lesser fraction of
the brushwood would be sold. The jurors were often at a loss
to value the lord's revenue from the common woods: *non
potest extendi quare est communis.*

The revenue from woodland varied from year to year. Thus
pannage is sometimes paid only *si boscus portat.*[1] At Hamsey
(Sussex) heybot and housebot are valued at £1 *plus vel minus.*[2]
A park with game in it would not bring in the usual revenues
of woodland.[3] The areas of woods are often given in acres,
but sometimes are omitted altogether. Sometimes they are
described in terms customary since the days of Domesday:
parcus 1½ *leucae et amplius in circuitu.*[4]

MILLS AND OTHER MONOPOLIES

Revenue from mills is sometimes reckoned in with the
demesne, sometimes along with the holdings. A mill might be
run by the manorial administration, but often it would be
leased out; sometimes a free tenant has it. Sometimes both
methods of working might be in use on one and the same manor.
But even a mill which is run by the manorial administration
does not represent solely an item of revenue from demesne.
It is also closely linked with the levies made on the tenants.
Secta molendini is a vital part of the mill revenue. We therefore
find special disclaimers to the effect that there is no suit
connected with a given mill. At Hadstone (Northumberland)
bondmen and free tenants bought themselves off from the
obligatory *secta molendini*. On this account £1 4s. was added to
the *firmae* of the bondmen, and 5s. to those of the freemen.[5]
Revenue from mills is usually given in terms of money. But
this is simply a valuation of the mill's revenue, which was only
partly made up of money, and partly of payments in kind.

[1] Birling (Kent), C. Hen. III, File 42/6.
[2] C. Hen. III, File 42/6.
[3] Weoley (Worcs.) C. Ed. I, File 2/6: herbage is valued at £5, *si fere non fuissent*.
Also Barrow (Leics.), *ibid.*
[4] Bentley (Essex), C. Hen. III, File 31/1.
[5] C. Hen. III, File 21/11.

In a number of cases we find nothing but payments in kind—flour, malt, barley, etc. The rent paid by the lessee of the mill might be in kind too.[1] Expenditure on the upkeep of the mill is often set against revenue.[2]

Mill revenue, then, was composed to a great extent of the levies on the tenants using the mill. These levies are, in fact, a form of rent in kind, which must be taken into consideration when we notice the insignificant part played by rent in kind, in the surveys of villeins' and free tenants' dues. Among other monopolies the oven (*furnus, pistrina*) and the brew-house (*bracina*) are occasionally mentioned. Sometimes the oven is leased out.[3] References to fulling mills (*molendina fullonica*) are not infrequent, but the way in which these were run and their connection with the system of monopolies, is not clear. Very often fisheries are valued, both those belonging to the demesne and those in common use (in the latter case the valuation is for the lord's share). They are sometimes leased out. Also mentioned is revenue from peat bogs,[4] from salt-pans (usually paid in kind), from game in the park,[5] and from rabbit-warrens.[6] Finally there are such items of revenue as wreck.[7]

REVENUE FROM TENANTS' HOLDINGS

That part of the revenue from holdings which is reckoned separately[8] falls into the following principal constituent items:[9] (i) money rent (*redditus assisae*) of freeholders; (ii) the money

[1] Beetham (Westmorland), C. Hen. III, File 16/8.

[2] Sometimes a mill, especially one which is leased out, is treated as part of a property, including also a piece of land and the mill-dam.

[3] Rothbury (Northumbr.), C. Hen. III, File 9/1.

[4] The revenues from marshland appropriated by the lord are sometimes very great. Marshes were used principally as pasture. At Carlton (Lincs.), C. Hen. III, File 6/12, the demesne marsh brings in £15 19s. 4d.—three times as much as the demesne arable.

[5] *Warenna de leporibus*, at Walton (Suffolk), C. Hen. III, File 37/17, valued at 10s. per annum.

[6] This is sometimes a real revenue of a commercial nature. At Disning (Suffolk), in 1295–96 a *cunicularium ad vendendos cuniculos* is valued, together with the pasture land it is on, at £16 10s.

[7] Wells and Warham (Norf.)

[8] Parts of it have already been counted as constituents of the revenue from the demesne (particularly revenue from pastures, woods and mills).

[9] In the inquisitions, however, these are not shown as separate items, or are not completely separated from one another.

rent of villeins; (iii) the labour dues of villeins (and occasionally of freeholders too); (iv) the payments in kind made by
both groups; (v) tallages and aids; (vi) various small customary
rents—churchscot and others ; (vii) the revenues of the manor
court.[1] The inquisitions usually give summary valuations of
these items of revenue. But in some cases the area of tenants'
land is given; sometimes all the holdings are listed and the
dues of each shown. The most essential of the above items for
our purposes are the first three, but they present special
difficulties in calculation. This is due to the fact that they are
not sufficiently clearly separated. First of all, it is a frequent,
almost customary, practice to lump together money rents
from both free and villein holdings. Only, therefore, if one
regards the amount of freehold land as insignificant can one
use the information in the inquisitions *post Mortem* as evidence
on the question of commutation as Gray used it—comparing
labour dues with the sum total of money payments.[2] However,
sometimes the rents of freeholders and villeins are reckoned up
separately; and these cases are sufficient in number to indicate
the relative proportion of these two classes of payment.

TALLAGE OR AID

Tallage or aid, one of the main payments made by villeins,
is not always mentioned. Sometimes it is noted that tallage
is paid at the lord's will, and then an approximate estimate of
its rate may be given.[3] Occasionally there is a note *nullum
tallagium*.[4] But the absence of any mention of tallage or aid
does not mean that they were not paid, especially as tallage
could be counted in with other items of revenue, e.g. the
court revenues.[5] In the inquisitions for Yorkshire rents and
tallage are counted together. All in all, the failure to include
cases of tallage or aid—which was sometimes a very considerable item—must on the average have artificially lowered
the money rent shown for villeins.

[1] A separate place is occupied by the revenue from the hundred, if it is annexed
to the manor, and by market dues, etc.
[2] *E.H.R.*, xxix (1914), 633.
[3] *Communibus annis valet* or *potest valere* or *plus vel minus*, etc.
[4] E.g. Elm (Somerset), C. Hen. III, File 6/12.
[5] E.g. Ashley (Hants.), C. Hen. III, File 14/13.

LABOUR SERVICES

These are not always separated from the estimate of money revenue. Gray assumes that rents and labour services were almost always set down separately, and that where there is no mention of services we are entitled to assume their absence—'such (he adds) is the exactitude of these documents'.[1] I cannot agree. Quite apart from the fact that there actually are a few summary estimates of 'rents and labour dues' as one item,[2] in a number of cases we have good grounds for presuming the existence of labour dues in places where there is no separate mention of them. A comparison of the parallel surveys (one short and one extensive) for Lambeth (Surrey),[3] shows the existence of labour dues where the short survey only speaks of 'rents'. The indeterminate nature of the terminology employed points the same way. Usually the term denoting money rents is *redditus*, that for labour dues is *opera* or *servitia*. But it sometimes happens that *servitium* refers to money rent, and *redditus* to labour rent.[4] Without checking all Gray's material, it seems possible that he was mistaken in taking the silence of the inquisitions on labour rents as evidence of their non-existence. In some cases he adduced very summary surveys which might easily have lumped together under one heading both money and labour rents.[5] It is also strange that as a basis for conclusions on the commutation of labour dues Gray should have chosen surveys which show clearly a complete absence of villeins.[6] How little the absence of mention of labour dues in the inquisitions proves either their existence or their non-existence is best brought out by a comparison of the contemporaneous surveys of the manor of Catworth from the inquisitions *post Mortem* and the 1279 Hundred Rolls.[7] The inquisition speaks only of villeins' money rents, payable over

---

[1] H. L. Gray, *op. cit.*, 630.

[2] *Redditus cum operibus*—see Sutton and Plumborough (Essex), C. Hen. III, File 36/14.

[3] C. Hen. III, File 29/2.

[4] *Idem habuit in servicium liberorum 34s. 7d.*, C. Hen. III, File 3/4, and many others. See also expressions such as *redditus averagia*—Walton (Suff.), C. Hen. III, File 38/17. *Redditus pro omni servicio* often means an overall assessment of all dues, including labour dues.

[5] Thus, at Muskham (Notts.) the heading is *redditus nativorum et cottariorum*—6s. 8d. We should read this as meaning an overall assessment of all villein dues.

[6] E.g. Eccleshall (Yorks.), *ibid.* Maurholme (Lancs.), C. Ed. III, File 69/25.

[7] C. Ed. I, File 22/8; and *R.H.*, ii, 625.

three different periods. The Hundred Rolls give only a list of labour dues. This is no more abnormal than the note appended to certain Ramsey extents after listing the labour dues of the villeins—*Ad censum autem potest dominus opera sua omnia ponere si voluerit*. We see, in short, an ordinary case of the system of alternatives which was in use on manors where labour services were prominent. The tenants' dues could be expressed either in terms of work-days or by a monetary estimate.[1] The form in which they actually were demanded was flexible and could vary from year to year. This should be remembered by all engaged in work on surveys, manorial as well as governmental. A true picture can only be gained by the study of a chronological series of ministers' accounts.

Sometimes a distinction is drawn in the surveys between works which must always be rendered as such, and works which can be replaced by money payments.[2] In some cases the documents give a clear enough indication that there were no labour dues on the manor concerned. Such phrases as *nullam operacionem faciendo*,[3] or *opera sunt posita ad firmam* or *ad redditum* speak for themselves. We have plenty of indications that the process of commutation was well under way. But in all doubtful cases extreme caution is necessary.

Even in those cases in which labour rent is marked off from money rent we are not always certain that the assessment of the former does not include other elements as well. A very common antithesis is *redditus assisae liberorum hominum* and *opera villenagii*. Here the assessment of the villeins' labour dues can include small customary rents in money and in kind. A term like *consuetudines*, in particular, can mean not only labour rents but all the customary dues of the villeins.[4]

---

[1] Such expressions, therefore, as *opera villanorum extenta in denariis, opera et consuetudines positae ad certum*, refer not to commutation but to the assessment of labour dues in terms of money. Even such phrases as *reddunt pro quieta clamantia operum suorum* (Ferrybridge, Yorks., C. Hen. III, File 6/6) do not mean irrevocable final commutation since *redditus* is reckoned separately; here we have only the possibility of commutation.

[2] *Opera vel redditus*—Wroxall (Isle of Wight), C. Hen. III, File 29/2.

[3] Matfen (Northumbr.), C. Hen. III, File 30/14.

[4] Some works, which were paid for by the manorial administration—at any rate in the form of victuals—were not included in the general assessment, since they did not count as revenue for the lord (or only their value after deduction of the cost of the food was reckoned. E.g. at Burham (Kent), C. Hen. III, File 42/6. Cases of this sort are quite common and often come to light when reference is made to ministers' accounts.)

All manner of small levies in money and in kind (e.g. pannage, churchscot) might be reckoned in with other heads in the account—money rents, labour dues, court revenues.[1] Pannage is often included in the revenue from the demesne woods, but it is also often entered separately and counted as a villein payment.[2] It tends to become divorced from the actual use of the woods and to turn into a regular money rent.[3]

The revenue of the court is given in the majority of surveys. It sometimes forms a considerable addition to the money rent of the tenants. But the inquisitions continually give estimates for this item which are suspiciously low compared with those found, e.g. in ministers' accounts. Evidently some reductions were made in order to obtain a figure of net revenue. Sometimes certain payments which are usually treated as part of the revenue of the court are counted in with other items.[4]

Revenue from markets (*mercatum, forum, stallagium, teloneum*) is very rarely given. Apparently it did not play any great part in the demesne revenue. Among the revenues of the hundred, one which attracts attention is *opera hundredi*.[5] But they play so minor a part that they may safely be ignored so far as the relative proportions of labour and money rents are concerned.

LIMITS OF ACCURACY OF THE INQUISITIONS

In summary, we may list the following points, which must be taken into account in using the inquisitions for statistical purposes:

1. The number of acres at which the demesne is assessed is on the average below the real figure.

2. The estimate of demesne revenues is quite unreal and signifies only that in the jurors' opinion the items mentioned could be leased out for the stated amount of rent.

[1] It is possible that the overall assessments of rents and labour dues sometimes included the value of contributions in kind which are not mentioned as such. Thus the revenues of manorial mills included payments in kind. In general, therefore, the assessments in the inquisitions artificially decreased the actual amount of produce, sometimes to a considerable extent. Payments in kind might be concealed among the revenues of the court—heriot, for instance. See also La Penne (Isle of Wight), C. Hen. III, File 29/2: *pro ingressu recognitione warranto 21 libra cere* (16*d*.), *4 capones* (6*d*.).
[2] Almer (Dorset), File 6/9, and many more.
[3] Cf. N. Neilson 'Customary Rents', *O.S.S.L.H.*, ii (1910), 71–72.
[4] A curious bracketing is that of *licentia maritagii* with *averagia*, at Yalding (Kent), C. Hen. III, File 27/5.
[5] Somborne (Hants.), C. Hen. III, File 21/12.

3. The revenue from pasture is in part not mentioned at all, in part assessed at a much lower figure than its real value.

4. The revenues from woodland and mills include payments made by tenants, which apparently include a money valuation of the greater part of the payments made in kind, as well as actual money payments.

5. The money rent of the villeins is on the average assessed at a lower figure than it really brought in, since aid and tallage are not always included.

6. The absence of any mention of labour dues does not entitle us to conclude that they did not exist, and such cases should not be used as evidence in comparing amounts of money and labour rent.

7. The assessment of labour dues may include some contributions in money and in kind.

8. Part of the labour rents listed in the inquisitions might be replaced in any given year by money payments.

9. The figures for produce rent, as given in the lists of tenants' dues, are on the average lower, and sometimes, much lower, than the actual rate of such rents.

10. The revenue of the courts is put very much too low in the source.

RELIABILITY OF INQUISITIONS POST MORTEM

How far, then, can one trust the figures of the inquisitions *post Mortem*? How honest (granted the conventional nature of their terms) are these figures? How free are they from distortions due either to mistakes or to deliberate concealing of evidence?

As a check on the accuracy of the inquisitions, we may compare the surveys made in 1269–1270 of the manors of Roger Bigod, Earl of Norfolk,[1] with the almost exactly contemporaneous series of ministers' accounts for the same manors preserved in the Public Record Office. I have made this

---

[1] C. Hen. III, File 38/17. These particular inquisitions are remarkable for their unusual thoroughness in listing all items of revenue, particularly tenants' dues.

comparison for fourteen manors.[1] It does not cover all the figures in the inquisitions and the ministers' accounts, since the reckoning is not made on exactly the same basis in both cases. While the accounts give figures for gross revenue, and then figures for expenditure, the inquisitions try to give net revenue, and in the case of a number of items make deductions the basis of which is not always clear. The accounts do not give the number of acres in the demesne. But they do give the number of acres sown to various crops. Unfortunately the two- or three-field system was not in use in the counties of Essex, Norfolk and Suffolk, to which the material relates, so that a connection between the area of the demesne arable and the area sown to crops cannot always be established. The heads of revenue used in the accounts and the inquisitions are not the same.

Nevertheless, a number of items can be checked. And these are the most vital ones: (i) the sum total of money rents; (ii) the amount of labour dues, for which the surveys allow us to make quite detailed comparisons; (iii) produce rents; (iv) revenue from mills; (v) court revenues; (vi) (in places) revenue from woods, marshes, peat, etc.

The sum totals of money rents given in the accounts are usually higher than those in the inquisitions, but the difference in the majority of cases is not great, and cannot lead us into any great errors. It is hard to say whether the low figures are to be explained by deliberate concealment (it was easier for the officials to conceal the sum of money rents from the Exchequer than for the reeve to hide it from the lord), or by some deduction made from gross revenue. The latter is probable. The sum total of money rents (*redditus assisae*) for all fourteen manors is given in the accounts as £195 13s. 6d. (or £195 1s. 0½d.) and in the inquisitions as £167 16s. 7¾d., or about 87 per cent of the figure in the accounts.

[1] Viz. Dovercourt (Essex), M.A., Bdl. 840, N. 1; Soham (Suff.), M.A., Bdl. 1004, N. 1; Cratfield (Suff.), M.A., Bdl. 995, N. 1; Walton (Suff.), M.A., Bdl. 1007, N. 4; Dunningworth (Suff.), M.A., Bdl. 995, N. 15; Staverton (Suff.), M.A., Bdl. 1007, N. 7; Framlingham (Suff.), M.A., Bdl. 936, N. 18; Ditchingham (Norf.), M.A., Bdl. 933, N. 20; Lopham (Norf.), M.A., Bdl. 937, N. 27; Acle (Norf.), M.A., Bdl. 929, N.1; Walsham (Norf.), M.A., Bdl. 944, N. 21; Suffield (Norf.), M.A., Bdl. 944, N. 1; Halvergate (Norf.), M.A., Bdl. 936, N. 2. For seven of these the ministers' accounts refer to 1268–69, in one case to 1269–70, while the rest are two to three years distant one way or the other. In only one case is there a difference of seven years, and in one other, of ten.

For a number of manors where the inquisition gives a list of the different categories of labour dues, a detailed comparison can be made. In some cases we have very close coincidences, but on the whole there is a steady depression of the figures in the inquisitions. Comparison with the accounts shows that this cannot be explained by allowance having been made for the practice of commutation, which was usual on the Earl of Norfolk's manors. Those services are as a rule excluded which the manorial administration did not assess on the grounds of the outgoings connected with them. Thus *precariae* are excluded and a number of minor works are not recorded at all—e.g. the preparation of malt, the carting and spreading of dung, harrowing, etc. Even when precise, the inquisition gives a simplified and incomplete picture. But in some cases we find major omissions, which can only be put down to negligence, and which bring down the sum total of labour dues extremely sharply. All in all, for five manors the figures of the inquisitions are close to those of the accounts, for five others they are considerably lower, while for three more we find them showing only 2–10 per cent of the labour dues listed in the accounts. The great carelessness shown in the surveys of labour dues may be due to the fact that the Exchequer was interested primarily in the money side of the accounts, so that the greatest attention was given to this. The sum total of labour dues for the fourteen manors is assessed by the accounts at £145 19s. 8d., and by the inquisitions at £81 3s. 3¼d., or 56 per cent.

Produce rents are almost invariably put too low in the inquisition, the difference occasionally being very considerable, while in one case they are omitted entirely. But for the most part the figures of the two sources are fairly close. Produce rents, however, constitute a very small part of manorial revenue in this particular group of documents.

Revenues from mills are as a rule considerably higher in the accounts than in the inquisitions. But here, perhaps, the inquisition is giving net revenue only. The accounts sometimes show expenditure on mills. At times these expenses are considerable; they vary greatly from year to year.

It is possible that in calculating net revenue the escheators took some figure, which they believed to be a fair average, and deducted it from gross revenue. In one case the figure in the inquisitions is higher than in the account; in four cases there is a close resemblance; but in the rest the inquisition gives a much lower figure. The sum total of mill revenue in the accounts is £56 3s. 1¼d.; in the inquisitions it is £36 1s. 8d., or 63 per cent.

The greatest discrepancies between the accounts and the inquisitions occur on the subject of court revenues. The sum total of these according to the accounts is £124 18s. 2d., and according to the inquisitions £28 12s. 4d. According to the inquisitions, therefore, the court revenue was only a quarter of that given in the accounts. Possibly deductions had been made here for the salary of the bailiff or steward, or for other expenses connected with the court.[1]

A number of sources of revenue, sometimes very large items, named in the accounts, are omitted from the inquisitions, or greatly reduced. Thus, at Staverton the accounts note a revenue from peat working of £16 16s. 9½d. (though the accounts for some years state *nihil in hoc anno*); at Halvergate the accounts assess the leasing of four marshes at £50 17s. 4d., the inquisitions allow for £14 from five marshes; at Ditchingham the accounts give the revenue from woodland as £21 19s. 3d., while the inquisitions only give £9 7s. 2d. (the accounts do note, however, a large sale of brushwood in this year); at Walsham the accounts value leases of marshland at £17, while the inquisition assesses this item, together with peat-workings, at only £4 3s. 4d.; at Acle the lease of a marsh is worth £35 9s. 0d. according to the accounts, and only £4 according to the inquisition. The omissions or reductions in the inquisitions sometimes give a distorted impression of the nature of the demesne revenue, which might, as at Acle or Halvergate, have revenue from marshland, i.e. principally pasture revenue, as its main item. The inquisitions often omit small rents, but they sometimes mention items not included in the accounts.[2]

Something has already been said of the difficulties of checking figures for area of demesne arable by means of figures giving areas sown to crops on the demesne, especially in East Anglian material. The sum total of land sown, for seven

[1] Rothbury (Northumbr.), C. Hen. III, File 9/1: it is stated of the revenue of the court that it *non sufficit ad sustentationem ballivi*.
[2] At Walton, for instance, the *warenna, lepores, piscario in stagno, cuniculi*, etc.

manors, comes according to the accounts to 1,412¾ acres and 34 perches. The area of demesne arable for the same manors in the inquisitions is 1,542½ acres. One may presume that here, as at Forncett,[1] the inquisition is giving only acres sown to crops.

There are many cases in which comparisons can be made between the escheators' surveys and those of the 1279 Hundred Rolls; but these comparisons yield little. The main reason is that we are comparing the inquisitions with a source whose own accuracy is in need of confirmation and may often be doubted. At times the inquisitions enable us to correct mistakes in the Hundred Rolls. Parallel examination of the inquisitions and the Hundred Rolls suggests that in listing tenants' dues these sources were guided by different principles. The example was given above of the surveys of the manor of Catworth in the inquisition *post Mortem* and in the Hundred Rolls.[2] Where the inquisition gives only money payments, the Hundred Rolls give only labour rents. In general the inquisitions—where we can compare them with the Hundred Rolls—give higher figures for money payments and lower ones for labour rents. There is the very good survey of the manor of Brailes (Warwickshire) belonging to the Earl of Warwick.[3] The Hundred Rolls give here five carucates in the demesne, while the inquisition shows 600 acres. The figures correspond perfectly. For villein holdings the Hundred Rolls give 60 virgates, the inquisition 62½. The difference is trifling, especially since the surveys are not quite contemporaneous (the inquisition is eight years earlier than the Hundred Rolls). But in the assessment of the villeins' dues the discrepancy is considerable. The Hundred Rolls give 27d. money rent per virgate, i.e. £6 15s. 0d. for 60 virgates. The inquisition gives £10 3s. 3½d. as the money rent from villein virgates. The labour rents which the Hundred Rolls do not assess but merely list cannot yield less than £30. But the inquisition assesses them at £10 8s. 4d. The inquisition makes no mention whatever of a quite considerable amount of rent in kind—420 bushels of oats and 60 hens. The court revenues are not given in the Hundred Rolls, while in the inquisition they are reckoned at £8. Tallage

[1] See F. Davenport, *op. cit.*, 27.   [2] Cf. above, pp. 55–6.
[3] C. 52 Hen. III, File 35/13, and *R.H.* (*War.*), fol. 79.

is assessed by the Hundred Rolls at eight marks, by the inquisition at nine. It is hard to suppose that in the eight years that had elapsed between the inquisition and the Hundred Rolls the manor had gone over in part from money rents to rents in kind. At the same time, the inquisition is hardly likely to have exaggerated the money revenue, since it was precisely the latter the escheators had to account for to the Exchequer. One may presume that as a rule part of the labour rents listed in the Hundred Rolls were 'sold' each year, but in that case the total of labour rents given in the inquisition is too low.

It is certain, then, that we are dealing with an extremely unreliable source. If, as in the case of Walsham, a survey gives the amount of money rent almost precisely (£9 in the inquisition, £9 15s. 8½d. in the accounts), but puts labour rents twenty-five times lower than they ought to be (5s. 11d. in the inquisition, and £7 8s. 2½d. in the accounts), what help is such a survey in forming conclusions on the real relationship between different kinds of rent? It would certainly be very dangerous to construct any independent conclusions, especially in matters of detail, on the sole basis of the inquisitions. On the other hand, a comparison of the figures they contain, carried out over wide areas, enables us to capture certain characteristic traits, certain peculiarities which, though vague, are vital. And the results thus obtained assume considerable weight, when confirmed by other sources, and by conclusions independently arrived at. All that is needful is extreme caution in using this material, and a refusal to jump to conclusions where the evidence is not sufficiently clear-cut. The picture derived from the inquisitions is extremely obscure, and in places fades out in mist; it needs to be pored over and deciphered in the fullness of time; but an attentive eye will pick out from it lines which it would be hard to perceive by any other means, and which we cannot afford to ignore if we are to succeed in reconstructing the social order of feudal England.

Use of the Inquisitions post Mortem

What questions, then, can we put to these documents, and by what methods are we to get answers to them? The following questions, I believe, are of basic importance for determining the type of feudal economy existing in thirteenth-century England, and are capable of more or less satisfactory solution from the material at our disposal: (i) what was the predominant form of feudal rent? (ii) what was the comparative role of freeholders' and villeins' rent? (iii) to what extent did the demesne economy depend on the villeins' labour dues, and to what extent on wage labour? All these questions may have different answers in different parts of England.

1. The first point is the predominant form of feudal rent. Here we may note that the relation of the different forms of rent to one another is determined by the relation shown in their assessment in the surveys of tenants' dues, if they are assessed separately. But we must remember that we have here the bulk of tenants' rents, but not by any means the whole. Part is included in the revenues from woodland and from mills, and to some extent in that from pasture land, and especially in the court revenue. On the other hand, this part cannot be distinguished from the remainder of the revenue from woodland and mills; information on court revenues is not always given, and when it is, it sets them much too low; in all these categories of revenue it is difficult, or even impossible, for us to distinguish money rents from rents in kind or even from labour dues.

Thus the basic material here is provided by the figures denoted as *redditus assisae* and *opera villanorum* (together, in some cases, with the labour dues of freeholders), and by the rents in kind which are noted among the dues of freeholders and villeins. The other items of revenue mentioned above may sometimes affect our estimate of the comparative incidence of the different forms of rent—especially in cases where they are very large (like the milling charges in the north). When it comes to considering the data on these different forms of rent separately, the following points should be noted.

The extent of money rent is undoubtedly minimized out of all proportion in our material; in addition to *redditus assisae*, the greater part of forest rents (pannage, herbage, etc.) were paid in money, as was part of the mill farms and charges, and practically the whole of the court revenue, which played an incomparably greater part in the demesne revenue than our source shows. As for labour rents, we have no reason to think that they were present to any great extent among revenue from demesne pastures, woods, mills, courts, though small labour rents might sometimes lurk here, e.g. payments for use of timber. Further, our source does not allow for the annual sale of works, the replacement of part of the labour rents by money payments, which must have brought the total of labour rent down considerably at times. For this reason we might expect an exaggeration of the relative figures for labour rent. But the carelessness and omission in the sources' listing of labour dues—which have been mentioned above—to a certain extent counterbalance the opposite tendency to rate the comparative importance of labour rents too high. Nor must we forget that the sale of works, which the inquisitions do not record, not only brought the level of labour rents down, but raised that of money rents correspondingly. There is therefore not much danger of our calculations underestimating the role of labour rent as compared to money rent.

In order to prove this essential point, I may adduce parallel calculations from the inquisitions and from ministers' accounts for the fourteen manors of the Earl of Norfolk discussed above.[1] Here our analysis has already shown that the inquisitions assess labour rents far below their real value and that consequently there is some risk of underestimating them. Let us take the figures which we have already cited for labour rents and *redditus assisae* on these fourteen manors. According to the ministers' accounts they amount to £145 19s. 8d. and £195 13s. 6d. respectively, that is, 42 per cent and 58 per cent. Thus there appears to be a considerable underestimation of labour rents in the inquisitions, where they are assessed at only £81 3s. 3¼d. But the accounts show that in the years to which the inquisitions apply works were 'sold' on these manors to the value of £43 8s. 4½d. Thus the relation between the real amounts of labour and money rent (plus sale of works) will be £102 11s. 3½d. to £239 1s. 10½d., or 30 per cent to 70 per cent; in other words, the actual proportion of labour rents to money rents is even lower than the inquisitions show it. To make the check complete, we should, however, add to the sum total of money rents in the accounts other money rents apart from *redditus assisae* and 'sale of works', e.g. court revenue. For the fourteen manors this comes to £124 18s. 2d. The ratio

[1] Above, p. 58 ff.

E

of labour to money rent will thus be £102 11s. 3½d. : £364 10s. 0½d. or 22 per cent: 78 per cent. In actual fact the preponderance of money rent is even greater.

The conclusion is obvious: our thesis that in comparing the figures from the inquisitions for *redditus assisae* and *opera* we run no risk of belittling the rôle of labour rents in comparison to money rents is not only confirmed, but could even be replaced by another thesis: that in making this comparison we risk exaggerating the role of labour rent.

The inquisitions undoubtedly belittle the role of produce rents. We must take this into account, especially for places where, as in the northern counties, the revenue from mills is very large and is for the most part clearly in kind. But there are grounds for assuming that a certain part of the rents in kind was in practice replaced by money payments. The numerous entries in ministers' accounts and in the escheators' accounts, showing 'sales' of corn *de exitu molendini* or of poultry and eggs *de redditu* often do not represent market operations but the replacement of these contributions in kind by money payments. Thus, while admitting that the role of produce rent is far from fully displayed in our source, we must also make a note of yet another item which may conceal unrecorded money rents.

2. The comparative parts played by free and villein holdings can be calculated from the rents of free and villein holdings. A considerable obstacle here is the fact that in a majority of cases the money rents of freeholders and villeins are given together. Still, it is sometimes possible to separate them and thus to obtain some figures to serve as rough guides, which are, however, in many cases far from accurate owing to the incompleteness of the material. The percentage of 'free' rent is not the same thing as the percentage of free land, nor is it an accurate guide thereto; there are wide variations in the rent-levels of free holdings, which sometimes do not correspond at all to the size of the holdings. Often a vast area of free holdings lies hidden behind an insignificant rent-entry. In general we can assume that the percentage of free land compared with that of villein land is much bigger than the percentage of free to villein rents. Of course, the free holdings conceal among them many non-peasant holdings, sometimes even small

manors. Nevertheless, the 'free' rents have a certain value as a guiding figure.

3. Knowing the approximate extent of the demesne arable and of the villeins' labour dues, we can draw more or less accurate conclusions on the adequacy of the supply of obligatory labour for the demesne and on the probable role of wage labour.

All the figures, of course, which we obtain from our calculations will be significant only as guides. The proportion, for instance, which we arrive at between labour rent and money rent or produce rent for this or that part of England is certainly not to be taken as the real one. It requires further checking and investigation on the basis of the general rules laid down above, and on the basis of the analysis we have made of the inquisitions and the data contained in them; when this has been done it will be possible to reach a general conclusion on the probable predominance, or sometimes the considerable predominance, of one or another form of rent in the given area. I do not intend to draw any more precise conclusions than this.

CHAPTER II

MANORIAL STRUCTURE IN THIRTEENTH-CENTURY ENGLAND

THE CLASSICAL THEORY OF THE MANOR AND ITS CRITICS

According to the classical theory rural England was an agglomeration of more or less uniformly constructed manors. 'Descriptions of English rural arrangements in the age we are studying always suppose the country to be divided into manors. . . . Whether we take the Domesday Survey or the Hundred Rolls, or the custumal of some monastic institution, or the extent of lands belonging to some deceased lay lord— we shall again and again meet the same typical arrangement.'[1] The typical manor coincides with a vill, and therefore represents a village community. At the head of the manor stands a lord (an individual or a corporate body), who holds the manor from the king or from another lord. The manor is divided into two basic parts, the demesne, which usually comprises a half to one-third of the territory of the manor, and which is cultivated by the obligatory labour of the peasants, and the land of the peasant serfs: to these must be added the free holdings, which make up 'a narrow fringe' on the territory of the manor. Each manor represents a separate unit from the point of view of economic administration, which in each case is entrusted to a reeve and a steward; each manor has a court; and each manor keeps annual accounts. This system, not yet fully elaborated in Domesday Book, takes on a perfected and systematic form in the Hundred Rolls. 'When we compare these shades of subjection (in Domesday Book) to the well-rounded, compact manors of the Hundred Rolls, we are struck by the progress made by unification and subjection.'[2]

But it was precisely on the material of the Hundred Rolls that Maitland based his attempt to demonstrate that the manor had no constant, definite features. There might, he showed,

---

[1] Vinogradoff, *Villainage*, 313.
[2] Vinogradoff, *Growth of the Manor*, 299–300.

be no lord's farm, or no lord's land, on a manor; there might be no free holdings; there might even be no villeins and no villein land. A manor may have no court. A manor may be enormous, taking in a number of villages; a number of hundreds may belong to it; but a manor may also be a tiny patch of land. Even as a unit of economic administration the manor has no exactly defined characteristics.[1]

Even if we cannot agree with Maitland's excessively sceptical conclusion that in view of all this the term 'manor' cannot be defined, and that to ask for such a definition is to ask for the impossible, at least Maitland's analysis has shown the extreme complexity and variety of structure among English manors in the thirteenth century, the classical epoch of the manor. Maitland pointed out the presence in medieval England of holdings or complexes of holdings which cannot be called manors and yet do not come within any manor. And more recently local investigations have brought to light the specific peculiarities of manorial structure in the northern Danelaw, East Anglia, Northumbria, Kent, and other regions, which do not fit in with the description of a typical manor.

But the centre of England, the southern Midlands, which are covered by the material preserved in the Hundred Rolls, still appears as the area of typical manors, in spite of the fact that it was precisely here that Maitland found his main arguments against the universal validity of the manorial system in England. An analysis of manorial structure in this region will, therefore, be our first task.

We must first answer the following questions:

1. To what extent did the countryside of the Midlands consist of manors, and what part was played by elements which cannot be classed as manors?
2. To what extent do the manors which we find described in our sources correspond to the classical characterization of a 'typical' manor?

The Manor in the Hundred Rolls

The Hundred Rolls provide unique material for answering these questions, since in them the manor is not isolated, as in

[1] Pollock and Maitland, i, 594–601.

manorial sources, but presented in relation to the vill, to the tenurial system and to other manors.

The character of the Hundred Rolls as a governmental, not a manorial, survey is clearly expressed in the arrangement of its material. It would be better to say that here we have not one system of arrangement, but three, which sometimes cut across one another. The first, which stands out most clearly and sharply, is the division into villages—vills and hamlets. Any, or practically any, estate lies within some village or in several villages. Linked up with this division is the communal organization of the village, which, however, is little in evidence in this source. The second network superimposed on England is the system of tenure, arranged in the form of the feudal hierarchy. Every estate is a tenement, or a complex of tenements. There are exceptions to this rule. There are tenements of which it is not known from whom they are held. But such cases are abnormal, due either to lack of knowledge or failure of memory. Finally, the third system is the division into manors. One may agree with Maitland that in the thirteenth century no precise legal definition of the term manor had been established, but it is beyond doubt that in the fields of agriculture, administration and law the manor played a decisive part.

A careful survey of the Hundred Rolls indicates that the living tissue of rural England, at least in the area covered by the enrolments was, in fact, composed of manors; that is, if we do not understand by 'manor' only the 'typical' manor with serfs and labour services. But this living tissue is remarkable for its complexity, and is, in certain areas in particular, far removed from 'unification' and systematization. The parts distinguished by the greatest simplicity of structure are Oxfordshire and Huntingdonshire, except in the latter case for the southern hundred of Toseland. The fabric of the medieval countryside is most complex and involved in Cambridgeshire and in those hundreds of Bedfordshire and Buckinghamshire for which enrolments survive. Nevertheless, the whole ground covered by the Hundred Rolls can be divided into manors with practically nothing left outside; 'extra-manorial' elements are on the whole insignificant, and in certain cases may be the result either of lack of information on the part of the juries who simply did not know in which manor to place this or that holding—or of the fragmentary nature of the rolls. Sometimes the jurors were unable to determine from whom a given individual held his land, and confine themselves to the comment that the land is held 'from various lords' (*de diversis dominis*) or 'from several fees' (*de pluribus feodis*).

Sometimes the jurors cannot sort out a mass of freeholders and place them under their respective manors, and instead list them with an indication of the individuals under whom they are direct tenants and to whom they pay rent. Thus at Haslingfield (Cambs.)[1] a survey is given of three typical manors with demesnes, villeins and freeholders. But in addition there is appended a separate schedule in which twenty-six further freeholders are listed. Except for the last two, they hold small parcels of land from various people; of some of them it is said that they hold *de diversis dominis* or *de perquisitione sua*. Thus in the jurors' eyes alienation and sub-infeudation have completely destroyed the manorial connection. Then there is the unusual manor of Filgrave (Bucks.),[2] where there are no villeins at all. In the demesne of the 'lord' (*Johannes filius Johannis clerici*) there is only half a virgate; the remaining nine and a half virgates are in the hands of freeholders; furthermore only two and a half virgates are held directly from the lord and pay rent to him, the rest being held from a number of other people, whose connections with the lord's manor are not indicated. Instances such as this are by no means uncommon.[3] Such cases were sometimes of recent origin and connected with recent alienations. Accounting, for instance, for the confusion of holdings at Bourn (Cambs.),[4] the jurors declared 'that the Lord Gilbert Peche and his forebears held direct from our lord the king the barony of Bourn, and that this holding has been altogether sold and given over by them to the following . . .' But on the whole such alienations were nothing new in England, in some regions at any rate. Douglas has shown from charter material that alienation and purchase of land were widespread among the peasants of East Anglia as early as the twelfth century,[5] and Stenton has shown the same for the northern Danelaw. A proportion of free

[1] *R.H.*, ii, 557–58.   [2] *R.H.*, ii, 348.
[3] E.g. Hanslope (Bucks.), *R.H.*, ii, 343–46.   [4] *R.H.*, ii, 520–27.
[5] *O.S.S.L.H.*, ix.

holdings remained outside manorial organization *de facto*, and a certain (though insignificant) number of holdings even stood outside the manorial system *de jure*. We find holdings which legally do not belong to any manor and which are not themselves manors.[1] Such, for instance, are the small tenements held direct from the king, which are scattered over several vills and not linked with any of the king's manors. In these cases rent was sometimes paid to the sheriff.[2] Among such holdings there are many petty serjeanties. Of a similar extramanorial character were often assarts cleared on forest land, the rents for which were paid to the king.[3]

But apart from such cases we find in the surveys both separate holdings and whole groups of holdings where connections with manors have either been lost or never existed. The manorial organization was not so all-embracing as the organization into vills and holdings. But even the latter admits of exceptions. There are fiefs that do not come within any vill.[4] Theoretically every holding must be connected through the chain of tenures with the king; but in practice subinfeudation sometimes leads to the intervening links being forgotten.

An interesting point is the presence of villein holdings which do not belong to any manor. We sometimes find separate villein holdings, or small groups of them, which pay rent to their lords but are not connected with any manorial organization. In the vill of Stewkley (Bucks.), for example, the abbess of Fontevrault holds one carucate of free land from the principal lord of the manor, the Earl of Gloucester; from the abbess Margaret Aspernil holds two virgates 'and has these two virgates in villeins' (*habet illas duas virgatas in villanis*); each of the virgates pays her 15*s.* 6*d.* a year. Besides this, she has two freeholders.[5]

'Extra-manorial' elements there certainly are in the Hundred Rolls. But their sum total is insignificant, scarcely amounting to 2–3 per cent of the whole material. And in this connection

---

[1] Cf. Pollock and Maitland, i, 610.

[2] See, for instance, Podington (Beds.), two holdings of a half-virgate each, held direct from the king, *per parvam serjanteriam* pay 2*s.* each in money, to be handed to the sheriff of Bedfordshire.

[3] See Stoke Goldington (Bucks.), *R.H.*, ii, 347–48, the holding of Robert de Penfeld in Shudy Camps in the same county, *ibid.*, 428, etc.

[4] See *R.H.*, ii, 725: *Hec sunt feoda exempta que non sunt in villis sita.* Cf. Pollock and Maitland, i, 560–62.   [5] *R.H.*, ii, 335.

it must be emphasized that 'extra-manorial' is not by any means equivalent to 'extra-feudal'. The manorial organization is not the one and only method of levying feudal rent. A holding which pays rent or renders services directly to a lord, by-passing the manorial organization, does not thereby cease to be feudally dependent.

MANOR AND VILL

Although the Midlands is the typical area of the pre-dominance of the manorial system, this system is even here distinguished by considerable complexity, and a number of the definitions of the classical theory need modification.

First of all it must be stated that the 'typical' coincidence of the manor with the vill[1] is in fact not typical at all, and this applies not only—as has frequently been observed[2]—to the eastern counties, but to the whole of the territory covered by the Hundred Rolls.

We shall not be surprised to find that in Cambridgeshire vill and manor seldom coincide. The fact has been commented on frequently. Cambridgeshire bears the deep imprint of the régime characteristic of the southern Danelaw and of neigh-bouring East Anglia. Out of 110 Cambridgeshire vills covered by my calculations, only 12 coincide with manors. All the others are split up in a most complicated fashion between manorial units of widely varying structure. But if we move farther west we still find that practically nowhere does the 'typical manor', coinciding with the vill, predominate. Fifty-six Huntingdonshire vills are almost evenly divided—in 29 cases we find vills coinciding with manors, in 27 they do not coincide. Of those that do coincide, in 19 cases out of 29 we are dealing with monastic manors, which predominate in this county; in only 10 cases do the manors of temporal lords coincide with vills. Out of 25 Bedfordshire vills, only 7 are not

[1] Cf. Maitland, 'Select Pleas in Manorial Courts', *S.S.* ii, xi; Pollock and Mait-land, i, 586. Vinogradoff practically identifies the vill with the manor in *Growth of the Manor*, p. 361 ff. For Rogers, parish and manor are one and the same (*History of Agriculture and Prices*, i (1866), p. 12). Cf. also Jolliffe, *E.H.R.* (1926) xli. Contemporary writers sometimes identified the vill with the manor—'villas quas a manendo manerios vulgo vocamus' (*Ordericus Vitalis*, ii, 233).

[2] For the Danelaw see Stenton (*Br. Ac.*, v, lx); for East Anglia, see Douglas (*O.S.S.L.H.*, ix, 210), though the latter considers that in the south and west it is not often possible to distinguish between vill and manor. Cf. also Savine, *Zhurnal ministerstva narodnogo prosvyeschcheniya*, xi, 214; Pollock and Maitland, i, 604.

split up between various manorial units, and even here there are only two cases of complete coincidence between manor and vill; in the others the manor is more extensive than the vill and takes in parts of other vills.

Out of 46 North Buckinghamshire vills, 23 coincide with manors, while 25 do not. In Warwickshire 52 vills coincide with manors or are wholly contained within them, while 57 do not. According to Hilton's calculations, out of 134 vills in the Leicestershire hundreds of Guthlaxton and Gartree only 37 (28 per cent) coincide with manors, while 97 do not.[1] Of all the counties for which surveys are extant, only Oxfordshire shows a predominance of vills which coincide with manors; this predominance is to a large extent due to small-sized vills and hamlets. In Oxfordshire the number of vills coinciding with manors or totally contained by them is 191, the number of those not coinciding 111. Thus out of a total of 784 vills covered, 433 do not coincide with manors, and 351 do so. In reaching these figures, all those cases in which several vills are completely within a manor have been reckoned as 'coincident'. In fact, the real question is not the number of vills which do not coincide with manors, but the number of manors which do not coincide with vills. Then the frequency of 'non-coincidence' would be much greater, since every non-coincident vill would have to be divided into two, three, four or more manors. In fact, less than a quarter of the manors coincide with vills.

The manorial system is thus superimposed anything but symmetrically upon the village communal system, and non-coincidence is the rule rather than the exception.[2] If we take into account that in the north and east of England the vill and the manor represent systems even less closely connected, it is clear that we must abandon its coincidence with the vill as being the most important feature of the manor. Even in the area of the most highly developed manorial system the manor more often than not fails to coincide with the village community, its boundaries are not the boundaries of the com-

---

[1] *Studies in Leicestershire Agrarian History*, 20.
[2] The same fact was observed for Germany by von Below, *Probleme der Wirtschaftsgeschichte* (1920), 41.

munity, its fields overlap with the fields of other manors[1]
lying within the same community, its stock grazes on pastures
shared in common with other manors. In some cases we can see
that the non-coincidence of vill and manor is a comparatively
late development, arising as the result of the fragmentation of
an originally combined manor and vill unit. Thus the structure
of five manors in the vill of Clapham (Beds.) clearly betrays
the break-up of one manor first into two parts, and then of one
of these parts into four.[2] In Domesday Book Clapham appears
as a single manor belonging to Miles Crispin.[3] Several more
such cases could be cited. In other cases the division of a vill
between several manors leads eventually to its breaking up
into several vills.[4] But on the whole the relation of manor and
vill is no less involved in Domesday Book than in the Hundred
Rolls. In some places a certain strengthening of the manorial
element subsequently takes place, a certain 'unification', but
in others we see the disintegration of large manors. In any case,
the constant lack of coincidence between village community
and manor is an argument against the idea of the community
being a product of the manorial régime. The basic unit of
agrarian organization was the village community, not the
manor. The village assembly, not a manorial one, regulated
agrarian matters in the Danelaw.[5] We do not know of non-
manorial assemblies in central England in the thirteenth
century. But Vinogradoff's remarks on the subject offer a very
probable hypothesis.[6]

OVERLAPPING MANORS

It is sometimes very difficult to allocate to specific manors
all the evidence provided by the Hundred Rolls. And this most
often is not because there are gaps between manors, but
because manors overlap one with another; not because there
are many 'extra-manorial' elements, but because the same lands
come within two or more manors. Many difficulties arise

[1] One must, however, remember that villages too could overlap (Pollock and
Maitland, i, 561).
[2] R.H., ii, 321.   [3] D.B., i, 212.
[4] Vinogradoff, Villainage, 392–3, 450; Maitland, Collected Papers, ii, 84–95.
Cf. also such vills as Bampton Regis, Bampton Pogeys, Swaffham Prior, Swaffham
Pogeys, and many others.
[5] Cf. Stenton, Br. Ac., v, lxi–lxii.
[6] Vinogradoff, Villainage, 393 ff.

when it comes to drawing the boundaries between manors, and it is worth while to examine some of them, since they allow us to see in more detail the complicated relationships that had arisen in the English feudal village.

First of all it is by no means normal for the manor to be held from a single lord. We continually find that the lord holds his manor from various lords, and that the manor itself is composed of various parts whose character is determined at different levels of the feudal ladder and fixed by different services. Thus John Hervis holds 2½ hides and one virgate in the vill of Milton (Beds.) from the Hospitallers for 10s. a year; in the same vill he holds 1½ hides and a half virgate from the Earl of Leicester against payment of scutage.[1] Such cases are fairly common. Sometimes manors are such involved complexes that the jurors find it difficult to state from which fiefs and baronies the lord of the manor holds the various parts. The Master of the Templars holds his demesne in Duxford (Cambs.) from seven different people, in different portions.[2] In Bampton Pogeys (Oxon.) Robert Pogeys holds one carucate from W. Valence and one from various individuals (*in perquisito de diversis*), only two of whom the jurors are able to name.[3] We find an even more complicated case in Harleston (Cambs.), where Robert Tybetot holds 176 acres of arable, 20 acres of meadow and 4 acres of pasture from John de Burgo, who holds from Gilbert Peche, who holds from the bishop of Ely, who holds from the king; against what service, the jurors do not know. The same Robert Tybetot holds 120 acres of arable and 8 acres of meadow from John le Bretun, of which John le Bretun held 40 acres of arable and 6 acres of meadow from John de Burgo, and 44 acres from Hugh Clement, and the remaining 36 acres of arable and 2 acres of meadow 'in many portions, acquired in different fiefs, but we cannot distinguish the fiefs'—so the jurors declare.[4]

The lord of a manor often held lands on other men's manors as a free tenant. The John Hervis mentioned above, apart from his manor in Milton, also holds three-quarters of a virgate in the same vill on the manor of Robert de Camera; furthermore

---

[1] *R.H.*, ii, 321–22.   [2] *R.H.*, ii, 581.   [3] *R.H.*, ii, 689.
[4] *Per plures particulas perquisitas et de pluribus feodis sed nescimus distinguere feoda* (*R.H.*, ii, 551–52).

Robert de Camera holds one quarter of a virgate on the manor of John Hervis and another quarter of a virgate on a manor in the neighbouring village of Thurleigh.[1] Such cases are not uncommon.

Among the lords who are also free tenants on the manors of others we sometimes find the names of men of importance. For example, in Gamlingay (Cambs.) among the tenants of Philip Burnel are named *dominus* John Avenel and *dominus* Baldewin de St. George, both high-ranking lords. Thomas Ellesworth holds 20 acres on the manor of Simon de Stantone. Thomas is himself the lord of a manor in the same vill, Stanton (Cambs.). In virtue of his holding he is obliged to attend Simon's court, but he has bought himself out of this obligation for one mark and has received a charter recording this.[2]

Sometimes quite important landlords, clerics and knights, are obliged to render in return for holdings on other manors not only money payments, but labour dues. On the manor of Chesterton (Cambs.) the rector, himself a quite considerable lord, *faciet tres aruras pro tenentibus suis*;[3] *dominus Johannes le Moyne Atteasse tenet unam messuagium . . . per servicium 4s. 5d., secabit in autumpno 3 acras ad cibum domini*.[4] Of course, these gentlemen did not render their labour dues in person, but they were none the less answerable for them.

Especially frequent are holdings of land on other manors by ecclesiastical lords, mostly monasteries. Probably in many cases the lands held by a lord on other manors were in practice fused with his own demesne. Thus manors become as it were intertwined and merged into one another. The demesne of one manor may include a free holding, or several free holdings, on other manors. This at times makes the tracing of the boundaries between different manors difficult; for the same piece of land may belong to two manors, appearing now as demesne, now as a free holding.

SUB-MANORS

Not infrequently we find among the free holdings of a manor very large holdings of complicated structure, with a demesne

[1] *R.H.*, ii, 321–22, 325.
[2] *Satisfecit eidem per unam marcam quod habeat cartam suam nec amplius faceret (R.H., ii, 468).*
[3] *R.H.*, ii, 406.   [4] *R.H.*, ii, 544, cf. 882 (Elyas Wytefeld), etc.

and dependent holdings of their own, which fully merit the
title of manor. Such 'sub-manors' are a fairly common phenomenon in the Hundred Rolls. Sometimes on such a sub-
manor a further sub-manor may appear in its turn. Thus the
Buckinghamshire vill of Stewkley[1] appears on the surface to
be one manor, belonging to the earl of Gloucester. But among
the free holdings of this manor there are no less than six
which are complicated in structure, having each their own
demesne, freeholders and even villeins, so that it is legitimate
to call them sub-manors. On one of these sub-manors (that of
the abbess of Fontevrault) there is the further sub-manor of
Margaret Aspernil, with two villein, and one free virgate.
But the most striking case of this kind is to be found in the
Oxfordshire hundredal manor of Thame.[2] Here John Clifford
holds a sub-manor, with its own villeins and manor court,
from the bishop of Lincoln's manor of Thame. L. de Chiselhampton holds a sub-sub-manor with its own villeins from John
Clifford; W. Bluntesdene holds a sub-sub-sub-manor (with one
villein) from L. de Chiselhampton; Nicholas Marmiun holds
a sub-sub-sub-sub-manor with its own villeins and court
from W. Bluntesdene. Among the holders on the small manor
of Nicholas Marmiun there is one who has his own sub-
tenants. On the Earl of Warwick's Buckinghamshire manor
of Hanslope, there are more than ten free holdings of complex
type, some of which could be described as manors.[3] Manors
are thus built up on different levels of the feudal ladder, and
the 'lords' of sub-manors are looked on as freeholders in relation
to the 'chief lord' (*capitalis dominus*), pay him more or less
considerable rents, and attend his manor court.[4] The tenants
on sub-manors are not infrequently obliged, over and above
their dues to their direct lords, to render various minor dues
to the 'chief lord';[5] sometimes they are under obligation to
attend the 'chief lord's' manor court;[6] sometimes the sub-manor
starts its own private court.[7]

[1] *R.H.*, ii, 334–35.   [2] *R.H.*, ii, 820–21.   [3] *R.H.*, ii, 343–46.
[4] J. de Haddon holds from W. de Valence, the lord of the manor of Bampton
(Oxon.), the sub-manor of Haddon; pays him £1 3s. 5d. a year; is bound to attend
his court; and even pays tallage to the sum of 6s. 6d. (*R.H.*, ii, 691).
[5] *Et quilibet istorum 4 tenencium dicti prioris debet Willelmo de Jaspervil* (the chief
lord) 1½d. *et unum hominem ad magnam precariam suam in autumpno. R.H.*, ii, 334.
[6] *R.H.*, ii, 467–68.
[7] *R.H.*, ii, 471: *J. de Beneit tenet . . . de domina Elena la Zuche . . . et habet curiam
suam de tribus septimanis extra curiam domine Elene.*

Until the passing of the statute *Quia Emptores* (1290) every alienation created new rungs in the ladder of holdings, and as land changed hands with increasing speed, especially in the eastern counties, practically every holding of any size sprouted out into a series of lesser holdings. The sale and purchase of land was often concerned with very small plots (this being furthered by the scattering of holdings throughout the fields of the community), but one must not think that the small scale of these holdings necessarily means that their tenants were small men—*anelepmen, undersettles*. Out of these small holdings much larger ones were often built up. In Bedfordshire, and even more often in Cambridgeshire, we find free virgates and half-virgates divided literally into scraps among small and very small tenants.[1] But if we start to reckon up the 'estates' of these 'small' tenants, we see that sometimes they had acquired quite considerable lands in parcels from different people. Alienation, which under the conditions of that day meant sub-infeudation, often detached holdings from the manor of the 'chief lord'. Many of the inhabitants of a village held their lands not from the 'chief lord', but from his tenants and often from the tenants of his tenants. The ladder of holdings intervening between the 'chief lord' and the last tenant might be very involved. We can sometimes count up to five or more 'rungs'. Katherine Sausiton held a farmstead and twenty acres of plough land by hereditary tenancy (*feodi firma*) in Pampisford from the Master of the Templars, the latter from Richard de Ecclesia, Richard from William Coc, who held from the heirs of Robert, son of Lawrence, who held from the abbot of Waldon, who held from Hugh Brock, the 'chief lord of the manor'.[2] Katherine paid 20s. rent to the Master of the Templars. Her connection with the manor of Hugh Brock must have been extremely slight. Consequently there are a number of cases where the precise relations of tenure were

---

[1] For instance, *R.H.*, ii, 474: Ric. Bradenham holds in the vill of Fen Drayton (Cambs.) 2 virgates. Under him 12 smallholders hold respectively (for simplicity's sake I give only arable land) 20 acres, 1 acre, 2 acres, 1 acre, 1 acre (held by two men), 1 acre, 3 acres, 1 acre, 6 acres, 7 acres, 2 acres, 2 acres. These smallholders have their own sub-holders. See also the holding in the same vill of J. Calvele. See also *R.H.*, ii, 438, 475, 476.

[2] *R.H.*, ii, 414.

forgotten.[1] The chain was especially weakened if the inter-vening links included a holding in free alms (*libera elemosina*), which might free the tenant from all rents benefiting the chief lord. In such a case the holding would be much more closely connected with the other lands of the individual to whom it had been granted in *libera elemosina*, than with the manor to which it really belonged.

COMPLEXITY OF FREE HOLDINGS

Similar relationships were often created by grants of rent. The alienation of the rent of freeholders, especially in favour of the church, occurs fairly frequently in the Hundred Rolls. With which lord has a holding the closer connection when its rent has been alienated? Usually it remains close in both cases, since other obligations to the original lord (especially attend-ance at his court)[2] remain in force, and furthermore a rent was often alienated not entirely but in part; it could also be alienated in favour of several persons.[3] In any case, the person in whose favour the rent was alienated came between the original lord and the tenant,[4] upsetting the manorial symmetry. This symmetry was further disturbed by the fact that free-holders frequently held lands under several lords on several manors; in this way quite considerable estates of an inter-manorial type might sometimes be built up. Apart from church estates, which are often composed of many small gifts,[5] we continually meet extremely involved holdings, often situated in several different manors and vills at once. Even if in some

---

[1] For cases of the loss of free holdings owing to their being sold in parts, see *Liber Memorandorum*, 166, 312–17. A tenant under the prior of Barnwell sold his holding to strangers (*extranei*), who refused to pay rent to the prior, while the prior was unable to compel them, not even knowing exactly where their lands lay. On complaint being made by the prior, an inquiry was carried out to establish the location of these lands and the names of the tenants.

[2] Certain freeholders *reddunt predictos 32s. dicte capelle de Herdwick per assignacionem dicti comitis Wintonie, et sectas et omnia alia servicia faciunt dicte comitisse. R.H.*, ii, 669.

[3] *W. H. tenet de predicto comite* (the lord of the manor) *5 acras prati et debet scutagium et preterea 8s. per annum, videlicet priori Hatefeld 5s. et priori de Coln 3s.* (*R.H.*, ii, 425).

[4] *Abbas de Lesnes tenet in villa predicta de dono quondam Ricardi Avenel* (an ancestor of the lord of the manor) *de redditu assiso per annum 20s. de quibusdam tenentibus suis* (a list of whom follows). There are many such cases. An alienated rent could be passed on further: *dominus Hunfridus de Bereford tenuit de domino W. Avenel in liberum maritagium 26 solidatas et 8d. de redditu assiso de quibusdam tenentibus, quos idem W. ei assignavit, et ille dominus Hunfridus dedit illum redditum cuidem filie sue nomine Phillippe, unde illi sunt tenentes.*

[5] E.g., the demesnes of the prior of Barnwell, which are made up of 17 gifts, at Madingley (Cambs.).

hundreds (Papworth, Flendish [Cambs.]) the compiler of the
rolls attempts to adhere consistently to the principle of feudal
tenure and to list all these small holdings under the name of
the person from whom they were held, in other hundreds such
holdings are lumped together under the name of the person
who holds them *in manu* (Longstow, Chesterton [Cambs.]).
We find complex holdings made up of 10, 12 or more parts,
each of which is held from a separate person for a separate
rent.[1] W. Eagle and his wife hold 9½ acres of arable and
meadow in parcels from 10 different people and pay a separate
rent to each of them.[2] M. de Northampton holds 29½ acres
from 18 different people.[3] Roger, son of John, and Richard of
Bassingbourne have a quite considerable estate in the vill of
Little Abington (Cambs.): they hold 199½ acres from 5 different
people, while 32½ of these are held from them by freeholders.[4]
As a model specimen of a complex inter-manorial holding we
may well take that of Roger Willey in Bedfordshire, which is
surveyed in part in the Hundred Rolls, but even more fully
in the inquisitions *post Mortem*.[5] It consisted of almost 50
holdings, mostly small, held from different people in various
vills, amounted altogether to over 200 acres, and brought in
revenues estimated at £5 17s. 4½d.

The complexity of these relationships is increased by the fact
that one and the same person may hold part of his lands on a
manor or on several manors as free holdings, and part as
villein holdings. An example is provided by the holding of
Thomas Dovenel in Sawston (Cambs.): he holds villein lands
in this village from two different lords, and free holdings from
three.[6] A man could have villeins on another manor and
settle them on his own free holding there. Thus in the vill of
Podington (Beds.) John de Pavenham holds one virgate on
the manor of Nicholas le Cruse as a freeholder. But two
villeins hold this virgate from him; in the same vill John has a

---

[1] For instance, the holding of Roger Wendut at Impington (Cambs.) was in
12 parts held of different lords for different rents. In the majority of cases the
rents were very small, and may be presumed to indicate that the land had been
bought (*R.H.*, ii, 465). For similar cases see pp. 402 sqq., 465, 511, 512, 572. See also
the holding of Wakelin of Coye which consisted of 21 small parts held of different
lords (Quy, Cambs., *R.H.*, ii, 495–96). The complex composition of military
holdings in the Danelaw is noticed by Stenton (*Br. Ac.*, v, cxxxii).
[2] *R.H.*, ii, 447.   [3] *R.H.*, ii, 450.
[4] *R.H.*, ii, 423–24.   [5] C. Ed. I, File 22/2.
[6] *R.H.*, ii, 575–80; cf. Maitland, *Domesday Book and Beyond*, 136, n. 2.

F

small 'manor' with five and a half virgates of demesne and half a virgate of villein land.[1] Thus the same two virgates were simultaneously a free holding on Nicholas's manor and villein land on John's. Complex relationships were created by the alienation of villein rents. Thus Henry de Childerley sold the rent of four villeins on his manor at Childerley Minor to Philip de Coleville; their rents include not only money payments and small dues in kind, but labour services as well.[2] It is not clear whether it was only the rents which were alienated or the villeins themselves and their land, nor whether they retained any connection with their original manor and its court. We know of cases of the alienation of part of villein rents; one villein of Walter de Pelham pays half his rent to his own lord and half to Simon le Wallis.[3] Here the villein, in spite of paying rent to two lords, obviously belongs to only one—Walter. But cases are not uncommon in which one villein belongs to several lords, who exercise an equal or proportional control over him, his land and his rents. We find men who are the serfs of two,[4] four[5] or five[6] lords. This was often the result of a partition between co-heirs, as a result of which the 'domain' of each would include a half, a third, a quarter or a fifth of a villein. Knotty points could arise in this connection—e.g. if one of the lords granted freedom to his part of the villein. Such a case took place at Barton (Cambs.); a certain villein, Thomas Hodierne, held half his holding from one lord (Walter lord of Barton) and half from another (the prior of Barnwell). The temporal lord freed him and made his holding free, owing a money rent and scutage. But after Thomas's death the prior claimed heriot and seized the entire holding. The court decided in favour of the prior, 'as all a serf acquires is acquired for his lord'.[7]

In ways such as this one manor might merge into another. Land which is freehold on one manor may on another be either freehold, or demesne, or villein land. The boundary lines of manors are anything but clearly defined. Of many parcels of

---

[1] *R.H.*, ii, 329.   [2] *R.H.*, ii, 408.   [3] *R.H.*, ii, 410.
[4] *R.H.*, ii, 696, 424, and many other cases.
[5] *R.H.*, ii, 620.   [6] *R.H.*, ii, 522.
[7] *Liber Memorandorum*, 165; *R.H.*, ii, 563–64. The Hundred Rolls survey this holding in the period between the partial emancipation of Thomas and his death; half his holding he has as a free man, half as a villein.

land we are unable to say to which manor they belonged.
Manors are entangled not only through the overlapping of
their arable and common pasture lands, but in matters of
overlordship, tenure and agricultural practice as well. As an
economic complex the manor is not necessarily identical with
its own structure as a system of holdings. Even within one
manor the dividing lines between the demesne, the villein land
and the free holdings are by no means always clear. I leave
out of account here the transformation of villein into free
holdings and the intermediate stages between the two (it is
sometimes hard to determine whether any particular holding is
free or unfree), the depression of the status of free holdings
which the lord wished to turn into villein tenements, villein
holdings in the hands of free men and free holdings in the
hands of villeins, and the holdings both free and villein taken
by the lord into his own hands. We see the demesne merging
into the free holdings even within the bounds of one manor.
Thus we continually find the lord adding part of the tenants'
land to the demesne. Such additions are carried out not only
by the appropriation of escheated or confiscated land, but also
by purchase and by the lord leasing land from his own tenants.
Thus Ralph Passeleve holds half a virgate from his own freeholder on the manor of Biddenham (Beds.), pays him 3d. rent
and renders 'foreign service'.[1] Robert Maudut in the vill of
Dornford (Oxon.) holds one virgate from Gilbert le More, his
own freeholder, and pays him 2d. a year, etc.[2] Some of these
relationships, which so confuse the boundaries of manors
and destroy manorial symmetry, are the result of alienations,
sometimes of recent alienations carried out within the recol-
lection of the jurors, and reflect the disintegration of the
manorial system. In a number of cases, on the other hand,
we are dealing with relics of an earlier régime, with incomplete

[1] *R.H.*, ii, 327.
[2] *R.H.*, ii, 865. Cf. *ibid.*, 575: Ralph Pyrot holds from W. de Swaston, who in
turn holds the land from Ralph Pyrot. See also p. 577. Cf. the holding of the
Abbot of Thorney from J. Folkesworth (p. 648), that of the Abbot of Ramsey
from Will f. John. (p. 481), and many others. In his interesting essay, 'Monastic
Demesnes and the Statute of Mortmain,' *E.H.R.*, xlix (1934). Bishop has shown
that the monasteries often acquired land from their own freeholders and even
from villeins, thus enlarging their demesnes. Bishop has made it clear that even
for such acquisitions licence was required, although no lords' interests would
appear to be damaged. In view of this, Bishop presumes that one of the objects
of the Statute of Mortmain was to hinder the growth of monastic demesnes.

'manorialization', unfinished 'unification'. But in spite of all this confusion, which is especially marked in Cambridgeshire, Bedfordshire and Buckinghamshire, we can still see sufficiently clearly the outlines of the manors which indubitably formed the basic fabric of agrarian England in the feudal period.

MANORIAL TYPES

We have already quoted the characteristics of 'the typical manor'; a large demesne, cultivated by the hands and tools of the servile peasants; villein land covering the greater part of the tenants' land on the manor, and assuring the demesne of a supply of obligatory labour; an insignificant amount of freehold—a mere 'fringe', consisting of small knightly holdings and the tenements of the few free peasants, who paid money rents. But in actual fact the organization for collecting and assessing feudal rent took on forms incomparably more involved than the 'typical' manor. Both in size and in structure manors reveal extreme variety. On many there were only free holdings, and undoubtedly the organization of such manors differed very considerably from what we know of 'typical' manors. There were manors without demesnes; there were manors without free holdings. We can, in fact, establish several types of manorial structure. *Type (a)* comprises all 'typical' manors with a demesne, villein land and free holdings. To *Type (b)* we refer manors with a demesne and villein land but no free holdings. Later legal theory maintained that a manor, to qualify as such, must have at least two freeholders. In the thirteenth century, when the theory of the manor had not yet been worked out in full legal perfection, there was no question of any such requirement; but generally speaking manors without free holdings are not common in the Hundred Rolls. *Type (c)*, a widely recurring type, is the manor with a demesne and free holdings but without villein land. *Type (d)* is the manor with villein land and free holdings but no demesne.[1] *Type (e)* comprises free holdings alone, without demesne or villein land. Douglas considers the use of the term 'manor' for such complexes of holdings to be incorrect;[2] but in the

[1] E.g. the manor of Roger Bewmis, *R.H.*, ii, 629; the manor of Henry Walpol, *ibid.*, 528; and many others.
[2] Douglas, *O.S.S.L.H.*, ix, 121.

Hundred Rolls we find cases of such estates being called manors.[1] *Type* (*f*) is villein land alone, without demesne or free holdings, e.g. the manor of John Ewe at Garsington (Oxon.), which consists of ten villein virgates each paying one mark.[2] *Type* (*g*) is demesne alone, without villein land or free holdings. Examples of this type, especially of any size, are very rare; but from time to time we find estates which nearly equate to it in structure—i.e. a demesne with an insignificant amount of tenants' land. Such is the holding of Walter, son of Roger, at Baldon St. Laurence (Oxon.): $7\frac{1}{2}$ virgates of demesne and half a virgate held *ad voluntatem*.[3] Such is the manor specifically referred to as the *manerium* of Thomas de Laungel[4]—a large demesne of 3 carucates and 8 virgates (in three different vills), the revenue of which is assessed at £15, and inconsiderable free holdings (3 virgates and 16 messuages, with rents amounting to £2 16s. 11d.). To this type also belong a large part of the Cistercian manors. Between all these types there are transitional forms, and the characteristics of the different types vary according to the proportional relationship of the three main elements—type *a* may be close to either *b*, *c*, *d*, *f* or *g*.

Properly speaking only types *a* and *b* can be classed as typical manors, as Seebohm and Vinogradoff understood the term; they alone have the characteristic peculiarities of manorial economy—labour rents and a demesne cultivated by the hands of the unfree peasantry. In types *d* and *f* we find villeins, but since there is here no demesne, labour dues have a secondary, incidental character (being mainly cartage dues). Close to this is type *e*, where the lord merely receives the rents of free holdings—a type closer to a 'soke' than to a 'manor'. On manors of types *c* and *g* we find a demesne, but unsupplied with serf labour, able to rely at best (type *c*) only upon the insignificant labour dues of free holders. Even in the case of manors of types *a* and *b*, however, their structure in itself is no guarantee of the predominance of labour rents or of a sufficient supply of unfree working hands for the demesne; in the last resort it is not the structure of a manor but the form of

---

[1] Staunton (Cambs.): ... *dominus N. de Segrave habet in homagio in villa de Staunton 11 virgatas terre in socagio ... et tenet illum manerium de S. de domino rege ...* This estate is called 'manerium' three times, *R.H.*, ii, 466.

[2] *R.H.*, ii, 854.   [3] *R.H.*, ii, 724.   [4] *R.H.*, ii, 739.

rent which there predominates that determines its economic characteristics.

What is the numerical relation between these types of manor? Undoubtedly the type characteristic of the manorial system, type *a*, is the predominant one. More than half of the manorial units belong to this type. And its predominance would be even more striking if we reckoned up the actual area occupied by the manors of each separate type. The vast majority of large manors belong to type *a*, and about three-quarters of the whole territory for which statistics can be produced is covered by manors of this type. And the predominance will be greater still if we include type *b* as well. If the typical manor, with its demesne and villein land, does not cover the whole of the territory dealt with by the Hundred Rolls, it is still over-whelmingly predominant. Probably not less than 80 per cent of the whole territory for which figures can be worked out was occupied by manors of types *a* and *b*. But the point has already been made that within the limits of these types very consider-able variations are possible; a manor of type *a* may come very close to one of the other types.

We are thus obliged, while emphasizing the predominance of 'typical' manors in the areas under examination, to note complexity, confusion and variety in the forms of manorial structure. The question arises whether this complexity is a new occurrence, connected with the disintegration of the manorial system, as Seebohm, for instance, thought; or whether it is a survival from the epoch when the manor had not yet become the formative force in the English countryside, as Vinogradoff observed in contrasting the complicated nature of manorial structure in Domesday Book with that in the Hundred Rolls. I have already remarked that the changes brought about by the increasing mobility of land, by alienation and subinfeudation, brought extreme confusion into the manorial structure. But it is also beyond doubt that the passage of two centuries had not brought about complete re-grouping of the English countryside into symmetrical manors, and that conditions depicted in Domesday still persisted in some degree. This is brought out very clearly by a comparison of the Hundred Rolls and Domesday Book, if we arrange the material of the

latter as it was arranged in the original, i.e. according to vills.
We shall return to this question.

In the villages of the English Midlands in the thirteenth
century, we find both incompleteness of manorialization and
the beginning of the disintegration of the manorial system,
and this leads to great variation and many departures from
type. Nevertheless it was precisely in this area and at this
period that the English manorial system reached its highest
development, and its outlines are clearly perceptible beneath
all the imperfections and variations.

METHOD OF CALCULATING COMPONENT ELEMENTS OF MANORS

Demesne, villein land, free holdings—the mutual relationship of these three elements determines, fundamentally, the
structure of a manor. Under free holdings we include holdings
for terms of years and those at the lord's will, though these are
not in a legal sense 'freehold'; in short, we bring under this
heading all non-villein tenements. Also included with free
holdings are the holdings of free sokemen. The holdings of
'villein-sokemen' or 'bond-sokemen' are reckoned in with villein
holdings.

One of the most important purposes of this chapter is to
determine the comparative importance of each of these three
elements. The establishment of the relationship of demesne,
villein land and free holdings both on individual manors and
over a wide region—hundred or county—is an important
preliminary step towards determining the type of feudal
production which predominates in a given territory. I shall
attempt to answer this question first in general terms, by com-
puting the figures for areas of demesne, villein land and free
holdings in each hundred. It must be noted that a precise
calculation of each of these elements is not everywhere possible.
In the enrolments the extent of the demesne is often not given.[1]
In a number of Cambridgeshire surveys the demesne is not
given separately, only the size of the manor as a whole (and
that often in such vague terms of measurement as knights'

[1] On this point the government surveys differ little in practice from manorial
extents, in which a survey of the demesne was by no means always given; see,
for instance, the majority of the extents of St. Peter's abbey, Gloucester. *C. Glouc.*,
iii, pp. 35-221.

fees, followed by a catalogue of the holdings and their dues). All this makes the calculation of the territorial extent of Cambridgeshire manors exceedingly difficult. For a number of hundreds approximate figures only can be given. The demesne land can be calculated in only six hundreds out of eleven—Chesterton, Chilford, Longstow, Thriplow, Papworth, Whittlesford. In my calculations I have included only those manors for which all the elements can be worked out.

Among the free holdings I have included all 'non-manorial' free holdings, holdings *de diversis dominis*, where the jurors were unable to assign the holdings to any manor, and finally, all small complexes of holdings (less than one hide) that had no villeins on them. I did not consider it possible to count these as separate manors and divide them up into demesne and holdings. In cases where in the rolls the size of the virgate and carucate is not defined, I have attributed the 'average' number of acres to each, viz., 30 and 120 respectively, except for Oxfordshire, where the average size of a virgate has been taken as 25 acres, and of a carucate as 100 acres.

The results of my calculations are summarized in Table 1.

This table, like the others contained in this chapter, requires some explanation. First of all, the conditional character of what appear to be precise figures must be noted. These figures do not represent the actual number of acres of arable in every hundred, since our source does not permit us to give such figures. In each hundred the following elements have necessarily been omitted: (1) manors and villages omitted by the source; (2) manors of which the survey is not fully decipherable in the manuscript; (3) manors for which the surviving surveys show obvious lacunae and major inaccuracies which cannot be corrected by reference to other sources; (4) manors which are described in such vague and summary fashion that even approximate calculations concerning them are impossible. All these omissions have a random incidence and cannot have any considerable influence on the final conclusions reached, but in certain cases they must be borne in mind. For instance, the predominance of ecclesiastical ownership in the hundred of Hirstingstone (Hunts.) is beyond all doubt, but in the enrolments it is further exaggerated owing to the seriously damaged state of the beginning of the survey.

A second cause of inaccuracy in our calculations is the extreme difficulty of disentangling the web of manorial and tenurial relationships, of which we have already spoken. Whether the properties of the same lord compose two manors or one, to which manor this or that free holding should be assigned, whether a certain holding should be counted as the demesne of one manor or as a free holding on another, whether small 'sub-manors' should be counted as holdings or as independent estates—such questions arise on practically every page of the source. They have to be answered on the basis of insufficiently precise data. Other historians may adopt other combinations and obtain slightly different final results.

The influence of inaccuracies in reckoning on the results of the work has already been discussed in Chapter I. Here I wish only to stress the conditional character of my total figures and to warn against their incorrect use. They are only meant to give an idea of the extent of the material used in each case. The percentage figures are another matter, and it is these which provide the basic material for drawing conclusions. I do not think they would be altered to any considerable extent, even if more precise calculations were carried out; and the possibility of minor variations is unlikely to have any substantial effect on the results achieved.

CAMBRIDGESHIRE FIGURES

Altogether my calculations cover over half a million acres of arable land, 32 per cent of which are comprised in demesnes, 40 per cent in villein land, and 28 per cent in free holdings. But the table omits five Cambridgeshire hundreds in which, owing to difficulties in calculating demesne land, it was only possible to calculate villein land and free holdings. Their relationship is as follows:

Name of hundred	Villein land	Free holdings
Flendish	2,233	2,997
Longstow	2,932	2,653
Staploe	4,845	4,079
Wetherley	3,528	4,312
Staine	1,424	3,079
For all five hundreds	14,962	17,120

TABLE I

DEMESNE, VILLEIN LAND AND FREE HOLDINGS

County and Hundred	Demesne	Villein land	Free holdings	Total Arable area
HUNTINGDONSHIRE				
Hirstingstone	*4,301	9,260	2,893	16,454
	26	56	18	
Leightonstone	9,728	18,934	7,281	35,943
	27	52	21	
Normancross	8,254	8,522	4,990	21,766
	38	39	22	
Toseland	8,094	7,127	4,888	20,109
	40	35	25	
For the whole county	30,377	43,843	20,052	94,272
	32	47	21	
CAMBRIDGESHIRE				
Chesterton	1,678	2,971	1,584	6,233
	27	48	25	
Chilford	6,795	2,041	5,054	13,890
	48	15	37	
Papworth	2,168	3,636	3,934	9,738
	22	37	41	
Longstow	6,201	4,077	6,049	16,327
	38	25	37	
Thriplow	3,602	3,398	2,509	9,469
	38	35	27	
Whittlesford	3,307	2,501	2,263	8,071
	41	31	28	
For all hundreds here given	23,651	18,624	52,143	63,728
	36	29	33	
BEDFORDSHIRE				
Stodden and Willey	8,086	5,086	10,930	24,102
	33	21	46	
BUCKINGHAMSHIRE				
Bunstow	3,276	2,312	3,427	9,015
	36	26	38	
Stodfold	3,818	3,894	4,282	11,994
	32	32	34	
Mucha	2,730	2,098	2,005	6,833
	40	30	29	
Mursley	3,697	6,220	3,374	13,291
	27	48	25	
For all hundreds here given	13,521	14,524	13,088	41,133
	35	35	32	

* The top figure denotes the area of land in acres (in Oxfordshire in virgates), the lower figure the percentage of the total arable area that this represents in each case.

TABLE I (*continued*)

County and Hundred	Demesne	Villein land	Free holdings	Total arable area
OXFORDSHIRE (in virgates)				
Banbury	142½	280	146½	569
	25	49	26	
Ploughley	486	751½	304	1,541½
	31	49	20	
Bullington	347½	404½	152	904
	38	44	17	
Wootton	473	770	405	1,648
	28	48	24	
Chadlington	487	606	382	1,475
	33	41	26	
Bampton	319	457½	294	1,070½
	30	42	28	
Thame	123	172	53½	348½
	35	49	16	
Lewknor	160	211	124	495
	32	43	25	
Pirton	123	98	188	409
	30	24	45	
Ewelme	191	201	286	678
	28	29	43	
Langtree	104	92	150½	346½
	30	27	43	
For all hundreds here given	2,956	4,043½	2,485½	9,485
	31	42	26	
The same in acres	73,900	101,088	62,138	237,125
WARWICKSHIRE				
Kineton	15,109	29,627	12,554	57,290
	28	52	20	
Stoneleigh	9,510	8,517	11,379	29,406
	32	29	39	
For both hundreds	24,619	38,144	23,933	86,696
	28	44	27	
For the whole material	174,154	221,309	151,594	547,057
	32	40	28	

The relationship of free holdings to villein land which this table gives is close to that obtained for the other six hundreds of Cambridgeshire. We shall therefore probably not be mistaken if we assume a similar percentage of demesne land here also, i.e. about 36 per cent. We then get a credible relationship of demesne, villein land and free holdings for the five missing hundreds of Cambridgeshire.

	Demesne	Villein land	Free holding	Total arable
For the 5 missing hundreds	18,046 36	14,962 30	17,120 35	50,128
For all Cambridgeshire	41,697 36	33,586 30	38,573 34	113,856
For the whole of the material	192,200 32	236,271 40	168,714 28	597,185

Of these figures, that for demesne land gives rise to doubts. On many manors the demesne is given in carucates, and we have already seen that the figure given for demesne carucates in a number of cases does not correspond to the real size of the demesne, but indicates only the number of ploughs on the demesne. Probably the figure for demesne land should be somewhat raised.

The figures for villein land and free holdings are more accurate. Here we get a proportion of 40 per cent to 28 per cent (10 : 7). Of course, this is not the proportion obtaining between the land of villeins and the land of free peasants, since the figure for 'free holdings' also includes lands held by persons of higher rank.[1]

PERCENTAGES OF DEMESNE, FREE AND VILLEIN LAND

Free holdings account for 28 per cent of the land covered by our calculations. This percentage varies considerably over the different hundreds and counties, falling to 16–17 per cent in some Oxfordshire hundreds and rising to 46 per cent in the hundreds of Stodden and Willey (Beds.). The percentage of villein land fluctuates within even wider limits—from 15 per cent in the hundred of Chilford (Cambs.) to 50 per cent

---

[1] The question of the respective proportions of land held by free and servile peasants will be dealt with in Chapter IV.

and over in a number of Huntingdonshire and Oxfordshire
hundreds and in the Warwickshire hundred of Kineton.
Thus we can distinguish regions characterized by a predominance of free holdings over villein land, and others in
which villein land predominates over free holdings. The latter
comprise all four hundreds of Huntingdonshire, two hundreds
of Buckinghamshire lying to the south of the Ouse (Mursley
and Mucha), a large part of Oxfordshire, and the adjacent
Warwickshire hundred of Kineton. Taking this territory as a
whole, the proportion of demesne, villein land and free holdings
respectively (in acres) is 115,363—173,101—84,511 = 372,975,
or (in percentages) 31—47—22. Regions with a high percentage of free holdings include Cambridgeshire; all that remains
in the enrolments for Bedfordshire, i.e. the hundreds of Stodden
and Willey; two hundreds of Buckinghamshire, to the north
of the Ouse (Bunstow and Stodfold); three southern hundreds
of Oxfordshire (Pirton, Ewelme and Langtree); and the
Warwickshire hundred of Stoneleigh. The areas of demesne,
villein land and free holdings here, expressed in acres, are
76,837—63,170—84,203 = 224,210, in percentages 34—28—38.
The territory with a predominance of villein land totals over
370,000 acres, that with a predominance of free holdings over
220,000, i.e. 62 per cent and 38 per cent respectively. Thus
free holdings represent a pretty wide 'fringe' round the demesne
and villein land, occupying for the whole area no less than 28
per cent of the arable. In certain regions, moreover, they
predominate over villein land. In the surviving material for
Bedfordshire free holdings contain over twice the area of
villein land. In the regions of the predominance of free holdings their proportion to villein holdings is on the average
about 4 : 3.

However, it may be that this proportional relationship was
in fact rather different even for the section of central England
which we have studied. Chance has preserved almost in their
entirety the surveys for those counties where there was a high
percentage of villein land (Oxfordshire, Huntingdonshire).
Meanwhile only a small fragment of Bedfordshire, for instance,
has survived. The Huntingdonshire, and especially the
Oxfordshire material, plays an exaggerated part in our
calculations. It is evident that the region of the predominance

of free holdings was considerably larger than our source shows. We should accordingly raise the percentage of free holdings in our final figures. Furthermore, my method of calculation reduces the actual area of free holdings, since it classifies the more sizeable of them (over one hide), those with dependent holdings, as small manors. We shall hardly be far wrong if we assume that in that part of England which is described in the Hundred Rolls, the percentage of free holdings was on an average over 30 per cent, and scarcely differed much from the percentage of villein land. But I decline to make any more precise inferences.

SOME PROBLEMS CONCERNING THE DEMESNE

We have already referred to the doubts arising from the figures of demesne arable as given in the Hundred Rolls. In a number of cases we may assume that the extent of the demesne is put too low. We must therefore approach with caution all interpretations of our figures where they concern demesne land. In general, the proportion of demesne to villein land shows a significant constancy, local variations notwithstanding. The overall average percentage of demesne land is 32 per cent, which is close to the individual average for each of the different counties represented in our table. The figures for the latter fluctuate only within narrow limits—between 28 per cent and 35 per cent—in contrast to the violent fluctuations which we noted in the figures for villein land and free holdings. It is hard to distinguish any local variations in the role played by the demesne arable. A certain fall in the percentage of demesne land, which it is possible to observe as one moves from east to west, is not sufficiently well defined for any conclusions to be based on it. More important is another observation. The area of the demesne does not, generally speaking, stand in any constant relationship to the area of villein land, with which one might have expected it to be very closely connected, if the labour services of villeins, performed on the demesne land, are considered to be the basis of the manorial régime. Fluctuations in the ratio between demesne and villein land are evident even within the class of 'typical' (type *a*) manors, but the relationship does not exist in other types of manors where there are demesnes but no villein land (mainly types *c* and *g* and those closely resembling them).

The Hundred Rolls show that there is a large area of demesne without a corresponding provision of villein land. Such, first of all, are the Cistercian monastic estates. But cases of lay estates where the demesne was quite unprovided with villein land are also far from uncommon. Even more numerous are the cases where the area of villein land is insignificant compared to the demesne and is clearly insufficient to provide for the cultivation of the latter. In the Cambridgeshire hundred of Chilford we find an unusually high percentage of demesne land and a very low percentage of villein land—48 per cent of the total arable calculated is in demesnes, and only 15 per cent is villein land. In this hundred, out of 30 manors surveyed, 11 have no villein land whatever, and on 10 there is plainly not enough to provide for the cultivation of the demesne. (There are really only three manors with what is beyond doubt an adequate provision of villein land.) In this hundred, where the total area of demesne is 5,773 acres, only 1,670 of these demesne acres are provided with villein land (436 acres). This is an extreme case. But even in such a typically serf county as Huntingdonshire we find over 4,000 acres of demesne against which we cannot set a single acre of villein land. In view of the doubts raised by the calculation of demesne areas, and of the difficulty of determining what proportion of demesne to villein land represents a satisfactory provision of villein labour on the demesne, I do not propose at this stage to draw any general inference. I merely consider it essential to point out the presence of a large percentage of demesne land totally or almost totally unprovided with villein land. We must remember, also, that the presence of villein land does not in itself necessarily imply an adequate provision of obligatory villein labour for the demesne. For this it is essential first to discover the ratio of labour to other forms of rent.

ANALYSIS OF MANORS ACCORDING TO SIZE

In studying the structure of the feudal manor we cannot avoid the question of its size. What was the usual size of a manor; what was the relative proportion of large, medium and small manors (both numerically and in relation to the total area they covered); and what structural peculiarities are connected with manors of different sizes? These questions are all the more pressing because, hitherto, historians have concerned themselves almost exclusively with the large manor. We, on the contrary, must take due account of the abundant small manors, which have left behind them neither manorial surveys, nor annual accounts, nor court rolls. On these manors there may even have been no courts.[1] The small manor is a peculiar social phenomenon. We know little of its organization. Yet many pages of the Hundred Rolls are studded with surveys of small manors, and this is practically the only source from which we can hope to learn something of them—to learn, first and foremost, how numerous they were and how much territory they occupied.

My calculations concerning these questions are summarized in Table 2. The manors included are divided into three groups—large manors, for which the rolls mention over 1,000 acres of arable; medium, from 500 to 1,000 acres; and small, under 500 acres. Only those manors have been included which we know to have possessed all three elements—demesne, villein land and free holdings. For this reason we have omitted the five Cambridgeshire hundreds in which the areas of demesne land are not clear. Likewise omitted are the free holdings which do not belong to any manor (or which the jurors are unable to assign to a definite manor), and those small complexes of free tenements which in sum amount to less than one hide (120 acres) and do not come within other manors, but which I did not feel able to describe as manors themselves. All these omissions, taken together, account for a small area only, about $3\frac{1}{2}$ per cent of the whole, and even if this material should have been included, in part or in whole, the effect on the figures and ratios reached as the result of the calculations summarized in Table 2, would have been insignificant.

Table 2 draws our attention to the important part played in the agrarian life of England by the medium and small manor. Out of a total of 1,031 manors included in this table, 139 (13 per

---

[1] Pollock and Maitland, i, 602.

Table 2. LARGE, MEDIUM AND SMALL MANORS

unty and Hundred	Large manors			Medium manors			Small manors			All manors		
	No. of manors	Total arable area	Average arable area per manor	No. of manors	Total arable area	Average arable area per manor	No. of manors	Total arable area	Average arable area per manor	No. of manors	Total arable area	Average arable area per manor
NTINGDONSHIRE												
irstingstone	7	12,335 75	1,762	3	2,172 14	723	13	1,946 12	149	23	16,453	715
eightonstone	13	24,430 69	1,880	5	3,787 11	757	35	6,623 19	188	53	34,840	660
ormancross	6	9,022 42	1,503	8	6,046 28	755	29	6,311 30	217	43	21,379	497
oseland	2	2,481 13	1,240	11	7,928 42	721	57	8,956 46	157	70	19,365	277
or the whole county	28	48,268 52	1,724	27	19,933 22	738	134	23,826 26	178	189	92,027	487
or the 3 northern hundreds	26	45,787 63	1,760	16	12,005 17	750	77	14,880 20	193	119	72,672	611
BRIDGESHIRE												
esterton	2	2,654 43	1,327	3	1,901 30	633	11	1,677 27	153	16	6,232	390
hilford	4	4,710 36	1,180	6	3,730 28	640	20	4,637 35	232	30	13,077	436
apworth	3	4,045 47	1,378	3	2,267 26	756	13	2,260 26	174	19	8,572	451
ongstow	2	2,451 17	1,225	10	6,531 46	653	27	5,697 36	211	39	14,679	376
hriplow	3	3,368 36	1,123	6	3,749 41	630	12	2,090 22	174	21	9,207	440
hittlesford	1	1,355 17	1,355	3	2,078 26	693	17	4,554 57	268	21	7,987	380
or all hundreds here given	15	18,583 31	1,225	31	20,256 34	654	100	20,915 35	209	146	59,754	407
FORDSHIRE												
todden & Willey	2	3,402 15	1,701	14	8,087 39	573	40	9,830 45	246	56	21,319	308
KINGHAMSHIRE												
unstow	1	2,364 27	2,364	4	2,890 33	730	19	3,608 40	189	24	8,862	369
todfold	2	3,023 26	1,512	9	5,844 46	690	11	3,028 26	273	22	11,895	540
ucha	2	2,721 40	1,360	6	3,902 57	650	2	205 3	102	10	6,827	682
ursley	6	7,807 59	1,301	6	2,997 22	749	12	2,487 18	216	24	13,291	5 54
or all hundreds here given	11	15,915 39	1,444	25	15,633 38	625	44	9,328 23	214	80	40,875	501
ORDSHIRE (in virgates)												
anbury	4	261 49	65	5	134 24	27	18	145 26	8	27	540	21
oughley	12	629½ 44	52	18	443½ 31	24	35	370 26	11	65	1,443	22
ullington	4	257 29	64	9	271½ 31	30	31	355 40	11	44	884	20
ootton	9	581 37	65	21	578 37	28	45	416 26	9	75	1,575	21
hadlington	13	884½ 60	68	13	338½ 24	26	12	244 17	12	38	1,467	39
ampton	7	369½ 35	53	11	311½ 30	28	31	361½ 35	11	49	1,042½	21
hame	4	223 62	56	3	74 20	25	9	53½ 18	6	16	348½	21
ewknor	5	258½ 52	52	3	100 20	33	15	134¾ 28	9	23	491¼	20
irton	1	72 20	72	6	167½ 47	28	11	120½ 33	11	18	360	20
welme	3	328 51	109	4	94 15	23	23	221 34	10	30	643	21
angtree	3	138 43	46	3	92 29	31	9	89 28	10	15	319	21
or all hundreds here given	65	4,002 45	61½	96	2,602½ 28	27	239	2,510¼ 27	10	400	9,115¾	23
he same in acres		100,050	1,588		65,062	675		62,750	250		227,868	575
RWICKSHIRE												
ineton	15	27,324 49	1,821	22	15,145 27	688	64	14,098 25	220	101	56,567	565
oneleigh	6	10,910 39	1,818	15	10,812 38	721	38	6,631 23	148	59	28,353	480
or both hundreds	21	38,234 45	1,820	37	25,957 30	702	102	20,729 25	205	160	84,920	531
or the whole material	142 14	224,452 42	1,580	230 22	154,928 30	674	659 65	147,378 28	223	1031	526,758	511

cent) are large, 229 (22 per cent) of medium size, and 664 (65 per cent) small. The average size of a manor—507 acres— is not far off the upper limit for a small manor in our classifica- tion. Large manors (average size about 1,600 acres) occupy 41 per cent of the total territory covered; medium-sized manors (average size about 675 acres) occupy 30 per cent of the total territory, and small manors (average size 224 acres) 29 per cent. We should not forget at this point that we have excluded five Cambridgeshire hundreds from our calculations, since Cambridgeshire shows a comparatively high percentage of small manors (35 per cent) and a low percentage of large ones (31 per cent). Had these manors been included in the table, we should have had to lower the overall percentage of large manors and raise that of small ones. We have already spoken of the effect this has on our figures. We may assume that large manors occupied something over a third of the whole territory under consideration, and that the rest was about equally divided between medium and small manors.

LOCAL VARIATIONS

Very considerable local variations are to be observed in the proportional relations of the three groups. In the Huntingdon- shire hundred of Hirstingstone (which we have already men- tioned more than once) we find an extreme instance of the predominance of the large manor, due to those of the abbey of Ramsey and of the bishopric of Ely. Here large manors occupy 75 per cent of the total territory, medium-sized manors 14 per cent and small manors only 12 per cent. But in the Bedfordshire hundreds of Stodden and Willey small manors occupy 46 per cent of the total arable, large manors only 15 per cent. These are extreme cases. But apart from these we can observe a definite unevenness in the distribution of large, medium and small manors over the territory covered by our material. Here also, as in the case of the relation of villein land to free holdings, we can perceive two quite clearly defined zones, marked by the predominance of the large and of the small manor respectively. The former predominates in Huntingdonshire, or, to be more accurate, in the three northern hundreds of the county, where it occupies more than 60 per

cent of the whole area calculated; in Oxfordshire, where in
spite of unevenness in the distribution of large manors in
different hundreds (60 per cent in Chadlington hundred, 20
per cent in Pirton hundred) the average percentage for the
territory of large manors throughout the county is 45 per cent;
and in the adjacent Warwickshire hundred of Kineton (49 per
cent). We find a high percentage of small manors in Cambridgeshire (altogether they make up 35 per cent of the total
territory, which is a higher figure than that for large manors);
in the adjacent Huntingdonshire hundred of Toseland,
which in this respect presents a sharp contrast to the other
hundreds of Huntingdonshire; and in Bedfordshire. The
percentage of small manors is high in the Buckinghamshire
hundred of Bunstow, which lies to the north of the Ouse;
in the remaining hundreds of this county large and medium-
sized manors predominate. The percentage of large manors
in the Warwickshire hundred of Stoneleigh is also low: there
the medium-sized manor is the predominant form. If we
compare the incidence of the large manor with the incidence
of villein holding, we see that to a considerable extent they
coincide, but that there are some divergences. Generally
speaking, the mere juxtaposition of these two factors is sufficient
to enable us to assume that the structure of large and small
manors was not identical, and that villein land played a larger
part in the former. This impression is confirmed by Table 3,
which shows the relations between the size of a manor and its
structure.

VARIATIONS OF STRUCTURE BETWEEN MANORS OF DIFFERENT SIZE

If we examine the totals of this table, we see that as one
passes from large manors to small the percentage of demesne
land increases and that of villein land falls. On large manors
the demesne accounts for only 25 per cent of the arable land,
on medium manors for 35 per cent, and on small manors for
41 per cent. This increase seems to be beyond all doubt,
although it is possible that the figures quoted exaggerate
slightly, in view of the fact that the demesne of large manors
is usually described in terms of carucates. Even more clearly

County and Hundred	Large manors			Medium manors			Small manors		
	Demesne	Villein land	Free holdings	Demesne	Villein land	Free holdings	Demesne	Villein land	Fre holdi
HUNTINGDONSHIRE									
Hirstingstone	2,636	7,469	2,230	612	1,223	336	1,053	567	32
	21	61	18	28	56	16	54	29	
Leightonstone	5,928	14,671	3,832	1,080	1,561	1,146	2,296	2,723	1,60
	23	60	16	28	41	30	35	41	2
Normancross	3,120	4,579	1,323	2,288	2,476	1,281	2,846	1,466	1,99
	35	51	14	38	41	21	45	23	3
Toseland	668	1,150	662	3,288	2,747	1,893	4,138	3,226	1,58
	27	46	27	41	35	24	46	36	3
For the whole county	12,352	27,869	8,047	7,268	8,007	4,656	10,333	7,982	5,5
	26	57	17	36	40	24	43	34	2
CAMBRIDGESHIRE									
Chesterton	464	1,417	775	660	999	240	552	555	5
	18	51	31	35	52	13	33	33	3
Chilford	1,993	1,359	1,359	1,953	435	1,342	2,849	248	1,54
	42	29	29	52	13	35	62	5	3
Papworth	740	2,030	1,275	613	1,027	627	744	579	93
	18	50	32	26	46	28	33	26	4
Longstow	640	1,064	747	2,638	2,071	1,822	2,863	942	1,89
	27	43	30	40	32	28	50	16	3
Thriplow	1,110	1,544	714	1,492	1,410	847	875	379	83
	33	45	21	40	38	22	42	18	4
Whittlesford	249	351	755	922	605	571	2,085	1,545	92
	19	26	54	44	29	27	46	34	2
For all hundreds here given	5,196	7,764	5,625	8,258	6,547	5,449	9,968	4,248	6,6
	28	42	30	41	32	27	47	21	3
BEDFORDSHIRE									
Stoddon and Willey	597	1,675	1,130	2,701	1,484	3,902	4,098	1,908	3,82
	17	49	34	34	18	48	42	20	3
BUCKINGHAMSHIRE									
Bunstow	805	400	1,159	1,076	759	1,055	1,395	1,147	1,00
	34	17	49	37	26	36	38	32	2
Stodfold	877	991	1,155	1,980	2,017	1,847	961	886	1,18
	29	33	38	34	35	32	32	29	3
Mucha	660	1,049	1,012	1,905	1,024	973	165	25	
	24	38	37	48	26	25	80	13	
Mursley	1,687	4,406	1,714	660	1,336	1,001	1,350	478	65
	21	57	22	22	44	33	54	19	2
For all hundreds here given	4,029	6,837	5,049	5,621	5,136	4,876	3,871	2,536	2,92
	25	43	32	36	33	31	42	27	3
OXFORDSHIRE (in virgates)									
Banbury	56	184	21	38½	47	48½	48	49	4
	22	70	8	47	36	37	33	34	3
Ploughley	162	375	92½	162	226	55½	162	145½	
	26	60	14	37	51	12	43	40	
Bullington	70½	159	27½	102½	110	59	174½	135½	4
	28	66	11	38	40	32	42	39	
Wootton	170	321	89½	169	250	157	134	194	8
	29	55	16	28	44	27	33	45	2
Chadlington	277	389	218	107	137½	94	103	79	6
	31	44	25	32	40	28	42	32	2
Bampton	89	184	96	104	145	62½	126	128	10
	24	50	26	33	47	20	35	35	3
Thame	71	113	39	33	33	7½	19	26	3
	32	50	17	45	45	10	36	51	
Lewknor	56	139	63½	44	36	20	60	35	3
	22	54	24	44	36	20	45	26	
Pirton	8	15½	49	56	56½	55	59	26	3
	11	21	68	33	34	33	49	22	
Ewelme	72	132	124	38	24	32	80½	45	4
	22	40	38	41	25	34	37	20	
Langtree	36	39	63	26	27½	38½	42	25½	
	26	28	46	29	30	41	47	29	
For all hundreds here given	10,671½	2,051½	883	880	1,092½	630	1,009	889	6
	26	51	22	30	47	23	37	39	
The same in acres	26,687	51,287	22,075	22,000	27,312	15,750	25,225	22,225	15,3
WARWICKSHIRE									
Kineton	5,880	15,650	5,794	4,146	8,045	2,954	5,083	5,932	3,0
	21	57	22	27	53	20	36	42	
Stoneleigh	4,250	2,433	4,227	3,434	4,013	3,365	1,734	2,071	2,8
	43	24	43	35	41	34	26	31	
For both hundreds	10,130	18,083	10,021	7,580	12,058	6,319	6,817	8,003	5,9
	27	47	26	30	46	24	39	33	
For the whole material	58,991	113,514	51,947	53,428	60,544	40,952	60,312	46,902	40,1
	26	51	23	35	39	26	41	32	
Average areas within the manor	416	800	366	232	263	178	92	73	

apparent is the fall in the percentage of villein land as one moves from large to small manors. On large manors the percentage of villein land is 51 per cent, on medium manors 39 per cent, and on small manors 32 per cent. Thus the ratio of demesne to villein land is 33 : 67 on large manors, 49 : 51 on medium manors, and 56 : 44 on small manors. A certain rise in the percentage of land held by free tenants may also be observed. On large manors 23 per cent of the territory falls to them, on medium manors 26 per cent, and on small manors 27 per cent. But if we take the percentage relationship between free and villein holdings, the differences between large, medium and small manors are brought out very sharply. On large manors this is 31 : 69, on medium manors it is 40 : 60, whilst on small manors it is 48 : 52. We are left with a very definite impression that on small manors, the demesne was much less linked up with villein land, and occupied a more independent position in the manorial economy, than on large manors. Moreover, it has already been observed that the majority of manors without villein land are small manors. In the Cambridgeshire hundred of Chilford, for example, the majority of manors, as we have seen,[1] were either totally unprovided or inadequately provided with villein land. But on the three largest manors in this hundred we find comparatively large areas of villein land; the manors without villein land are here almost exclusively small manors.

A similar relationship of demesne, villein land and free holdings on large, medium and small manors respectively is maintained almost everywhere. An exception is presented by the hundreds of Whittlesford (Cambs.), by the Buckinghamshire hundreds of Stodfold and Bunstow, the hundreds of Langtree and Pirton in Oxfordshire, and the hundred of Stoneleigh in Warwickshire. Almost always these exceptions are due to the structural peculiarities of single large manors. Thus in the hundred of Stoneleigh the low percentage of villein land on large manors is due to the part played by the large manor of the Cistercian abbey of Stoneleigh, which had an immense area of free land (1,796 acres, 113 cottages, and 48 messuages), but only 14 acres and 2 cottages of villein land, and by Theobald Verdon's manor of Bretford, which had no

[1] Cf. above, p. 95.

villein land but 956 acres in burgage. Apart from these two, there is one other large manor in the hundred, Itchington, which belonged to the bishop of Chester, and here we find the ratio characteristic of the large manor—600 acres of demesne, 1,020 acres of villein land, and $266\frac{1}{2}$ acres and 16 cottages in free tenure. In the hundred of Bunstow there is only one large manor, Hanslope,[1] belonging to William Beauchamp, which has an unusually large area of free land. The predominance of free over villein land on the large manors of the hundred of Stodfold is also produced by a single manor, that of Hugh de Chastillon at Leckhampstead.[2] A second large manor in this hundred, John Somery's manor of Radclive,[3] also has an unusual structure, reminiscent of a Cistercian estate, which consists of a huge demesne practically without tenant land. In exactly the same way one manor at Watlington,[4] belonging to the Earl of Cornwall, causes a considerable predominance of free holdings among the large manors of the hundred of Pirton, and a single manor of Hugh Rivell at Goring[5] causes a similar predominance to appear among the large manors of the hundred of Langtree.

Thus almost everywhere where we find deviations from the average they are accounted for by special circumstances. Is it possible, however, to observe specifically local variations in the structure of large, medium and small manors? Are there any differences in this respect between the areas with a high percentage of villein land and those with a low one? A certain difference, which does not, however, always come out clearly, may be observed. In the areas with a low percentage of villein land and a high percentage of free holdings, in Bedfordshire and Cambridgeshire in particular, the structural differences between large and small manors are more sharply expressed. Here on the small manors—which incidentally cover the major portion of this territory—the area held by free tenants is considerably in excess of villein land, while at the same time on the large manors the area of villein land is considerably in excess of free holdings. In the areas where villein land has an overall predominance it is predominant on small as well as on

---

[1] *R.H.*, ii, 343.   [2] *R.H.*, ii, 338.   [3] *R.H.*, ii, 342.
[4] *R.H.*, ii, 815.   [5] *R.H.*, ii, 777.

large manors, though on the former the predominance is not so marked as on the latter.

SIGNIFICANCE OF STRUCTURAL VARIATIONS

We may ask to what extent the analysis of large, medium and small manors, and the comparative study of their structure, contributes to a solution of the problem of the part played by large, medium and small feudal estates in medieval England, and to an understanding of the specific features of their respective economies. It is certain that our analysis does not help us to draw conclusions as to the overall territorial area covered by large, medium and small estates respectively. As a rule large feudal estates are composed of a number of manors of varying sizes, and although large manors may predominate in the domains of great lords, both church and lay, nevertheless even here there are many medium and small manors, not to mention free holdings on other manors. On the other hand, the 'large' manor is not so very large after all; its average size is about 1,600 acres of arable, and manors of 3,000 acres are a rare exception. A manor of 1,600 acres does not, however, constitute a large feudal domain; it would normally be the estate of a knight of middling rank. At the same time we must remember that we have before us only a fragment of a large survey, and what appears in this fragment often represents only insignificant portions of large domains of complicated structure, extending over a number of hundreds and counties. It is thus very difficult, without referring to other sources, to pick out, among the manors surveyed in the Hundred Rolls, those which belonged to great feudatories and those which belonged to medium and small lords; but it may be done in the case of church domains, which are better known to us than lay estates from other sources and have been most thoroughly studied in the past.

MANORS ON ECCLESIASTICAL ESTATES

In the surviving fragments of the Hundred Rolls we find estates belonging to about a hundred different ecclesiastical institutions, mostly monasteries. Of these the majority hold either small manors or else individual tenements on other lords' manors. In Table 4, which excludes these individual holdings and includes only manors, 66 per cent of all the church manors are small manors. Among the lords of these small manors there are many small monasteries, but there are some very large ones as well. Within the area surveyed by the Hundred Rolls large monasteries such as Gloucester and Cirencester[1] hold only small manors, as also does the great abbey of St. Mary, York.[2] Three manors in Buckinghamshire belonging to St. Albans fall with the 'medium' category, but come close to its lower limit (570, 540 and 660 acres).[3] Also in the medium category are the two Huntingdonshire manors of the large abbey of Peterborough.[4] The manors of the priory of Ely are either of medium size or small. The domains of the Hospitallers are almost entirely made up of small parcels of land; of nine estates of theirs which can be reckoned as manors, only one may be called large, and one medium. The Templars have four medium and twelve small, but not a single large manor. And many other similar examples might be adduced. The large ecclesiastical bodies situated some distance away hold for the most part small and medium-sized manors, and their large manors are concentrated nearer to the main centre. However, some large monasteries situated a considerable distance away possess large manors within the area covered by the Hundred Rolls. There is a very large manor belonging to Winchcombe abbey,[5] and two large manors belonging to Westminster.[6] Large manors are the rule on the domains of the episcopal sees, among which Lincoln possesses the most numerous estates in the territory covered by the Hundred Rolls. There are large blocks of its lands in Oxfordshire in the hundreds of Banbury and Thame; indeed, the whole of the hundred of Thame is a hundredal manor of the bishop of Lincoln although subdivided into a number of manors, in the hands of either the bishop himself or his vassals. Altogether the bishop of Lincoln holds within this area six large, two medium, and five small manors; the bishop of Ely three large and two medium-sized manors; the bishop of Chester three large manors and one of medium size; and the bishop of Winchester has one large manor, in the hundred of Bampton.

---

[1] *R.H.*, ii, 695, 696.   [2] *R.H.*, ii, 556–57.   [3] *R.H.*, ii, 337–38.
[4] *R.H.*, ii, 638–39.   [5] *R.H.*, ii, 739.   [6] *R.H.*, ii, 831–32.

The relationship between the total size of estates and the size of the separate manors included within them comes out clearly in the case of those church lords the centres of whose domains lay either within the territory covered by the Hundred Rolls or in close proximity to it. First among these is the ancient Benedictine abbey of Ramsey, famous for its cartulary, its manorial accounts, and its court records, all of which have played a great part in the study of the medieval manor. The rolls survey eighteen manors of Ramsey abbey. Of these, eleven are large, six medium-sized, and only one is small. The hundred of Hirstingstone is almost entirely covered by large manors belonging to Ramsey abbey. Ramsey is the only large monastery lying within the territory covered by the surviving fragments of the Hundred Rolls, but among the large monasteries lying near by is the abbey—also Benedictine— of Abingdon, in Berkshire, which held two large manors in Oxfordshire.

Monasteries of medium size lying either within or close to the area surveyed, and having more or less considerable estates within it, include the Benedictine abbey of Eynsham (Oxon.), the slightly larger Augustinian abbey of Osney (Oxon.), the Benedictine abbey of Thorney (Cambs.), the Benedictine priory of Coventry, and the Augustinian priory of Kenilworth. Among their estates large manors are rare. For the five houses together there are only seven large manors in all: Kenilworth has none, the rest one or two apiece. Their medium-sized manors amount to twelve, and their small ones to forty-three.[1] From these, however, quite considerable holdings are built up; Osney has as many as eighteen manors, Eynsham fourteen, and Kenilworth twelve.

Among the small monasteries situated in the counties to which the Hundred Rolls refer, the following may be named: in Huntingdonshire, the Augustinian priory of Huntingdon and the Benedictine priories of St. Neots and St. Ives (both very small); in Cambridgeshire, the Augustinian priory of Barnwell and the Benedictine nunneries of Swaffham and Chatteris; in Oxfordshire, the Augustinian priory of Bicester and the Benedictine nunnery of Godstow; in Bedfordshire, the Augustinian priory of Bushmead and the Benedictine priory of

[1] I exclude small holdings on other manors.

Chicksands. These ten monasteries account for only two large manors (Barnwell and Huntingdon have one each),[1] three medium-size, and twenty-six small manors. Even those houses which hold comparatively large complexes of lands have them made up almost exclusively of small manors.

Of the medium and small size monasteries lying outside the area covered by the Hundred Rolls and its immediate neighbourhood, but holding lands within it, only rarely does any hold a large or medium-sized manor,[2] and those mentioned in the Hundred Rolls are almost all small.

Large manors are more frequently found in the possession of Cistercian monasteries of small or middle size. The rolls describe manors belonging to eight such monasteries: Bruerne and Thame (Oxon.), Bittlesden (Bucks.), Combe and Stoneleigh (War.), Sawtry (Hunts.), Woburn (Beds.), and Tilty (Essex), of which all, save Woburn and possibly Combe, are small. We find in their possession six large, five medium, and twenty-five small manors. But their large manors are manors of a peculiar type, sharply distinguished from the normal large manor by the complete or almost complete absence of the element most typical of a large manor—villein land.[3]

If we leave aside the domains of the Cistercian monasteries, with their peculiar manorial structure, we can say that a considerable majority (about 32 out of 45) of the large church manors surveyed in the Hundred Rolls are in the possession of large ecclesiastical establishments. The number of small and middling manors in their possession is considerably less. On the other hand, among the possessions of the medium-sized and smaller monasteries small manors are definitely predominant.

MANORS ON LAY ESTATES

Can this observation be extended to cover non-ecclesiastical manors? The enrolments do not, in fact, reveal any large groupings of estates under lay lords comparable to the domains

---

[1] R.H., ii, 402, 626.

[2] E.g., the small monastery of Deerhurst (Glos.) holds quite a large manor in Oxfordshire. Cf. R.H., ii, 742.

[3] On the Cistercian manors, see below, p. 112.

of Ramsey abbey or of the see of Lincoln. Indeed, it would appear that thirteenth-century England had very few really large lay domains. At the end of the reign of Henry III the only person whose income could properly be called 'vast' was the king's brother, Richard, Earl of Cornwall. The income of Prince Edward came to something like £10,000 a year. We can count a scanty half dozen barons with incomes of over £3,000 or £4,000 a year—among them the Earl of Gloucester, the Earl Marshall, and the Countess of Devonshire. Rather later, the five earldoms of Thomas of Lancaster yielded about £8,000. The earldom of Ferrers was valued at 2,000 marks a year, that of Richmond at 1,200 marks. A rich baron, the father of St. Thomas of Cantilupe, had an income of 500 marks.[1] The largest complex of lay domains in the Hundred Rolls belongs to Edmund, Earl of Cornwall, Richard's son. He has up to ten manors in Huntingdonshire and Oxfordshire. Three of them seem to be parts of larger manors, for which the survey is incomplete. If we exclude these three, all the others except one come within the category of large manors—very large, even, with up to a hundred virgates of arable on each of them.[2] The one and only manor of the Earl of Warwick which is described in the rolls, is very large (about 3,800 acres of arable). The Countess of Warwick's manor at Kirtlington (Oxon.) is in the 'large' category, but she also has a manor of medium size at Garsington (Oxon.). Of very considerable size is the Huntingdonshire manor of John Bohun, Earl of Hereford.[3] But Gilbert Clare, Earl of Gloucester, has only one large manor (very large, it is true), one small one and one of middle size.[4] Robert de Vere, Earl of Oxford, has four manors, only one of which is large, while one is of medium size (but close to the upper limit of this category) and two are small.[5] Henry de Lacy, Earl of Lincoln, had a medium-sized manor at Bicester (Oxon.).[6] From the inquisitions *post Mortem*, however, we know that the estates of these earls consisted mainly of large manors.

It seems to me that while the fragmentary nature of the surviving rolls precludes any judgment on the comparative

[1] See Denholm-Young, *Seignorial Administration in England*, 22–23.
[2] *R.H.*, ii, 650, 715, 716, 751, 815, 824, 826, 855.
[3] *R.H.*, ii., 621.   [4] *R.H.*, ii, 334, 676, 734.
[5] *R.H.*, ii, 422, 424, 427, 774.   [6] *R.H.*, ii, 828.

incidence of large-scale, middle-scale and small-scale feudal
landholding, they provide a basis for conclusions regarding
peculiarities of manorial structure on the estates of large,
small, and possibly also middling feudal lords. While the
estates of the great feudal lords undoubtedly included small
and medium-sized manors (especially in districts far removed
from the main estate centres), the large manor is predominant,
and the organization of the large manor, characterized first
and foremost by a high percentage of villein land, can be
considered the distinguishing mark of large-scale feudal
landholding. As for the smaller lords, it is quite clear that
among their lower strata the small manor and the organization
that went with it was predominant. The line we have drawn
between the 'small' and the 'medium' manor was apparently
approximately that which determined whether a holding was
knightly or not. The middle ranks of the feudal lords would
appear to have occupied an intermediate position not only in
wealth but also in the manorial organization of their estates.

LAY AND ECCLESIASTICAL MANORS COMPARED

In this chapter we have more than once found ourselves
confronted with the problem of church lands. We may state
this problem here in the form of the following questions:
(1) What proportion of the total of manors belonged to the
church, and in what proportion did the area comprised by
church manors stand to that of lay estates? (2) Are there
structural differences between church and lay manors?

Table 4 summarizes calculations which provide the answer
to the first question. I am well aware of the difficulties facing
the investigator who attempts to define the area of the church's
estates, or the share of the church in the national income.[1]
Nevertheless, our calculations do provide a basis for some
conclusions concerning the role of the church as a land-holder
in England at the very time when its growth had been checked
by the Statute of Mortmain. We see that in the region under
consideration, where there were no especially large complexes
of church lands, apart from Ramsey abbey and the see of
Lincoln, the church held 274 manors out of a total of 1,031, or

[1] *O.S.S.L.H.*, i (1909), 78–89.

26 per cent, while these manors included 31 per cent of the total arable in the region. It is, of course, true that the rights exercised by churches on these manors were very varied, that they were not the same for demesne land, villein land and free holdings, that the number of arable acres tells us nothing about woodland, pastures, meadows, mills, and that we have no data on revenues from ecclesiastical boroughs. But we still can draw certain conclusions about the share of the church in the appropriation of feudal rent. The church held, as feudal lord, almost one-third of the agricultural land under consideration. Would it be incorrect to say that about a third of the feudal rent therefore went into the hands of the church? In fact, much more than 31 per cent of it went to the church. It is common knowledge, which will be confirmed in the following analysis, that the rents of villeins are much higher than those of free holdings. And the ratio of free holdings to villein land is not the same on church as on lay lands; for although holding 26 per cent of all manors, and 31 per cent of all arable in the given area, the church holds 37 per cent of all villein land, the main source of feudal rent, and only about 23 per cent of the relatively unremunerative free holdings. One must also take into account that the church held the greater part of its lands by free alms and was, therefore, not obliged to share the feudal rent it received with the lords from whom it was held. Furthermore, the enrolments take no account of the 'spiritual' revenues of church establishments, tithes in particular. But even if we limit ourselves to *temporalia*, we may assert with confidence that it received not less, and probably more, than a third of the total feudal rent. And in saying this we are still not taking into account the extra-manorial holdings of the church, in other words its holdings on the manors of other lords.

STRUCTURAL PECULIARITIES OF ECCLESIASTICAL MANORS

Is a high percentage of villein land a special characteristic of church manors, distinguishing them from other manors? I do not think so. This high percentage is explained by the fact that the proportion of large manors is higher among those belonging to the church. The average size of a church manor,

TABLE 4
ECCLESIASTICAL AND LAY ESTATES

County and Hundred		Ecclesiastical Estates				Lay Estates			
		Total arable (acres)	Number of estates	Number of large, medium and small estates	Average size of estates	Total arable (acres)	Number of estates	Number of large, medium and small estates	Average size of estates
Huntingdonshire									
Hirstingstone	.. %	15,269 93	14	7–3–4	1,084	1,185 7	9	— — 9	131
Leightonstone	.. %	13,232 36	14	6–1–7	945	21,608 64	39	7–4–28	554
Normancross	.. %	12,047 57	19	4–5–10	631	9,332 43	24	2–3–19	385
HUNTINGDONSHIRE									
Toseland	.. %	2,280 12	9	1 — 8	253	17,086 88	61	1–11–49	280
County Total	.. %	42,828 46	56	18–9–29	782	49,211 54	133	10–18–105	370
Three Northern Hundreds	.. %	40,548 55	47	17–9–21	884	32,125 45	72	9–7–56	446
CAMBRIDGESHIRE									
Chesterton	.. %	3,695 60	5	2–1–2	740	2,537 40	11	— 2—9	230
Chilford	.. %	497 4	4	— — 4	248	12,580 96	26	4–6–16	488
Papworth	.. %	4,374 52	7	2–2–3	625	4,198 48	12	1–1–10	350
Longstow	.. %	4,268 28	9	1–2–6	474	10,411 72	30	1–8–21	347
Thriplow	.. %	3,798 41	4	2 — — 2	950	5,409 59	17	1–4–12	317
Whittlesford	.. %	1,905 24	5	—1—4	381	6,082 76	16	1–2–13	380
Total of Hundreds Covered	..	18,537	34	7–8–19	545	41,217	112	8–23–81	368
BEDFORDSHIRE									
Stodden and Willey	.. %	747 4	3	— — 3	249	20,572 96	53	2–14–37	390

	[virgates]	%		£—s—d		acres	%		£—s—d	
Mucha	3,526	51	6	—5—1	586	3,307	49	4	2—1—1	850
Mursley	6,406	49	8	2—2—4	801	6,885	51	16	4—4—8	430
Total of Hundreds Covered	13,761		22	3—9—10	625	27,120		58	8—16—34	467
OXFORDSHIRE										
Banbury	297	54	8	—4—4	37½	243	46	19	—5—14	12½
Ploughley	359½	25	16	4—2—10	22½	1,083½	75	49	8—16—25	22
Bullington	256½	30	17	1—2—14	15	627½	70	27	3—7—17	23
Wootton	342	21	21	3—3—15	17	1,233	79	54	6—18—30	23
Chadlington	305	22	8	2——6	38	1,162	78	30	11—13—6	39
Bampton	311	30	15	1—4—10	20½	731	78	34	6—7—21	21½
Thame	164½	47	3	3——	53	184	53	13	1—3—9	13
Lewknor	142	28	4	2——2	35	351	72	19	3—3—13	17
Pirton	30	8	3	——3	10	330	92	15	1—6—8	22
Ewelme	163	25	9	—1—8	18	480	75	21	2—4—15	23
Langtree	13	4	2	——2	6	306	96	13	3—3—7	23
Total of Hundreds Covered	2,383½	32	106	21—11—74	22	6,731	68	294	44—85—165	23
In acres	59,587				550	168,275				575
WARWICKSHIRE										
Kineton	13,619	24	26	5—4—17	525	42,948	76	75	10—18—47	572
Stoneleigh	16,415	58	24	4—6—14	684	11,938	42	35	2—9—24	341
In both Hundreds	30,034	35	50	9—10—31	600	54,886	65	110	12—27—71	499
Total of all material used	165,494	31	271 / 26	58—47—166	611	361,281	69	760 / 74	84—183—493	475

in our material, is 615 acres; that of a lay manor 467 acres. On church lands large manors make up 20 per cent of the total number of manors, on lay estates 11 per cent. Out of 138 large manors dealt with in the enrolments, 56, or 40 per cent, are in the hands of the church. Therefore the characteristic structure of the church manor is, in general terms, identical with the characteristic structure of the large manor.

But even among church manors we find many deviations from the 'typical' structure of the large manor. If the estates of the old Benedictine house of Ramsey provide an example of the purest type of the manor cultivated by servile tenants, with a large area of villein land and an insignificant percentage of free holdings, it is, on the other hand, precisely among church manors that we find the widest deviations from that type— manors with a large demesne but without villein land, or with an insignificant amount of it. This is the characteristic Cistercian type.

Here are some examples of the structure of Cistercian estates. The abbey of Sawtry had its principal property at Sawtry itself. This consisted of 1,440 acres of demesne land, 10 acres of villein land, and 14 cottages on the demesne.[1] On the seven manors of the abbey[2] we find no more than 50 acres of villein land, but over 2,500 acres of demesne. Free holdings come to about 445 acres. On the principal estate of Thame abbey at Thame itself, there are 31 virgates of demesne, and no villein land whatsoever; in addition there are some free holdings, but they are not large compared with the demesne.[3] On the other five manors of Thame abbey we find, all in all, four cottages on villein land, and two virgates and 38 cottages in free holdings, while there are almost 55 virgates of demesne.[4] But the same monastery has a manor with a typical 'manorial' structure (Sidenham, Oxon.), with 12 virgates of demesne, and 28 virgates of villein land, without any free holdings.[5] On the manor of the abbot of Stoneleigh, in Warwickshire, there is a huge demesne with an insignificant amount of villein land, but with extensive freehold. There is rather more villein land on the manors of the abbot of Combe, but even

[1] *R.H.*, ii, 663.   [2] *R.H.*, ii, 623, 624, 653, 663, 673, 529, 539–40.
[3] *R.H.*, ii, 820–21.   [4] *R.H.*, ii, 834, 836, 819, 764.
[5] *R.H.*, ii, 784.

there it is only about a third as big as the demesne. Somewhat nearer to the typical manorial structure are the manors of the abbot of Woburn, but even on them there is less villein land than there is demesne.[1] On the manors of the abbot of Bittlesden the amounts of both villein land and freehold are very small.[2] The part played by the Cistercian monasteries in medieval economic history is well known; in England they were pioneers in commercial sheep-raising. But it would be a mistake to think that they had begun to go over to capitalist methods of production; in other words, that they cultivated their large demesne by means of hired labour. The labour force on the Cistercian manors was provided by the *conversi*, who lived in the monasteries on the footing of servants bound to the house. Although such an economy as this does not altogether fit in with the conception of a feudal economy, since the *conversi* were not provided with plots of land, it certainly did not embody any progressive principles of the development of free labour. The *conversi*, personally free, were bound to the monastery by non-economic ties.

The lands of the Hospitallers and Templars consisted for the most part of small manors and holdings on the manors of other lords.

The property of the church was very unevenly distributed over the territory under study. While in some hundreds church land comprised a considerable part of the whole—for instance, in the three northern hundreds of Huntingdonshire, in some hundreds of Oxfordshire, and in the Warwickshire hundred of Stoneleigh—there are hundreds in which there are practically no church lands, and in particular no large church estates. Such, for example, are the Bedfordshire hundreds, the Buckinghamshire hundred of Bunstow, and the Oxfordshire hundreds of Pirton and Langtree.

THE NON-MANORIAL HOLDINGS OF THE CHURCH

In discussing church manors we cannot ignore the numerous small tenements held by ecclesiastical bodies on other manors. The descriptions of free holdings in the Hundred Rolls are full of such instances. They are often very small, only a few

[1] *R.H.*, ii, 335, 337.   [2] *R.H.*, ii, 340, 343, 350.

H

acres, sometimes even a rood or less, but in sum they reach very imposing figures, amounting often to as much as 25 per cent of all free holdings in the hundred (e.g. the hundred of Banbury, Oxon.). But in other hundreds the percentage of land held in this way is insignificant (e.g. Bampton, Oxon.).

In a majority of cases these possessions are held by free alms, but sometimes rent is paid, and not always only a nominal rent. Thus, the prior of Ely pays 2 marks for 2 virgates in the hundred of Thriplow, and the abbess of Chatteris 6s. o½d. (and three *precariae*) for 32 acres in the same hundred, while the prior of Chacombe pays 10s. for one virgate and 80 acres which he holds for life. Sometimes a church holding land in this way paid rent to begin with, but later tried to turn it into free alms (*trahitur nunc in elemosynam*, as the source puts it). In the majority of cases, we are dealing with small gifts to the church, but sometimes one may assume the acquisition by the church of lands by purchase or lease.

Some problems are raised by these numerous church holdings on lay manors. In the first place, it is not clear how the individual churches exploited them. If they were situated close to the church's own manors, it may be assumed that they were included in the demesne land. But much more frequently the church in question had no manor in the vicinity to which the holdings could be attached, and in that case we must assume that they were leased out to tenants. This is sometimes explicitly stated in the Hundred Rolls, but in the vast majority of cases no such explanation is made. Why do the Hundred Rolls, which list so scrupulously all tenants, free and villein, depart from their usual practice in this case? And if these plots were not leased out, then in what way were they exploited? The Bedfordshire Hundred Rolls indicate clearly when small free holdings of the church were leased out to tenants. The prioress of Harrold holds a virgate *cum suis tenentibus*.[1] St. John's Hospital in Bedford holds 1½ virgates in Biddenham, a quarter virgate of which is *in dominico*, while the rest of the land is leased to two tenants for a rent of 7s. 4d. and forinsec service.[2] The prior of Canons' Ashby holds a virgate in Thurleigh *que est tenta de eo in villenagio, quam quidam nativus tenet de eodem Priore*.[3] But such indications are comparatively

[1] *R.H.*, ii, 327.   [2] *Ibid.*   [3] *R.H.*, ii, 325.

rare. The fact that a very small plot, a quarter of a virgate, is definitely stated to be *in dominico*, indicates the possibility of exploitation by other means than leasing out; but it is difficult to see just how this was done. Nevertheless, the Hundred Rolls confirm the well-known fact that church holdings were firmly established within lay manors, and by means of small donations and acquisitions churches had secured control of what was sometimes a considerable percentage of free holdings. The donations might be made either by the lord of the manor or by free tenants. Following the dissolution of the monasteries these holdings were transferred to the hands of laymen, and so facilitated the encroachment of the gentry on the peasants' holdings.

However, we have already seen that by the thirteenth century lay as well as church lords possessed holdings on other lords' manors,[1] and quite considerable estates might be built up in this way. Even the English nobility of the thirteenth century shared the ambition to make itself 'a motley but warm cloak of patches'. It would be of interest to determine, even if only approximately, what proportion of free holdings was in the hands of lay lords; but it is very hard to reach any conclusions on this point, since we cannot always determine the status of a freeholder, and as the survey is fragmentary it is always possible that an individual whose holdings appear to be small, may have been a considerable landowner in districts not covered by the Hundred Rolls. We have succeeded in tracing only a very small percentage of freeholdings held by lay magnates, but in actual fact there may have been more.

A review of the church lands surveyed in the Hundred Rolls suggests the following conclusions. A large number of big manors, which display the characteristic features of the typical serf-economy, were concentrated in the hands of the church. As far as the estates of the church are concerned, they play a decisive role. But side by side with these there were large numbers of small and middle-sized manors with varying structures, and even among the large manors we find departures from the basic type. Finally, another characteristic feature of

[1] Such an entry as the following is typical: *Dominus Henricus de Lacy* (the Earl of Lincoln) *tenet 2 acras pro 6 denariis*. Cf. *R.H.*, ii, 523.

the church's possessions was the large number of small holdings and rent rights held on the manors of other lords.

These characteristic features have probably a historical explanation. Comparison with other sources, particularly with Domesday Book, shows that the main body of typical large manors, with a high percentage of villein land, were in existence on the lands of the church by the end of the eleventh century, or even earlier. The majority of the large church manors of this type belong to the episcopal sees and to the old Benedictine monasteries. Already in Domesday Book a large number are found in the hands of the same church lords who held them at the time of the compilation of the Hundred Rolls.

On the other hand, the rapid growth in the landed property of monastic houses which took place in the twelfth and continued into the thirteenth century, brought into being comparatively few typical large manors. The new estates of the monasteries, mainly of the Cistercian and to some extent of the Augustinian order, consisted of manors of a peculiar type, with a predominance of demesne land and an insignificant number of villeins. The estates of the new monasteries, and of the orders of chivalry, the Templars in particular, are often composed of small manors and of holdings on other lords' manors. It appears also that in the twelfth and thirteenth centuries the possessions of the older ecclesiastical bodies were often divided into smaller units; the charters of Gloucester and Ramsey abbeys are eloquent on this point.

REGIONAL DISTRIBUTION OF MANORIAL TYPES

Let us now try to build into a general picture the preceding observations about the amount of land occupied respectively by demesne, villein tenements and free holdings, by large, medium-sized and small manors, and by church and lay manors, in the different districts within the area under study.

The Midland districts covered by the extant fragments of the Hundred Rolls may within limits be regarded as a unity so far as manorial structure is concerned, just as they are a unity from the point of view of economic geography. Throughout these districts the serf-cultivated manor, with demesne land, villein land and free holdings, predominates. In view of the fact that villein land is virtually always peasant land, whereas free holdings include lands of other types (lands held by parish churches, by monasteries, and by lay lords), we are entitled to conclude that taking the area we are studying as a whole, the servile peasantry predominated over the free peasant.

In the same way, so far as total area covered is concerned, the large manor is the predominant type, though its predominance is not very great, and the areas comprised by small and medium-sized manors are almost as large. Church manors occupy something under a third of the total territory under study, and are unevenly distributed. All in all, we may consider the territory surveyed by the Hundred Rolls to be typical of the classical manorial order.

Nevertheless, in spite of the overall unity in character, there are considerable local variations, if we review the different counties included in the Hundred Rolls, one by one from east to west. Here we must note first of all two large areas distinguished by different historical backgrounds. The eastern area—the counties of Huntingdonshire, southern Cambridgeshire, Bedfordshire (so far as the Rolls survive), and the two northern hundreds of Buckinghamshire—all comes within the territory which can be described as the southern Danelaw.[1] The remaining part—the two hundreds of Buckinghamshire to the south of the Ouse, Oxfordshire, and the two hundreds of Warwickshire—belonged to the English kingdom of Mercia.

THE EASTERN AREA

In the east our material shows a large massif formed by Huntingdonshire and south Cambridgeshire. Here we have the surveys of fifteen hundreds. Those with the most clearly defined characteristics are the three Huntingdonshire hundreds of Hirstingstone, Normancross and Leightonstone. Here the large manor is unquestionably predominant—the typical manor with its high percentage of villein land, and insignificant free holdings. In the majority of cases the vills coincide with the manors. If we exclude the manors of the Cistercian

[1] Cf. G. B. Dodwell, 'The Free Tenantry of the Hundred Rolls', *Ec. H. R.* xiv (1944). The author considers the great number of free peasant farms and of small manors in this area to be the legacy of Scandinavian influences.

monastery of Sawtry, almost all the manors in these hundreds belong to type *a*. At the same time the percentage of land in these hundreds which belongs to the church is very high, covering more than half the total area. Huntingdonshire is an old-established 'church' county—a characteristic clearly evident as early as Domesday—and over forty ecclesiastical bodies held lands in this county. A number of them—Ramsey abbey, Huntingdon priory, St. Ives priory (a 'cell' of Ramsey), St. Neots priory, Sawtry abbey, Stonely priory, the Hospital of St. John the Baptist, and St. Margaret's Leperhouse—were actually situated in Huntingdonshire; others, such as the Cambridgeshire abbey of Thorney, the Lincolnshire abbey of Crowland, the Northamptonshire abbey of Peterborough, and the sees of Ely and Lincoln had from time immemorial owned manors, holdings and revenues in the county.

Let us start our survey with the Huntingdonshire hundred of Hirstingstone, the centre of the lands of the famous abbey of Ramsey, which lies in its northern part. The classical picture of the manorial order, based on serfdom and serf labour, was to no small extent created on the basis of the material from the Ramsey cartulary.[1] Certainly it would be hard to find more perfect examples of the supremacy of the typical, large serf-worked manor, than the hundred of Hirstingstone presents. One after another they pass before us—the large, symmetrical manors with their demesnes, their villein land, and their small freehold plots. These large manors comprise a whole village in the majority of cases, or even two or three villages. Among twenty vills we find only seven which are split up between manors, and even in those the division is not far advanced. Church lands occupy almost the whole of the hundred. Except for the vill of Great Stukeley with the hamlet of Baldewinho, almost all the villages are held by Ramsey abbey; one (with a complicated structure) is held by the bishop of Ely (Somersham *cum socha*). Some small manors belong to the priors of Huntingdon and St. Ives. A few small lay manors are dotted about among them. Ramsey abbey and the bishop of Ely had long held the manors which are recorded as theirs

[1] The Ramsey manorial accounts were a main factor in forming the conclusions of Page, convincing him how tenacious of life labour rents had been. Cf. T. W. Page, *Die Umwandlung der Frohndienst in Geldrenten* (1897); *The End of Villeinage in England* (1900).

in the Hundred Rolls; they are in their possession even in Domesday Book.[1] The survey of the vill of Great Stukeley is so defaced that it is impossible to use it for calculation. Consequently it is difficult to enumerate lands in lay possession. Our calculations are based almost exclusively on church material, and there is therefore some risk of exaggerating the already pronounced ecclesiastical character of the hundred's manorial structure.

The church is also the dominant landholder in the northern hundred of Normancross. Here almost 60 per cent of the total territory falls to the church, and about two-thirds of this church territory is occupied by large manors. Pride of place goes to the lands of the abbots of Thorney.[2] This hundred, too, presents a typical manorial picture, with the decisive role played by the large church estates, which include the Sawtry manor of the Cistercian abbey of Sawtry.

In the western hundred of Leightonstone church estates account for 38 per cent of the land, and more than 80 per cent of this church land is contained in six large manors, first among which are the great manors of the see of Lincoln.[3] The hundred presents a picture of the supremacy of the typical large manor— about two-thirds of the total territory reviewed is occupied by twelve large manors—and its typical features are very pronounced; villein land occupies over four times the area of free holdings.

These three Huntingdonshire hundreds represent a solid block of manors worked by servile labour. They show an overall percentage of something like 30 per cent demesne, 50 per cent villein holdings and 20 per cent free holdings. Servile tenements account for half—in some hundreds more than half— the arable of the county. Large manors (over 1,000 acres) occupy almost two-thirds of the total area; more than half is covered by church manors. The total number of manors in these three Huntingdonshire hundreds is 25, of which 17 are church manors; the average size of a large manor is about 1,800 acres of arable. There are 18 manors of medium size, averaging about 755 acres, and 6 small manors, with an average

[1] *D.B.*, i, 204–204v.
[2] Almost all the Thorney abbey lands in the hundred are already recorded as such in Domesday Book (*D.B.*, i, 205).
[3] *R.H.*, ii, 615, 616 sqq.

size of about 200 acres. Among the large manors there are
very few exceptions to the usual manorial plan, but the manors
of the Cistercian abbey of Sawtry may be noted, and also the
manor of Imbert of Montferrand, at Offord Cluny, with 300
acres of demesne and 642 acres of free holdings, but no villein
land.[1]

Quite different features characterize the southern hundred
of Huntingdonshire. The hundred of Toseland is distinguished
by its low percentage of church land. Only 12 per cent of
the total arable accounted for is included in the church manors,
and a much smaller part is played by the large manor. There
are only two manors of over 1,000 acres, of which one (Heming-
ford) belongs to Ramsey abbey.[2] Almost half the hundred is
distributed among small manors. Extensive splitting up of
vills between manors is characteristic of this hundred, and the
coincidence of vill and manor is rare. In the smallness of its
manors this hundred is reminiscent of Cambridgeshire, to
which it lies adjacent geographically.

From the Cambridgeshire surveys, only those for the southern
part of the county have survived (with the exception of three
hundreds). As early as the time of Domesday the Cambridgeshire vills were distinguished by the complicated character of
their manorial structure; indeed, it was from the Cambridgeshire
Domesday that Maitland drew the material for his description
of a village of the non-manorial type.[3] After the Conquest
villeinage and the manorial system grew up here, but the latter
never assumed its typical, fully-fledged form, and this remained
true even at the period of the Hundred Rolls. Maitland quotes
Duxford in Cambridgeshire as an example of the extremely
complicated web of manors and holdings within one vill
which existed in the thirteenth century. Like the counties of
East Anglia, Cambridgeshire shows a considerable development of free holdings, which passed rapidly from hand to hand
at an early date. The alienation of free holdings, in whole or in
part, created here complications of tenant relationships so
extreme that they are not easily disentangled.

Extremely small manors are characteristic of the whole of

---

[1] *R.H.*, ii, 683.   [2] *R.H.*, ii, 680.
[3] The Cambridgeshire village of Orwell and the Cambridgeshire hundred of
Wetherley served as his examples of complicated vill structure that did not accord
with 'manorial' characteristics. Cf. *Domesday Book and Beyond*, 129–38.

Cambridgeshire, and large manors occur only as isolated instances in different hundreds. In the six hundreds of Cambridgeshire for which it is possible to give figures for demesne land, we find no more than fifteen manors with more than 1,000 acres of arable, and these manors are not really large—they average about 1,225 acres of arable each. Small manors of varying types account for 35 per cent of the land in these hundreds, and in some occupy nearly 60 per cent of the total area. If we also take into consideration the fact that free holdings within the larger manors often include sub-units of a manorial type, which cannot always be fully distinguished, the importance of the small manor in these hundreds is even clearer.

Church manors comprise about 31 per cent of the total territory accounted for in these hundreds, which is the overall average. To this should be added 2 per cent, representing church holdings on lay manors. Of the fifteen large manors seven belong to churches. On the large manors the percentage of villein land is on the average twice that on the small manors, and the church manors show a considerably higher percentage (45 per cent) of villein land than is found on those of the laity. But even here there are manors without villeins, such as that of the Augustinian abbey of Waltham,[1] and those of the Cistercians. It is difficult, therefore, to speak of a predominance of the large church manor in Cambridgeshire. We have before us an area, little manorialized in the eleventh century, in which the process of manorialization was far from complete in the thirteenth century, and complicated by the fact that frequent transfers of land began early here. This latter factor cuts across and confuses the manorialization which was taking shape.

These conclusions, derived from the material provided by the six hundreds for which figures of demesne land are available, may be extended to cover the other five Cambridgeshire hundreds (Longstow, Staine, Flendish, Staploe, Wetherly). Here, too, we can observe the small size of manors, the predominance of free holdings over villein land, the sharp structural distinction between large and small manors, while on the former, which are for the most part church manors,

[1] Horseheath, *R.H.*, ii, 421.

we find large accumulations of villein land, many times greater than the free holdings. On the small manors great variety of structure reigns.

In the material relating to our eastern grouping we can thus distinguish two sections—the northern and the southern. The distinguishing features of the northern section are the predominance of the large manor, a very considerable proportion of church land and typical 'manorial' traits. The southern section is characterized by the small size and varied nature of its manors, by a very considerable development of free holding, and by the comparatively secondary role of ecclesiastical tenure. The free holdings of the southern section are unusually small in scale and involved in character, and it is from this area that we have examples of free virgates fragmented into a multitude of small and very small holdings—a striking picture of the rapid circulation of free land. It is true that we also find a fair number of large manors with typical manorial characteristics, especially among the church possessions. But on the whole manorial structure in this area is close in character to that which we find in the directly adjacent parts of East Anglia.

How are we to explain this sharp distinction between north and south? Cambridgeshire and Huntingdonshire are twin counties, which for a long time formed one administrative unit. Both came within the area of the southern Danelaw. There is little difference between the soil conditions and the economic connections of the one and the other. It would appear that the peculiarities of the three northern hundreds of Huntingdonshire are due to the marked and early development in them of large-scale church estates, and to the consequent early manorialization of the county. Historians have already pointed out that the organization of church estates had a noticeable influence on surrounding districts.[1] Coulton is inclined to explain the greater freedom of the Danelaw, compared with the rest of England, by the fact that the Danes destroyed the churches and monasteries.[2] The predominantly lay hundred of Toseland is sharply distinguished from the

[1] Stenton, *Br. Ac.*, v, liii. See also Neilson, *Camb. Econ. Hist.*, i, 444.
[2] *Medieval Village*, 170.

other Huntingdonshire hundreds; and this difference, striking in 1279, existed already at the time of Domesday.

The extent of manorialization in Cambridgeshire is not the same in all hundreds. There are hundreds with insignificant amounts of villein land, e.g. Chilford, Longstow, Whittlesford, Staine, Flendish, in all of which the large manor is little developed. But there are also more 'manorialized' hundreds, such as Papworth, where large manors occupy 47 per cent of the total area and villein land 37 per cent of it. Even so, this hundred contains only three large manors. The percentage of villein land is considerable in the hundred of Chesterton, which lies in three separate patches around Cambridge. But this is attributable in part to the existence of villein land in the hands of the bond sokemen of the ancient crown demesne of Chesterton. Furthermore, the survey of this hundred in the Hundred Rolls is fragmentary; there is no record of the large vill of Dry Drayton, which was responsible for four of the hundred's jurymen, and the apparently high percentage of villein land may therefore be deceptive.

The type of agrarian structure characteristic of East Anglia and southern Cambridgeshire extends far to the west. In the northern sector it comes up, on the west, against the fens and the ancient groupings of church lands in the Isle of Ely and northern Huntingdonshire, but further south it extends westwards through southern Huntingdonshire to Bedfordshire, and northern Buckinghamshire.

Chance has preserved for us the surveys for an almost unbroken stretch of land extending west of the southern hundreds of Huntingdonshire and Cambridgeshire, up the river Ouse to its head-waters, where we come to a number of villages in the counties of Bedfordshire and Buckinghamshire.

For Bedfordshire only a part of the 1279 record has been preserved, covering the hundred of Willey[1] and four adjacent villages in the hundred of Stodden.[2] These comprise the northwestern corner of the county. In the Bedfordshire hundreds the 'abnormal' features evident in the south Cambridgeshire hundreds are even more noticeable. The relation between

---

[1] A composite hundred (*Hundredus de Wilye et dimidius hundredus de Bukkelawe*), comprising two parts which had been separate at the time of Domesday, but had merged into one by 1279.

[2] The survey of one of these is incomplete.

manor and vill is extremely variable. Only in three instances do they coincide and in the vast majority of cases the manor is only part of a vill, though sometimes it consists of parts of different vills. Almost all the vills are broken up into small manors, sometimes as many as ten. Altogether, in twenty-five vills there are something like a hundred sub-divisions, manors or parts of manors. The Bedfordshire hundreds show a high percentage of small manors—46 per cent as compared with 15 per cent large and 37 per cent medium manors. The percentage of free holdings is also very high, comprising 46 per cent of the total arable recorded, whereas that of villein land is very low (21 per cent). Free holdings thus account for more than twice as much land as villein holdings. The total area of demesne land is close to the average figure for all areas (33 per cent).

If we examine more closely the distribution of villein land in different villages, we shall observe that it is extremely uneven; thus, in one village there is none at all (Souldrop), in another it accounts for 76 per cent of the total arable (Chellington). But these are extreme cases, and in general we can divide all the villages into two groups: those with a trifling amount of villein land (which form the majority), and those with a large amount. The first group includes villages with 0–16 per cent of villein land, the second group those with 33–76 per cent. The first group includes fourteen out of the twenty-five villages, with an arable area of about 4,000 acres (out of a recorded total of 24,000). Here free holdings cover more than five times the area of villein holdings. The second group includes only eight villages, with about 6,000 acres of arable, and here villein land amounts to almost two and a half times as much as free holdings. An intermediate group is formed by the two villages of Stagsden and Podington.

Comparing these two groups, we may note a number of other differences. The vills of the second (serf economy) group either coincide with manors, or contain only two or three manors or parts of manors. The most pronounced fragmentation in this group is found in the vill of Clapham, but it is clearly of recent date. The majority of vills in the first group have disintegrated into small manors (or parts of manors). The three largest manors surveyed in the enrolments, manors of over 1,000 acres (including the 'former' manor of Clapham), are all distinguished by a notable development of villein land, the proportion of demesne to villein land and free holdings being 22–47–31 per cent. The majority of manors under 1,000 acres, on the other hand, are distinguished by an extremely slight development of villeinage. Church estates are a negligible factor in this hundred. It is interesting that the vills of Great and Little Odell, Pavenham, Stevington, Clapham, Chellington, where the development of villein land is marked, lie adjacent to one another and represent a sort of island in an area which in general is only slightly manorialized.

The incomplete manorialization, which is typical of southern Cambridgeshire, is thus even more marked in Bedfordshire. And the same trait is found again, as we move further west, in north Buckinghamshire.

The extant Hundred Rolls provide surveys of forty-eight vills in the northern part of Buckinghamshire. Taken in conjunction with the Bedfordshire vills, they form a strip stretching from the southern hundreds of Huntingdonshire and Cambridgeshire, along the southern boundary of Northamptonshire, to north Oxfordshire. Adjacent to the Bedfordshire territory described in the Hundred Rolls lies the Buckinghamshire hundred of Bunstow. Here we find much in common with the agrarian structure of Bedfordshire, from which we may conclude that the hundred of Willey and the half-hundred of Botlowe, with their peculiar manorial forms, were not chance islets isolated in the middle of England. In Bunstow hundred we find a considerable predominance of free holdings over villein land. Small manors comprise 40 per cent of the whole hundred, and only one manor has over 1,000 acres of arable. Church estates are negligible. The same characteristics appear, in a slightly less marked form, in the more westerly hundred of Stodfold. Here there are only two large manors, one of the usual 'manorial' type,[1] the other, belonging to the abbot of Bittlesden,[2] a typical Cistercian estate, with a large demesne and insignificant holdings. Church estates occupy 25 per cent of the total area.

This is where the boundary of the southern Danelaw runs,

---

[1] Magna Leckhampstead, the manor of Hugh de Chastillun, *R.H.*, ii, 338–39.
[2] In Bittlesden, Whitfield, Dadford and Evershaw. *R.H.*, ii, 343, 340.

and where Mercia begins; and here ends a strip of territory, only superficially manorialized, with a predominance of the small manor, slight development of villeinage, and great complication of manorial structure—a region where the typical manorial régime occurs only on 'islands' of large (frequently church-owned) manors.

The two Buckinghamshire hundreds lying to the south of the Ouse (Mursley and Mucha) are distinguished by rather different features. Here large and medium-sized manors predominate, and small manors are an insignificant factor. Villein land, especially in Mursley hundred, exceeds the area of free holdings, and this predominance of villein land is not confined to large manors, but is found on medium and small manors also. Manorial structure here is more symmetrical than in the regions hitherto surveyed, and we can already perceive the transition to the regions of highly developed manorialization. Church manors are unevenly distributed, occupying a greater proportion of the territory of those Buckinghamshire hundreds which lie to the south of the Ouse than of those in the north.

THE WESTERN AREA

The second great area depicted in the Hundred Rolls, the western area, is formed by Oxfordshire and the two hundreds of Warwickshire which are its continuation. This is a wide belt running from south to north, from the middle Thames to the headwaters of the Avon. For this area the surveys of over four hundred villages are extant.

The Oxfordshire surveys vary widely in quality and are mostly very rough and ready, with omissions and simplifications. The demesne is usually given in carucates, the holdings in virgates, and acres are much more rarely used. The size of cottars' holdings is not usually defined, but though they varied greatly, their average size was not large, and we shall not be far wrong if we place it at two acres. The virgate here is on the average smaller than in the east; a virgate of 20 acres is not exceptional, but I shall assume the average to have been 25 acres. In Oxfordshire we find a very considerable percentage of large manors; church manors occupy 32 per cent of the total area—a figure close to the general average.

We can distinguish two regions in Oxfordshire: the flat and fertile north, which includes the greater part of the county, and the hilly and wooded south. The river Thame may serve as an approximate dividing line. In the north we find very large hundreds, with scores of villages and manors in each. In the south the hundreds are, as a rule, small. We shall see a certain difference in manorial structure also.

The northern group consists of the large hundreds of Banbury, Ploughley, Bullington, Wootton, Chadlington and Bampton,[1] which account for three-quarters of the area of the county. They are all typical manorial hundreds, where large manors predominate, vills usually coincide with manors, villein land is well developed and free holdings play a minor role. In these hundreds the overall extent of villein land is about twice that of free holdings, and this predominance of villein land over free holdings is to be observed on the small as well as on the large and medium manors. Nevertheless it is greater on the large manors. Thus on the large manors (all belonging to the church) in the hundred of Banbury the area of villein land is almost nine times that of free holdings (70 per cent and 8 per cent).

Further to the south lie the small hundreds: Thame, Dorchester, Lewknor, Pirton, Ewelme and Langtree—hundreds which sometimes cut across one another, and occupy about a quarter of the total area recorded for the county.

Among these hundreds Thame, which is a hundredal manor belonging to the bishop of Lincoln, and Dorchester, which also belongs almost entirely to the same bishop, are typical manorial hundreds. Here we see a considerable predominance of villein land over free holdings, of large manors over small (especially in Thame, where large manors contain 62 per cent of the arable land, and where villein holdings are three times the size of free holdings).

Typical manorial traits appear in Lewknor also, where villein land comprises 43 per cent of the recorded arable as against 25 per cent in free tenure, and large manors cover 52 per cent of the total recorded area. On the large manors here villein land covers five times the area of free holdings,

[1] The survey of the hundred of Bloxham is missing.

but on the small manors its total area is slightly less than that of the free holdings.

Quite different features distinguish the hundreds of Pirton, Ewelme and Langtree, where land in free tenure is considerably greater in extent than villein land, accounting for 44 per cent of the recorded arable as against 27 per cent held in villeinage. This characteristic comes out most sharply in Pirton hundred, where free holdings make up 45 per cent of the total area recorded, and villein land only 24 per cent. Yet this predominance of free holding is not accompanied by a predominance of small manors. In Pirton hundred medium-sized manors are predominant, covering 47 per cent of the total area, while in the hundreds of Ewelme and Langtree the large manor is predominant. Here even the large manor is distinguished by a predominance of free holdings.[1] Perhaps the farming conditions of the wooded Chilterns were not favourable to the development of servile labour dues and villeinage.

The southern extremity of Oxfordshire runs down into Berkshire, for which no enrolments survive. Thus unfortunately the fragmentary nature of our source does not permit us to establish whether the three southern hundreds of Oxfordshire were an accidental and isolated patch, or part of a larger area with the same characteristics.

The territory described in the surviving fragments of the Warwickshire surveys lies adjacent to north Oxfordshire. The Warwickshire material falls into two distinct parts: the southern, formed by the hundred of Kineton, and the northern, consisting of the hundred of Stoneleigh. Kineton, contiguous with north Oxfordshire, is characterized by the same traits. The figure of demesne land, villein land, and free holdings, the average size of manors, the proportion of territory occupied by large, small and medium manors respectively, and the structure prevailing in these different categories—all this approaches closely to the conditions prevalent in north Oxfordshire. Indeed, the manorial features are even more sharply defined here than in north Oxfordshire itself; the large manors account for upwards of 50 per cent of the total area, and villein holdings comprise 52 per cent of the land as against 20 per cent held

[1] In Pirton and Langtree; in Ewelme free tenements and villein land are about even.

y free tenure. The hundred of Stoneleigh, however, is very different. Here we see a comparatively insignificant amount of villein land and extensive free land (39 per cent). Stoneleigh is a hundred with a very high proportion of church estates; but even on church manors villein land is only slightly developed, considerable area is held by free tenants, and, in particular, here are large demesnes with no corresponding provision of villein land.[1] This is mainly due to the large demesne of the Cistercian abbey of Stoneleigh (seventeen carucates). The extensive free holdings and negligible villein land range Stoneleigh hundred with the most characteristic hundreds of southern Cambridgeshire.[2]

We thus see that the southern hundreds of Oxfordshire, leading to Berkshire, and the Warwickshire hundred of Stoneleigh, which leads to Leicestershire and the northern Danelaw, show considerable departures from manorial type.

It has been noted above that it is precisely the church manors which show typically 'manorial' features, and that these manors exerted a strong influence over the manorial structure of the surrounding countryside.[3] How, then, are we to explain the fact that Stoneleigh Hundred, where the church's possessions amount to over one-half of the total recorded area, shows such sharp departures from the typical manorial order? The difference is explained principally by the fact that in Huntingdonshire it is the estates of the ancient great Benedictine monasteries—Ramsey with its 'cells', and the abbey (later the bishopric) of Ely—that are the dominant factor,[4] and have left a deep mark on the whole manorial structure of Huntingdonshire. What we see in Stoneleigh hundred is quite different. The church estates there are for the most part of recent origin; the principal ecclesiastical landlords are the Cistercian abbeys

---

[1] The largest concentration of villein holdings is found on the manor of Itchington, belonging to the bishop of Chester.

[2] Cf. R. H. Hilton, 'Social Structure of Rural Warwickshire in the Middle Ages', *Dugdale Soc. Occasional Papers*, No. 9 (1950), where the difference between the hundreds of Stoneleigh and Kineton is attributed to a large extent to the geographical differences between the wooded northern part of the county (Arden) and its southern region (Felden), although the boundary between Arden and Felden does not coincide exactly with the boundary between the hundreds.

[3] Cf. above, p. 118–9, for the three northern hundreds of Huntingdon.

[4] The estates of the new foundations (the Augustinian foundation of Huntingdon, and, in particular, the Cistercian abbey of Sawtry) are distinguished by their peculiar structure; cf. above, p. 112.

I

of Stoneleigh and Combe, the Benedictine priory of Coventry, and the Augustinian priory of Kenilworth, the estates of none of which conform to the classical manorial type. The only typical large manor in the hundred is Itchington, an ancient manor of the bishop of Chester. Church estates in Stoneleigh hundred thus exerted no 'manorializing' influence over the local agrarian organization.

Conclusions

As a final conclusion from our calculations, we may attempt to answer the question: which approximates more closely to the truth, the theory of the classical manor set out by Seebohm and Vinogradoff, or the picture drawn by their critics? Can we say that England was covered with manors of a uniform type, or should we agree with Maitland that England was not primarily a land of manors? We must, of course, bear in mind that the Hundred Rolls provide no answer for England as a whole; but it seems to me that neither view can be accepted without qualification. So far as concerns the areas we have studied, which lie in one of the most manorialized parts of England, I should suggest the following conclusions:

1. The typical manor, with a demesne and a large amount of villein land—more, that is, than is occupied by free holdings —is on the whole predominant in the area covered by the enrolments. Its importance is emphasized by the fact that the overwhelming majority of large manors, which account for more than a third of the total recorded land, belong to this category. The organization of the large manor is characteristic of the large-scale feudal landed property, which played the leading role in English society and government in the thirteenth century. The highest development of feudal relations of production, i.e. the highest degree of 'manorialization', is to be seen precisely on the lands of the great estate-owners, of the great ecclesiastical lords in particular. The process of feudalization had laid its firmest hold on the large manor, especially the large church manor, and this is expressed first and foremost in the development of villein holdings, which is closely linked up with the labour-rent system.

2. The typical self-worked manor appears, however, in company with manorial forms of a different structure, most

of these being small and having as their distinguishing mark only a slight development or even the complete absence, of villeinage.

3. Even in the specifically manorialized areas we have been studying, certain zones may be distinguished where manorialization is less marked, villein land on the whole occupies a smaller area than free holdings, and the large serf-worked estate does not play the decisive role.

While noting, therefore, the major part played by the typical large manor in the structure of the English countryside in the thirteenth century, our study of the most highly manorialized areas of England compels us to give more attention than hitherto to (i) the freeholdings, which are far more than a 'narrow fringe' around the typical elements of the manor, the demesne and the villein land; (ii) the organization of the smaller manorial formations, which represent different degrees of manorialization, but which in general are distinguished by a comparatively slight development of villeinage and by the fact that the demesne did not depend on villein labour.

But, on the other hand, the analysis of manorial structure gives us only external evidence from which it is by no means always possible to form a picture of the economic organization of a manor. For example, villein land will perform a completely different economic function on a manor where labour rents predominate, from that which it plays where money rents are the rule. And since the form of rent changes more easily than does the manorial structure, analysis of the latter is useful as an indication of the degree of manorialization achieved in the past, but it is the former which provides the clue to the direction in which manorial development is moving and will move in the future.

It is, therefore, essential at this stage to consider the question of the predominant form of rent (i.e. labour services or money rent) in the area with which we are dealing.

MANORIAL STRUCTURE OUTSIDE THE AREA COVERED BY THE HUNDRED ROLLS

It would be of great interest to extend our observations beyond the limits of the territory dealt with by the Hundred

Rolls. This territory includes the most highly 'manorialized' areas of England, while outside its boundaries we have every reason to expect many more departures from the 'typical' manorial structure. In fact, we have already mentioned certain major regions distinguished by peculiarities of manorial structure. Thus conditions in Cambridgeshire recalled in many ways those of East Anglia, and, in fact, Cambridgeshire, Bedfordshire and the northern hundreds of Buckinghamshire may be considered part of the southern Danelaw. The Warwickshire hundred of Stoneleigh, which also showed considerable departures from the usual manorial type, brought us to the boundary of Leicestershire,[1] i.e. to the northern Danelaw. Conditions in the northern Danelaw and East Anglia deviate more sharply from typical manorial structure than those in the southern Midlands.

THE NORTHERN AND SOUTHERN DANELAW

Stenton[2] has expounded the characteristic peculiarities of manorial structure in the northern Danelaw (the counties of York, Derby, Nottingham, Leicester, Lincoln and Rutland). In this area a number of local peculiarities which had their origin as far back as the Danish colonization of the ninth century, long persisted; they included the units of local government, a special agrarian terminology, and Scandinavian place-names. Up to the very end of the Middle Ages the estates of the Danish zone bore little resemblance to the manors of southern England. The estates of the early Norman period were here made up of holdings scattered over wide areas, linked with the manorial centre by the payment of customary dues and attendance at the manor court. Even the unfree peasantry did not here perform heavy labour services. As a direct result of the Danish military colonization, the free peasantry formed a very considerable percentage of the population (in places as much as 60 per cent). The mass of the free

[1] R. H. Hilton in his works devoted to Leicestershire manors (*The Economic Development of some Leicestershire Estates* (1947); 'Kibworth Harcourt' in *Studies . . .* ed. W. G. Hoskins) notes as features characteristic of Leicestershire the predominance of small manors and the weakness of the link between the peasant holdings and the demesne.

[2] F. M. Stenton, *O.S.S.L.H.*, ii (1910). See also his essay 'The Danes in England' in *History* (1920).

peasantry, the so-called sokemen (settlers from the ranks of the Danish warriors), was grouped around the nobility in various degrees of dependence. The unfree peasantry was formed partly from the native population, partly from Danish settlers who for one reason or another lost their freedom. But a social order based on the free peasantry and the incomplete development of the manorial system, are characteristic of the Danish zone. The soke, which continues to be a characteristic feature of the Danelaw in the twelfth and thirteenth centuries, and the seignorial link between lords and freeholders, played a greater part here than the manor and its offshoot, the berewick. This area is remarkable for the extremely varied array of tenurial relationships it presents. The decisive part played by the free peasantry, and the limited degree of manorial control, led early to a free traffic in land; many surviving documents of the twelfth and thirteenth centuries record alienations of land by small owners.

Stenton notes that the southern Danelaw was subjected to 'manorialization' to a far greater extent than the north, and that villeinage made considerable progress here. But even here certain features were preserved which probably go back to Danish institutions.

Douglas[1] has described the peculiar agrarian organization of East Anglia, that is Norfolk and Suffolk. Here peasant holdings are not divided among the different fields of the village, but every tenant tries to concentrate his strips in one part of the fields. The virgate is practically unknown; where it does appear, it is a late and artificial formation concocted out of the old smaller holdings. 'Disintegration and reintegration' of tenures occurred at an early stage, in the course of frequent transfers of land beginning perhaps as early as the eleventh century, which resulted in a great variety of levels and types of rents paid from individual holdings. Vill and manor rarely coincide in East Anglia. As a rule the vill is divided up into several manors, of differing sizes and with widely differing seignorial rights. The fiscal and judicial functions of the village, as distinct from the manor, appear nowhere more clearly than in East Anglia. Here we find a peculiar type of symmetrical hundred, and a peculiar territorial

---

[1] D. C. Douglas, *O.S.S.L.H.*, ix (1927).

unit, the 'leet', of ancient origin. Scandinavian influence has left its mark on East Anglian agrarian organization (e.g. the soke, and the bovate as the basic unit of peasant allotments). But East Anglian organization was considerably more varied than that of the Danelaw, and even more distinct from the usual manorial arrangements. The revenues of the East Anglian lords were made up principally of dues, very various and heterogeneous, paid by scattered groups of freeholders. The non-feudal elements in English medieval society are most strikingly apparent in East Anglia, where the most characteristic feature is the numerous free peasantry; a free village—a village without lords—is not uncommon. But from the twelfth century onwards we can observe increasing pressure on the peasants by their lords, the development of manorial institutions, and the transformation of some of the former sokemen into villeins. Characteristic of East Anglia is the early development of money rents side by side with labour dues, partly in the form of commutation, and partly in that of ancient customary payments. In spite of the depression of the status of the peasantry, the social structure of Norfolk and Suffolk, even in the thirteenth century, does not fit into the classical manorial scheme, though here a distinction should be made between the manorialized and the non-manorialized areas of East Anglia. Most of our sources emanate from the former.

Northumbria

Different again from the typical manorial organization is that of Northumbria—i.e. the counties of Northumberland, Cumberland, Westmorland, Lancashire, Durham, and the northern mountainous part of Yorkshire[1]—which has been studied by Jolliffe.[2] The distinctive features of Northumbria are the minor part played by the demesne, and the comparative independence of the village community. Here an estate usually signifies a very considerable stretch of territory, with a central farm that has dozens of dependent vills attached. Large domains bore the name of 'shires', and an estate might often be a whole hundred, all in the hands of one owner. The pasturing of stock is the predominant economic activity,

[1] The Yorkshire plain belongs to the Danelaw.
[2] J. E. A. Jolliffe, *E.H.R.*, xli (1926).

and labour dues are insignificant, the main source of seignorial income being court dues and payments in kind, e.g. the provision of grain and stock for the lord's table, the 'feeding' of the lord as he travels around his domains, and payments for pasturing of cattle. The vill, not the manor, is here the unit for fiscal and judicial obligations. Dues are connected not with the holding, but with the individual—based, in other words, on the personal dependence of the peasant on his superior lord. Therefore they are not proportionate to holdings; some small labour dues are owed by all categories of peasants, both free and unfree, and the different ranks and classes of the peasantry are scarcely distinguished so far as dues are concerned. The division of peasants into 'villein' and 'free', characteristic of the southern manors, can only with difficulty be applied under northern conditions. Both free and unfree pay heriot, merchet and leyrwite. By the thirteenth century the 'shire' and its peculiar institutions are in process of disintegration, though many characteristic features remain; it splits up into manors, and this process is not infrequently connected with the elevation of seignorial officials to the position of lords of manors. Demesne farming starts to be developed; but the predominance of pastoral farming hinders the development of labour rent and makes easier the advance of commutation. The manorial court is not developed; instead the old 'shire' (hundred) court remains operative. Taken as a whole, the institutions of Northumbria are reminiscent of those of Wales, and possibly represent a survival of Celtic organization.[1]

According to observations based on the thirteenth-century inquisitions *post Mortem*, the manorial system had undoubtedly made considerable advances in the Northumbrian region, but a number of typical historical peculiarities still survived. Many manors appear as agglomerations of villages, in one or two of which there is a demesne, while the others contain only holdings. Nine out of 28 manors which I have investigated are focal points for about 30 villages inhabited by their tenants,

---

[1] Wales, where demesne farming begins to develop in the thirteenth century, offers a number of analogies with Northumbria. A certain resemblance can also be traced between them and early Anglo-Saxon institutions. Cf. *Survey of the Honour of Denbigh, Br. Ac.*, i (1914). Many of the questions touched upon here were raised by Maitland; cf. *Collected Papers*, ii, 96.

and some manors can boast of as many as 6 dependent villages. These manors are not the old 'shires', but they are very considerable fragments of them. With this is connected the insignificance—in the vast majority of cases the complete absence—of revenue from manorial courts, which sometimes was not even sufficient to pay the bailiff. Nevertheless, the manorialization of the old shire is an undoubted fact. I cannot accept Jolliffe's assertion that in thirteenth-century Northumbria, if the church lands be left out of account, demesne farming is insignificant in scale, and that the evidence does not allow us to assume that it had any significance in the past. The examples which Jolliffe quotes from the inquisitions—the capital manor of a barony, Wigton, where there were only 36 acres of demesne arable; Lydell, where the demesne was 'negligible'; and the vill of Singleton and Ribby, where the demesne was represented by *quedam placea grangie*—are very characteristic of the economic conditions of the north, but as survivals only. Leaving the more distant past aside, we find demesnes which cannot be called 'negligible' as early as the reign of Henry III on the majority of Northumbrian manors. The demesne of the manor of Prudhoe, for instance, with 1,108 acres of arable and meadow, is considerable even by southern standards. The average size of the demesne in the 28 manors I have investigated is about 220 acres of arable (allowing an average of fifteen acres to the bovate), which cannot be called very small. On the other hand, the extent of these northern manors is such that, relatively, these large figures are less significant than at first sight appears. The revenue derived from demesne arable and meadow land is no more than a quarter of that derived from dependent holdings. Although farming in the north is extensive rather than intensive in character, the revenue from the average northern manor (not counting revenue from pastures) is almost twice that from the average manor of southern England. Tenants' land, a good part of which would appear to be held in free tenure, is considerably greater in extent than the demesne arable; bondmen's land accounts for more than twice the area of the demesne. The area of free holdings cannot be calculated with accuracy, but the rents they brought in show that it was undoubtedly very great.

The Vale of York

T. A. M. Bishop has drawn attention to the singular agrarian organization of the Vale of York, an area which was not covered by the investigations of either Stenton or Jolliffe.[1] The area studied lies between York and the Tees, taking in about three hundred civil parishes grouped in seven wapentakes; it was subjected to the most severe devastation in 1069 and 1070. In most of the villages here there is no sign of the manorial system; in particular no sign of a demesne. In the thirteenth and fourteenth centuries they were occupied by large groups of freeholders associated by complicated tenurial relationships. Their farms (mostly of peasant type, one or two bovates) reveal an unusual mixture of open fields broken up into small *culturae* and assarts. Villages of this type arose in places where Domesday Book records complete devastation, and are the result of colonization in the twelfth century and the gradual reclamation of the abandoned land. In places, on the other hand, where elements of the population had survived, we find in the thirteenth century typical manors with demesnes, although here also considerable groupings of peasant freeholders are in evidence; they are found even where Domesday Book showed the presence of sokemen. The development of the manorial system and of villeinage was the result of the depressed conditions resulting from the punitive expeditions of William the Conqueror. In rare cases a whole village that had been devastated was turned into a demesne, worked by villeins from the neighbouring villages, which all became part of the one manor. Since Bishop classifies manors according to the presence or absence of demesne land and does not deal with tenants' dues, it is not altogether clear to what extent the 'manorialized' part of this region reflects the characteristic features of the classical manor. But in any case the majority of the villages in the region were not 'manorialized' at all.

Kent

Many historians have commented upon the singular agrarian institutions of Kent, which do not share the usual characteristics

[1] T. A. M. Bishop, 'The Distribution of Manorial Demesne in the Vale of Yorkshire', *E.H.R.*, xlix (1934), and the same author's 'Assarting and the Growth of Open Fields', *Ec. H. R.*, v (1935).

of the manor. In the Domesday account Kent is in no way distinguished from other counties. The bulk of the population were villeins, and sokemen are not mentioned; Norfolk, or the counties of the northern Danelaw, are to a far greater extent representative of 'peasant freedom'. But the terminology of Domesday may well be misleading; for in the thirteenth century there is a clearly defined distinction between Kent and other counties. In Kent local custom prevailed—that is, the *Lex Kantiae*, which in the Kentish local courts played the part performed by common law in the courts of other counties. The principal peculiarity of Kentish custom was that those sections of the population to which it applied—and this would appear to have been the bulk of the Kentish peasantry—were accounted personally free. In the courts of common law it was sufficient to plead Kentish origin for *exceptio villenagii* to be admitted. Kentish custom severely limited the rights of the lord over peasant tenures; in particular, the peasants were free to alienate their land, and the lord could only require that, in such alienations, the services and dues owed to him should be maintained. By the well-known system of gavelkind the peasant holdings of Kent were divided between sons, although in practice they might be jointly farmed. Gavelkind brought with it also other peculiarities of land tenure and inheritance. The manor was little centralized; scattered groups of peasants paid rents in money and produce to the lord's court, and rendered cartage and other slight labour services, amounting only to a few days' work per year. Dues were apportioned on the basis of large units known as 'sulungs', which correspond to hides (about two hundred acres) and which had once been units of tenure. But by the thirteenth century the 'sulungs' had been split, as the result of alienations, into a multitude of small holdings, often so minute that they were totally insufficient to maintain a livelihood. Yet even at this stage the sulung was preserved as a unit for the allocation of rent.[1]

Vinogradoff sees in the position of the Kentish peasants a survival of Anglo-Saxon institutions, which were ignored by the compilers of Domesday Book but reappeared later. The Kentish peasants retained their former status, which recalls that of the sokemen of other counties, thanks to the fact that

[1] See Neilson, 'Custom and Common Law in Kent', *Harvard Law Review* (1925).

labour dues were not developed in Kent. But why is it that Kent succeeded in retaining Anglo-Saxon institutions which were undermined in other counties by the development of feudalism? The reason is that, even in Anglo-Saxon times, Kent was the high road between England and the continent; and the special economic conditions arising from this situation account for the fragmentation of the earlier peasant allotments into small individual holdings. Their owners could live not only by working for wages on the lands of local magnates, but also by employment in non-agricultural trades, or by working for the merchants engaged in trading in London or in the Cinque Ports. From this point of view conditions in Kent are more reminiscent of Normandy or Italy than of Surrey or Essex. Lying on the most important trade route in England, Kent assumed 'a mobilized, commercial, pecuniary aspect'.[1] Since the end of the Anglo-Saxon and the beginning of the Norman period was the time of Kent's greatest prosperity, the peasants, because of their additional resources, could defend their freedom against the rising manorialism, and the land-lords were unable to impose the manorial structure, and com-pelled to accept the 'liberties' expressed in Kentish custom. This process began in Anglo-Saxon times, and it is therefore not surprising that many survivals from that period should have been preserved. 'In short, Kent seems to have proceeded from the tribal system and the independent village system directly towards commercial husbandry, without going through the intermediate stage of manorial husbandry which was common to the rest of England.'[2]

Maitland, while in the main adopting these views, main-tained that Kentish customs are to be explained principally by developments in the twelfth and thirteenth centuries, which made it possible for the Kentish peasants not only to preserve but to extend the earlier liberties which elsewhere were lost.[3] This continued development, he argues, was far more significant than the mere survival of former freedom. 'Kent is no mountain home of liberty, no remote fastness in which the remnant of an ancient race has found refuge; it is

---

[1] Vinogradoff, *Growth of the Manor*, 317.
[2] *Ibid.*, 318. See also his *Villainage*, 205, 247.
[3] Pollock and Maitland, ii, 271 sqq.

the garden of England, of all English counties that which is most exposed to foreign influences. The great roads which join London to the seaboard are the arteries along which flows money, the destructive solvent of seignorial power.'[1] The Kentish lords came to know the value of money early, and preferred ready money to their manorial rights. Maitland thinks that the incomparable position of Kent for trade in the twelfth century led to a rapid development of the county which proved advantageous to the peasants as well. Thanks to the early development of a money economy, produce-rents are transformed directly into money rents, by-passing the stage of the predominance of labour rent. For this reason the germ of primitive freedom was able to take hold and develop. Kent was a prosperous county; its peasants were rich, and purchased a royal charter from Henry III.[2]

In view of this prosperity, on the other hand, it is fair to ask why Kent is the most revolutionary of all the English counties and why it was Kent that put forward the most radical programmes and produced the most resolute leaders in the rising of 1381. The reason seems to be that, as early as the thirteenth century, Kentish prosperity was accompanied by the impoverishment of the mass of the peasants, and that one reason why Kent jumped the labour-rent system was the early formation there of a numerous class of landless or nearly landless peasants, who were ruthlessly exploited, while the 'liberties' of the more prosperous 'gavelkinders' were preserved. In contrast to the Mile End programme of the Essex villeins in 1381, the programme of the Kentish rebels puts in the fore-ground the restoration of the common rights usurped by the lords, the division of church lands among the peasants, and the repeal of all laws except the Winchester law—i.e. first and foremost the repeal of the 'labour legislation' that bore so hardly on the poor peasant labourer.

In Kent there comes out more clearly than elsewhere the characteristic feature of the feudal development of England—the preservation of pre-feudal institutions side by side with the early disintegration of feudalism.[3]

[1] Pollock and Maitland, i, 187.   [2] *Ibid.*, i, 188.
[3] On the manorial system in Kent, see also *Camb. Econ. Hist.*, i, 455.

The West

Even more considerable local modifications of manorial structure may be expected to distinguish the comparatively thinly populated mountainous and wooded regions of north-west England, and the regions bordering on Wales, in which the peasantry had to render military service and be in constant readiness either to repel a raid by, or to attack, their warlike neighbours. Hewitt, in his interesting work on medieval Cheshire,[1] brings out a number of peculiarities in the natural conditions and in the economy of the county which hindered any wide development of villeinage and labour dues, although the existence of manors—sometimes quite large ones—is beyond doubt. The wooded and marshy nature of the land was not very suitable for the growing of grain; there was scarcely enough corn for the needs of the comparatively small population, corn exports are rare, and more often than not the county had to import corn from Ireland. Labour services were in existence, but in many parts of the county money rents and wage labour were the rule. A very important part was played by stock-breeding—not sheep-raising, but the breeding of cattle and pigs. Cheshire scarcely played any part in the export of wool, but it provided meat for the army, and may have exported some by-products of stock-breeding. On the whole the social conditions of Cheshire are close to those of North Wales, and its field system also is reminiscent of what in Scotland, Wales and Ireland is called 'run-rig'.[2]

This review of the order of things prevailing in East Anglia, the northern Danelaw, Kent and Northumbria, has shown us how variegated the manorial system is throughout the extensive territories of northern and eastern England. If we bear in mind the Welsh influences in the west of the country,[3] it is beyond doubt that the 'typical' manorial structure is modified in a number of ways over at least half of England. Miss Neilson limits the predominance of the typical manorial system to the area where the two- and three-field systems were prevalent;[4]

[1] H. J. Hewitt, *Medieval Cheshire. An Economic and Social History of Cheshire in the Reigns of the three Edwards* (1929). Cf. also G. H. Tupling, *The Economic History of Rossendale* (1927).
[2] Gray, *English Field Systems*, 258.
[3] W. Rees, *South Wales and the March* (1924).
[4] *Camb. Econ. Hist.*, i (1942), 451.

but evidently even this area requires to be considerably reduced.

FACTORS CAUSING REGIONAL VARIATIONS

In the case of regions whose social structure was formed far back in history, it is obvious that historical tradition was a factor of importance. Undoubtedly many of the special features of these districts can be explained by their preceding history—the role of the free peasantry, for example. But in addition, other factors also stand out. We have seen that the manorial organization of the southern Danelaw is not everywhere the same, and even comprises areas—for example, the three northern hundreds of Huntingdonshire—where the 'typical' manor was developed. This feature was due, more than anything else, to the early development there of church estates. Again, there was the influence exerted in certain regions by trade, money, and production for the market. This applies to the Danelaw in particular, the eastern and southern parts of which were the richest and most thickly populated region of England. As early as the time of Domesday the three counties of Lincolnshire, Norfolk and Suffolk accounted for a quarter of the population of England. The figures for the 1297 lay subsidies and the surveys made for the levying of poll tax prove that the eastern counties maintained this pre-eminence from the eleventh to the end of the fourteenth century.[1] If we include with them the other counties of the southern Danelaw, they probably account for more than a third, perhaps nearly a half of the total population of England. This region included King's Lynn, the main centre for the export of grain, and was in close proximity to the main centre of consumption, London. Within it lay Norwich, Lincoln and Colchester, and the locations of a number of fairs (Stourbridge, St. Ives, Boston). In other words, here we have the core of the population of England, and a series of important centres of industry and trade, and here consequently were the prerequisites for the development of agriculture as a commodity-producing industry.

This aspect of the economy of eastern England is of particular

---

[1] Cf. Maitland, *Domesday Book and Beyond*, 21–22.

interest in our context, since here we find the survival of pre-feudal relationships—or, more correctly, the incomplete development of the manorial order—side by side with the early penetration of money-commodity relationships into agriculture. The development of production for the market leads to the rapid disintegration of the manorial order, especially in places where it has not taken a sufficiently firm hold. Nevertheless it is precisely in this area that we also find the most striking examples of the typical manorial system, and to this problem we shall have to return later. The impact of money-commodity relationships is uneven. Their influence is felt first along the great trade routes, along the courses of navigable rivers, and in the neighbourhood of towns. We shall have more than one occasion in the course of these studies to observe this fact.

Finally, geographical factors, the terrain and the soil, necessarily influenced economic conditions and consequently the manorial structure, which evidently was unlikely to be exactly the same in grain-growing and in stock-breeding areas, on fertile plains and wooded hills. This accounts, in part at least, for the peculiar characteristics, which we have already noted, of the southern hundreds of Oxfordshire, which lie in the Chilterns.

A number of historians have discussed the factors which determined local variations in English manorial structure. Miss Neilson, in an interesting essay,[1] emphasizes natural conditions and the local terrain. G. T. Lapsley, interpreting the Boldon Book,[2] distinguishes villages with a predominantly pastoral economy, villages predominantly agricultural, forest villages, and embryonic town settlements; they are differentiated both in manorial structure and in the dues rendered by the tenants. Miss Neilson has drawn attention to a particular type of village, that lying in marshy country, with dykes whose upkeep was a heavy burden. Another special type is provided by the forest villages of Essex. Unfortunately the Hundred Rolls, because they provide information principally on the arable, and pay scant attention to the common lands and the economy they supported, rarely enable us to establish any

[1] Neilson, 'English Manorial Forms', Amer. Hist. Review xxxiv (1929).
[2] V.C.H., Durham, i, 269 sqq.

connection between local peculiarities of terrain and the peculiarities of manorial structure.

The fundamental importance of natural conditions in creating different types of manors was stressed by Eileen Power,[1] in whose opinion natural conditions were the decisive factor in the agrarian world. 'The rustic world is a local world.' It is a world of differences. The geographical location of a place, its climate, the predominant occupation dictated by geographical conditions—these, in her view, are the factors which determine the type of a settlement, its field system, and even the personal status of the peasants. Her theory, set out very cautiously, is that wide stretches of flat country, suitable for agriculture, are usually characterized by village settlements with open fields, large manors, villeinage, and serf-worked economy. This is where 'the text-book manor' takes root. Hilly pasture-lands, on the other hand, are marked by settlement in isolated farmsteads, the predominance of stock-raising, a limited development of labour dues, and the predominance of payments in kind and in money. These are the areas of incomplete manorialization; serfdom here is superficial and easily disappears. In remote mountainous regions the peasantry is as a rule free. There are also specific types of settlement and manor connected with the reclaiming of forests and marshes, with colonization. Besides the geographical factor, Miss Power also takes account of 'racial' and of 'historical' factors (in particular the growth of towns).

While not denying the importance of the geographical factor, I should hesitate to attribute the decisive role to it; for even in those days of comparatively primitive technique there was a considerable transformation of natural conditions by the hands of men. Forests and marshes were transformed into fertile valleys suitable for agriculture, and on the open hills, occupied in the first place for agricultural purposes, a pastoral economy only developed later. Whether a particular region was used primarily for agriculture or for stock-raising was often dictated by economic rather than by 'natural' conditions. Economic conditions not infrequently determined the ruling form of rent, as well as the predominance of a free or servile status among the peasantry.

[1] *Camb. Med. Hist.*, vii, 716 sqq.

The 'text-book manor' did not play in thirteenth-century England such an all-embracing part as was attributed to it by the classic manorial theory. On the contrary we find the most varied forms of manor and the most varied degrees of 'manorialization', determined by very complex historical conditions. But this variety does not mean that generalizations are impossible. Although 'the manor' is certainly not the key which will unlock all the riddles of the medieval agrarian order, the large serf-worked manor nevertheless played a very important part in the medieval countryside. The manor based on serfdom and labour dues is the most finished form of feudal exploitation. But other forms were numerous, and a study of these 'incomplete' forms is essential in order to fit the manor into its historical setting and to understand its development. The 'incomplete' forms of the feudal manor determined the direction in which the English countryside would develop no less than did the 'text-book manor'.

The Evolution of Manorial Structure, 1086–1279

In the thirteenth century it would appear that the process of manorialization was making great advances in the parts of England we have just described—Northumbria, the northern Danelaw and East Anglia. The inquisitions *post Mortem*, which enable us to survey the whole of England, together with other documents from different parts of England, indicate the universal diffusion of the typical manor in the thirteenth century. But we have seen that typical manors may be located in areas with manorial forms of a totally different type, and there is every reason to assume that the estates of tenants-in-chief of the crown, which are surveyed in the inquisitions, were among the most 'manorialized' of lands. Nevertheless, the process of manorialization was far from complete even in the estates surveyed in the inquisitions, and in certain districts incomplete manorialization is found in conjunction with the beginnings of the disintegration of the manorial order.

In order to elucidate this question it is desirable to turn from an analysis of the English countryside as it was in 1279, and instead to look both backwards and forwards, starting at the time of Domesday Book, when the manor appears in a setting

K

which has not taken shape and crystallized, and which bears all the marks of incomplete feudalization. At this time, the large manors, which occur more frequently in the west than in the east, were everywhere mixed with small properties of varied structure, and had not yet reached a definite form, though less variegated than in the time of Edward the Confessor. When we compare these varied, often rudimentary forms with 'the well-rounded compact manors of the Hundred Rolls', we cannot fail to be struck by the success achieved in the direction of subordination and unification. Vinogradoff, tracing the path of manorial development between Domesday and the Hundred Rolls,[1] speaks of 'the engulfing and organizing tendency of the rising manor'. For although many artificially created manors disappeared, and some manors disintegrated, the fundamental tendency was towards the formation of large manors which absorbed not only individual holdings but also other incompletely developed manors. This process began long before the Norman Conquest and proceeded with increased vigour after it.

Vinogradoff's description of the variegated small-scale manorial formations or 'maneriola' of Domesday Book, incompletely developed, inchoate and disjointed, recalls in some degree what we see among the small manors of the Hundred Rolls. On the other hand, even in Domesday Book we find a considerable number of fully 'rounded' large manors, no less complete in their development than the large manors of the Hundred Rolls, even if described in a more summary fashion. If, therefore, the process of manorial development appears on the whole to have pursued the path sketched by Vinogradoff, the presence of uniform large manors, on the one hand, and variegated small manors on the other, is no less characteristic of the eleventh than it is of the thirteenth century. Consequently we must ask ourselves to what extent the manorial order which we see in the Hundred Rolls had already taken shape in the eleventh century. Do we see, after Domesday, a concentration of the various types of small manorial formation around the large serf-worked manors, and, if so, how far had that process of concentration advanced? Did the significance

---

[1] Cf. *Growth of the Manor*, p. 300.

of the small, variegated, incomplete manorial types decrease between the eleventh and the thirteenth centuries?

A comparison of the Hundred Rolls with Domesday Book can give us some indications, though not completely clear results, because the methods of reckoning used in the two sources differ too radically. Sometimes it would appear that considerable changes in the distribution of land between villages have taken place, but we must not ignore the probability of inaccuracies or omissions in one or both of the sources. My conclusions are based upon detailed comparisons for the hundreds of Hirstingstone, Leightonstone, and Toseland in Huntingdonshire, Whittlesford and Thriplow in Cambridgeshire, and Stodden and Willey in Bedfordshire.

It is common knowledge that the main estates of the old Benedictine monasteries had taken shape before the time of Domesday Book. Hirstingstone hundred, which takes pride of place in the Rolls of 1279 for the predominance of large, typical serf-worked manors, appears in exactly the same guise in Domesday Book also. Ramsey abbey and the bishopric (or at the time of Domesday the abbey) of Ely are here the main landowners. Small manors appear only as exceptions. But perhaps a hundred with a predominance of old church estates is not typical. Let us therefore consider Leightonstone in the same county. Here large manors predominate at the time of the Hundred Rolls, but a large part of these are not church property. In the eleventh century also Leightonstone is characterized by large manors. Furthermore those manors which figure as large in 1279 were large in 1086 also. Here we have the king's great manors, Alconbury and Brampton; in the thirteenth century these are manors of the ancient demesne of the crown. Here are the great church manors, Leighton, Spaldwick (with villages), Weston and Ellington (with villages), and the manors of the great lay lords, Buckworth, Kimbolton (with its 'soke'), Hamerton and Covington.

Now let us consider some hundreds where small, variegated manors are preponderant in the thirteenth century, and large manors are the exception. Outstanding in this respect are the Bedfordshire hundreds of Stodden and Willey.[1] The

---

[1] Cf. the detailed comparison with Domesday in my book *The English Village in the 13th Century* (in Russian), 83, 258–59.

manorial structure of these hundreds changed little between the eleventh and the thirteenth centuries. In the eleventh century also small, variegated manors were predominant, and each vill was normally divided into a number (sometimes a very large number) of manorial units of varying structure. If Domesday Book and the Hundred Rolls are compared, we find in the majority of cases that extremely small manorial units are characteristic of most of the vills in both sources, though both reveal the existence of large manors at Odell, Stevington, Pavenham and Harrold. But the largest of the manors found in Domesday Book, the manor of Clapham with land for 30 ploughs, had by the time of the Hundred Rolls broken up into five manors, all save one of which were small. On the other hand a large manor of about 40½ virgates mentioned by the Hundred Rolls at Bletsoe, figures in Domesday Book as two small manors of equal size, with 4 carucates of land in each.

The two Cambridgeshire hundreds of Whittlesford and Thriplow are both distinguished in the Hundred Rolls by the predominance of small manorial formations. In 1279 Thriplow shows a very exact reproduction of the manorial divisions prevailing in 1086. The larger manors of the Domesday period (there are no really large manors in the hundred) have their counterparts in the Hundred Rolls, and in the case of church manors they are in the same hands. The one major discrepancy is at Fowlmere, but it is possible that the information in Domesday is incomplete. Both sources similarly show exceptionally small manorial formations in Whittlesford hundred, but the largest manor mentioned in Domesday Book, Ickleton, which belonged to count Eustace of Boulogne and contained 24 carucates of land, had by 1279 split up into 10 small manors, of which 7 belonged to the church. In Whittlesford itself, on the other hand, where Domesday Book describes 4 manorial units, of which one is fairly large, the Hundred Rolls specify one manor only, in the hands of J. de Akyni.

In 1279 Toseland was remarkable among the Huntingdonshire hundreds for the unusually small size of its manors. Here comparison with Domesday is made difficult by a number of discrepancies; but it is significant that in Domesday Book also we find a large number of petty manorial formations, though the number in the Hundred Rolls is far greater. Thus the large manor of Paxton, belonging at the time of Domesday to the countess Judith, contained land for 41 ploughs, 60 villeins, and 8 borders. By the time of the Hundred Rolls, on the other hand, the village of Paxton had split up into Magna and Parva Paxton, each containing at least fifteen manors, and there were a number of freeholders as well, whom the jurors did not assign to manors.

Vinogradoff had ample grounds for considering the manorial order described in Domesday as evidence of the incomplete manorialization of the English village in the eleventh century; but he is not altogether correct in contrasting the variety of Domesday Book with the uniformity of the Hundred Rolls. Small size and variety of structure is just as characteristic of the latter as of the former. On the other hand, Domesday Book also presents us with a very considerable number of fully 'rounded and compact' manors which look, on the surface at any rate, no less finished than the manors of the Hundred Rolls. A detailed comparison, hundred by hundred and village by village, might yield valuable results; but even without that we may draw the following preliminary conclusions:

1. The bulk of the large manors in the area we are examining was in existence even before 1066; especially stable is the solid block of the old Benedictine manors.

2. After 1066 we see individual cases of large manors arising in place of small manorial formations.

3. But even more frequently we see the opposite tendency for large manors to split up into a number of small ones.[1]

4. On the whole the ratio between typical large manors and small manorial formations appears to have undergone no essential change between the time of Domesday Book and that of the Hundred Rolls.

Does this mean that no essential changes in the manorial structure of England took place between the days of William the Conqueror and Edward I? This would, indeed, be remarkable, when we consider that this was the period when the English

---

[1] My pupil, M. A. Barg, in a thesis devoted to a comparison of the Hundred Rolls and Domesday Book for Cambridgeshire, and the *Inquisitio Comitatus Cantabrigiensis*, has discovered a general tendency for small manors to increase at the expense of large ones.

state, English law, the English towns, and English internal and foreign trade took shape. Without doubt changes took place also in the agrarian structure. What was the character of these changes, and the direction which they took?

The period between 1086 and 1279 is characterized by most important changes in the distribution of landed property. First, the huge royal demesne, which occupied first place in the Domesday survey, almost completely disappears. Almost all the royal manors were alienated, and the Hundred Rolls relate in detail when, by whom and to whom. These alienations created a series of large manors of a special type—the manors of the ancient demesne of the Crown, where the villeins were in a position bordering on that of freeholders, with important effects upon the manorial structure, in particular considerable mobility of the land of the 'villein sokemen'. Secondly, the estates of the church increased to an enormous extent, especially the estates of the new monastic and military orders, among which the Cistercians took first place, followed by the Augustinians, Hospitallers, and Templars. But these new orders by no means always created or built upon a system of classical serf-worked manors. On the contrary, their estates were often composed of a varied series of petty acquisitions, often separate holdings on the manors of other lords, and even their large manors were frequently virtually without villeins and the cultivation of the demesne was carried out by other methods.

More difficult are the questions whether the landed possessions of the feudatories had increased or decreased, and in what direction transferences of property among the lay lords themselves were tending. Do we find large landowners growing at the expense of small landowners, or the reverse? As far as the ratio of large to small manors is concerned, we have already seen that it had changed little. A lively transference of property was in progress among freeholders, and internal changes were in progress in the structure both of the large manors and of the incompletely manorialized forms. The intensification of feudal exploitation after the Conquest, the sharp demarcation between villein and free status and tenure as a result of Henry II's legal reforms and of the development of the common law, the growth of the towns and the development of the foreign market —all these could not fail to have a considerable influence on the life of the manor. The emergence of the villeins as a single class from a number of intermediate gradations, on the one hand, and on the other hand, the disintegration of the villein class, as individuals left it to enter the category of freeholders, together with the development of various forms of leasehold, were bound to cause far-reaching changes in the structure of manors, both large and small. But the fundamental factor determining the structure of the manor was the form of exploitation to which the dependent peasantry was subject, the form of appropriation of the peasants' surplus employed by the feudal lords, in other words the predominant form of rent. It is to this theme that we must now pass.

CHAPTER III

LABOUR RENT AND MONEY RENT

METHOD OF ANALYSIS

What form of rent predominated in England in the second half of the thirteenth century? The answer to this question is not, of course, provided by estimating the proportion of one or other form of rent, within the general total of feudal rent paid over by the English peasantry to lords ecclesiastical and secular, but it is from such an estimate that we have to start. At once we come upon a number of difficulties.

How are we to estimate the relative importance of different types of rent? The way is pointed by the practice of both government and manorial records, in which both labour rents and produce rents are often estimated in terms of money. We know the purpose of these estimates from bailiffs' accounts and other sources. They provided the basis for *venditio operum*, that is, the substitution of money payment for labour obligations in cases where the prescribed works were not required. Contributions in kind were also 'sold', that is, replaced by money payments on the basis of these estimates. But if we are to make a quantitative comparison of the different forms of rent, we need to know to what extent these monetary estimates were the equivalent of the labour rents they replaced. It has been stated that the estimates for works done by villeins that are given in manorial and government documents are, as a rule, lower than the accepted rates of pay for hired labourers at the same time.[1] In cases where it is work by the day (*dieta*) that is being estimated, the explanation is that those villagers owing labour service were not always required to work for a full working day. In the case of task work (a given quantity of a specific kind of work) the estimates are close enough. For instance, harvesting one acre is estimated at three to six pence in the Cambridgeshire Hundred Rolls of 1279. The pay per

---

[1] J. T. Rogers, *op. cit.*, i, 82. Cf. Levett, *O.S.S.L.H.*, v, 156.

acre given to harvesters (for the period 1272–80), according
to Rogers,[1] varies between the same figures. The thirteenth-
century material is very scanty, but it seems that at this period
there was no significant difference between the manorial
estimates and the normal rates of pay.[2] The manorial estimates
may therefore be used as a basis for comparison. But here
begins a fresh series of difficulties.

If the documents give an estimate of labour dues as a whole,
or an estimate of separate varieties of dues, calculations are
comparatively simple. If they do not, difficulties arise, since
the works might be variously estimated, owing both to the
varying length of the working day,[3] and to differing principles
of assessment. For example, the use by peasants of their own
draught-animals made a large difference in the estimate of
work done. Carting manure in one's own cart was estimated
at 6d. a day, in the lord's cart at 1d. It is not always clear
whether work was assessed on a working-day or a piece-work
basis. Works listed in summary form leave us in doubt whether
they were done with food provided by the lord or not. This
makes a difference to the estimate, about a penny a day being
allowed for food on the average. Sometimes certain kinds of
work, when food is provided, do not come into the estimate
at all; in other cases they are assessed, but at a reduced rate.
This lowers the total money estimate of labour dues. The
quantity of work is not always given precisely, most often
in the case of haymaking, but also in connection with other
works. Sometimes it was not easy to determine precisely the
necessary number of days on which services would be demanded
because of the weather, or the possibility of finding supplementary supplies of labour. Some of the works due (especially
carrying services and boon services), were in general not fixed
by manorial practice, but were left at the will of the lord.

We cannot always make the necessary corrections for
festivals, still less for illness.[4] The allocation of work is often

---

[1] *Op. cit.*, i, 309–21.
[2] Vinogradoff even supposed that the estimates were computed on a basis to
the advantage of the lords and that money rates were higher than the value of the
work they replaced (*Villainage*, 311). This shows that the difference cannot have
been a significant one. Cf. *Villainage*, 342.
[3] *Averabit ter in anno ita quod possit redire ad prandium*—estimate ½d (*R.H.*, ii, 426).
[4] *R.H.*, ii, 453 (and many other passages).

very peculiar and based on movable feasts. The number and variety of kinds of work are very considerable, and the ways of reckoning them and assessing them vary infinitely. Precise calculation of the general over-all estimates of villeins' services is therefore extremely difficult, and where such estimates are given we have every reason to doubt their accuracy.

Nevertheless some estimate is necessary, and I have observed the following rules in estimating villein services. In reckoning up week works I have assumed that about four weeks a year are lost through holidays, bad weather and illness, though this figure is probably much lower than the actual loss. That leaves eight weeks for autumn work (from St. Peter in Chains [August 1st] to Michaelmas [September 29th])[1] and forty for the rest of the working year. In estimating separate kinds of work the average rates I have used[2] (in cases where there were no more precise indications) have frequently had to be altered according to local conditions, taking into account varying ways of reckoning up work, and assessments current in a given hundred or village (or in the neighbourhood). The estimates of obligations 'at the lord's will', too, have had to be calculated by rule of thumb, or by taking into account the practice of the neighbouring manors.

Even complicated calculations give only approximate figures, but they can nevertheless give a general picture of the dimensions of labour rents in the separate manors and regions.

We have seen that produce rent plays quite a secondary part in the Hundred Rolls, amounting on the average to not more than 2–3 per cent of villein obligations. Produce contributions include eggs, hens, capons, more rarely geese, still more rarely grain, (mostly oats as fodder corn), and from freeholders pepper, cummin, and wax. The monetary estimate

---

[1] In doing this we exaggerate the total amount of work estimated, since reaping and harvesting rarely went on more than a month or six weeks, according to the weather (Rogers).

[2] Autumn work $1\frac{1}{2}$–$2d$. per day's work, for the rest of the year 1–$1\frac{1}{2}d$. per day's work; boon services—$2d$. without food provided, $1d$. with; ploughing—$3d$.; carting—$2\frac{1}{2}d$.; mowing—$2d$.; haymaking—$\frac{3}{4}d$.; harrowing—$1d$.; weeding—$\frac{1}{4}d$.; for work reckoned 'by the piece': reaping 1 acre—$4d$.; salting one quarter—$2d$.

For comparison with these figures, which were worked out on the basis of data in *R.H.*, we give the assessment of Walter of Henley: ploughing 1 acre—$6d$., harrowing—$1d$., weeding 1 acre—$\frac{1}{2}d$., reaping 1 acre—$5d$., carting in August—$1d$. *Walter of Henley*, pp. 18–19.

of these rents presents no difficulties, and is frequently given in the source. But possibly a significant proportion of produce rent escapes us—that part which may be extracted in the form of heriot and banalities. These rents are sometimes commuted. At the same time, certain produce rents are closer to money rent than to rent in kind, being paid in products which have to be bought with money. Examples are payments in the form of pepper, salt, salted herring, spurs, gloves, and the like.

The calculation of money rents presents the greatest difficulties of all. The extremely complicated nature of tenurial relationships prevents the proper calculation of the rents of free holdings, especially in counties where there has been large-scale disintegration of free holdings, such as Cambridgeshire. The free tenant not only pays rent but often receives it himself from his own quite numerous tenants. And so between the freeholder actually farming his own land and the lord there often stands a whole chain of intermediate tenants through whose hands the rent passes, being partially distributed among them. Moreover, in precisely those regions where the rent of freeholders predominates, cases of the alienation of rent, or part of it, make calculation even more difficult. In a number of cases, therefore, we have succeeded in obtaining only approximate indicatory figures, and where calculations can be made easily, we may be justified in suspecting some simplifications in the material.

It would be too complicated a task to reckon up all the rents given in the Hundred Rolls, nor should we even then obtain reliable figures. Furthermore the extremely varied character of the data prevents us from laying down constant principles on which to base our reckonings. I have therefore reckoned up in full villein labour services for only a few counties and hundreds. In many cases I have limited myself to general estimates only, based on rough comparisons, particularly in those cases where there was no doubt as to the predominant kind of rent and where a careful calculation could only confirm the conclusion that might have been reached by simpler means. As a result, instead of neat tables I shall have to set down something of a patchwork review of our material, hundred by hundred, going from east to west.

LABOUR RENT AND MONEY RENT—A REGIONAL SURVEY FROM
   THE HUNDRED ROLLS

In the three northern hundreds of Huntingdonshire we find
fresh support for our impression of the predominance there of
typical manorial relations.

Hirstingstone hundred is dominated by the great manors of
the abbey of Ramsey, with their heavy labour dues. The huge
manor of Somersham, belonging to the bishop of Ely is similar
in organization, although the labour dues are somewhat
lighter. Money rent plays a purely secondary role. On the
average, a villein's virgate in the Ramsey manors carries labour
dues to the value of approximately 20s., and money payments—including tallage, heusire, maltsilver, fishsilver, etc.—
2s. to 3s.[1] Sometimes there is a small assize rent. In Wistow
the villeins pay 3s. per virgate; 3 virgates in Needingworth
pay 5s. each; in Broughton 30 virgates and 5 cottars together
pay £5.[2]

Boon works and carrying services were often undefined, and
consequently labour dues would be particularly heavy. It is
only among cottar holdings that money rent occasionally
predominates over labour rent. Nevertheless, we must still
remember the statement of the compiler of the Ramsey
cartulary—*ad voluntatem domini possunt opera poni ad censum*.[3]
At any time money payment could be taken instead of labour
service. This remark could well undermine all conclusions
based on the Hundred Rolls.

The rents of freeholders in Hirstingstone hundred are insignificant. Even in the bishop of Ely's manor of Somersham,
where free rent is found, it (or more precisely that part of it
paid in money) only amounts to £10 6s. 6d. On the other hand
the assessment of the labour dues of the villeins comes to
£56 12s. 4d., not counting carrying services at the lord's will,
while their money rents bring in £3 14s. 3d., not counting
arbitrary tallage, pannage, and other unfixed dues.

Here, therefore, we have a typical manorial system based on
labour services, as depicted by the classical exponents of the
manorial theory, who derived their views from practically

---

[1] In the Ramsey manors we find a fairly high money assessment of labour dues.
See *C. Ram.*, i, 325.

[2] *R.H.*, ii, 600, 602, 603   [3] *C. Ram.*, i, 325, etc.

the same body of material. In the other two northern hundreds
of Huntingdonshire, Normancross and Leightonstone, matters
are somewhat more complicated. Generally speaking the
labour service system predominates here also, although we also
find, especially on small estates, a complete or almost complete
absence of labour rents. Villein land held predominantly for
labour rent comprises about 70 per cent of the whole in
Normancross and 60 per cent in Leightonstone. This total
includes the villein land of practically all the large manors.
The rents from free holdings could not make any vital difference
as the amount of free land was comparatively insignificant.
Labour rent predominates in the southern hundred of Toseland
also, where there was a considerable development of small
estates. Here, too, villein lands held for labour rent, or mainly
for labour rent, make up more than half of all villein land.
Free holdings in the hundred are not sufficiently important
to swing the scales to the side of money rents. Thus, in
Huntingdonshire we have a clear picture. With all its variations, our source everywhere shows a predominance of labour
rent for the villeins.

For Cambridgeshire I attempted to calculate all dues paid
by villeins. This is involved and difficult, since in many cases
assessments of works were not given, the amounts of others
were only vaguely indicated, and some were 'at the lord's
will'. Consequently a great deal that was hypothetical had
to be included, and I doubt whether my figures are always
exact. But they cannot differ greatly from reality, and for
our purposes their accuracy is sufficient. Altogether my
calculations cover 241 manors in south Cambridgeshire, comprising about 34,000 acres of villein land and 4,210 villein
holdings, and I have taken into account only those complexes
of holdings which included villein land.

My figures show[1] that for those manors of south Cambridgeshire which included villein land the predominant form of rent
was money rent, which makes up more than half (52 per cent)

---

[1] Labour rents of villeins—about £725. Money rents—£474 17s. 4d. Produce
rents—£31 13s. 8d. Money rent of free holdings, paid to the lords of these same
manors—£344 4s. 1¼d. Labour rent of free holdings—£4 11s. 0½d. Produce
rent of these holdings—£4 11s. 0½d. Thus for the total number of manors dealt
with, labour rent comes to about £730, money rent—£819 1s. 5¼d., produce
rent—£36 4s. 8½d. Total amount of rent—about £1,585.

of the total sum of rent, while labour rent comes to about 46 per cent, and produce rent to about 2 per cent. But this predominance of money rent is due to the inclusion in the calculations of the free holdings, which paid practically entirely money rent with only insignificant services and payments in kind. In the rent paid by villeins labour services predominate, making up about 60 per cent of the total, while money rent makes up only 37 per cent, and produce rent about 3 per cent.

We have not, of course, taken into our calculations all the rents of free holdings. In Cambridgeshire there were many manors in which there were no villeins at all: these have not been included in our reckoning. Furthermore a considerable amount of rent was paid to persons other than lords of manors. Therefore the total amount of free rents must be greatly increased if we are to obtain a figure approaching reality. According to my approximate calculations free rent amounted to about £500.

So we may say that south Cambridgeshire is an area where money rent predominates, but where at the same time labour rent is predominant on villein holdings. The predominance of money rent must be put down to the exceptionally strong development of free tenure in this county. In some hundreds where it is possible to reckon up more accurately the rents of free holdings the balance in favour of money rents is even greater. For example, in Chilford hundred the money rent of free holdings amounts to over £50, the money rent of villeins to £12 13s. 1½d., and the labour rent of villeins to £35. In the hundred of Flendish the money rent of free holdings is over £47, that of villeins is £39 14s. 3½d., and the labour rent of villeins over £43. In the hundred of Longstow, on the other hand, the assessment of villein labour dues exceeds the combined total of money rents of both villein and free holdings.[1] But in all the hundreds labour services predominate among villein rents.

When we turn to the area linking the east (Huntingdonshire —Cambridgeshire) to the west (Oxfordshire—Warwickshire), it becomes impossible to separate the money from the labour dues of villeins. The Bedfordshire records describe villein obligations by a short formula—usually in the form *quelibet*

---

[1] The figure for the last is only very inexactly calculated.

(virgata) valet per annum ... s. vel opera ad valorem. The rent of a
virgate is assessed variously at 25*s.*, 20*s.*, 17*s.*, 14*s.*, at 1 mark,
at 12*s.*, 10*s.*, 8*s.*, 5*s.*, but most frequently of all at 20*s.*,[1] and
always in round figures. Thus the assessors gave only an
approximate overall estimate of all dues, without troubling
to define the proportionate amount of each form of rent
separately. Apparently money rent was a significant part of
villein obligations, but how big a part it is difficult to say.
The sum total of villein rents is £131 1*s.* 1*d.*, of free rents[2]
£78 4*s.* 9¾*d.*, or 65 per cent and 35 per cent. Even if the greater
part of villein rents took the form of labour dues, it seems
probable that there was a balance in favour of money rent.

The proportions of labour and money rents of villeins in
the Buckinghamshire records are equally unclear, since the
same formula (or an equivalent) as that found in Bedfordshire
is also used here. The sum total of villein rents is about £345,
the rent of free holdings £108 5*s.* 2*d.*

We are better informed about the western zone, Oxfordshire
and Warwickshire, where the Rolls give exact figures for a
number of hundreds and the proportion of labour and money
rents can be approximately calculated.

Thus, in the hundred of Bampton money rents *(redditus)*
and an assessment of labour dues *(opus et servicia)* are separately
enumerated. The assessment of labour dues—which could
evidently be demanded in the form of money payments—
here reaches a maximum figure, and we may assume that part
of it was, in fact, money rent. The labour rents of villeins
amount to £169 0*s.* 9½*d.*, their money rents to £139 16*s.* 2¼*d.*,
while the rent of free holdings totals £98 17*s.* 9*d.* Thus money
rent amounts to a minimum of 60 per cent of the overall total.[3]

For Banbury hundred rents can be fully calculated. Money
rent predominates not only in the general total, but even in
the rents due from villeins. They owe about £56 in money,
and labour services are estimated at rather more than £38.
The money rents of free tenants come to somewhat more than
£26. Hence, money rents comprise 57 per cent of villein rent

---

[1] In the case of the lower assessments it is possible that rents of half-virgates are
being given.

[2] The free rent total includes only money rent.

[3] An insignificant produce rent, and the petty labour dues of free holders, have
not been included in the calculations.

and 67 per cent of total rent. This predominance of money
rent can be seen to have been even more marked when we
consider that arbitrary tallage was common in this hundred
and that the obligations of villein and free tenants often
included scutage payments.

In the hundred of Thame, where in the majority of manors
labour and money dues can be easily calculated, we find an
immense predominance of money over labour rent. Labour
rent, in those manors where it can be reckoned up separately,
comes to £17 0s. 7d., the money rent of villeins to £41 7s., and
the money rent of free holdings to £25 15s. 5d.[1] The sum total
of money rent is thus two-and-a-half times as great as the
assessment of labour rent.

In a number of other hundreds only approximate calculations can be made. Labour rents are usually not assessed,
but are described either in a very summary manner, or in
such a way as to present great difficulties in calculation, or
as being at the lord's will. Sometimes an overall estimate of
dues is given with an indication that it was at the lord's will
to exact them as labour dues or in money. For the purpose of
approximate calculation we can use either those cases in which
money and labour rents are given separately, or money rent
totals, which are usually given, or the average amount of the
sum total of rent which falls on one villein virgate, which we
can work out for the separate hundreds. On this basis we
can presume in Bullington hundred a considerable predominance of money over labour rent in the dues of villeins, and
this predominance is emphasized by the considerable amount
of land in the hands of free tenants. In Ploughley and Wootton
hundreds we can presume something like an even balance
between the labour and the money rents of villeins, but a considerable amount of free land in both hundreds results in an
undoubted balance in favour of money rent.

In Ewelme, Pirton, Lewknor, Langtree and Dorchester
hundreds the money rents of villeins are precisely indicated,
and the labour dues are recorded sufficiently clearly for us to
get a general idea of their extent, although an exact assessment
is sometimes difficult. In all these hundreds there is a clear
predominance of money rents in villein obligations without

---

[1] Tallage and scutage have not been included in the calculations.

taking into account the free holdings which in Pirton, Ewelme and Langtree hundreds exceed the villein land in area.

Somewhat apart among the Oxfordshire hundreds stands Chadlington hundred, one of those where the large manor was well developed. Here in most cases figures are given both for money rent and for the assessment of labour dues. There is a considerable balance in favour of labour rents, the assessment of which stands at £217 13s. 5d., as against £85 18s. 10d. for villein money rents. Even if we add tallage,[1] which amounts to about £40 to the last figure, no essential difference arises in the relation of the two kinds of rent. There is in the hundred quite a considerable amount of land in the hands of free tenants, but even taking this into account, money rent still does not outbalance labour dues.

Money rent, therefore, predominates in Oxfordshire.[2] In the majority of hundreds we find that villeins render more money than labour rent. Only in Bampton and Chadlington is the labour rent of villeins higher, and in Wootton and Ploughley they are perhaps equal. But Bampton, Chadlington, Wootton and Ploughley are among the largest hundreds of Oxfordshire, and we can therefore on the whole presume an approximate equilibrium between the two forms of rent for villein holdings. On the other hand the money rent of free holdings creates an undoubted balance in favour of constant money rent, while the commutability of a considerable part of labour rent, together with arbitrary tallage, pannage, gifts (*exennia*), and court revenues, emphasizes even more that Oxfordshire was an area where money rent was predominant.

In the Warwickshire hundred of Stoneleigh (as in Oxfordshire) the week-work system is the exception rather than the rule. We find it only in one large ecclesiastical manor, Bishop's Itchington.[3] In the remaining manors there are no week-works, and labour dues are on the whole insignificant

---

[1] Tallage is mainly arbitrary throughout the hundred, but can be approximately calculated on the basis of the fixed instances.

[2] In our calculations of money rents we have excluded those cases (not uncommon in the Oxfordshire records), in which even though rents are given in money terms the lords retain the right to demand quit-payments in kind for labour dues, or are free to demand either money or labour. The money rent for which we have made estimates is in all cases described as *certum, certitudo, redditus assisae*, i.e. it is not such that other forms of rent might be substituted for it.

[3] R.H. (War.), 28v.

L

and are defined by a certain number of days per annum. Finally, in thirteen cases the villeins have no labour obligations whatever. This slight development of labour rent is accompanied by a correspondingly heavy monetary levy on the villeins. While the labour dues of villeins in the hundred of Stoneleigh can be assessed at approximately £80, their money rents amount to £132 5s. 7½d., and their produce rents are trifling.[1] The money rents of free tenants come to £122 6s. 2½d.; their labour dues to £2 5s. 1½d.; produce rents being insignificant. Thus in Stoneleigh hundred money rent and labour rent bear the relation of 77–23 per cent.

The same characteristic features appear also in the Warwickshire hundred of Kineton. Here in the vast majority of manors we find no week-work system, although it is more frequent here than in the hundred of Stoneleigh. I have made calculations for ninety manors,[2] on which the money rents of villeins come to £354 15s. 9d., their labour rents to about £234.[3] In many manors we find tallage or aid at the lord's will. As in the hundred of Stoneleigh, freeholders not infrequently have labour obligations, but their money rents are far more important, amounting to about £124 for the hundred (excluding manors omitted from my calculations of villein dues). The relation of money to labour rent in this hundred is 67 and 33 per cent respectively, for the two Warwickshire hundreds together 70 and 30 per cent.

This review of all our material shows that, in the area to which it relates, money rent was undoubtedly quantitatively predominant. The sole exception is Huntingdonshire. If one gives the term rent a wider interpretation, and includes in it payments to the government, then one must add to money rents scutage, hidage, sheriff's aid,[4] and ward money, all of which together made up a considerable sum. All this without doubt increases the importance of money rents. And yet we have every reason

---

[1] For the whole hundred these came to 230 hens, 20 eggs and 35 loaves.

[2] Excluding those whose records were illegible in the manuscript, also those few cases in which the method of detailing dues in the source made their results for our calculation doubtful. I was unable to read the record on ff. 70–72 and 117v.–23 covering 17 vills in the hundred of Kineton.

[3] The reckoning is approximate, since assessments of works are not given and their extent is not always precisely defined.

[4] This was often in the hands of lords of franchises and formed part of the revenues of the court.

for supposing that the role of money rent was even more considerable than the Hundred Rolls indicate.

RENTS IN THE MINISTERS' ACCOUNTS

The full amount of villein rent is difficult to determine, and only one source—ministers' accounts—offers us more or less adequate information. Manorial and government records, including the Hundred Rolls, as a rule list rents in so summarized a form that it is not possible in all cases to reconstruct a full picture. Usually they record the following types of rent: (1) *redditus assisae*—an annual more or less fixed money rent, which forms the larger part of the rent of free tenants and usually a certain part of the rent of villeins; (2) the labour obligations of villeins (*opera, consuetudines*), and to a certain extent of free tenants also, often given with their monetary assessments; (3) regular (annual) contributions in kind made by both classes, sometimes with an indication of the monetary equivalent. The remaining forms of rent are not always given, and some are normally never given at all. For instance, references to cartage, which was often at the lord's will and might vary widely, are very irregular. All manner of petty customary rents, of which there were many in the medieval village, are also often omitted. Unfixed dues (*consuetudines non taxatae*), heriot, merchet, duties on the sale of stock and on trading in beer, which usually figure in ministers' accounts among the court revenues, are omitted, and indeed it would have been extremely difficult to reckon them up. Payments arising from monopolies are also omitted, as well as fines, duties and levies derived from the lord's judicial rights. The Hundred Rolls themselves sometimes note that the enumeration of rents is incomplete.[1] State and ecclesiastical taxes, which in a number of cases were 'manorialized', and might therefore reasonably be included under the heading of feudal rent, were irregularly recorded. It is very difficult to determine how large a proportion of the total feudal rent was made up of these various levies. It is easier to define their form. However, the majority of these supplementary payments had to be made by the villein in money, and a smaller number in kind

---

[1] See for instance *R.H.*, ii, p. 741: *Summa tocius valoris preter cartagium perquisita et fines terrarum.*

(particularly multure). Only as a rare exception do we find them in the form of labour.

If we try to determine the relation between labour and money rent purely on the basis of a comparison of *redditus assisae* and the money assessments of labour dues, the danger of under-estimating the significance of money rent, and to a smaller extent of produce rent, is considerable. Furthermore, it is essential to bear in mind that the assessment of labour dues in our sources is normally considerably greater than their actual incidence, since labour rents could at the lord's will be replaced by money payments, by means of the annual *venditio operum*.

I have attempted, on the basis of the ministers' accounts for the manors of Roger Bigod, Earl of Norfolk, to compare the relation of labour and money rent as shown by works and assize rents owed, with that which existed in practice.[1] The comparison covers thirteen manors. Seven accounts are for 1268–69, one for 1269–70, and the remainder for a few years before or after. Some difficulty in calculation was caused by the fact that the ministers' accounts give only a single figure for *redditus assisae*, the rent of the villeins not being separated from that of free tenants. To resolve this difficulty I have also used the inquisitions *post Mortem* for the Earl of Norfolk's manors in 1269, where the two sets of rents are given separately.[2] Although the figures in the inquisition are somewhat lower, the relation between the rent of villeins and freeholders is probably correct, so I have made a corresponding proportionate division of the sums of *redditus assisae* in the ministers' accounts.

To begin with, let us compare the figures for the assessment of works and for the *redditus assisae* of the villeins, without in the first place taking account of *venditio operum*. As is seen in Table 5, such a comparison suggests a preponderance of labour over money rents. But when we take into account the replacement of part of the works by money payments, the picture is reversed, and money rent considerably exceeds the assessment of works. In the first case labour dues amount to 54 per cent, in the second, to only 38 per cent of the total rent. Actual practice, in fact, departed considerably from the assessment.

[1] P.R.O.: M.A., Bdl. 840, no. 1, Bdl. 1004 no. 1, Bdl. 995 nos. 1, 7, Bdl. 1007 no. 4, Bdl. 995 no. 15, Bdl. 1007 no. 7, Bdl. 935 no. 22, Bdl. 936 no. 18, Bdl. 933 no. 20, Bdl. 937 no. 27, Bdl. 929 no. 1, Bdl. 944 no. 21, Bdl. 944 no. 1, Bdl. 936 no. 2.   [2] C. Hen. III File 38 (17).

Although the lord retained the right to exact works in full, a comparison of ministers' accounts over a number of years shows that the practice of *venditio operum* was repeated annually,

TABLE 5

Manor	Nominal assessment		Actual assessment	
	Works	Redditus assisae	Works	Redditus assisae
	£ s. d.	£ s. d.	£ s. d.	£ s. d.
Dovercourt	10 12 5	8 4 0	4 19 3	13 17 2
Earl Soham	17 19 6	10 6 5	11 14 2½	16 11 8½
Cratfield ..	10 10 11	5 18 0	7 17 7	8 11 4
Walton ..	19 3 4	39 1 0	12 11 1	45 13 3
Dunningworth ..	1 10 6	6 4 0	1 5 0	6 9 6
Staverton ..	8 16 4	8 1 2	6 15 6	10 2 0
Framingham ..	12 5 4½	6 3 5	9 1 5½	9 7 4
Hanworth ..	15 19 9¾	8 10 9	5 13 4	18 17 2¼
Ditchingham ..	6 12 6¾	7 0 0	5 14 3¾	7 18 3
Lopham ..	12 4 1½	2 4 0	10 14 2	3 13 11½
Acle	10 17 5	7 6 0	10 16 0	7 7 5
Halvergate	7 14 4	5 4 0	6 19 2	5 19 2
Walsham ..	7 9 2½	8 8 0	6 6 3½	9 10 11
	141 15 10	122 19 9	100 8 4½	163 18 2¾
	54%	46%	38%	62%

with considerable variation in detail, but with a general tendency to become more far-reaching. Even if we suppose that the sale of works was practised more widely on the manors of the Earl of Norfolk than on those of other lords (and we have no reason to do so), it is still clear that the extents and the governmental inquisitions give an exaggerated figure for labour rents and an unrealistically low one for money rents. We must always remember that, although works could be replaced by money payments, *redditus assisae* could not be replaced by works.

In our table, however, as in most of our sources, not all the villein's rent is included. A considerable part of it appears in other sections of the ministers' accounts, and these I have tabulated for the same manors in the same years. The revenues mentioned in Table 6 are not confined to villein rents, since court revenues and contributions in kind might include a certain income from freeholders. But it is beyond doubt that the greater proportion is accounted for by the villeins' payments. We do not know the real significance of the headings 'sale of wood' and 'letting of marsh'. They might mean the sale of wood and handing-over of marshes to individuals outside the manor, but it is also possible that the transactions took place within the manor when the lord 'sold' or 'gave over' to the peasants their lost rights to wood and marsh, that is, extracted additional rent from them. In this case a part of villein rent might be concealed under these headings too.

Taking all these elements into account, together with the data in Table 5, it is evident that, if we only take into account the assessment of works and the amount of *redditus assisae*, we are dealing with approximately half of the villein's rent. For example, the court revenues, made up almost entirely of payments by villeins, amount to more than the assessment of works actually performed, yet neither the extents nor the Hundred Rolls ever mention them. None of these concealed forms of villein rent took the form of labour services. Court revenues and the petty rents (*faldagium, herbagium, pannagium, capitagium*) were money payments, though *capitagium* was often paid in the form of poultry. *Auxilium* is often included with the court revenues and was always levied in money. *Venditio bosci* and *firma marisci*, if (as suggested) they consisted of the sale and letting of wood and marsh to the peasants, also required money payments. Contributions in kind, mostly multure in grain, were by comparison very small. Some other duties were levied in kind—for instance, the duty on beer brewed for sale.[1] If multure and other levies in kind are taken into account, the size of the villain's produce rent should be increased perhaps fourfold.

TABLE 6

Manor	Court revenues £ s. d.	Mill revenues £ s. d.	Petty rents £ s. d.	Auxilium £ s. d.	Assessment of payment in kind £ s. d.	Various £ s. d.	
Dovercourt ...	9 18 2	3 6 8	1 9 0½	inc. in court revenues	7 4 2		Sale of wood
Earl Soham ...	3 1 6	2 0 0	1 9 10	6 0 0	10 8	1 3 4½	,,
Cratfield ...	10 11 6	2 19 0	3 19 0	2 13 4	13 4	2 7 6	,,
Walton ...	23 11 2	14 8 4	1 11 8	inc. in court revenues	2 5 10	—	
Dunningworth ...	3 11 10	3 6 8	1 12 11½	,,	7 0	2 11 3½	,,
Staverton ...	2 19 4	2 11 11½	4 8 4½	—	10 10	5 9 1	,,
Framingham ...	9 18 0	4 13 4	4 5½	12 0 0	6 8	—	
Hanworth ...	20 18 2	6 8	—	8 0 0	1 10 8	—	
Ditchingham ...	5 7 3	7 6 8	2 4 8	—	10 2	21 19 3	,,
Lopham ...	3 10 0	4 7 10	4 17 0	—	16 5	—	
Acle ...	4 12 4	1 6 8	—	—	10 8	35 9 0	Letting of marsh
Halvergate ...	11 2 4	2 12 0	—	—	—	50 17 4	
Walsham ...	6 5 8	4 4 0	2 4 1	—	9 0	17 0 0	,,
	115 3 3	53 7 9½	24 1 0½	28 13 4	16 15 5	136 18 9¾	

[1] *Si braciaverit ad vendendum dabit 14 lagenas ad tonnutum.* C. Glouc. iii, p. 170.

If we add court revenues and aid to *redditus assisae* and sale of works the ratio of money and labour rent rises from 62 : 38, as in Table 5, to approximately 75 : 25. In actual fact the preponderance of money rents must be even greater. For the nominal assessment of produce rent was only about one-ninth of that of labour rent, but in actual fact it probably amounted to something over one-half. Thus the analysis of ministers' accounts shows that on the Norfolk manors, where at first sight it seemed as though labour rent was predominant, in fact we find a significant preponderance of money rent, with produce rent playing quite an important role. The masterly analysis of villein rents by Miss Levett in her work on the Winchester estates[1] in the fourteenth century also shows the great importance of minor levies made on the villeins, such as those found under the headings *Fines et maritagia* and *Exitus manerii*. Thus her table of fines paid on entering into possession of a villein holding shows that £4, £8 and even £10 might be paid. Such cases occur in the thirteenth century too, though not so frequently. Payments of this kind considerably raised the money rent of a villein without being reflected in state and manorial documents.

It is clear that in many cases, if not always, the Hundred Rolls give an unduly low estimate of the money and produce rent of villeins and an unduly high estimate of their labour rent. We must therefore emend our conclusions accordingly. The actual role of money rents was greater, perhaps much greater, than our source indicates. Furthermore, as Ballard has observed, the Hundred Rolls have a tendency to minimize the amounts of money rents while detailing labour dues fairly precisely.[2]

RENT AND MANORIAL STRUCTURE

In addition to the foregoing conclusions we may also make, though in a very generalized form, some comparisons between different regions and between manors of varying types. Our material, in spite of the comparative economic homogeneity of the territory it covers, shows certain local peculiarities in

[1] *O.S.S.L.H.*, v.
[2] We must also make certain, though probably small, additions to the amount allowed for the money rent of freeholders.

the proportionate division between the various kinds of feudal rent. The main feature is the progressive decrease of labour rent in the obligations of the villein, as one moves from east to west, though even in the western region we find such cases as the hundreds of Bampton and Chadlington, where labour dues predominate.

How does this geographical distribution of labour and money rent relate to the local variations in manorial structure which we described in the preceding chapter? The predominance of villeinage coincides with the predominance of labour rents only in Huntingdonshire. Elsewhere it is different. In Cambridgeshire, where villeinage was less strongly developed than in Oxfordshire and Warwickshire, villein labour rents are nevertheless high. In the latter counties villeinage is more strongly developed, but labour rents are less important. The differentiation between free and villein holding is stronger in the east. Here the villein holds his land predominantly for labour services. On the other hand, in the west, especially in Warwickshire, free tenants owe more works than in the east, while villeins owe comparatively more money rent. Still further to the west, in Wales, the obligations of free and unfree resemble each other even more closely. However, the geographical region covered by our material is too homogeneous for observations of any real breadth to be possible.

Besides the regional differences noted above, we also find different relations of labour rent to money rent on manors of different sizes. A brief study of the pages of the Hundred Rolls is sufficient to show that it is chiefly on large manors that labour rents predominate, though even here there are exceptions. It is on the small manors that we most often find that there are no labour dues, as well as in many cases a complete absence of villeinage. The average size of manors with money rents alone is very small, and the highest average figures for villein land are found among manors where labour rent predominates.

Another feature to be borne in mind is that the nature of rent varies not only as between different types of manor, but within each manor as between different types of tenant. As a general rule it seems that money rent is more important for small villein holdings than for large. Most small (cottar) holdings are either free from labour dues, or owe very few by comparison with their money rent. According to my calculations, based on material from nine hundreds in Cambridgeshire, Huntingdonshire, and Oxfordshire, the percentage relation between money and labour rent is for villein virgaters 45 and 55 per cent respectively; the same for half virgaters; for the holders of quarter virgates approximately 50—50 per cent, for small holders (less than five acres of arable) 70—30 per cent. It is at times difficult to establish whether some small holders are free or unfree, since there is no noticeable difference in the character of dues as between the two categories. Probably the manorial authorities did not always know where the line should be drawn, and were not very concerned about it. A cottar was of interest to them less as a source of feudal rent than as a reserve of hired labour.

The principal significance of the rent of free tenants in relation to feudal rent as a whole is its predominantly money form. Thus the money rent of free tenants creates a balance in favour of money rent in Cambridgeshire, where on villein holdings labour rent plays an important part; and it makes this general balance in favour of money rent very marked in Oxfordshire and, particularly, in Warwickshire. We have seen that there is more land in free tenure on small manors than on large, and in general the money rent of free holdings plays a more important part on small than on large manors.

If we now ask what form of rent predominates on ecclesiastical and lay manors respectively, we shall come up against the same difficulty as we met when discussing manorial structure, since it is not clear whether the undoubted tendency of church manors to favour the labour service system is a peculiarity of their ecclesiastical character or whether it is connected with their large average size. The large ecclesiastical manors, of which there are so many in Huntingdonshire, give us the purest types of labour service economy—unless, of course, works were replaced by money payments at the lord's will. In Cambridgeshire there is a heavier balance of labour rents over money rents on church manors than on secular ones, in spite of certain special features of the county. In Cambridgeshire there were, apart from the bishopric and priory of Ely, few large religious foundations, and only Ely and Chatteris held large manors.

The highest percentages of money rent are found on the manors of monasteries situated outside the region. In Ickleton (priory of Montmorel [*Monte Maurilii*]), money rent is three times as much as labour rent (£4 3s. 4d. to £1 4s. 4d.),[1] in Oakington (Crowland Abbey) it is also considerably higher (£7 2s. 7d. to £4 19s. 10d.).[2] But particularly remarkable is the development of money rent on the manor of Histon (Eynsham Abbey), where money rent reaches the enormous figure of £43 8s. 6d., while labour rent is only £5 6s. 0d.[3] On the Cambridgeshire manors of the abbey of Ramsey we observe as usual a predominance of labour over money rents, but on the whole this predominance is not so marked as on the same monastery's Huntingdonshire manors. The fact is that rent-systems depended on the greater or lesser proximity of the manor concerned to the centre of its lord's domains. Labour rent was developed most on the nearer manors, money rent on the more distant.[4]

TABLE 7

VILLEIN RENT ON CHURCH AND LAY MANORS IN CAMBRIDGESHIRE

	Money rent	Labour rent	Produce rent
Church manors ..	£145 15 10	£267 19 3	£9 17 1
	34%	64%	2%
Lay manors	£329 1 6	£457 8 6	£21 16 7
	41%	57%	2%

The predominance of labour rents on ecclesiastical manors is far less clear-cut in the western region, Oxfordshire in particular. Here the labour-rent type of manor is, on the whole, rare. Labour rent and money rent are approximately equal. Even on large church manors we sometimes find examples of a purely money-rent system, or of an insignificant development of labour rent. But on the whole the tendency for labour rent to predominate on the large (and especially the old) ecclesiastical domains is to be observed even in Oxfordshire. In the Warwickshire hundred of Stoneleigh the largest manor basing its economy on labour rent was Bishop's Itchington, belonging to the bishop of Chester—a large manor with 33¼

[1] *R.H.*, ii, 587.   [2] *Ibid.*, ii, 448.   [3] *Ibid.*, 411–12.
[4] This observation can be supported by references to other sources. Gloucester Abbey, while it based its economy exclusively on labour rent in its Gloucestershire manors, admitted money rents to a certain extent on remote manors like Littleton and Linkenholt.

irgates of villein land.[1] The huge manor of Stoneleigh, which
ontained the villages of the Cistercian abbey, is distinguished
y a manorial structure typical of Cistercian estates, and by the
orrespondingly small part played by labour rents. In the
undred of Kineton, where, as we saw, the level of develop-
nent of labour rent is very low, we find nevertheless a series
f large church manors of the type based on labour rent:
Chadshunt, Gaydon and Bishop's Tachbrook (Bishop of
Chester),[2] Honington and Broad Moor (Prior of Coventry).[3]
However, on the large Coventry manors of Hardwick and
Prior's Marston, money rent predominates.[4] Thus the descrip-
ion given for Oxfordshire is, on the whole, correct for Warwick-
hire also.

Thus we can confirm the view, set out in the preceding
chapter, that the typical feudal manor, with numerous villeins
nd the labour-rent system reigning supreme, is developed
n its most clearly defined form on the lands of the old Benedic-
ine abbeys. Here the manorial system found its earliest
levelopment, here it appears in its most typical form, here it
naintains itself longest and most obstinately. The manorial
égimes of the great monasteries and the episcopal sees exerted,
as we have seen, a great influence on the adjacent countryside.
The same can be said of their system of labour rents. The solid,
table and conservative character of the economic arrange-
nents of the old religious foundations can be explained to a
arge extent by the inflexibility of their seignorial rights;
here was no change of lords, and so their estates were not
ubject to alienation or fragmentation as much as lay or
smaller ecclesiastical estates. Hence they established a strict,
ponderous, conservative tradition, which, however, was compatible with intensification of exploitation, on the basis of
old and typically feudal forms. It is quite understandable, therefore, that the 'classical' historians of the manor, basing their
work on the material provided by large, and mainly by
ecclesiastical, estates, should have exaggerated the role of
labour rent in the manorial life of the thirteenth century,
assigning it a dominant position which it did not in fact
occupy.

[1] *R.H.* (War.), fol. 28v.   [2] *Ibid.*, 66–67.
[3] *Ibid.*, 104–07.   [4] *Ibid.*, 74–75.

The Commutation of Labour Rent—Critical Survey of Previous Interpretations

The problem of feudal rent has been raised by historians principally in connection with that of commutation—the transition from payments by the villeins in labour or kind to money payments. But it is in the treatment of this problem perhaps more clearly than anywhere else, that the unsatisfactory character of current theories of the economics of feudal society is revealed.

Broadly speaking, the causes and the progress of commutation were outlined by an earlier generation of historians as follows in the twelfth and thirteenth centuries the 'classical' manor based on the labour dues of unfree peasants, reigned supreme in England. From the end of the thirteenth century, and to some extent much earlier as well, labour dues began to be replaced by money payments. This commutation is connected with the development of a money economy, through which the 'natural economy' basis of the manor was undermined. The growth of the division of labour, the separation of the town from the country, the development of the internal and external markets, all complicate the previous purely consumer aims of the economic activity of both landowner and husbandman, by bringing in commercial motives. The important part played by the state in developing the money economy is also stressed. The prerequisites of commutation are assumed to be the newly-developing link between the peasant economy and the market, and those interests of both the peasant and the lord which were furthered by commutation. The lord had an interest in getting his revenues in money form, as he was developing new requirements as a consumer. From time to time the state levied heavy land taxes, and military campaigns devoured large sums. On the other hand, the lord was eager to free himself from the unprofitable system of labour dues, a system in essence belonging to a natural economy, and to replace this system (under which he was tied hand and foot by manorial custom) by one of hired labour. Commutation was advantageous to the peasants also, freeing them from their most burdensome obligations, and in practice creating a transitional stage on the way to full liberation. To begin with

ie lord could either take money or demand the performance
f works, and there were no definite rules governing money
ayments. But gradually the money payments turn into
dditus assisae and acquire fixed dimensions sanctified by
ianorial custom. Commutation began earlier on the lands
f the king and of the temporal lords than on the manors
elonging to religious bodies, where economic development
toved more slowly.

J. T. Rogers linked the question of the tempo of commuta-
on closely with that of the influence of the Black Death on
ie agrarian development of England, and even to-day the
ommutation problem is often discussed in this connection.
'o a great extent this explains the form of its presentation;
iat is to say, the extent to which the process of commutation
ad advanced by the time of the Black Death is first considered,
nd then the influence of the Black Death on commutation.
'he period immediately preceding the Black Death has there-
ore been the starting-point for most discussions of the subject.

In 1886 Rogers stated that by the middle of the fourteenth
entury only insignificant traces of labour dues remained.[1]
ut later Page demonstrated on the basis of statistical calcula-
'ons that in the middle of the fourteenth century the labour
ues system was still very firmly rooted on the English manor,
t least in the eastern, southern, and midland counties of
.ngland, except Kent.[2] 'As far as labour dues are concerned',
'age concluded, 'it is clear that the villein holding of the mid-
iurteenth century is comparatively little changed from what
was a hundred years before.'[3] But the following objections
ave been made to Page's methods.[4] First, his main source, the
iinisters' accounts, is precise and detailed, but it is very
.ifficult to derive from it information about commutation,
xcept in so far as annual 'sales of works' are concerned.
'urthermore, as Page has nowhere indicated his methods, his
ssertions have to be taken on trust, and a cross check has
ometimes revealed them to be incorrect.[5] Secondly, his
naterial is insufficient since it covers manors in only 19 counties.
'urthermore, it is unevenly distributed geographically; out of

---

[1] *Op. cit.*, i, 81. [2] T. W. Page, *op. cit.* [3] *Ibid.*, 47.
[4] Cf. Vinogradoff, *E.H.R.* xv, 774; Feiling, *E.H.R.*, xxvi, 335; Gray, *E.H.R.*,
xix, 627 sqq.
[5] See, for instance, Levett, *O.S.S.L.H.*, v, 147 sqq.

19 counties, 7 are represented by only one or two manor
Finally, the material relates for the most part to ecclesiastic;
estates, the fullest use of all being made of the documents (
Ramsey Abbey. Out of 81 manors, 33 belong to persor
unknown, and only 8 are known to belong to lay person
including 3 royal manors, while 39 belong to religious found;
tions, and 10 of these to Ramsey Abbey. It is thus understanc
able that little Huntingdonshire, where the main complex (
the Ramsey domains lay, is the best represented of the countie;
with 11 manors. Page's material, therefore, only justific
conclusions of a very limited character—namely, that on
number of manors, mostly ecclesiastical, in southern an
eastern England and the Midlands, we find a well-develope
system of labour services. If, using Page's material, one make
separate calculations for the lay manors, the conclusion
reached are quite different conclusions.

The discussion of commutation was guided into a completel
new direction by H. L. Gray[1] who introduced a new source
well known to genealogists, but little used by economi
historians—the inquisitions *post Mortem*. Gray studied thes
inquisitions for the period 1334–42, using 521 documents in al
The material is more or less evenly distributed over th
counties, and relates exclusively to lay estates. Gray's calcula
tions are based on slightly different principles from those c
Page. According to Gray, Page loses sight of one very importan
class of rent, namely the *redditus assisae*, regular money pay
ments made by both villeins and freeholders. Other payment
by villeins such as aid, cartage, court revenues, and the revenu
from mills (which were often let out at rent), were ignored b
Page, and thus led him to construct a false picture of th
character of manorial economy. In view of this, Gray base
his calculations on a comparison of labour dues (or rathe
their assessed value) with *redditus assisae* and aid. He leave
aside other money dues as of secondary importance. He doe
not separate the *redditus assisae* of free and unfree tenants, as i
the majority of cases the source does not allow this to be done
On the basis of these comparisons Gray divides all his manor
into four groups, and considers the geographical distribution o

---

[1] 'Commutation of villein services in England before the Black Death', *E.H.R.*
xxix.

hese groups over the various counties. Page's proposition
hat proximity to London had an influence on the rapid
progress of commutation turns out to be unjustified; the exact
opposite is more correct.

To the west and north of a line drawn from Boston to the
mouth of the Severn there are no labour services at all to be
found, or only insignificant traces. In the south-east,
none are found in Kent. For the rest of south-eastern England
Gray studied 309 manors. On half of them there are no labour
services, or they are very insignificant. A well-developed
labour-dues system was found only on one-sixth, a more rudimentary one on one-third of the total number of manors.
At the same time labour dues increase as one moves towards
the south-east, especially in the counties of Norfolk, Suffolk,
Essex, Hertfordshire and Sussex.

Gray considers material relating to church domains
separately, especially the ministers' accounts of the estates of
nine bishoprics, during the time when they were in the hands
of the king. This material is more dispersed chronologically.
The conclusions reached are practically the same as those
indicated by the inquisitions. In the north and west labour
dues have been commuted; in the south-east the labour-dues
system, generally speaking, is still preserved. He also uses
monastic material, namely documents concerning the lands of
alien priories (taken over in 1325), the 1338 survey of the lands
of the Hospitallers (including those lands taken over from the
Templars), and several other sources, but omits that material
which was the main basis for the work of Page and others,
namely that relating to the manors of the great monasteries.
His conclusions are that commutation followed the same course
in both lay and church estates; that in the north-west by the
time of the Black Death only a few labour services were left,
while in the south-east they are met with everywhere, and in
some places are the rule rather than the exception. Thus,
broadly speaking, he returns to Rogers' point of view; to a
certain extent Page is correct so far as the south-eastern area
is concerned, but it would be incorrect to apply his conclusions
to the whole of England.

In Gray's researches the question of commutation is directly
linked with that of the growth of a money economy in medieval

England. This produces in the last resort an unresolved con
tradiction. In establishing a relation between labour service
and money payments (not only of villeins but of free tenant
as well), does Gray solve the problem of commutation? Ar
money payments always the result of commutation of labou
dues? Without a doubt he has shown very clearly that by th
middle of the fourteenth century the labour-service systen
was not nearly so strongly developed in the north and wes
as in the south and particularly the south-east. But does thi
mean that in the north and west commutation has gon
further—that is, that the system had once held sway here
to give way later to a system of money payments? If thi
is so, how is one to explain the rapidity of the process c
commutation in the most economically backward areas of th
country? And why do labour services keep their hold longe
in the areas of the liveliest circulation of money? There is n
doubt that Gray made important discoveries; but, because h
accepted current ideas about the universal supremacy of th
labour-due system in feudal times, and regarded commutatio
as a natural result of the development of a money economy
he was unable to explain the results of his researches.

A question of central significance for the whole history c
the manorial system is the origin of the money payments mad
by the villeins, *redditus assisae* in particular. Gray's whol
argument presupposes that the main constituent is commute
labour dues. Vinogradoff believed that money rents had a dua
origin;[1] in part they represented *gafol*, the immemorial pay
ments from those holding land, in part they represented *ma
mol* or *mail*—the result of commuted labour dues. Payment
such as *aid* and *tallage* were not the result of commutatior
though some small customary money rents were the result c
services not connected with the demesne.[2] But what was th
origin of the main body of payments by the villeins? Fo
Vinogradoff the answer to this question was clear, in as muc
as his main material came from the estates of the great religiou
foundations of the southern half of England, where in the thir
teenth century the system of labour services reigned supreme.

Miss Levett, on the other hand, analysed the *redditus assisa*

[1] Vinogradoff, *Growth of the Manor*, 329, and *Villainage*, 291, 307.
[2] N. Neilson, *O.S.S.L.H.*, ii.

in the manorial accounts of the estate, and concluded that these payments did not result from the commutation of labour dues.[1] Her cautious conclusion was that the basis of *redditus assisae* was the early money payments (*gabulum* or *gafol*) which in their turn may have been the result of commuted produce rents. Her analysis of the constituent parts of *redditus assisae* showed that they included no commuted labour dues but a good number of commuted produce levies. At times money rent may even have preceded labour dues and been replaced by them. But, if that is the case, what remains of Gray's arguments so far as commutation is concerned? If the money payments dealt with by Gray (*redditus assisae* and *auxilium*) are not the result of the commutation of labour rent, then the whole argument is incorrectly framed.

So far, however, no adequate study of the relative extent of the labour service and money-rent systems in twelfth- and thirteenth-century England has been made. But a number of historians in the last half century have shown that the process of commutation (in other words, the growth of money rent) cannot be regarded as a continuous line of development resulting from the growth of a 'money economy'.[2] Miss Neilson, in her book on Ramsey Abbey, noted cases of an increase in labour services and a fall in money rent between the twelfth and thirteenth centuries. Professor Gras's book on the English corn market demonstrated (perhaps with some exaggeration) that in the thirteenth century there was a growth of economic activity generally, and in particular a development of the corn market, with a rise in corn prices, when labour services were at their height. And, of course, Gray's calculations show that it was in the economically most developed areas that labour services were kept longest in the fourteenth century.

By 1935 I had come to the conclusion[3] that while money rents were prevalent in the thirteenth century, nevertheless the development of the corn market sometimes led to the growth of labour services, even at the expense of money rent, but mainly in the most advanced areas and on certain types of

[1] Levett, *O.S.S.L.H.*, v, 14–20. See also her article 'Financial Organization of the Manor', *Ec. H.R.*, i (also printed in *Studies in Manorial History*, 1938).
[2] Leaving aside the dubious question of the 'feudal reaction' after the Black Death.
[3] In *The English Village in the Thirteenth Century* (in Russian).

M

manor. And in fact local studies have shown that developments of money rents and labour services are by no means uniform in different parts of the country.

The theory that the thirteenth century was a period of increasing labour services has been developed by Professor Postan.[1] It would appear that he proceeds from Dopsch's conception of the medieval estate as a quasi-capitalist organization closely connected with the market. Consequently he assumes that the amount of labour service is determined by the labour requirements of the demesne. This demand, as well as the size of the demesne farm, was in turn determined by the profits to be made from the sale of corn. Hence, the demand for villein services rose and fell with the rise and fall of these profits. In the twelfth century, the contraction of the demesne and development of money rent at the same time, were thus a consequence of unfavourable market conditions. On the other hand, the increase in population in the thirteenth century, the growth of the corn market and a steep rise in the price of corn caused an increase in demesne farming and a growth in labour services.

Whilst I do not agree with Professor Postan's conception of the manor as a quasi-capitalist organization, nor with his theory of the development of money rent in the thirteenth century, his observation that the development of the corn market and of the profits of corn production caused a considerable development of labour services in certain parts of England in the thirteenth century, is certainly correct. Yet this tendency could only slow down—it could not stop—the general trend towards the development of money rent which had begun in the twelfth century.

FIELD OF STUDY WIDENED BY USE OF INQUISITIONS POST MORTEM

Our work on the 1279 Hundred Rolls led to the conclusion that money rent was even then the quantitatively predominant form of rent in the Midlands. At the same time we noticed a certain unevenness in the distribution of the different forms of rent over the various regions. But the territories covered by the

[1] 'The Chronology of Labour Services' in *T.R.H.S.*, 4th S., xx, and subsequent publications.

Hundred Rolls are economically too homogeneous for it to be possible to establish any general rules from them for the whole of England. In order to decide whether money rent was as common in other regions, and to explore the connection between regional peculiarities, both economic and geographical and the predominant form of rent, we must therefore extend our observations over a wider area. This can be done on a reasonably wide scale, with the help of the inquisitions *post Mortem*. The dangers involved in the use of this source have been explained; but since our object is not a detailed analysis of individual documents, but a general picture of the distribution of different forms of rent, we may, observing all due caution, use the inquisitions in order to seek an answer to our questions.

In my study of the inquisitions *post Mortem* for the first forty years of their existence, that is, for the approximate period 1230–70, I tried to choose material more or less evenly distributed over the whole of England, and fixed on the figure of 10 manors per county, which should have made a total of about 400 manors for the whole country.[1] It nevertheless proved impossible to attain a completely even distribution. For some counties there was abundant and detailed material, but for others inquisitions for 10 manors could not be found. In quality, too, the material proved to be very uneven. For Essex I found ample material (61 manors) and enough for eastern England generally (33 manors for Suffolk and 21 for Norfolk), but there was a shortage for other counties; and while there was detailed and clear information for Northumberland, other counties, such as those of the northern Danelaw, yielded only unprecise and summary accounts.

Should we then refuse to use the material in the inquisitions? Independent, and especially, detailed conclusions based solely on this material would be risky, since the figures derived from it are neither clear nor reliably accurate. But a comparison of these figures over large areas does reveal some characteristic features, even if somewhat vague in outline. And if these results are confirmed by other sources and by conclusions

---

[1] For each county I have taken the earliest documents available, trying not to go outside the reign of Henry III (that is, beyond 1272), and only in cases when the material thus selected was insufficient have I passed on to the first years of the reign of Edward I.

previously reached, their significance is considerable. Therefore although the picture built up from the inquisitions is
not always clear, the attentive eye can distinguish in it lines
which it would be difficult to make out without their help.

One of the most important achievements of modern scholar-
ship is its insistence on careful local differentiation where both
material and conclusions are concerned. We cannot speak of
England in general, as Seebohm and Vinogradoff did, assemb-
ling indiscriminately data from various places throughout
the country. Before putting forward arguments concerning
England as a whole we must analyse the separate regions with
their local peculiarities, and then unite the results we have
obtained into one complex but differentiated whole. The more
or less even distribution of the inquisition material I have
collected to a certain extent ensures the fulfilment of this
fundamental requirement. Of course, the boundaries of
counties do not coincide with the geographical demarcation
lines of the distribution of rent-forms. The problem of the
division of medieval England into economic regions is still a
very debatable one. Scholars such as Stenton, Douglas and
Jolliffe have shown the historical peculiarities of certain
regions, especially during and before the twelfth century. But
by the thirteenth century regional historical peculiarities had
begun to be evened out. In this process the conditions of the
market began to play a large part. However, the division
proposed by N. S. B. Gras, based on the average levels of corn
prices, does not appear to me convincing.[1] H. L. Gray's
division of England into two parts, according to the extent
to which labour services predominated and his further division
into regions according to the prevailing field systems, are
inapplicable or irrelevant to my purpose.[2] The division into
regions which I follow is tentative and is partially determined
by the unevenness of my material. There are before us two
regions with well-defined individual characteristics: the
northern, including Northumberland and Cumberland (with
a small amount of material for Westmorland and Lancashire);
and the eastern, including the counties of Lincolnshire,
Huntingdonshire, Cambridgeshire, Norfolk, Suffolk, Hert-

[1] *Evolution of the English Corn Market*, Chap. ii.
[2] See *E.H.R.*, xxix, and *English Field Systems* (1915).

fordshire, Essex and Middlesex—an economically advanced area.[1] The characteristics of Yorkshire attach it partly to the northern and partly to the eastern group. The southern counties—Surrey, Sussex, Hampshire, Dorset, Wiltshire, Somersetshire, Devonshire and Gloucestershire—are little distinguished from the southern Midlands, Bedfordshire, Buckinghamshire, Berkshire, Oxfordshire and Warwickshire. For the other counties there is little material in the inquisitions, and even that is not always clear. Thus the characteristics of the western counties (Herefordshire, Worcestershire, Shropshire, Cheshire) and of the northern Midlands (Rutland, Leicestershire, Nottinghamshire, Derbyshire and Staffordshire) can only be tentatively sketched, with many qualifications, and need further confirmation.

NORTHERN GROUP OF MANORS

I shall begin my survey with the northern group. The basic material was provided by 14 manors in Northumberland, 12 in Cumberland, and 2 in Westmorland. The 4 Lancashire surveys are very summary and far from clear. Durham is not represented at all. Thus the material relates to the most northerly marches of England. In most cases the surveys are clear and detailed (especially for Northumberland); but there are also gaps in vital places. It is common knowledge that in the northern counties the pasturing of stock played a decisive part. The inquisitions, however, rarely refer to pasture lands and their value, and where the revenue from pasture grounds is given, it is quite insignificant. It seems that owing to the difficulty of calculating it pasture revenue was commonly omitted from the assessment.

We have already seen that in thirteenth-century Northumbria manorialization had made considerable advances, but that the Northumbrian manor still preserved many characteristic features of the former 'shire'—namely, a large total area, a comparatively small demesne, and a considerable area of land in free tenure. Free holdings in Northumbria paid a very small rent. Thus, in Skelton (Cumberland), the whole

---

[1] This latter is one of the most fertile, thickly-populated and richest regions of England, including London, the main corn export centre, King's Lynn, and a number of the most important commercial and industrial centres.

quite considerable area in free tenure (5 carucates and 6 bovates) pays only 6*d*. Many of the holdings pay nothing at all, or involve services of a non-agrarian character, particularly military service. Sixty acres in free tenure in Hadstone (Northumberland) pay ½ lb. of pepper, and so on. Nevertheless, the total sum of rent from free land is very considerable; for 17 manors where the free money rents can be isolated they amount together to £53 12*s*. 3*d*.

Corresponding to the slight development of the demesne, we find a still slighter development of labour service. In 9 manors there is none; in most cases it is reckoned in with other dues. It can be extracted for 9 manors only, on which it amounts only to about 10 per cent of the dues of tenants.

By contrast with the south, a large part was played by produce rent on the northern manors. Part was paid directly to the lord of the manor in the form of levies of malt, iron and salt; and in Warkworth (Northumberland) contributions in kind make up the major portion of the rent of the bondmen. But the major part of this produce rent was levied by means of seigniorial monopolies. Revenue from mills, usually insignificant on southern manors, is huge in the north, much greater than the revenue from the demesne arable. As far as one can determine its composition, it was mostly in the form of flour and malt. Sometimes it was a regular rent independent of the amount of milling actually done. Sometimes it was linked with full or partial commutation, when the payment of multure was included in the rent of tenants both free and unfree.[1] Mills were sometimes let (*firmantur*) for a rent consisting of contributions in kind, flour for the most part.[2] Apart from mills we find other monopolies, such as the oven (*furnum*), the bakehouse (*pistrina*) and the brew-house (*bracina*).

Comparing the separate constituents of rent revenues, so far as they can be distinguished, we can reduce them to approximately the following proportions: money rents, 54 per cent; produce rents and monopoly charges, 36 percent;[3] labour

---

[1] Thus at Linton, Northumberland, the freeholders pay 5*s*. *pro multura*. At Hadstone *multura computatur in firmis bondorum*.

[2] Beetham, Westmorland.

[3] Not all this amount was paid in kind, however, and some part of it should probably go in with money rent.

rent, 10 per cent. Since, however, labour rent is distinguish-able on only 9 out of 32 manors, it should probably be lowered considerably for the whole region. Money rent was paid by free tenants (9 per cent), bondmen and cottars (45 per cent).[1]

Thus, in the north we find a manorial system, but one of a peculiar type. Labour dues are very insignificant. On the other hand produce rents play a comparatively large part. But the dominating role is still played, even in this far-off corner of England, by money rents, which make up more than half of all the payments made by tenants; and it is the rents of the unfree peasantry which predominate. The demesne stands out quite clearly, but is nevertheless insignificant in comparison with the large total area of the manor, which sometimes takes in several villages. A major gap in our picture is due to the absence of information on the pastoral economy of the demesne and the holdings. We can only guess at its importance.

NORTHERN DANELAW

It would be extremely interesting to carry out a similar analysis for the northern Danelaw, whose characteristic features have been described by Stenton. But the inquisitions for this region are extremely scanty and summary, except for two counties—Yorkshire (20 manors) and Lincolnshire (16). It may be that the scanty and summary nature of the material hides peculiarities common to the whole region, but it is also possible that by the thirteenth century the process of economic development had already partially erased the historical peculiarities of this settlement area of Danish warriors. Thus Lincolnshire, economically, seems very similar to the eastern region lying adjacent to it on the south, though this may be due to the fact that it is represented in our material mainly by manors lying in its southern part. Yorkshire has an indivi-duality of its own. Our material for the most part relates to the southern or 'Danish' part of the county, not to the 'Northumbrian' section, and the Yorkshire manor seems to be of a type lying midway between the northern and the southern. It is akin to the northern type in the limited development of

[1] This proportion can be arrived at on the basis of material relating to 18 manors.

labour rent. On the 9 manors where one can distinguish such rents, they amount to only £4 5s. 5d. as against £37 18s 4d. in money rents and £9 14s. 1d. from monopolies, and even then £2 5s. 5d. of these labour rents might be commuted into money payments. Another point of similarity is the extent of seigniorial monopolies, especially the lord's mill, and the fact that a considerable part of the monopoly payments were made in kind, but, apart from the monopolies, produce rent was insignificant. The tenants of Yorkshire manors were frequently spread over several villages. Court revenues are very small, but this may be partly due to the fact that some of them were included in rents.[1] But even where the court revenues are given separately, they are quite insignificant.[2] As in the north, the extent of the pastoral economy, on which only the barest of information is given, cannot be ascertained, although it was probably important. This is as far as the resemblance to the northern manors goes. The average size of the Yorkshire manor is not great—half as large as in the north. The demesne is much more important, as is free tenure, though there is no evidence that free land was proportionately greater in area. The proportions of free rent, villein money rent, labour rent, and mill revenue are (for 9 manors), 21, 52, 8, 19 per cent respectively, but as part of the labour rents may have been commuted, the percentage figure for labour rent should be lowered still further. The area of villein land is approximately one-and-a-half times the area of the demesne arable. The extent of free land cannot be calculated in all cases, but we have sufficient evidence to indicate that it was very considerable. The development of assarts among the lands of the villeins is noteworthy: 415 acres at Slaidburn (where assart rent makes up the major portion of villein money rent), and 100 acres at Bradford.

The material for the remaining counties of the northern Danelaw is only scanty, and difficult to use for our purposes, since labour rents are only reckoned separately in a very few cases. I have examined inquisitions for 4 manors in Rutland, 8 in Leicestershire, 12 in Nottinghamshire, and 10 in Derbyshire;

---

[1] At Linton (Wharfedale) the rents of villeins are reckoned *cum mercheto et tallagio* (C. Hen. III File 23–7).
[2] Topcliffe (ibid.).

but only for 1 manor in Leicestershire, 2 in Nottinghamshire, and 2 in Derbyshire, can labour rents be calculated separately. In Derbyshire (Staveley and Walton) they are insignificant; in Leicestershire (Evington) and Nottinghamshire (Holme) they are quite large. Often it is stated that there are no labour rents. But there is not sufficient evidence to estimate the comparative extent of labour rent in the northern Danelaw, though perhaps one should not follow Gray in minimizing its significance. Free rent, on the other hand, is almost always given separately, showing a small percentage in Rutland and Leicestershire (9—13 per cent) and a higher one in Nottingham and Derby (23—27 per cent). Generally speaking, free rent is comparatively small for counties where we may assume that a considerable amount of land was held in free tenure. This suggests that free holdings carried only light rents. Mill revenues on some manors are quite high,[1] but the average is no different from that of the southern counties, indicating that monopolies played only a secondary role. The material is still more unpromising for Staffordshire. Here we have only two surveys, which, of course, provide no basis for any conclusions whatever. But it should be noted that on one of these two manors (Clayton) there are no villeins, while on the other (Madeley) there are no labour rents and all dues are translated into money form (*firma*).

WESTERN GROUP

The information on the counties lying west and south-west of this group—Cheshire, Shropshire, Worcestershire and Herefordshire—is equally unsatisfactory. For Cheshire we have inquisitions for 6 manors, for Shropshire 10, for Worcestershire 8, and for Herefordshire 5, but not all are sufficiently detailed, nor do they always give the essential information, and it is difficult to pick out any local peculiarities. Only in Cheshire do we see, as in Northumbria and Yorkshire, enormous revenues from mills, exceeding the revenues of the demesne arable, and providing evidence of a great development of monopolies. If one counts multure as rent, mill revenue is 34 per cent of the total—nearly as much as in Northumbria. But by the time we reach Shropshire these levies fall to one-

---

[1] Empingham, Rutland—£13 6s. 8d. Staveley, Derby,—£8.

third of this figure, and they are still lower in Worcestershire and Herefordshire. Thus we can outline the region of high monopoly charges—it is the north of England, bounded on the south by the southern borders of Yorkshire and Cheshire. Labour rent here can be reasonably accurately assessed. It amounts in the different counties to between 14 and 26 per cent of the total rent, and on the average to about 20 per cent. It is more difficult to isolate the rent of free holdings; but it seems to amount to something like 16–18 per cent of the total. The greatest proportion is accounted for by the money rents of villeins, which come to 53–61 per cent. About 11 per cent is accounted for by mill revenues.

It must be admitted that the vast and less studied area which takes in the northern and western parts of England is far from fully or evenly represented in our material. Durham is not mentioned at all; there are too few figures for Lancashire, Westmorland, and Staffordshire, and for a number of counties the documents are insufficiently detailed. It is in fact only the northern marches—Northumberland and Cumberland—and Yorkshire (mainly its southern part) that stand out more or less clearly. The remaining parts of west and north England appear only in very dim outlines in the inquisitions. But it is at any rate possible to note some sort of outline, even if it is a vague one. In particular, we can recognize (or have at least good reason to presume) the presence of labour rent in all the counties; but it plays everywhere only a secondary part, especially in those counties which are best represented in our material. Everywhere it is outweighed by money rents, and in the northern counties by produce rents. On the other hand, the inquisitions provide singularly little information on revenues from pasturing, and this is an important limitation in a region predominantly mountainous in character and rich in pastures.

The south-eastern half of England is represented more fully and evenly in our material. For convenience, this region may be divided into three groups—the *eastern*, including the counties of Lincoln, Northampton, Cambridge, Hertford, Norfolk, Suffolk, Essex, and Middlesex; the *central* (southern Midlands), including Bedford, Buckingham, Berkshire, Oxford, Warwick, and the *southern*—the counties of Surrey, Sussex,

Hampshire, Dorset, Wiltshire, Somerset, Gloucester, Devon. Kent, of course, stands apart because of its peculiar manorial structure.

EASTERN GROUP

The basic material for the eastern group comes from Essex (61 manors), Suffolk (33 manors), and Norfolk (21 manors). These numerous surveys indicate very clearly the various forms of rent, and distinguish labour from money rents particularly well. The Northampton and Lincoln surveys are also quite numerous (16 manors each) but often summary, and they do not always distinguish the various forms of rent. The Cambridgeshire surveys are scanty and summary (8 manors), as are those for Hertfordshire (9 manors), and Huntingdonshire (7 manors). But for two of these counties we have abundant material available in the Hundred Rolls of 1279. For Middlesex we have only three surveys, but they are quite detailed. For the eastern region, I have used 175 surveys in all, but the geographical distribution of this material, both qualitatively and quantitatively, is uneven.

The eastern group is marked by the greatest development of labour rent in the whole country, varying over the different counties from 31 to 55 per cent, and averaging 39 per cent of the total sum of rent. In no single county included in the other groups does the percentage figure for labour rent reach even the lowest figure found in the eastern group; though it should be said that in the counties of the eastern group labour rent is not always precisely distinguishable from other forms of rent. It is most exactly defined in Essex, where it can be distinguished on almost all the manors, in Suffolk, Norfolk and Hertfordshire. It can be defined for all the 8 Cambridgeshire and the 3 Middlesex manors. But in Huntingdonshire considerable labour services are distinguishable in only one case, and then not very clearly. But other sources, particularly the Hundred Rolls, confirm a very considerable development of labour services in this county. The Hundred Rolls also reinforce our conception of Cambridgeshire as a county with comparatively high labour rents owed by villeins. In any case, in spite of all unevenness, our material shows us very definitely a strong development of labour rents in the region. Some qualifying statements are necessary in the case of Lincolnshire and Northamptonshire. Although in both counties we have material for 16 manors, in Lincoln extensive labour services appear on 4; on 2 there were apparently no such dues, and on 8 they are reckoned in with the money rents of the villeins. In 2 out of these 8 cases labour services seem to make up the greater part of the general rent assessments (Tallington, Uffington), but the other cases are not clear. Nevertheless, the Lincolnshire manor is closer in type to the eastern than to the northern. Very striking is the great development of revenues from meadow and marsh land, connected with the peculiarities of the Lincolnshire landscape (a marshy coastal area).

Northamptonshire, which stretches away far to the west of the main body of eastern counties, represents a certain departure from the scheme we have indicated of a geographical distribution of the incidence of labour services. It is here that we find what seem to be the highest figures for labour rent, though this impression is based on the inquisitions for only 6 manors, and the bulk of labour dues are found on 1 manor alone, the earl of Gloucester's manor of Rothwell. But on at least 2 or 3 other manors we are entitled to assume if not a pre-dominance, at least a significant percentage of labour rents (Houghton, Paulerspury, and perhaps Aynho). These heavy labour dues may be peculiar to Northamptonshire, suggesting conditions similar to those of the eastern counties, but the impression may also be the result of a chance selection of material. The labour and money rents of villeins in the eastern grouping are approximately equal. In the eastern counties also a comparatively high percentage of rents is received from free tenants, highest of all in Cambridgeshire and lowest in Huntingdonshire. On the average free rent makes up 28 per cent of the sum total of rent—a much higher percentage than is found anywhere in the northern and western half of England, not excluding Yorkshire. But this tells us more of the comparative territorial extent of free tenure than of the comparative rate of rent.

SOUTHERN AND CENTRAL GROUPS

Our material is evenly distributed in the southern group of counties and the south Midlands. Here we have examined inquisitions for an average of 10 manors per county, the smallest number being in Surrey (6), the largest (17) in Hampshire. The structural difference between the two groups is insignificant and they can be considered together. The figures for labour rent as a percentage of total rent almost coincide when averaged for the two groups (23 and 24 per cent), varying from 17 per cent (Devonshire) to 30 per cent (Somersetshire and Gloucestershire), and thus being higher than those for the north and west and lower than those for the east. In all these counties there is a marked predominance of money rent, which averages about 77 per cent, and is nowhere lower than 70 per cent of the total. Free rent grows proportionately less from east to west: the highest figures are in Bedfordshire (41 per cent), Buckinghamshire (31 per cent), Sussex (34 per cent) and Surrey (27 per cent), falling to 13 per cent in Devonshire, 12 per cent in Somersetshire, and 8 per cent in Gloucestershire. Everywhere the greater part of both villein rent and total rent consists of money payments by villeins. These vary from 38 per cent of total rent in Sussex to 70 per cent in Devonshire, and on the average are more than double the amount of labour rent.

Kent is unique. On the Kentish manors villeins and labour services are to be found, but the latter are insignificant, coming to only 6 per cent of the total rent, less than in any other county in England. The form of the inquisitions does not allow us to separate the money rents of freemen and villeins. The revenue from demesne arable and meadow is small compared with total rent, but we find here a considerable revenue from pasture and woodland held in severalty. Evidently the seizure by the lords of common lands went forward more rapidly in Kent than in the other counties. Considerable revenues, in comparison with the neighbouring counties, are received from mills and from courts.

LABOUR RENT AND MONEY RENT ON SOME LARGE LAY ESTATES

Owing to the character of the inquisitions we cannot compare the proportions of the various forms of rent on lay and church, or on large and small manors. The inquisitions deal exclusively with lay, and almost exclusively with large or medium-sized manors, in whose structure we cannot expect to find noticeable differences. Furthermore, the material is too scanty and too dispersed for detailed generalizations. Nevertheless, on a number of manors belonging to great magnates we find figures showing a very high percentage of labour rent to total rent,[1] and this is particularly true of the manors of Richard Clare, seventh Earl of Gloucester, the famous baronial leader who was one of the greatest of feudal lords, and whose estates were an outstanding example of the labour service system. Sixteen of his manors are surveyed—13 in the eastern group (4 in Essex, 4 in Norfolk, 3 in Suffolk, one each in Hertfordshire and Northamptonshire respectively), and 3 in Kent.[2] On some manors the demesne arable is exceptionally large,[3] and these evidently form part of the main complex of the earl's domain. Generally speaking, labour rents on the Earl of Gloucester's manors are very considerable. On the manors in the eastern counties the percentage relationship of free rent, villein money rent and labour rent, is 23–30–47 per cent. On his Kentish manors labour rent accounts for 13 per cent of the total.[4] If we omit these manors, the average percentage figure for labour rent to total rent in Kent falls from 6 to $4\frac{1}{4}$ per cent. Hugh de Vere, Earl of Oxford, was another great feudal lord. On seven of his manors, in the counties of Suffolk, Cambridgeshire, Middlesex and Oxfordshire, the labour services of the villeins were worth more than twice their money rents and account for about half of the total of rent. However, he also owned manors of another type. On the lands of the Earl of Devon (in Devonshire and the Isle of Wight), the labour dues and money rents of villeins about balance one another, and free rent is a negligible quantity. The Earl of

[1] On the manors of the Earl of Gloucester—Bardfield, Claret, Hersham, Thaxted (C. Hen. III, File 27/5); of the Earl of Oxford—Canfield, Earl's Colne, Bentley, Doddinghurst, Ramsey, Bumpstead, Hedingham, Yeldham, Downham, Messing (C. Hen. III, File 31/1); of the Earl of Norfolk—Chesterford, Dovercourt, Hardwick (C. Hen. III, File 38/17).

[2] In Essex—Bardfield, Claret, Hersham, Thaxted; in Norfolk—Wells and Warham, Walsingham, Bircham, Crimplesham (File 27/5); in Suffolk—Hundon, Clare, Disning (ibid.); in Huntingdonshire—Stanton (ibid.); in Northamptonshire —Rothwell (ibid.); in Kent—Eltham, Luckiñgdale, Yalding (ibid.).

[3] 1,146 acres at Thaxted, 1,109 acres at Hundon, 1,199 at Clare, 1,256 at Disning.

[4] It is only on the Earl of Gloucester's manors (Eltham) that we find villeins mentioned in Kent.

Norfolk's estate also was not dominated by the labour service system.

Conclusions

In all the territorial groupings, and in almost all counties where it is possible to distinguish labour dues from the villein's other dues, money rent predominates over labour rent. The highest average figures for labour services come from the eastern group of counties, but even there the overall average figure for labour rent, compared on a percentage basis with money rent, is only 39 per cent. This figure falls, in the central and southern groups, to 23–24 per cent, declines still further in the west, and descends to next to nothing in Yorkshire, Northumbria and Kent. Produce rent is insignificant over the whole country except the north. Furthermore, we must recall once again that the government surveys and extents regularly minimize the relative importance of money rent, and in part also of produce rent. Thus, after widening our material to cover almost the whole country, the conclusion previously reached on the basis of the Hundred Rolls is confirmed; that is, that the quantitatively predominant form of rent in England in the thirteenth century was money rent. In the material we have surveyed, money rent comprises certainly not less, and probably more, than two-thirds of the total sum of rent. And even in the dues owed by villeins money rents predominate throughout all England, with the possible exception of the eastern region.

Money rents come in part from free holdings, in part from villein holdings. Usually, but not always, our sources enable us to distinguish between the two. The result we obtain by doing so is once again considerably at variance with the common conception of the manorial system. The rent from free holdings in the eastern and central counties comes to 28–29 per cent of the total rent, and in no single group of counties does it fall lower than 18 per cent, except for Northumbria, where, as we have seen, free holdings were very large but paid very little rent. On the average one-quarter, certainly not less than one-fifth, of the whole sum of rent came from the money payments of free tenants. Since free holdings paid on the average much lighter rents than villein holdings, these facts attest the existence of a considerable percentage of free land among the general mass of holdings. More precise conclusions would be incautious, but we can at any rate conclude that free holdings paying money rent played a far more conspicuous part in the English village of the mid-thirteenth century than it has been customary to suppose. Nevertheless the greatest proportion of rent was supplied by the money payments of villeins. The unfree English peasant paid on the average more than half his dues in money.

Money rent, then, predominates quantitatively in thirteenth-century England over labour rent, and even more so over produce rent, which played a significant part only in the most economically backward areas, those of the north. But a quantitative analysis alone is not enough to determine the real significance of one or the other form of rent. Here we must note two further important points. First, the analysis of the Hundred Rolls, confirmed by research into the inquisitions *post Mortem*, has shown that labour rents play a greater part on larger manors than on small. Secondly, the geographical distribution of labour rent has a very specific character. Table No. 8 and Map No. 2 show very clearly that labour rents were concentrated principally in the east of the country, with a gradual decrease as one moves farther away—insignificant as one moves south, more noticeable as one moves west, and very noticeable as one moves north. This, however, reflects the distribution of population in England, which was most dense in the east, and it reflects also—with the exception of Kent, whose development was abnormal—the rate of development of monetary and commercial relations. As we have already seen, the special features of the eastern region favoured the development there of the agriculturalist as a commodity-producer; and at the same time it is in this very area that we find the heaviest labour dues. Thus the traditional picture of the manorial system at its classical period of development appears to be almost inverted. Instead of the usual picture of the predominance of labour rent, which was gradually commuted under the influence of the development of a money economy, we see the predominance of money rent, with the highest percentage of labour rent in the areas of the greatest development of economic activity. The major role played by labour services in the most thickly populated and economically best developed regions of England, and likewise on the large estates of the politically most powerful group within the class of feudal land-owners, is a warning that we must not underestimate the social importance of labour rent.

The characteristic peculiarities of the eastern group of counties continued into the fourteenth century. In Gray's table[1] showing the level of labour rents in the middle of the fourteenth century the first four places, also the sixth and seventh, are occupied by counties of the eastern group. Thus the eastern grouping clung to the labour-service system for a long time; and it is noteworthy that this is the very region which gave birth to the peasant rising of 1381. Essex was the main centre of the revolt. Among the other counties which were caught up in the rising we find almost all those belonging to the eastern group—Suffolk, Norfolk, Hertfordshire, Cambridge-shire, Huntingdonshire, Northamptonshire, Lincolnshire. It was the Essex peasants who put forward the Mile End programme, of which the basic demand was the abolition of serfdom and labour dues. Outside the eastern group there was a wide revolutionary movement in Kent alone, where the rebels put forward a programme of their own (the Smithfield programme), concerned primarily with the seizure of common rights by the lords, the landlessness of the peasantry, and labour legislation. Outside these counties we find only minor dis-turbances, and these are often directed against the great ecclesiastical lords: in Buckingham against the abbot of St. Albans, in Bedfordshire against the prior of Dunstable, in Derbyshire against the abbot of Dale. We know little of the disturbances in other counties, especially how widespread they were among the population, or of the part played by the peasantry in them. But in the eastern region the revolt expressed the conflict between the peasant who was turning

---

[1] *E.H.R.*, xxix, 635. We differ from Gray's observations with regard to Lincoln-shire and Northamptonshire, where on the majority of manors labour dues are not distinguishable as separate entities in the general assessment of rents (which Gray mistakenly assumes to mean an absence of labour dues), and Huntingdon-shire, where his material is confined to four manors in all, three of which belong to the 'D' group and are suspect for our purposes.

N

TABLE 8

PERCENTAGE RATIO OF MONEY AND LABOUR RENT ACCORDING
TO THE INQUISITIONS *POST MORTEM*

Group and County	Money rent (of freehold)	Money rent (of villein land)	Estimate of labour rent of villeins	Number of surveys used
EASTERN GROUP:				
Essex	32	31	37	61
Suffolk	16	42	42	38
Norfolk	27	41	32	21
Cambridgeshire	45	15	40	8
Hertfordshire	69*		31	9
Huntingdonshire	12	88*		7
Northamptonshire	22	23	55[1]	17
Middlesex	38	29	33	3
Lincolnshire	17	51	32	16
FOR THE WHOLE GROUP:	28	33	39	175
SOUTH MIDLANDS:				
Bedfordshire	41	42	17	9
Buckinghamshire	31	41	28	10
Berkshire	24	58	18	8
Oxfordshire	25	46	29	10
Warwickshire	23	54	22	9
FOR THE WHOLE GROUP:	29	48	23	46
NORTH MIDLANDS:				
Rutland	9	91*		4
Leicestershire	13	87		8
Nottinghamshire	23	77		10
Derbyshire	27	73		10
FOR THE WHOLE GROUP:	18	82		32
SOUTHERN GROUP:				
Surrey	27	52	21	6
Sussex	34	38	28	11
Hampshire	22	53	25	17
Dorset	15	65	20	11
Wiltshire	25	55	20	18
Somersetshire	12	58	30	10
Gloucestershire	8	62	30	11
Devonshire	13	70	17	11
FOR THE WHOLE GROUP:	19	57	24	107

* The figures half-way between columns indicate that a single total only is
available for money rent from free and villein holdings, or that the money valuation of villein labour rent is included in total villein rent.

[1] The unusually high percentage figure for labour rent is due to the influence
of a single manor (Rothwell, of the Earl of Gloucester). If this manor is omitted
the percentage falls to 37, while that for money rent of villeins increases to 41.

TABLE 8 (*continued*)

Group and County	Money rent (of freehold)	Money rent (of villein land)	Estimate of labour rent of villeins	Number of surveys used
WESTERN GROUP:				
Herefordshire ..		83*	17	5
Worcestershire ..	22	59	19	8
Shropshire	15	59	26	10
Cheshire	17	62	21	6
FOR THE WHOLE GROUP:	18	61	21	29
Kent		94*	6	12

	Money rent Freehold	Money rent Villein	Produce rent		
NORTHERN GROUP:					
Northumbria[1] ..	9	45	36	10[2]	35
Yorkshire	21	52	18	8[3]	21
(Cheshire)[4] ..	11	41	34	14	6

into a commodity-producer and the feudal exploitation of serf-labour that was still tenaciously enforced.

Comparing the results of our calculations on the different forms of rent from the inquisitions and from the Hundred Rolls, we find that, allowing for certain differences, the evidence of the two sources points in the same direction. In Cambridgeshire, according to the Hundred Rolls, the percentage relation of the money rent of free tenants, the money rent of villeins, and labour rent was 32–28–40 per cent; according to the inquisitions it was 45–15–40 per cent. In Bedfordshire villein rent accounts for 61 per cent of the total according to the Hundred Rolls, and for 59 per cent according to the inquisitions. In Buckinghamshire the corresponding figure was 76 per cent according to the Hundred Rolls, 69 per cent according to the inquisitions. The figures for Yorkshire are 23–47–30 per cent according to the Hundred Rolls, 24–54–22 per cent according to the inquisitions. The relative importance of free rent compared with villein rent in Huntingdonshire, and the importance of free tenure in Cambridgeshire and Bedfordshire are fully confirmed by the inquisitions. A difference appears only in the case of Oxfordshire, where the

[1] Northumberland, Cumberland and Westmorland.
[2] This figure should really be lowered yet further.
[3] Not less than half of which could be commuted.
[4] Cheshire (included in the western group) is here reckoned again, taking into account produce rent (mill revenue).

Hundred Rolls show approximately equal labour and money rents from villeins, while in the inquisitions the money rents of villeins are considerably higher than their labour rents. But in the Oxfordshire inquisitions there are only four surveys which draw any distinction between the two.

On the whole the inquisitions give a lower percentage for labour rents than the Hundred Rolls, and that is surprising when we take into account the fact that the average size of a manor in the inquisitions is larger than that in the Hundred Rolls. Do the Hundred Rolls exaggerate the importance of labour rents, or do the inquisitions underestimate it? All the evidence speaks in favour of the first alternative, though it is possible that in individual cases the second may apply. In any case, the inquisitions confirm the conclusions we reached on the predominance of money rent in England in the thirteenth century. They also indicate that this predominance was already a fact by the middle of the thirteenth century. The geographical distribution of rent-forms indicated by the inquisitions does not disagree with the conclusions deduced from the Hundred Rolls.

CHAPTER IV

ECONOMIC AND SOCIAL DIFFERENTIATION
AMONG THE ENGLISH PEASANTRY IN
THE THIRTEENTH CENTURY

THE PROBLEM STATED

The peasants, the basic producers of feudal society, were not a homogeneous class. This is common knowledge. In the earlier period the elements of which the peasantry was composed were still clearly distinguishable—slaves, laets, and members of the village community who had lost their freedom and fallen into various degrees of serfdom. But even at the time of the full development of feudalism when many of the previous distinctions were ironed out, various groups may be observed. Between personal freedom and unfreedom there were many intermediate stages. In the field of tenure this distinction is expressed in the counterposing of villein and free tenure. Nor is there any uniformity in the size of peasants' holdings. It is well known that the villeins in England were divided into virgaters, half-virgaters, fardel-holders[1] and cotters, and the composition of the free peasantry was even more varied. Considerable differences within the peasantry resulted from their forms of rent—not only as between free and unfree peasants, but within the two groups themselves. We may distinguish holdings carrying labour services and holdings paying money rent, holdings burdened with heavy services and holdings paying an insignificant symbolic rent *pro recognitione*. Finally, as a result of the early phases of the disintegration of feudal relationships, a group of tenants holding for limited periods, the forerunners of the tenant farmers, begins to separate itself off from the rest of the peasantry.

All these are well-known facts, which have been more than once subjected to analysis. Nevertheless, the classical theory does depict the main mass of the peasantry as something more or less homogeneous, or at any rate only slightly differen-

---

[1] Tenants of quarter virgates.

tiated. Only comparatively small and unimportant groups are divided off from the main body. The main group, taking in the vast majority of peasants, consists of villeins reasonably well provided with land and stock (mostly virgaters and half virgaters) and performing work on the lord's land. The general line of research on the history of the English peasantry is concerned with this group, its origin and obligations, the changes taking place within it, its emancipation, the copyhold tenure to which it gives rise, and its fate in the future.

Without denying in the least the decisive part played by this main body of the peasantry in feudal production at the time of both its genesis and its disintegration, I should like to draw attention to other elements and to attempt a definition of their historical role, which was, perhaps, not so insignificant after all. What we have discovered so far of the relations of villein and free holdings and of labour and money rent is in itself enough to make us pause and consider anew many questions in the history of the peasantry which have been regarded as settled. And yet whatever distinctions and contradictions may have existed within the peasantry, they do not preclude our seeing in the peasantry of the epoch a single class, occupying a definite place in the feudal mode of production, and characterized by the anti-feudal direction of its interests and its class struggle.

THE EVOLUTION OF FREE AND UNFREE TENURE

The first difference in the field of tenure which strikes one on reading through manorial and governmental documents is the difference between free and unfree—or, to use the terminology of our sources, between villeins and free tenants (*liber tenentes*). But by no means all *liberi tenentes* were peasants. Free tenure, *liberum tenementum*, is any holding that is hereditary or for life according to Common Law. To be contrasted with it is tenure at the lord's will and according to the custom of the manor—villein holding; likewise the privileged villein holding of the ancient demesne of the Crown. Among free tenures are included tenure by knight service, tenure in frankalmoign, serjeanty, socage, and burgage. The common distinguishing mark of free tenure is that it carries with it the right of pleading in the king's courts. For its defence is created the system of *brevia originalia* and trial by jury at the assizes. On this conception of tenure is built up the whole system of the Common Law.[1]

In this general sense both the greatest of barons and the tenant of the smallest 'free' holding were free tenants. Every lord of a manor was at the same time a free tenant under another lord or the king. But in manorial documents, and in government surveys composed on the same lines as manorial records, 'free tenements', or, more often, 'free tenants' (*liberi* or *libere tenentes*), has a narrower meaning. The whole manor is as a rule divided into three main parts—demesne, villein holdings, free holdings; the last are contrasted with the demesne as well as with villein holdings. Among free holdings those of the peasant type predominate.

The judicial reforms of Henry II and the development of the Common Law drew a sharp line between free and villein holdings. Protecting the former, they refused protection to the latter. At the same time the Common Law grouped under the one heading of free tenure peasant free tenure (socage), the tenure of the upper class (the knight's fee), and the privileged ecclesiastical tenure (frankalmoign). The main demarcation line ran not along the division between the noble and base estates, as in France, but along that between free and villein. An important influence, of course, was the preservation of a considerable free peasantry in medieval England, and the role assigned to it in the organization by the government of the police and of the judicial and financial machinery of the localities. Also working in the same direction was the early replacement of the military service of knights by money contributions (scutage). Not infrequently representatives of the ruling class, even great barons, held land by right of socage. At the same time knights' fees become fragmented. In the Hundred Rolls we find holdings of one-twentieth of a knight's fee, which is equivalent to a virgate—a typical peasant holding, and some even of one-fortieth of a knight's fee, which equals a half-virgate. But a number of specific obligations continued to distinguish military tenements from

[1] On this point see in particular the article of Joüon des Longrais, 'La tenure en Angleterre au moyen age', *Recueil de la Société Jean Bodin*, iii, Bruxelles, 1938.

socage—right up to the famous Acts of the Long Parliament
and of Charles II which abolished military tenure and replaced
it by socage.

All the sharper was the line drawn between free and villein
tenure (if we leave aside the special ancient demesne tenures).
Exceptio villenagii is the principle not only of the Common Law,
not only of the practice of the king's courts, but of the whole
policy of the Crown and of all the legislation of the twelfth
and thirteenth centuries. However, until the end of the thirteenth century there were no precise criteria by which free
holding could be distinguished from villein holding. The line
between them, so clear in legal theory, in practice was not clear
at all. Vinogradoff has shown how even such a characteristic
sign of villein tenure as the payment of merchet can also be met
with among free holdings.[1] Neither heriot, nor pannage, nor
subjection to seigniorial monopolies, nor aid is peculiar to
villein tenure; they are met with on free holdings, even if
rarely. Vinogradoff rightly sees the most essential difference
between free and villein holding in the payment of money rent
by the former and labour rent by the latter. But this criterion,
although in practice it provided the most obvious indication
where the dividing line came, is also vague, since villeins do not
always render labour dues, while freeholders perform minor
works.

Some recent historians of the English village—notably G. G.
Coulton and his school—have argued that in general one should
not assign the same importance to legal distinctions as Maitland
and Vinogradoff, both legal historians, did, and that in real
life, in manorial practice, the difference between free and villein
holding was often not noticeable.[2] The free tenant of a small
plot, who had to pay a considerable rent, usually rendered
some labour dues, had to attend the manor court, and was
bound to the routine of the community, was in fact scarcely
to be distinguished from the villein. The position of a villein,

---

[1] Though the Hundred Rolls, for example, regularly distinguish villeins by
precisely this characteristic—*isti sunt servi de sanguine suo emendo* and similar formulae.
[2] See in particular H. S. Bennett, *Life on the English Manor 1150–1400* (1937);
and Homans, *English Villagers of the Thirteenth Century* (1942). The tendency of
some authors to ignore juridical differences and stress the economic ones is because
they overlook the unpleasant fact that a large part of the population of England
consisted of serfs bereft of all rights, and they treat freemen and serfs together as a
coherent body of 'villagers'.

especially of one whose labour dues had been commuted, might be better than that of a free tenant whose 'freedom', in so far as he remained on his holding, was very relative. So far as the protection of personal and property rights is concerned, even on this point doubt may be expressed whether the rights of the 'free' peasant were always better protected than those of the villein. We have not the least wish to exaggerate the role of the manor court and manorial custom in protecting the property rights of the villeins. But, we may ask, how much better did the king's courts protect the interests of the free peasant? The complicated nature of a suit in the king's court, and particularly the fact that it had to be paid for, undoubtedly made it a course open only to the upper layer of the free peasantry. It is difficult to suppose that the judges were insensible to various approaches which might be made to them by rich and powerful lords, and that a peasant could always expect a just verdict from them. It can scarcely have been a frequent occurrence for a peasant, even a free man, to take it upon himself to go to law against his lord. In daily life, probably, the distinctions between free and villein holders used often to disappear.

Interesting material on this question has been provided by Helen M. Cam.[1] Using a number of cases in the Curia Regis Rolls, in which the question of proving free or villein status arose, the author reconstructs several peasant genealogies, some of them very minutely. Their main interest lies in the frequency of marriages between villeins and free, so that some of the relatives of individuals discussed are villein and some are free. Miss Cam rightly remarks that in village life where mixed marriages were so frequent, class distinctions cannot have followed that between legal freedom and serfdom. Even if this latter distinction had a practical meaning for the king's lawyers and for the landlords, in ordinary life a villein might be an important and respected personage in the village.[2] On the other hand, even the most important rights of the free man —his 'freedom', i.e. the absence of attachment to the land and to the person of the landowner, his right to leave the manor

---

[1] 'Pedigrees of Villeins and Freemen in the Thirteenth Century' (*The Genealogist's Magazine*, Sept., 1933, reprinted in her book *Liberties and Communities in Mediaeval England*, Cambridge, 1944).

[2] *Ibid.*, pp. 134–5.

and give up his holding—might be to a great extent illusory, given the prevalence of natural economy relationships, and the slight development of town industries. The peasant was practically, if not legally, attached to his holding, to his village community and to the common lands where his stock grazed, to his farmyard and his kitchen garden. And if a free peasant were in debt to his lord, the distinction between freeman and serf was further diminished.

Nevertheless, both the manorial records and the governmental surveys always divide the tenants of a manor into freemen and villeins. It is well known that personal freedom or unfreedom did not always coincide precisely with free or unfree tenure, that there were cases when a villein holding was in the hands of a personally free man, and when villeins held free tenements. But the records and government surveys look on these cases as exceptions. It was usually presumed—and it evidently was usually so in practice—that the holders of villein plots were villeins, and that free holdings were occupied by free men.

In manorial records free holdings can for the most part be easily distinguished from villein holdings. In contrast to the villein holdings, they are usually not divided into symmetrical groups of virgates, and half-virgates, but are extremely varied in size. Furthermore, the dues they carry bear no relation whatever to the size of the holding. But these are only the external signs behind which lie real and essential distinctions. The most important distinction is that a free holding, as a rule, carries no labour dues, or only insignificant ones, while the villein holding is usually burdened with labour services, though their amount varies widely. The peculiar characteristics of peasant free tenure are comprehensible only as a function of its freedom from the system of labour services.[1] These characteristics are, first and foremost, the freedom to leave the manor; then freedom to alienate one's holding, divide it, hand it on to one's heirs, and lease it out (within the limits, after 1290, laid down by the statute *Quia Emptores*). It was all the same to a lord of the manor in what way a

---

[1] Even if there should be evidence of some labour service, due mainly from small holdings.

money rent was paid. But the organization of serf labour on the demesne demanded the strict subjection of the peasant to manorial discipline—and the indivisibility of holdings.

Even the *Rectitudines Singularum Personarum*, an early eleventh-century document, divides the main body of the peasantry into *geneat* and *gebur*, that is, into peasants paying rent and those performing labour dues. Both these classes of peasant, not yet divided into 'free' and 'unfree', are included under the general title of 'villein' in the broad terminology of Domesday Book. The ancestors of the free tenants of the thirteenth century are to be found, not only among the *liberi homines* and sokemen, but also among the villeins and borders of Domesday Book.[1] Similarly, the ancestors of the later villeins are to be found not only among the geburs, but in many of the geneats of the Anglo-Saxon epoch, who later fell under the yoke of labour rent and so of unfreedom. But in the twelfth century, especially after the time of Henry II, the legal division into 'villein' (labour-rent) and 'free' (non-labour-rent) holdings became established. Free tenements increased in the twelfth and thirteenth centuries owing to felling and clearing (*assarta*), to the leasing out by the lords of part of the demesne, and finally owing to the process of commutation and the development of money rent. Commutation in itself did not make a villein a free man or a villein holding free. But it was a step towards emancipation, and in a number of cases apparently led to this result. By the end of the thirteenth century, free holders make up a very considerable section of the English peasantry. Vinogradoff in fact maintains that a considerable majority of free holdings are of late appearance, connected with the distintegration of the manorial system.

PEASANT HOLDINGS IN 1279

My own investigations into the question of free tenure suggest views different from those of Seebohm and Vinogradoff. An analysis of the 1279 Hundred Rolls shows the very significant place of free holdings on thirteenth-century manors, where they comprise about 30 per cent of the total arable

[1] Vinogradoff, *Villainage*, p. 352.

mentioned in the rolls.[1] The percentage of free holdings is undoubtedly higher than this in the northern and eastern counties
of England, and somewhat lower in the western counties; it is
higher where the manorial system had already reached the
stage of disintegration and also where it had not yet taken final
shape. It is higher on small manors than on large, higher on
lay manors than on church lands. It would seem that it should
be higher in the regions where pastoral farming prevailed.
Eileen Power[2] has noted that a pastoral economy favours the
preservation of peasant freedom, and that freeholders with
comparatively small arable allotments might possess considerable grazing rights.

Since all villein holdings are undoubtedly of a peasant
character, all the villein land—40 per cent, according to my
reckoning, of the total arable which can be traced in the
Hundred Rolls—can be called peasant land. But matters
are much more complicated when it comes to free holdings.
Even where free holdings can be counted as 'peasant' in
point of size, they nevertheless include many other elements.
Among free tenements we often find holdings of various
sizes in the hands of ecclesiastical foundations, usually monasteries. According to my approximate reckoning these come to
about 4 per cent of the total territory under consideration,
or about 10 per cent of the total area of free holdings. Glebes,
likewise, which make up about 5 per cent of all free holdings,
must not be confused with peasant lands. Not infrequently
priests have free tenements apart from the glebe, but these are
very insignificant as a percentage of the whole. Finally, as
we have seen, lay landowners sometimes had free tenements on
either their own or other manors. Holdings in the hands of lay
lords are not always easy to identify, especially if they are
situated at a distance from the main domains of the owner,
and if the latter is not a great lord. According to my somewhat
inexact observations, such lands were not large in total extent.

[1] By the method of calculation which I followed, I to some extent under-
estimated the real role of free holdings. In any case, the figure of 30 per cent
is certainly not exaggerated. I should point out that under the heading 'free
holdings' I included all non-villein holdings, taking in holdings for terms of years
and at the lord's will, which are not freehold if one keeps to strict legal terminology.
These are not at all numerous in the Hundred Rolls, and it is very difficult to
separate them from the free holdings.

[2] *The Medieval English Wool Trade*, pp. 6, 30.

But in any case about 20 per cent (in some hundreds more, in some less) of the total area of free holdings must be excluded from the total area of peasant land (free and villein). On the other hand, part of the peasant land is concealed because it appears in the form of tiny manors. A peasant holding of any size (sometimes very small) might collect around itself a number of small free and even villein holdings. A prosperous peasant not only paid rent, but received it too, was not only the object of feudal exploitation, but himself exploited his sub-tenants. He became transformed into a small landowner. Hence, on the basis of our sources, it is not possible to draw a clear demarcation line between the well-to-do peasant and the small landowner.

There are thus great difficulties to contend with when we try to calculate the total area of peasant land, and this cannot in fact be done with precision. To sum up our estimates so far, it seems that 40 per cent of the total calculable arable was in the hands of villeins, and that the area of free holdings can be approximately estimated at 30 per cent. Approximately one-fifth of the territory of free holdings was not in peasant hands. Thus the peasant part of the free holdings came to about 24 per cent of the territory covered by the rolls. This being so, the relation of villein land and freehold land of peasant type can be given as approximately the relation of 40 to 24, or more simply 5 : 3 (62 : 38 per cent).

It would be very much to the point to define not only the ratio of the area, but also that of the numbers of villein and free holdings. This I have done for ten hundreds, containing in all 9,934 peasant households. Of these 5,814 (58 per cent) were villein and 4,120 (42 per cent) free, but with considerable variations between different counties and between different hundreds. In some hundreds, both the number of free holdings and the area covered by them exceed those of villein holdings. In the hundred of Chilford (Cambridgeshire) the number of free holdings of peasant type is 491, the number of villein holdings 216; in the Bedfordshire hundreds of Willey and Stodden the number of peasant free holdings is about 930, that of villein holdings 505. But the reverse ratio is much more common. In the Oxfordshire hundred of Ploughley, there are 1,081 villein holdings to 231 peasant free holdings.

TABLE 9

NUMERICAL RELATION OF VILLEIN TO FREE PEASANT
HOUSEHOLDS

County and Hundred	Villein households	Free households	Total number of households
HUNTINGDONSHIRE			
Normancross	972	359	1,331
CAMBRIDGESHIRE			
Chilford	216	491	707
Flemditch	373	429	802
Staploe	600	285	885
Stow	376	407	783
BEDFORDSHIRE			
Stodden and Willey ..	505	930	1,435
BUCKINGHAMSHIRE			
Bunstow	255	263	518
OXFORDSHIRE			
Bampton	736	335	1,071
Chadlington	700	390	1,090
Ploughley	1,081	231	1,312
Over all the given hundreds	5,814	4,120	9,934

I see no reason for not extending this ratio of villein to free
households to cover the whole area taken in by the Hundred
Rolls. It could, of course, hardly be taken to apply far outside
the boundaries of this area. So far as we can judge, the percentage of villein holdings was greater in the west, and that of
free holdings greater in the north and east.[1]

ECONOMIC DIFFERENTIATION AMONG THE PEASANTS

The development of money rent presupposes the existence
of a considerable degree of stratification of the peasantry. This
stratification is very considerable among the English peasantry,
both serf and free, in the thirteenth century. It would, however, be wrong to attribute all stratification to the development

[1] We would like to know the ratio of the free population of the English countryside in the thirteenth century to the villein population. Probably the percentage
of free peasantry as opposed to the villeins would be lower than the percentage of
free households to villein ones, since among the free holdings a more considerable
part was played by small units, where we must assume a lower average number
of individuals present. This would scarcely be counterbalanced by the high percentage of large free holdings.

of commodity and money relationships and the disintegration of the manor. The deep-seated causes of peasant differentiation probably lie as far back as the disintegration of the pre-feudal lands into the ownership of separate families. The formation of allodial holdings, and the development of land alienation, were bound to result in the creation of private estates, both large and small. The imposition of bondage on the village community should, it might seem, have halted this process, but in fact it did not do so. The lord of the serf-worked manor had an interest in maintaining the indivisibility of the peasant household and holding, since it was necessarily equipped with everything required for the performance of labour dues and other services. As the population increased,[1] holdings were sub-divided, but this was a very slow process, and there was always a considerable number of peasants without land, or with only small plots without draught stock. It would seem that some of these small holdings came into existence through the settlement of slaves on the land of the demesne. Finally, the villein holdings themselves, indivisible and equal at first glance, in fact presented a picture of extreme inequality.

First of all, families of various sizes might occupy villein holdings of equal size, and very varied and complicated groups might be found occupying villein virgates.[2] There were often several generations living on the virgate, while brothers continued to live on the same holding, sometimes receiving small plots within it for their private use. Thus, behind a full land-allocation might be concealed overcrowding of the land, which found no reflection in the manorial documents, since these were concerned only with the dues arising from the allotment as a whole. On the other hand, dues were levied from the different holdings without any consideration being given to the size of the holders' families, and this could only lead to extreme inequality. Behind the equality of the 'typical' villein holdings, in other words, behind the symmetrical virgates and half-virgates, was concealed a very considerable stratification, leading to accumulation of resources in some

[1] In the time of Bede the typical peasant holding was the hide; at the time of Domesday Book it was land cultivable by between a half and a full plough team; in the thirteenth century between half a virgate and one virgate.
[2] Cf. Homans, op. cit., Book II.

households and extreme want in others. Again, the administrative system of the manor furthered the differentiation of the
villein peasantry in yet another direction. The 'ministers',
the manorial bureaucracy, used their official position to enrich
themselves personally. If, to a certain extent, the manorial
system preserved external equality, it was not able to hinder
effectively the development—which had begun at a very
early date—of sale, purchase and lease of peasant holdings.
The manor court sought only to control these transactions,
though without doubt a considerable part of them escaped
control. This development was facilitated in places where the
predominance of money rent made it of no consequence to the
manorial administration whether or not the indivisibility of
the peasant allotments was preserved. The connection
between the peasant economy and the market was an even
more effective factor in the enrichment of some and the ruin of
others; and among the free peasantry the process of differentiation was even more intense than among the villeins.

CRITIQUE OF THEORY OF I. I. GRANAT

The problem of the sub-divisions and social stratification of
the peasantry in medieval England was discussed by Granat,[1]
on the basis of calculations from Domesday Book and more
particularly from the 1279 Hundred Rolls. Analysing the
latter he counted the number of households of villeins and freeholders separately. His total of villein households is 10,581,
divided as follows:

Up to 5 acres	3,580 households, or 33·8% of the total
From 6–9 ,,	1,126 ,,	10·6% ,,
,, 10–19 ,,	3,573 ,,	33·7% ,,
,, 20–30 ,,	2,261 ,,	21·3% ,,
Over 30 ,,	41 ,,	0·4% ,,

In the first category (up to 5 acres) only 601 households have
3 to 5 acres of land, 1,319 have not more than 2 acres, and
1,660 cottars have either no land at all, or only insignificant
plots. Granat's total of free tenants is 2,826 households, and

[1] Granat, I. I., *The Divorce of the English Peasantry from the Land* (Russian),
Moscow (1908). Granat made his work the basis for an attack on Marx's theory
of primitive accumulation. But his calculations are not altogether convincing, and
the conclusions which he tries to draw from them are unacceptable.

about them his conclusion is that economically they differed little from the servile peasantry, or at any rate were much closer to the latter than to the 'land-owning class'. Here is a summary of his calculations:

Up to 6 acres	1,508 households, or	53·4% of the total	
From 6–9 ,,	374 ,,	13·2%	,,
,, 10–19 ,,	464 ,,	16·4%	,,
,, 20–30 ,,	299 ,,	10·6%	,,
Over 30 ,,	181 ,,	6·4%	,,

Granat was well aware that not only well-to-do but also small free tenants often had land on several neighbouring manors, and in his methods of calculation he tried to make allowance for the fact. Nevertheless, it is easy to see that he minimizes the relative importance of the well-to-do. Free holdings of any size, especially in the east of England, are regularly made up of several parts, and unless we carry out the complicated task of combining the parts (which Granat does not do) we always run the risk of belittling the importance of the top layer of free tenants. Without doubt Granat has counted as 'landless' or 'inadequately provided' many households which were really well-to-do. Finally, from the evidence of certain ecclesiastical records,[1] Granat concludes that in the western and northern counties the peasants were better provided with land than in the central and south-eastern counties. Small peasants (with up to 5 acres) make up a quarter to a third of the peasantry in the former counties, and two-fifths to a half in the latter. Thus at least a third of the whole English peasantry was inadequately provided with land.

Whence came such a vast 'landless proletariat'? Granat finds the answer to this question in the peculiarities of the English village community and, in the last resort, in the peculiar nature of the English soil. One peculiarity of the English village community was, he considered, the indivisibility of the peasant household, which he explained by the fact that the heavy English soil demanded an especially large amount of stock to work it—the cardinal fact, in his view, in the whole agrarian development of England. Not lack of land, but lack of draught stock produced the landless proletariat

---

[1] From Glastonbury and Gloucester Abbeys, St. Paul's Cathedral, Battle Abbey, and the See of Durham.

o

that is such a striking feature of the medieval English village.
Thus the 'proletariatization' of the English peasantry is not
the result of forcible expropriation due to primitive accumulation, as Marx supposed,[1] but a natural and inevitable result
of the soil-peculiarities of the country! 'For several centuries
prior to the rise of capitalism there existed in the country an
extensive class of hired labourers; as industry producing for
the market developed, it only remained to transfer these landless peasants from the country to the town, and impel them to
break finally the feeble link that bound them to the soil.'
Landless peasants began to leave the land and go to the
towns, because town industry offered them a higher wage.
The differentiation of the peasantry, according to Granat, is
thus an immemorial phenomenon of the English countryside.
The 'peculiar' organization of the English village community
'drew a wide demarcation line between the cottar and the
household with arable land.' The virgaters formed 'a powerful
stratum of prosperous peasants', using much hired labour.
The half-virgaters, who according to his figures were the most
numerous group of the peasants with arable land, are also
assigned by him to the category of 'solid' peasants. Reconstructing the budget of a peasant holding of 15 acres of land
in the thirteenth and fourteenth centuries, he calculates that
the net income of such a holding was two or three times more
than the minimum necessary for subsistence.[2] From the sixteenth century, in Granat's opinion, these prosperous peasants
enter the ranks of the capitalist leasehold farmers; they
part with their own holdings because the status of farmer
brings in greater profits. Thus there was no forcible expropriation from the land. The peasants expropriated themselves,
because it was advantageous for them to do so.

We see in this analysis an unsuccessful attempt to make
primitive accumulation respectable. The expropriation of the
peasants is lifted from the consciences of the landlords, since
the rural proletariat has existed from time immemorial by
virtue of the peculiarities of the English soil. Similarly the
exploitation of the rural proletarian by the 'solid' peasant was
a natural peculiarity of the English village. The well-known
fact, noted by Marx, of the transformation of the top layer of

---

[1] *Capital*, i, Section 8.   [2] For peasant budgets, see below, p. 230.

the peasantry into capitalist farmers is incorrectly extended by Granat to cover the whole of the peasantry except the cottars. Straining to draw a line of demarcation between the prosperous households provided with arable land, and the cottars, Granat forgets the middle peasantry, living by their own labour on their own land and not, as a rule, exploiting the labour of others. For him the whole of the English peasantry was from earliest times divided into the 'solid peasants' who exploit the labour of others, and the 'proletarians'—the cottars.

Granat's attempt to explain the appearance of a 'proletariat' in the English medieval village by the natural conditions of the English soil must be rejected. We have already explained the connection between the appearance of a stratum of practically landless peasants and the peculiar characteristics of the serf-worked estate. There is nothing specifically English here. Another cause working to develop a near-landless peasantry was the growth of money rent, which hastened the process of the differentiation of the peasantry and to a considerable extent made 'solid' villein holdings no longer necessary. Granat's explanation could, in any case, apply to villein holdings only. Free tenure was not subject to the rule of inheritance by the younger son, and here a complicated differentiation was soon created, due to the freedom of division and alienation.

LIMITATION OF HUNDRED ROLLS AND EXTENTS AS EVIDENCE OF STRATIFICATION

To what extent can one rely on the Hundred Rolls and the manorial extents as evidence for the stratification of the English peasantry in the thirteenth century? In the thirteenth-century village, various forms of lease (at will, for life, for a term of years) were common. From at least as early as the beginning of the reign of Edward I there are numerous cases of the leasing-out of demesne land and of inter-peasant leasings, for short-terms and for money rent. Neither the Hundred Rolls nor the extents are suitable sources for the study of such things. The essential evidence is to be found in the records of the manor courts, in which leases were registered and where suits concerning their breach were heard. What information do these records give us? Petrushevsky, who analysed this material, found that for the most part the leases concern very small plots, of 1, 1½, 2 or 3 acres, or frequently of fractions of an acre. Alongside the development of leasing goes the accumulation of peasant land in fewer hands by means of sale and purchase. Cases of this sort are common in the records of manorial courts from the beginning of the fourteenth century. But we have evidence of them in the thirteenth century also; for example, from the instructions of Abbot Roger of St. Albans (1260–90), where a number of procedures are prescribed for the lease and sale of villein lands.[1]

Cases of peasants leasing and buying both peasant and demesne land are not infrequent in the manor court records of the thirteenth century.[2] Sometimes peasants tried to arrange the deal without the knowledge of the court, and it is possible that a number of such transactions escaped the court's control. In her description of the court-records of St. Albans,[3] Miss Levett gives first place to cases dealing with alienation of lands, which fill the pages of the registers from 1240 onwards. She also notes the predominance in these cases of small plots of land upwards of half an acre. From 1267 there begins a long series of disputes over whether villeins had the right to alienate their land without the consent of the court. Plainly such cases were common. Miss Levett notes the considerable influence which such small alienations had on the character of rent; they confused the allocation of labour services and led to commutation.

What were the social results of the alienation and leasing-out of land? Who leases out land and who rents it? Some investigators have supposed that land was leased out by those holding full or considerable holdings, and was rented by the landless or near-landless people. Leasing thus levelled up unequal holdings. But was this so in actual fact? It is well known that inter-peasant leasing and alienation often take a different direction. The small peasant leases or sells his plot to the prosperous peasant who aims to profit from enlarging his

[1] *Gesta Abbatum Monasterii Sancti Albani*, i (1867), pp. 453–55.
[2] Cf. *Select Pleas in Manorial Courts*, ed. F. W. Maitland.
[3] *T.R.H.S.*, 4th Series, vii; *Studies in Manorial History* (1938).

holding. In this way the leasing of land leads not to a levelling-up, but to a further differentiation of peasant economies.

The latter process seems to me the more probable. A well-known passage from the records of the manor court of Elton[1] indicates what may often have happened. There the reeve Michael is accused by his fellow-villagers of using serf labour to mow his own meadow, to reap his own harvest, and to plough his own land. Furthermore, he lightened the villeins' labour dues on condition that they sold or rented their land to him at a low price. The jury found that the accusation was unjustified, but we are left with a different impression. We seem to see before us the figure of a 'kulak', who utilizes his position as reeve to round off his own possessions and to exploit the labour of his fellow-villagers, in which he is supported by his own men in the hallmote. The peasants who accused him were fined, but the fine was reduced at Michael's own request. Such generosity was probably evoked by the desire to hush up an unpleasant affair as quickly as possible. From being a safeguard of the interests of the village community at large the hallmote could easily become an instrument for strengthening the peasant élite. Jurymen were usually chosen from a small circle of individuals; it was easy to form a party of one's own in the hallmote, which would make verdicts accordingly.

We know that all sorts of petty alienations were carried through secretly without being registered in the records of the manor court. We have the impression that the manorial and communal authorities, and the more prosperous peasants who carried most weight in the court, sheltered one another in this activity, and that such transactions were largely carried through to the disadvantage of the poor peasants. All this compels one to suppose that the increased negotiability of land led to an intensification of differentiation between peasant economies, not to its moderation.

Thus the information available in the Hundred Rolls and the manorial extents does not fully reflect the stratification of the thirteenth-century village. This applies particularly to villein holdings, for which these documents provide only the

[1] Maitland, *op. cit.*, p. 95.

original 'official' allocation.[1] As far as free holdings are concerned, their fluidity is far better reflected in these sources. But even here not all cases of leasing are given. Thus the picture we get from statistics derived from the Hundred Rolls will not be accurate. Its degree of inaccuracy depends on how far the process of disintegration of villein holdings had advanced by 1279. But in any case even a statistical analysis of land as first allocated gives sufficiently striking results.

STRATIFICATION OF VILLEIN HOLDINGS IN THE HUNDRED ROLLS

First let us consider villein holdings. I have repeated Granat's calculations, not because I consider them to be inaccurate, but in order to bring in more detail.[2] To simplify the reckoning I divide all villein holdings into five basic categories. In the first are holdings of over one virgate; in the second, those of one virgate; in the third, those of half a virgate; in the fourth, those of a quarter-virgate; and in the fifth, small holdings (cottages, crofts, tofts, eighths of a virgate). I have counted the comparatively infrequent holdings of three-quarters of a virgate as virgates, those of one-third of a virgate as half-virgates. Where holdings are given not in virgates but in acres, I have counted holdings of 20 to 40 acres as one virgate, those of 10 to 20 acres as half a virgate, those of 5 to 10 acres as fardels, and holdings of less than 5 acres as cottar holdings. Very small virgates (10 acres and under) I have counted as half-virgates, and their halves as fardels. In cases where cottar holdings were over 5 acres, I have put them up into the corresponding category. I have divided manors into three categories, according to their amounts of villein land. In Group A are included those manors where the area of villein land does not exceed 240 acres (two hides), in Group B those with villein land between 240 and 360 acres, and in Group C those with villein land exceeding 360 acres.

---

[1] [The distinction between the official holding for the rent of which the tenant was responsible to the lord, and which was entered opposite his name in the public or private survey, and his actual working holding which might be quite different, is more easily expressed in Russian than in English terminology, but it is hoped that the distinction appears from the sense of the translation.]

[2] In connection with the problem of the structural variations between large and small manors, I needed to arrive at the character of peasant holdings on manors of different sizes, and their economic role in each of the various categories. Therefore, I have introduced into my calculations the division of manors into categories according to the amounts of villein land on them.

My calculations relate to those counties covered by the Hundred Rolls—Huntingdonshire, Cambridgeshire, Bedfordshire, Buckinghamshire, Oxfordshire and Warwickshire.

My figures do not vary greatly from those produced by Granat. On the whole I get a slightly lower percentage of near-landless peasants and a slightly higher one for half-virgaters, virgaters and holders of allotments over one virgate. The difference is probably to be explained not so much by different methods of calculation (the calculation of villein holdings is comparatively simple) as by the fact that I have included in my material the Warwickshire surveys which Granat did not use. Some explanation of the heading 'holdings of over one virgate' is needed. The vast majority of these are only a little over a virgate, most often $1\frac{1}{2}$ or 2 virgates. Holdings of 3 or 4 virgates are the rarest of exceptions.

In Table 10 we see, alongside a very considerable percentage of peasants with inadequate land, a comparatively small number of the peasants in the 'top layer'. But this, as already indicated, may be deceptive. Let us recall Lenin's table showing land held by, and land actually used by, separate groups of the peasantry in the Dnieper district in the 1880s. Comparing the amounts of holdings in this table, we note there, too, only a slight differentiation as one nears the upper stratum. The average area of the holdings of the upper group is only 17.4 desyatins, not very different from the holdings of the main mass of the peasantry. But the peasants in this group had on the average 30 desyatins of purchased and 44 of rented land in addition to their holdings, that is on the average 91.4 desyatins altogether. Lenin showed that it is predominantly the rural proletariat that lets its land. The holdings of this rural proletariat are rented principally by the peasant bourgeoisie.[1]

Without having the least wish to draw parallels between the Russian village after the emancipation of the serfs and the English village of the thirteenth century, it seems highly probable that the development of the English village had begun to move along similar lines. We have already given some foundation for such a supposition. It seems that the top

[1] Lenin, S.W., i, p. 173. (*The Agrarian Question in Russia at the End of the Nineteenth Century*, 1908). [The table quoted was based on Zemstvo statistics of the 1880s. The *desyatin* equals about 2.7 English acres.]

stratum of the villeins could extend the area of land in their use by renting land from the near-landless and the demesne, and that those with small holdings did not actually use all the land allotted to them. The Hundred Rolls give only a modified picture of the differentiation of peasant economies at the end of the thirteenth century. But even the differentiation of their nominal holdings gives us material for certain conclusions. Noteworthy is the predominance of holdings of half a virgate, which amount to 36 per cent of all the holdings taken into our reckoning. Virgates make up 25 per cent, holdings over a virgate only 1 per cent of the total. Thus a considerable majority of the peasantry—62 per cent—are sufficiently provided with land, 29 per cent are provided more or less inadequately. Probably the holders of fardels, who usually had no draught stock and were not liable to labour dues requiring it, can also be added to the number of those inadequately provided with land. They compose a comparatively small group of 9 per cent of the total.

TABLE 10

STRATIFICATION OF VILLEIN HOLDINGS, ACCORDING TO THE HUNDRED ROLLS

County	Over 1 virgate	1 virgate	½ virgate	¼ virgate	Petty allotments	Total
Huntingdonshire	2	525[1]	1,554	161	1,231	3,473
		15	45	4	35	
Cambridgeshire	1	196	1,602	673	1,725	4,197
		5	38	16	41	
Bedfordshire	—	15	248	131	111	505
		3	50	26	20	
Buckinghamshire	3	154	235	161	283	836
		19	28	20	32	
Oxfordshire	116	2,319	1,492	125	948	5,000
	2	46	30	2	19	
Warwickshire	51	731	593	127	389	1,891
	3	38	31	7	21	
	173	3,940	5,724	1,378	4,687	15,902
	1	25	36	9	29	
Group A	11	524	1,762	791	2,113	5,201
		10	34	15	40	
Group B	12	501	760	127	652	2,052
		25	38	6	32	
Group C	150	2,915	3,202	460	1,922	8,649
	2	34	37	5	22	

[1] The upper figure denotes the number of holdings, the lower one the percentage of the total this represents.

We note a considerably greater fragmentation of holdings in the east than in the west, on which Granat had previously remarked. If we moved farther to the west, we should find even larger peasant holdings. A villein holding of more than one virgate is a rare phenomenon in Huntingdonshire, Cambridgeshire and Buckinghamshire, and does not occur in Bedfordshire. In these counties the typical holding is the half-virgate. The percentage of peasants with too little land for subsistence is very considerable. True, in Bedfordshire the number (20 per cent) is below the average, but this is compensated by an exceptionally high percentage of fardels (26 per cent), so that the two together come to 46 per cent. The highest degree of fragmentation is in Cambridgeshire, where small holdings make up 41 per cent of all villein holdings—57 per cent if the fardels are added.

EAST AND WEST CONTRASTED

If in order to bring out the implications more clearly we divide all villein holdings into: (1) those more or less adequately provided with land (holdings over 1 virgate, of 1 virgate, and of half a virgate), (2) those insufficiently or totally inadequately provided (fardels and holdings less than five acres); and if then we divide the counties under consideration into two groups—the eastern (Huntingdonshire, Cambridgeshire, Bedfordshire and Buckinghamshire), and the western (Oxfordshire and Warwickshire)—we get the following ratios between the two classes of peasant economy:

Eastern Group
Huntingdonshire .. 60 : 39
Cambridgeshire .. 44 : 57
Bedfordshire .. 53 : 47
Buckinghamshire .. 47 : 53

51 : 49

Western Group
Oxfordshire .. 78 : 21
Warwickshire .. 72 : 28

75 : 25

For all counties .. 63 : 37

The ratio is analogous if we compare the percentage of virgates and half-virgates in the eastern and western groups. Holdings of over a virgate have been included with the virgates. The first figure gives the virgates and the second the half-virgates, as percentages of the total number of holdings in the county:

> *Eastern Group*
> Huntingdonshire   ..   15 : 45
> Cambridgeshire   ..   5 : 38
> Bedfordshire   ..   3 : 50
> Buckinghamshire   18 : 28
>
> *Western Group*
> Oxfordshire   ..   48 : 30
> Warwickshire   ..   41 : 31
>
> *For all counties*   ..   21 : 37

These figures speak clearly enough for themselves. The holding, the 'natural wage' of the servile peasant, is considerably lower in the east than in the west. It is in the thickly populated east, where money-commodity relationships had become more deeply rooted in agricultural life, that we find the small peasant holding. The low level of this 'natural wage' suggests that there was a higher degree of exploitation of the peasant in the east than in the west. Alongside this we must put the fact, previously noted, of the greater development in the east of the heaviest form of feudal rent—labour rent. It is common knowledge that the dues owed from a peasant's holding were in some measure proportionate to its size; nevertheless the smaller the holding, the greater was the relative exploitation of the peasant.

Varying Degrees of Stratification on Different Types of Manors

Before drawing further conclusions from the differences in the degree of stratification of the peasantry on a geographical basis, let us consider the differences that appear as between large and small manors. The majority of villein holdings belong to manors of Group *C* (manors with more than 360 acres, that is, 12 virgates of villein land). Manors of this group have their own peculiar characteristics. The percentage of full holdings of 1 virgate is considerably above the average (34 per cent as against 25 per cent), the percentage of small holdings is below the average (22 per cent as against 29 per cent), and that of fardels is insignificant, but the percentage of half-virgates is close to the average. Thus for a manor of Group C the ratio between peasant holdings adequately provided with land and those not so provided will be different from that established for all manors irrespective of size. On such a manor, peasants inadequately provided with land will not be one-third of the total number, as Granat supposed, but only about one-fifth; even if we include the holders of fardels it only brings the figure up to a little over one-quarter (27 per cent). The peasantry more or less adequately provided with land, on the other hand, amounts to 72 per cent.

The proportions on smaller manors are very different. On manors of Group B, where there is villein land of 240 to 360 acres (8 to 12 virgates), the proportion of half-virgates is also close to the average, but the proportion of virgates is considerably lower than in Group C, being only 25 per cent. The percentage of small holdings, however, is considerably higher, amounting almost to one-third of all villein holdings (32 per cent). These characteristics stand out still more sharply for manors of Group A, where there is less than 240 acres of villein land. Here holdings of 1 virgate make up only 10 per cent of all villein holdings, while small holdings rise to 40 per cent. The percentage of half-virgates here again is little different from the average. If we go further and subdivide off a further group, AA, of the very smallest manors, where there is less than 120 acres of villein land, the percentage of virgates on these falls to 5, that of half-virgates to 26, while the percentage of petty holdings rises to 52, and that of fardels to 18, which amounts to 70 per cent!

If we compare the percentages of peasants adequately and inadequately provided with land, as we did for the separate counties, we get the following ratios for the different categories of manor:

Group C .. .. 73 : 27
„ B .. .. 63 : 37
„ A .. .. 45 : 55
Sub-group AA .. .. 30 : 70

The method of division into groups followed here does not correspond exactly with that used in previous chapters for dividing manors into large, small and average. But in any case our figures show clearly enough the considerable difference between a large and a small manor in the numerical relation between the different strata of peasants, especially if we take into consideration the fact that it is precisely the large manors that are distinguished by a high percentage of villein land. Hence, while confirming Granat's observation of a high percentage of peasants with land inadequate for subsistence, we observe also that a high percentage of near-landless villeins is characteristic chiefly of small manors. On large manors it is not so high. This makes even more dubious the attempt to derive the stratification of the English peasantry from the natural peculiarities of the English soil. I shall not stop to analyse the differences between ecclesiastical and lay manors with regard to the size of their villein holdings. A higher percentage of virgates and half-virgates and a lower one of fardels and small allotments on church manors may be attributed to the more important part played by large manors on the church estates.

STRATIFICATION OF PEASANT FREE HOLDINGS IN THE HUNDRED ROLLS

The calculation of peasant free holdings presents great difficulties. First of all one has to exclude lands held by ecclesiastical bodies (this is not so difficult) and then those of lay estate-owners (which is very difficult). Then one has to piece together the holdings of the various peasants, since many of them have complicated holdings scattered over several manors. Thomas de Camera, whose land in the hundred of Flendish (Cambs.) totals 70 acres, but consists of 25 different holdings, is no exception. Inevitably the task of comparing the names of tenants involves the risk of combining the holdings of two peasants with the same name or of dividing up those of one peasant who had more than one appellation. But it is the only way to get even an approximate solution. Nevertheless, in view of the difficulties involved in a reckoning of this sort, I have not been able to carry out calculations on all the material provided by the Hundred Rolls, but have limited myself to a few hundreds, and in reckoning up complicated holdings I have not gone outside the bounds of the hundred with which I have elected to deal. This is evidently not altogether correct, since any individual peasant might hold lands in another hundred. But to take these into account would have further complicated my work and made possible fresh mistakes.

The following table summarizes my calculations, indicates the hundreds which have been covered, and sums up the results for those counties which are represented by several hundreds. I have used the same headings as for the calculation of villein holdings. Since among free holdings the very smallest plots (less than three acres) play a larger part than they do among villein holdings, I have divided the fifth category (petty holdings) into two: small holdings (3 to 5 acres) and very small plots (less than 3 acres).

There are some inaccuracies in this table. We have reason to believe that in the Oxfordshire surveys small holdings are sometimes omitted, and the same applies in part to the Buckinghamshire surveys. Thus for these two counties the percentage of small and very small holdings should be increased. For Warwickshire, on the other hand, the figures for these two categories of holdings are almost certainly exaggerated, since I had not at my disposal the names of the tenants, and so probably failed to put together small parcels of land which formed parts of one large holding. For this reason the percentage of large holdings in this county should be increased slightly. Furthermore, it should be noted that while in the case of villein holdings the majority of tenements classed as 'over one virgate' amounted only to 1.5 to 2 virgates, in the case of free peasant holdings the upper limit is much higher. In Oxfordshire we find free holdings of 5, 6, 7 or 8 virgates. In fact, the free peasantry are more sharply differentiated than the villeins. One is struck by the huge percentage in the eastern counties of peasants with insufficient land; in Cambridgeshire it reaches 68 per cent, and rises, if the holders of fardels are included, to 80, of which no less than 60 per cent are the very smallest plots—less than three acres. In Huntingdonshire the percentage of small holdings is lower, but still great—52, or 59 including fardels; 42 per cent being under three acres. The percentage of those badly off for land falls as one moves to the west. In Bedfordshire it is 40, in Buckinghamshire 30 (or perhaps a little more). But in these counties the percentage of fardels is unusually high, and if their tenants are included in the class of those badly off for land, it brings the percentage up to 66 in Bedfordshire and 60 (or a little more) in Buckinghamshire. In Oxfordshire, however, the percentage of those inadequately provided with land is not considerable, being only 20, or 27 including the fardel-holders. In Warwickshire we find a high percentage of poor peasants. Although the figure is probably somewhat inflated as a result of the inevitable inaccuracy of calculation, it is still undoubtedly very considerable, and causes us to view the Oxfordshire figures with mistrust. Generally speaking, we have no reason to decrease the over-all figure of 47 per cent for small holdings; or 59 per cent including fardels; 37 per cent being very small holdings.

Holdings of a virgate and half a virgate, which are typical of the middling villeins, are met with considerably less frequently among free tenants. On the average they make up only one-third of the free holdings calculated, the ratio by comparison with insufficient holdings (small holdings and fardels taken together) for the separate counties being as follows:

Huntingdonshire	..	32 : 59
Cambridgeshire	..	17 : 80
Bedfordshire	..	31 : 66
Buckinghamshire	..	36 : 60
Oxfordshire	..	53 : 27
Warwickshire	..	36 : 55

The greatest difficulties of all are involved when it comes to defining the top stratum of free peasant holdings. Our heading of 'holdings over one virgate' comprises only part, and probably the lesser part of this stratum, as it includes only individual free holdings. In actual fact, as we have said, the large free peasant holding tended to turn into a small manor. In the eastern counties especially we can mark quite clearly the process by which large peasant estates were built up out of small

TABLE II

STRATIFICATION OF PEASANT FREE HOLDINGS ACCORDING TO THE HUNDRED ROLLS

County and Hundred	Over 1 virgate	1 virgate	½ virgate	¼ virgate	Allotments of 3–5 acres	Allotments of less than 3 acres
HUNTINGDONSHIRE						
Normancross ..	26	44	72	26	34	157
	7	12	20	7	9	44
Hirstingstone ..	20	15	27	10	16	54
	14	11	19	7	11	38
	46	59	99	36	50	211
	9	12	20	7	10	42
CAMBRIDGESHIRE						
Flendish	9	17	42	46	24	291
	2	4	10	11	6	67
Chilford	26	35	49	61	42	278
	5	7	10	12	9	57
Staploe	17	18	32	35	22	161
	6	6	11	12	8	57
Stow	8	21	53	54	35	236
	2	5	13	13	9	59
	60	91	176	196	123	966
	4	6	11	12	8	60
BEDFORDSHIRE ..	27	118	164	243	248	130
	3	13	18	26	26	14
BUCKINGHAMSHIRE	12	35	57	77	27	55
	5	14	22	30	10	20
OXFORDSHIRE						
Bampton	47	91	93	35	31	38
	14	27	28	10	9	11
Chadlington ..	64	114	68	29	26	89
	16	30	17	7	6	23
Dorchester ..	21	21	13	3	2	2
	34	34	21	5	3	3
Ploughley ..	57	82	61	4	7	20
	25	35	27	2	3	8
Banbury ..	42	33	25	3	2	6
	38	30	22	3	2	5
	231	341	260	74	68	155
	20	29	24	7	6	14
WARWICKSHIRE						
Stoneleigh ..	42	100	191	90	60	38
	5	12	22	10	7	44
Kineton	103	160	136	59	24	246
	14	22	19	8	3	33
	145	260	327	149	104	634
	9	16	20	9	6	40
FOR ALL COUNTIES	521	904	1,083	775	620	2,251
	8	15	18	12	10	37

acquisitions. Around them were formed complexes of dependent holdings both free and villein, paying rent to the 'estate-owner'.

SUB-TENANCIES

The process of differentiation advanced more easily and rapidly among the free tenants than among the villeins, since here there was no obstacle to the formation of the peasant upper layer. It could not come into being so freely among villeins, where the acquisition and accumulation of land were under the control of the manorial administration, and where, according to Common Law (as Glanville understood it), such acquisitions could at any time be taken by the lord of the manor as the legal owner of all that belonged to his villein. A careful study of free holdings, therefore, is of especial interest in the study of the stratification of the feudal village. The processes taking place among the free peasants are almost as important for the study of the disintegration of the feudal order as are the better-known changes in the position of the villeins.

A characteristic feature of the free holdings is their instability and mutability.[1] While villein holdings and even the dues attached to them appear without change for centuries, or with only insignificant changes, it is often impossible to recognize free holdings after the lapse of a generation, or sometimes even less. This is not only because various forms of limited lease—for life, for a term of years, at the lord's will—were counted as free holdings, but also because of the ease with which these tenures could be alienated or divided among heirs. Alienations of free holdings (or more often of parts of them), preserved a link between buyer and seller in the form of a symbolic rent and created within the limits of freehold intricate tenurial complexes. Feebly linked to one individual

---

[1] According to Homans, 'if we may properly speak of a main principle governing the organization of families in the champion country of England, this principle was that an established holding of land ought to descend intact in the blood of the men who had held it of old.' (*Op. cit.*, p. 195).

This idea is quite erroneous. Where we notice phenomena of this order among villein holdings, they are due to the requirements of the manorial administration. The domains of the king, of the great lords, and of middle and small freeholders are continually being alienated. The domains of the church are inalienable, but this has no connection with 'blood'.

by minute rents, they had no common organization. Such complexes of tenants 'dependent' on the same person are often found scattered over several vills and manors.

Here, for instance, are the holdings of Walter Bonde. His name is purely peasant; perhaps he came from a serf (bond) family.[1] He holds under various people—60 acres at a rent of 3s. 6d., 1 acre at 8d., 3 roods at 3d., ½ acre at 1d., and 1 rood of meadow at ½d., altogether 62½ acres for the fairly low rent of 4s. 6½d. But he does not farm all this land; *non tenet in dominico nisi 14 acras.* What does he do with the other 48½ acres? In the Hundred Rolls we can trace 34¾ of them. They are let out in small and very small plots to 19 sub-tenants, who pay small rents for them. Here is a list of these plots, and the rents paid for them:

1 acre at 2½d.; 3 acres at 3d.; 3 acres at 2¾d.; ½ acre at ½d.; 1½ acres at 1½d.; 1 acre at 2d.; ½ acre at ½d.; 2 acres at 2d.; ½ an acre at ½d.; 3 acres at 3d.; 1½ roods at ½d.; 3 roods of garden and 1 acre of croft at 4d.; 1 acre at 1d.; 6 acres at 6d.; 3 roods at 1d.; 5 acres—rent unknown; 1 acre of arable, 1 rood of meadow at 1½d.; 2 acres 1 rood of arable at 3d.; altogether 34¾ acres at 2s. 11¼d. I was unable to find any more holdings under Walter Bonde. For the untraced land (altogether 13¾ acres) and for the 5 acres whose rent is unknown, one should add a further 1s. 7¼d. (the usual rent for an acre in the plots leased out by Walter Bonde is 1d.). Thus Walter receives from his sub-tenants 4s. 6½d.—exactly the same amount as he pays himself. A rent of 1d. an acre is very low. The income brought in by all these leases, 4s. 6½d., is insignificant. Can we call Walter an estate-owner, exploiting his feudally dependent peasants and receiving feudal rent from them? Walter Bonde, like many similar husbandmen in the eastern counties, does not much resemble a 'lord of the manor'. In his 'demesne', *in dominico*, he has only 14 acres, half a virgate, the typical peasant holding. His 'tenants' can by no stretch of the imagination be called feudal dependents. Their insignificant rent does not look like a typical feudal rent. Furthermore part of these small holdings come within other complexes

[1] *R.H.*, ii, 466.

P

resembling the holding of Walter Bonde himself. Most probably, then, we have before us a case of the sale of land in small plots, which under the provisions of feudal law at this time created subinfeudations, confusing to an extreme degree the structure of the feudal 'ladder' of holdings.[1] The contract of sale itself, accompanied by the payment of *gersuma*, is unrecorded and so escapes us. In other cases the rent received by the person selling land is far less than the rent which he himself pays to the lord for that land. Michael Woleward holds 25 acres at a rent of 1 mark. Eight of these he keeps as his 'demesne'; the other 17 are let out to 17 tenants. Their rent altogether comes to 1s. 8½d. only. Michael had to pay dearly for those 17 acres.[2] But fairly frequently there are cases in which the person letting land in free tenure receives for it a more or less considerable rent, many times greater than that which he pays to his lord. For example, Geoffrey de la Huse holds a virgate at a rent of a halfpenny and lets it to Stephen, son of Jacob, for 15 shillings.[3] A large free tenant could receive a quite considerable sum of rent from his sub-tenants. It is under these conditions that a large tenants' estate would assume all the hall-marks of a small manor.

There are hundreds of these sub-manors in the Hundred Rolls, not all of which grew up out of the holdings of prosperous peasants. Many originated in the breaking up of large manors due to division, partial alienation, and the setting aside of marriage portions. Their owners form an intermediate group between the lesser knights and the rich peasants of free status, between whom, as we know, there was no sharp legal distinction. The top layer of the free peasantry could pass over into the class of small knights; indeed, it was obliged to do so, since the law prescribed that persons having a certain revenue from their land must become knights. Not that the well-to-do freeholders were anxious for this honour; on the contrary, they tried to avoid it, as the transformation of simple socage into military tenure brought with it the threatening prospect of a number of fresh burdensome obligations (principally marriage and wardship).

---

[1] This situation was ended by the Statute of *Quia Emptores*.
[2] *R.H.*, ii, 464.   [3] *R.H.*, ii, 330.

COMPARISON OF STRATIFICATION AMONG FREE AND VILLEIN
  TENANTS

Table 12 shows that differentiation had advanced much
further among the free peasants than among the serfs. The
vast majority—73 per cent—of the typical middle peasants
of the medieval village were villeins. But free holdings predominate among the fardels and small holdings, as well as
among the holdings of the rich peasants. Of course, the
absence of data on the alienation of villein land and the omission
from our figures of the quasi-manorial holdings of peasant type
leave much that is unclear in our final results. The picture we
obtain undoubtedly underestimates the extent of the differentiation in the medieval village. Even so the figures are expres-
sive enough. The basic mass of the peasantry—the villein
virgaters and half-virgaters—form a very numerous group
among the 35,000 peasant holdings covered by our calculations; but they cover at most only 35 per cent of the total
number of holdings. Even if we include the free tenants of
similar holdings, it only raises this percentage to 47 per cent.
Furthermore, although the virgaters and half-virgaters made
up the main body of peasants burdened with labour services,
even among them money rents predominate over labour rent.
Thus the percentage of the typical servile peasantry, performing labour services and adequately provided with land, must
be still further lowered. Moreover, we must not forget that
behind the symmetry of virgates and half-virgates are as a
general rule concealed actual working holdings with varying
degrees of economic security. Both the composition of the
family occupying the allotment, and unrecorded leases, could
create considerable economic differences among the virgaters
and half-virgaters.

A far-reaching differentiation of the peasantry does not
imply a far-reaching capitalist transformation of the countryside. The near-landless peasantry develops under the conditions of feudal, manorial production. The formation of an
upper layer among the free peasantry may be partially connected with processes taking place even in pre-feudal society,
with the advance of early property differentiation, and may
represent, as it were, certain elements of incompleteness in

the feudalization of English society. But the beginning of the development of money-commodity relationships, and of the market for land, were of course bound to add force and speed to this process. Since, however, it took place under the conditions of feudal society, it took on feudal forms. We can speak not so much of the appearance of a rural bourgeoisie as of that of small manor owners. However, an analysis of the small manor will reveal embryonic forms of capitalist relationships, too, in the midst of this singular social group.

TABLE 12

SERF AND FREE PEASANTRY

County and Hundred	Over 1 virgate		1 virgate		½ virgate		¼ virgate		Petty holdings	
	Villein	Free	Villein	Free	Villein	Free	Villein	Free	Villein	Free
HUNTINGDONSHIRE										
Normancross	—	26	244	44	239	72	6	26	483	191
CAMBRIDGESHIRE										
Chilford	—	26	16	35	76	49	48	61	76	320
Flendish	—	9	5	17	97	42	42	46	229	315
Staploe	1	17	31	18	209	32	45	35	314	183
Stow	—	8	3	21	128	53	121	54	124	271
BEDFORDSHIRE										
Stodden and Willey ...	—	27	15	118	248	164	131	243	111	378
BUCKINGHAMSHIRE										
Bunstow	—	12	6	35	77	57	128	77	44	82
OXFORDSHIRE										
Bampton	12	47	259	91	269	93	30	35	166	69
Chadlington	3	64	509	114	138	68	15	29	135	115
Ploughley	5	57	529	82	356	61	22	4	169	27
WARWICKSHIRE										
Stoneleigh and Kineton	51	145	731	260	593	327	127	149	389	738
Over all the hundreds	72	488	2,308	835	2,430	1,018	715	759	2,240	2,689
	0.5%	3%	17%	6%	18%	8%	5%	5%	16%	20%
	510		3,143		3,448		1,474		4,929	
	3.5%		24%		26%		10%		36%	

Our analysis so far leaves many questions unresolved. Conclusions based on the arable area of holdings are of limited value, for such acreage figures give only a partial idea of the peasant economy. We know next to nothing of the relation of arable and pastoral farming to one another—a relation which varied greatly from region to region. Although the region studied is predominantly grain producing, stock-breeding must have played some part, especially on the hills of the south and in the marshes of the east. We do not know the part played in the countryside by non-agricultural occupations, though many names indicate the presence in the peasantry of persons doing non-agricultural work.[1] These names, it is true, are not always a reliable indication of the non-agricultural occupations which were being followed. Not every craftsman received a name from his craft; blacksmiths (who can be distinguished by the special dues they had to render) do not in the Hundred Rolls always have the name 'Faber' attached to them. On the other hand, some of these names had already assumed the character of patronymics and we cannot be sure that every Taylor cut cloth or that every Cooper made barrels. However, the very abundance and variety of names indicating non-agricultural work remind us forcibly that our sources which fix the social position of the rural population purely on the plane of the arable field, give a far from full and very one-sided picture of the English village. Some of the counties, where in 1279 we see an abundance of very small holdings, have in the fourteenth century become places where the village textile industry was developing (Cambridgeshire, for instance). Finally, the economy of many villeins, and even more of the free tenants, need not have been based on arable farming, or not on it alone.

We use the terms virgate, half-virgate and so on, but what degree of economic security do these represent for the peasant family occupying them? Granat thought virgaters were 'rich peasants', exploiting the labour of hired hands. Half-virgaters are, for him, 'solid' peasants. Other investigators have reckoned that a half-virgater could hardly make ends meet. Analysing the living conditions of the English medieval peasantry,

[1] The textile industry is suggested by such names as Textor, Textrix, Draper, Comber, Fullo, Fuller, Cissor, Webbe, Parmentarius, Napper, Taylur, Teynter, Tinctor; the leather-working industry by such as Tannur, Sutor, Sutrix, Cobeler, Pelter, Cirotecarius; the metal-working, by Faber, le Ferrour, le Plumer, Iron-monger; the wood-working and building trades by Carpentarius, Couper, Turner, Cementarius, Masun, Thechare, Pictor; the victualling businesses by Carnificus, Carnifex, Cocus, Coquinarius, Braciator, Braciatrix, Baker, Pistor, Espicer; commerce is indicated by the names Chapman, Monger, Mercer, Mercator, Mercatrix, Wollemonger, Cornmonger, Haringmonger, Caperun; others speak of occupations rural though not agricultural—Bercarius, Gardiner, Graziere, Porker, Vaccarius, Kuherde, Piscator, Venator, Molendinarius; yet others of various functions within the manorial administration and economy—Prepositus, Messer, Bedellus, Forester, Spencer, Wodeward, Hayward, Porter; there are even some like Barbedor, Medicus, Medica, Capellanus, Scriptor; very frequently met with are the appellations Clericus, Clergis.

Bennett concluded that as a rule the peasant was poor and lived on the borderline of want, though a distinction should be drawn between the upper few and the mass.[1] On the solution of this problem depends the way in which we are to understand such conclusions as we have reached on the stratification of the peasantry.

ESTIMATES OF MEDIEVAL PEASANTS' BUDGET

Here we are faced with the very difficult question often asked but not yet satisfactorily answered, of the medieval peasant's budget. The answer is not easy, but we may note some facts which, if they do not solve it once and for all, will at least shed light on some of its most important aspects.

J. T. ROGERS

Rogers devotes many pages to proving that the English peasant in the Middle Ages was well off. He attempts to determine the income of a free peasant with 20 acres.[2] He uses as his starting-point the revenue which the lords of manors received from their lands. By this standard he reckons up the income from the land and common rights of the free peasant. His conclusion is that with a 'capital' of £15 the peasant from his 20 acres makes £3 10s. p.a., of which 10s. go to paying his rent to the lord. Over and above this, he can earn another £1 by working for wages at peak working times. Thus £4 net income is produced. Expenditure on food for the family Rogers calculates thus: four quarters of wheat (£1 3s. 6d.), two quarters of malt for beer (7s. 7d.), 800 lbs. of meat at ¼d. a pound (16s. 8d.); for clothing he allows 17s. All this, in his opinion, comes to £3 (really it is £3 4s. 10d.). In this way the freeholder is left with £1 over. Quite an idyllic picture—good food, including the roast beef of Old England, and £1 over for spending-money. But it is not difficult to see that such a result is produced only by stretching the evidence. Even if we accept Rogers' own hypothesis, what the peasant has left is not £1, but 15s. 2d. But this, of course, is a trifling point. What is more important is that this extra £1 can be earned only by day-labour 'on the side'. Furthermore, Rogers

---

[1] *Op. cit.*, p. 225. [2] *History of Agriculture and Prices*, i, 683.

has treated the expenditure side of the budget in an extremely simplified form. But, most important of all, Rogers takes as his standard a *free* peasant. If, instead, one takes a villein, whose rent is considerably higher than the supposed rent of the free tenant, then even making the most optimistic interpretation it will hardly be possible to make ends meet in his budget.

I. I. GRANAT

Rogers' conclusions can therefore hardly be taken seriously. Granat's attempt to reconstruct the budget of a peasant household with fifteen acres (a half-virgate) under the three-field system appears at first sight more scientifically based. Granat, who wanted to prove that the half-virgaters were 'solid' peasants, comes to even more optimistic conclusions than Rogers. To fix an average for harvest-yields he uses Rogers' figures for 11 manors of Merton College, in the years 1334–36, and in part follows Walter of Henley. Walter, however, depicts English agriculture not as it was, but as he thought it ought to be, and harvests such as he considers normal practically never happened. Granat was also well aware that yields on peasants' fields were lower than on the lord's land, though even the lord's farming did not always produce such large harvests as those quoted by Rogers. According to Ballard,[1] on the manor of Witney (Oxfordshire) in the period between 1340 and 1349 wheat yielded $4\frac{3}{4}$–$7\frac{1}{2}$ bushels per acre, after sowing $2\frac{1}{2}$ bushels, whereas Granat assumes a yield of 10.2 bushels, after sowing 2 bushels.

Granat also follows with some simplification the Merton College evidence in calculating the division of the area to be sown under various crops. On the basis of the average prices of 1340–50, he gives the total income from field crops of his half-virgater as £2 7s. 8d. But he adds a number of other items of revenue—from hay, straw, garden land, kitchen gardening, stock, and various home crafts. In calculating these supplementary sources of revenue Granat uses the accounts of another seigniorial demesne, namely the manor of Forncett (Norfolk) from 1272 to 1305.[2] Comparing revenue from corn crops and revenue from meadow, woodland, and

[1] *O.S.S.L.H.*, v, 192.
[2] F. G. Davenport, *The Economic Development of a Norfolk Manor* (1906).

stock-breeding in these accounts, he reckons the first to be 70 per cent of the total, the second 30 per cent. But he then modifies these proportions, since, in his view, a much more important part would be played in a peasant budget by revenue from garden land and from stock, forgetting that the peasant had a far smaller revenue from hay, peat and wood than the manorial lord. Besides this, according to Granat, the peasant could earn something extra by carting. All this permits him to double the income which was allowed for grain crops, and to estimate the total income of a half-virgater as £4 15s. 6d. He then estimates the half-virgater's expenses. He mentions that there are such expenses as forage for cattle, general maintenance of livestock, repair and renewal of tools and buildings. He does not, however, include these in his calculation to obtain net income, but takes out of the peasant's gross income only his money payments and dues to the lord, which, on his reckoning, should come for a half-virgater to not less than 10 shillings. Thus the half-virgater still has an income of £4 5s. 6d. This is 20 per cent more than Rogers' freeholder with twenty acres. Further, the sum of £4 5s. 6d., representing the net income of the half-virgater, reckoned on the basis of the price of wheat, corresponds to 112 bushels. Granat reckons the half-virgater's family at five persons. In this case he would need, in order to maintain his family on purely vegetable food, 62.1 bushels a year, or, on a mixed diet of animal and vegetable food, 45.5 bushels (the cost of the animal food is for some reason never calculated).

In this way, concludes Granat, the income of a peasant holding with 15 acres is more than twice as much as the subsistence minimum. For the half-virgater received in terms of wheat up to 225 bushels, that is, three to five times more than the subsistence minimum. Therefore he still had left, after paying all expenses, 49.9 bushels of wheat if he lived on a purely vegetable diet, or 66.5 bushels, if his diet was mixed. Translating this into money terms, we get £1 18s. or (on a mixed diet) £2 9s. 5d. over and above the subsistence level, which, according to Granat, is determined solely by food.

Ignoring such curiosities as the saving of 11s. 6d. if the half-virgater's family eats meat instead of bread alone, it is evident that Granat's calculations inflate by all possible means the income of the half-virgater, and minimize his expenditure. The translation of income first into money, then into bushels of wheat, and then back again into money, does nothing to clarify the matter, but only confuses it. Moreover, he ignores the fact that where part of the income of a half-virgater was translated into money (i.e. when he sold some of his produce), the sale was usually made at prices lower than those of the open market. The 10s. which the peasant paid as rent corresponded to a much greater proportion of his income than Granat imagines. In fact, the rent of a half-virgater, especially a villein, was usually much more than 10s. In calculating amounts of rent Granat takes only the fixed payment (*redditus assisae*) plus the money value of labour services, and this sum is actually fairly close to 10s. or even lower. But the very source that he was using,[1] should have shown him that this did not by any means exhaust the payments which the peasants had to make. The court revenues vary greatly from year to year, but on the average they are little lower than the *redditus assisae*, while in 1274–75 and 1279–80 they are even greater. Granat also ignores the seigniorial monopolies. The series of 'sales' (of pasture, wood, etc.) in the accounts really represent levies on the peasants. Aid accounts for no small sum. No consideration is given to *servitia forinseca* while tithes and the whole array of church dues are not taken into account. In short, we can without exaggeration double the allowance out of net income which Granat sets aside for money rent and dues.

On a more careful inspection of Granat's calculations, not only is there nothing left of the surplus which the half-virgater is supposed to have, but even his subsistence level will probably have to be considerably lowered. It would not be often that wheaten bread and the roast beef of Old England appeared on the half-virgater's table. More probably he had to rest content with oatmeal porridge and black bread.

N. S. B. GRAS

Just as optimistic and unconvincing is N. S. B. Gras's attempt to calculate the money budget of a peasant household.[2] Gras works out the budget of a virgater in south Crawley and that

---

[1] The ministers' accounts of the manor of Forncett.
[2] *Economic and Social History of an English Village*, 69–74.

of a fardel-holder in north Crawley. Like Granat, he bases his figures on data for the crop-yields of a lord's economy. But in his calculations there are some interesting points which are worth attention. For his analysis he takes two years—one with a good harvest (1257–58) and one with a bad (1306–07). The Crawley virgater had a holding of 16 acres, which is about equal to the usual half-virgate (in my calculations I have included such virgates among the half-virgates). The fardel equalled $5\frac{1}{2}$ acres.

Gras starts from the assumption that all surplus over what was required for consumption was sold by the peasant at the market price prevailing in that year. As opposed to Rogers and Granat, Gras, although inclined to exaggerate the prosperity of the peasant and the rural labourer, considers that the peasant ate only indifferently well, and first and foremost that he did not eat wheaten bread. It is still assumed that he sowed wheat at his autumn sowing, with the object of selling the crop. Meat was not eaten by the peasant, or only that of beasts that had fallen sick or died. Barley was used for making beer and bread, oats for making porridge. From 5 acres of wheat the virgater might in a good year get in 5 quarters, 4 bushels of which went in payment of the tithe, while the rest was sold. Thus in the year 1257–58, the virgater might make 36s. by the sale of his wheat (at 8 shillings a quarter). It must be said that both the crop-yield and the price given are exceptionally high. According to Rogers' data, the average yearly prices of wheat throughout the whole of the thirteenth century only twice rose higher than 8s., usually being considerably lower. The average price for the decade nearest to the year taken by Gras (1261–70) is 4s. $8\frac{5}{8}d$. According to Gras's own calculations the average price of wheat in Crawley for the period from 1231 to 1314 was 5s. 11d. a quarter.[1]

According to Gras, the income accruing from the sale of stock and animal products was very considerable. In the Middle Ages a customary tenant in Crawley could keep on the common pasture 25 sheep, 1 cow, 1 horse, and unlimited numbers of pigs. Gras assumes that every half-virgater had 2 horses,

[1] One should not forget that Gras takes a good harvest year, when prices could not be particularly high. The oats and barley were used in the peasant's own economy, and were not put on the market.

of which could be sold each year, 25 sheep, 4 of which might
e sold yearly; the wool from 10 sheep and 4 lambs could
lso be sold. Besides these, he had 2 cows, and 2 calves 1 of
which might be sold, and 10 pigs, at least 4 of which could be
old. We see here that Gras is going beyond the limits indicated
y the customs of Crawley. The sale of hides, of chickens, geese,
ggs, milk and cheese could not bring in any considerable
im. On the whole Gras reckons the cash income from stock
nd the produce of stock at 25s. 4d., which, together with the
income from the sale of wheat, amounts to 61s. 4d. Among
ems of expenditure we find 5s. allowed for rent and 9d. for
xtra payments for pasturage. Thus the net profit of the
enant of 16 acres came to 55s. 7d.

In a bad harvest year (1306–07) the virgater could sell
nly one-and-a-quarter quarters of wheat at 7s. a quarter
cheaper than the good harvest year 1257–58). However, he
ells the same amount of stock, including the horse, but at
igher prices. His total income comes to 42s. 5d. His expenses
emain the same, and he is left with 33s. 8d. It is hard to
nderstand how he managed to avoid buying oats and barley
or the family larder, if the harvest for these crops was also bad.
Iowever, it is possible that he had reserves.

For the fardel-holder the sale of produce from his beasts
nd poultry provides the whole of his money income. He does
ot sow wheat and has only enough oats and barley to feed his
amily. At the same time, according to Gras, the fardel-
iolder maintains as large a complement of stock as the virgater,
nd sells as much stock as he does (the exception being that he
ias no draught stock). His money rent is less (2s. 8d.). Con-
equently, he is left with 15s. 11d. in a good harvest year, while
n a bad one he has to buy 4.3 quarters of oats and barley at
s. the quarter. In such a year he sells more wool, leaving
ione for domestic use. In this way he has a surplus of 6s. 9½d.

How did the peasant spend his money? Gras lists the repair
of buildings, purchase of tools, also the lures of the village
nn and of St. Giles' Fair, the purchase of spices and of
nedicines. The virgater had to repair his plough and his cart.
Ie was able to buy himself a cap, and a coloured dress for
iis wife. The fardel-holder could not count on buying such
hings. The greater part of his clothing was made at home.

No wages are included in the fardel-holder's budget. He is too loaded down with labour dues and work on his plot to earn money on the side. The conclusion reached is as follows: the virgater (holder of 16 acres) was fairly prosperous, the fardel-holder had only the bare necessities of life. But it is only stock-breeding, based on the right of pasturage on the commons, that makes life easy for the one and possible for the other. Gras adds that the peasants could rely on the help of the lord in case of need.

As we have seen, much in Gras's figures is based on optimistic assumptions. But in any case, the comparative prosperity of the peasants of the manor of Crawley is dependent on stock-breeding. It must be remembered that Hampshire is sheep-raising country, and Crawley a sheep-raising manor. On the downs there was plenty of grass, and the chalky soil was more favourable to the health of the sheep than the soil of damp and low-lying places. But Gras himself states that the stock-breeding methods of Crawley were fairly primitive, and did not yield high profits. Very many ewes and heifers remained barren. In spite of good soil conditions, the flocks were constantly subject to disease. In the year 1355–56, the lord of the manor got 254 lambs from a total number of 475 ewes. In 1365–66 there was no cheese nor milk available for sale owing to disease among the stock. If things stood thus in the lord's economy they could hardly be any better in that of the peasant. Gras's calculations concerning the peasants' revenue from stock-breeding therefore appear extremely dubious. But Crawley was exceptionally well placed for stock-breeding. What of the population of those villages not enjoying such favourable conditions?

H. S. BENNETT

An attempt to work out the budget of a half-virgater is made by Bennett.[1] On the basis of new research, he reckons the average yield of a peasant virgate at 68 bushels of wheat, 95 bushels of barley and 70 bushels of oats—233 bushels in all. He assumes that these three varieties of grain were sown over equal areas. After allowing grain for the next sowing, 163 bushels are left. A sixteenth of these must be set aside as pay-

[1] *Op. cit.*, chapter iv, especially 85 ff.

ment for milling. This leaves 153 bushels. He does not think it necessary to allow for tithes, sinces these were, as Lennard has shown, taken as sheaves from the harvest-field and were not counted when the yield was reckoned up. Bennett finds it difficult to determine the annual consumption of grain in a peasant household, even using as a basis the issues of corn made to the workers on the demesne, as recorded in ministers' accounts. These issues usually came to 36 bushels a year, but it is not clear whether this was for an individual worker or a whole family. Bennett leans towards the latter supposition. In any case, the virgater gets in much more grain than he needs for home consumption. Bennett takes it that the virgater did not eat wheaten bread, but sold his wheat, receiving (at Rogers' average prices for the years 1261–1400) 35s. 4½d. for his 48 bushels.

But Bennett admits that these calculations are too optimistic. The harvest is reckoned on a very high standard, and not every year was a good one. Besides, this is the income of a virgater—one of the village aristocracy.

But the revenues of the villein do not begin and end with his income from the sale of grain. The stock resources of the peasant present one of the hardest problems, since there could be very considerable variations, depending on the character of the locality. Furthermore, the high mortality among the stock due to epidemics and the difficulties of providing fodder during the winter has to be taken into consideration. Bennett lists sources of food—oxen, cows, sheep, pigs, hens, geese, also game (poached), fish (in spite of prohibitions on fishing)—and comes to the conclusion that the virgater was quite well able to support his family and still have something over for sale or exchange. But this applies to the *virgater*; and the greater part of the villagers held smaller holdings. If one takes 30 to 40 bushels as the minimum amount of grain required to live on, 5 to 10 acres (and nearer 10 than 5) was the minimum holding that could provide a livelihood. On smaller holdings side earnings became a necessity. Bennett does not detail the dues paid by the peasant to his lord and to the state. He supposes that a considerable part of the rural population lived on the borderline of want.

Author's Conclusions

All the attempts to calculate the budget of an English medieval peasant which we have reviewed have one common feature—an underestimation of the feudal exploitation of the peasant. Calculations are either performed for a freeholder, or if not, the villein's dues are given anything but fully. This is partly to be explained by the tendentiousness of some of the sources; but it must be admitted that often the historians, too, make incomplete calculations.

As has already been shown, government and manorial surveys commonly specify only part of the dues which the peasant, the villein especially, had to pay to the lord, thus concealing large amounts of money and produce rent. Furthermore, one must allow for payments to the state, which usually remain outside our field of vision, unless they have been manorialized. Among these should be noted the payments for view of frank pledge, scutage, hidage, contributions to the sheriff, payments to the hundred and to the county, and many others. Further, the peasant was liable to pay levies to the church. Gras allows for tithes, but Granat and Bennett ignore them. Even if Lennard is right in thinking that tithes need not be taken into account in calculating the peasant's budget, since they were taken direct from the field, while the reckoning up of the harvest was done in the barn,[1] they were still a heavy burden on the peasant, and were not the only payment made for the benefit of the church. The spiritual revenues of the church also included payments for various services, as well as offerings on feast days.

Another point which was liable to play an increasing part in the expenses of the peasant should not be forgotten. The help of the lord, or of a rich neighbour, in lean years or in case of economic difficulties of any sort, was not given for nothing. The small and middle peasant became more and more involved in debt. The paying off or working off of debt to the landlord or rich peasant cannot be left out of a calculation of the peasant's expenditure. This indebtedness was particularly likely to increase as money rent became more widely developed. Further, one must not forget all kinds of

[1] *Economic Journal, Supplement,* Feb., 1936.

illegal levies made by the manorial administration. These only occasionally found their way into the records of the manor courts. Bribes, extra work, even the surrender of part of one's land at a low rent—all these were ways of avoiding interference from the manorial administration. Finally, even the temptations of the tavern and the fair, of which Gras speaks, transferred part of the peasant's income to the lord's pocket, since to him belonged the assize of ale and the profits of the fair. It is not easy to list all that the feudal manor, the church and the state took from the peasant, but in sum it must far exceed the figures with which Granat and Gras work.

On the other hand, caution is necessary in calculating the revenue of the villeins. The yield from peasant land is low, because the lord takes the manure for himself, because he disorganizes work on the peasant's fields by taking away every available pair of hands at the most vital working times, and because he takes potential labour away from the peasant's holding to work in his own household. Bad harvests must have been more frequent on the peasant's holding and their effect more catastrophic, since we cannot suppose that a half-virgater, for instance, had any significant reserves. The peasant could count on the help of the lord or of a rich fellow-villager, but this help was not given for nothing, and repayment became a fresh burden. As the date for paying his money rent approached, he might be obliged to sell his corn on the market at low prices to secure ready cash. All the budget reconstructions err in exaggerating the degree of production for the market in the medium peasant's economy. The lowest percentage of money rents in the thirteenth century was amongst virgaters and half-virgaters. The development of a monetary economy fell heavily on precisely these peasants. 'Only in good years and under particularly favourable conditions is the independent husbandry of this type of peasant sufficient to maintain him, and for that reason his position is a very unstable one. In the majority of cases the middle peasant cannot make ends meet, without resorting to loans to be repaid by labour, etc., without seeking 'subsidiary' earnings on the side, which also partly consist of selling labour power, etc.'[1]

We must, of course, note those factors in the peasant economy

[1] V. I. Lenin, *S.W.*, i, p. 235.

of which no details are recorded, such as the part played by pastoral farming and by all kinds of local industries, variations in the size of the virgate, in its fertility, and in the nature of the links between the peasant and the market. Without stretching the evidence, we can assume that the villein half-virgaters, and still more the virgaters, could have made ends meet without great difficulty, had it not been for the weight of feudal exploitation. It was this which not infrequently took from them almost all their surplus product, hindered them from raising the technical level of their farming, put them at a disadvantage in relation to the market, created an oppressive atmosphere of insecurity both of their persons and of their property, and threatened any reserves they might accumulate. But the occupier of a quarter-virgate (5–10 acres) could not—according to the calculations of Bennett, which cannot be called pessimistic—maintain himself on the produce of this plot, even without paying dues. Bennett reckons that the subsistence level, in terms of land held, comes somewhere between 5 and 10 acres, probably nearer the latter.[1] It can, perhaps, be taken to lie somewhere near 10 acres, admitting of course the extreme relativity of such general pronouncements.[2] And the half-virgate is the typical peasant holding.

The main body of the English peasantry, the villeins occupying virgates and half-virgates, were not rich, solid peasants, but a middle peasantry crushed by feudal exploitation. The Ramsey cartulary mentions the case of a virgater who wishes *propter indigentiam* to hire his services to the abbot as a ploughman.[3] The half-virgater might not have draught stock—*et si non habeat animal quo posset arare, liceat ei triturare unam travam frumenti.*[4] There was not (as Rogers thought) a general improvement in the position of the English peasantry in the thirteenth century as a result of which even the cottar could earn good wages in the lord's service. The latest investigations

---

[1] *Op. cit.*, 95.

[2] In the middle of the fourteenth century a bovate (that is, half a virgate), still less a half bovate (fardel), was not accounted sufficient to provide a livelihood. In the parliament of 1354 (28 Ed. III) the Commons complain that labourers take up a bovate or half a bovate of land from the lord, in order to have a pretext for not hiring themselves out as the Statute of Labourers demands, and in actual fact do hire themselves out in their free time for money payments. . . . *prenent bovees de terre ou demy bovee des seignours quele n'est pas sufficancie pur eux dount vivre ou estre occupez. Rot. Parl.*, ii, 261.

[3] *C. Ram.* i, 473.   [4] *R.H.*, ii, 616.

do not justify such optimism. Miss Neilson, while describing the thirteenth and the early fourteenth century as the period of the greatest prosperity of manorial economy ('a golden age for the lords,' 'the heyday of a great estate'), is very doubtful whether this prosperity was equally advantageous to the peasant.[1] The free peasant was not altogether free. He paid feudal rent, was often bound to attend the manor court along with the villeins, shared the common rights of the villeins, was in one degree or another subject to the manorial administration, and was sometimes liable to render certain labour services. But his dependence was less burdensome, his rent as a rule was less heavy, he enjoyed personal freedom and certain guarantees of his property rights. Accumulation of reserves was easier for him. That is why the formation of a peasant upper rank proceeds more quickly among the free tenants.

Undoubtedly the large hereditary free tenant, not obliged by law to attend the hallmote, bound only—and that not always— to the lord's special court for free tenants, paying only a symbolic rent of a few pence or a pair of gloves, entitled to defend his personal and property rights against his lord in the king's courts, and free to alienate and to bequeath his holding, was something very like the owner of his land, in so far as the concept of ownership is compatible with the system of feudal tenure. His place on the feudal ladder was sometimes hard to determine, especially if his holding, as often happened, consisted of many portions of land held from different lords. But lower in the scale of free tenants we find cottars, whose position was so far indistinguishable from that of the unfree cottars that the manorial administration sometimes does not distinguish them, and sees no inconvenience in this, since their role on the manor was exactly the same. In the vast majority of cases we cannot determine exactly the connection between a particular free tenant and the manorial organization. The fact that the obligation to attend the manor court is not mentioned, does not prove that the obligation itself did not exist. Merchet, heriot and so on are generally not mentioned in the Hundred Rolls among the dues of free holdings. Therefore the main, if not the only, material by which to judge the degree of feudal dependence of a free holding consists of the

[1] *Camb. Econ. Hist.*, i, 466.

Q

information on the extent of the money rent (and other forms of rent, if these are present),[1] which it owed.

We have seen[2] that on the manors of the Earl of Norfolk the figure given for *redditus assisae* together with the money value of labour services accounts for not more than half the total rent which the villein in fact paid to the lord. The other half was made up of aids, payments on account of the lord's monopoly rights, and tolls which are recorded in the accounts but usually not in the surveys. But while in the case of the villein about half his rent is concealed by the surveys, in that of the free tenant we can say that his fixed rent, in the majority of cases, represented the major portion of his dues, and hence that it is possible to judge the degree of his exploitation by the amount of his rent.

VARIATIONS IN THE BURDEN OF RENT ON DIFFERENT TYPES OF HOLDINGS

What was the degree of exploitation of free holdings as compared with villein holdings? Table 13 enables us to compare the average rents of free and villein holdings. A quick glance through the table is sufficient to show that villein holdings are incomparably more heavily burdened with rent than free holdings. The villein virgate and half-virgate carry rents on the average two-and-a-half times heavier than those of free holdings of the same size; villein fardels have rents twice as heavy as those of equivalent free tenements; only in the rents of small holdings is there no particular distinction observable, though even here the load on the villein holdings is somewhat heavier. As has already been said, part of the dues for both villein and free holdings escapes calculation. This hidden part is much smaller in the case of free tenants, who did not usually pay aid, were not subject to the seigniorial monopolies, were far less tied to the manor court, and were not as a rule liable to pay taxes on the sale of stock, pannage, and many other levies which taken together bore heavily on the villeins. Hence it seems clear that the villein virgate and half-

---

[1] The reservation must be made that the amount of fixed rent (*redditus assisae*) plus other, mostly very minor, dues, does not represent an exhaustive survey of all the forms of feudal exploitation to which a free holding was liable. Thus all the conclusions based on this material are only approximate.

[2] Above, pp. 164–7.

virgate bore on the average a load three or four times as heavy as that of the free holdings of equal size.

This constitutes a fundamental economic difference between free and villein tenure. If, on the whole, feudal rent devoured almost entirely the surplus product of the villein, in the case of the freeholder it left a certain part still in his hands, and thus there were far greater possibilities of accumulation for him than existed for the villein. And we must further note the greater legal security for the accumulations of a freeholder.

It is not difficult to see that as a rule the larger a free holding was, the lighter comparatively was its rent. In Cambridgeshire, holdings of over one virgate on the average pay a lower rent (in absolute terms) than holdings of one virgate. Rent per virgate is on the average half as much for holdings over one virgate as for those of one virgate; in some hundreds (Thame, Normancross) it is little more than a quarter. But the rents of half-virgates are proportionately higher than those of virgates. This, as is well known, also applies to villein holdings.

The table also confirms and amplifies the observation already made that the exploitation of villein holdings in eastern England is greater than in counties further to the west, and that in the east villein households were less well provided with land. The most oppressive form of rent, labour rent, bulked larger among the dues of villeins in the eastern counties, in spite of the greater development there of a monetary economy. The rent of a virgate in the Oxfordshire hundreds included in our calculations is, on the average, two-and-a-half times lighter than the corresponding rent in the Huntingdonshire hundred of Normancross. The rent of a half-virgate in Huntingdonshire is nearly twice as high as in Oxfordshire.[1] Since the amounts of other feudal levies are unknown it is difficult to reach a final conclusion, but in any case our figures confirm yet again the observation made earlier, that the feudal exploitation of the unfree peasant is heaviest in the regions of the greatest development of money-commodity relations.

They also provide partial confirmation of another observation—viz. that it is in the eastern counties that the distinction

[1] It may be that some part in this is played by the comparatively small size of an Oxfordshire virgate, which is on the average about 25 acres. But differences in the average size of villein virgates are still not enough to explain the differences in the amount of rent.

TABLE 13

RENTS (in shillings and pence) OF FREE AND VILLEIN HOLDINGS
(average figures)

County	Hundred	Free holdings					Villein holdings			
		Over 1 virgate	1 virgate	½ virgate	¼ virgate	Under 5 acres	1 virgate	½ virgate	¼ virgate	Under 5 acres
Bedfordshire	Willey and Stodden ...	£0.5.1 (0.3.9) 22	£0.3.0 80	£0.2.8 171	£0.1.10½ 143	£0.1.0 192	£0.16.4 13	£0.8.0. 244	£0.3.7 84	£0.1.1 85
Buckinghamshire	Bunstow, Stodfold, Mursley, Mucha ...	0.3.1 (0.1.2) 58	0.4.6 121	0.3.6 145	0.4.1 58	0.1.10 144	0.8.8 125	0.8.10 296	0.7.2 69	0.1.10 342
Huntingdonshire	Normancross ...	0.7.6 (0.1.4) 35	0.6.3 71	0.7.2 62	0.1.4 28	0.1.3 307	0.5.2—0.15.6 1.0.8 244	0.6.0—0.5.2 0.11.2 239	0.3.8—0.1.0 0.4.8 6	0.1.5—0.0.4 0.1.9 483
Cambridgeshire	Stow ...	0.3.10 (0.1.4) 8	0.3.11 20	0.4.3 58	0.2.0 56	0.0.11 499	[0.10.4] 4	0.4.7—0.6.8 0.11.3 114	0.3.0—0.4.0 0.7.0 115	0.0.10—0.2.2 0.3.0 104
	Thriplow ...	0.6.11 (0.3.1) 6	0.5.11 29	0.4.0 37	0.2.9 39	0.1.4 162	[1.0.0] 3	0.1.7—0.7.7 149	0.1.5—0.3.10 92	0.1.6—0.0.11 0.2.5 202
	Chesterton ...	0.3.6 (0.2.10) 2	0.4.8 10	0.3.10 17	0.2.4 9	0.1.10 38	—	0.8.0 170	0.3.6 46	0.3.3 114
	Whittlesford ...	0.5.7 (0.1.2) 14	0.4.3 13	0.2.8 38	0.1.7 50	0.0.9 299	0.6.10—0.8.0 0.14.10 9	0.2.10—0.5.7 0.8.5 114	0.1.10—0.3.3 0.5.1 47	0.1.5—0.0.9 135
Cambridgeshire	For all hundreds together ...	0.5.0 (0.2.1)	0.4.6	0.3.8	0.2.2	0.1.3	0.14.8	0.9.7	0.5.4	0.2.9
Oxfordshire	Bampton ...	0.10.0 (0.3.4) 52	0.5.6 95	0.3.9 107	0.4.0 33	0.1.6 81	0.4.3—0.7.2 0.11.5 249	0.2.8—0.4.3 0.6.11 270	0.2.5—0.4.0 70	0.3.1—0.0.9 93
	Banbury ...	0.5.6 (0.2.4) 37	0.2.10 35	0.1.1 16	0.4.4 5	0.1.6 7	0.4.0—0.3.7 0.7.7 28	—	—	0.1.8—0.0.11 93
	Bullington ...	0.6.7 (0.2.4) 30	0.3.4 35	0.2.8 31	0.1.11 10	0.1.4 89	[0.7.9—0.0.10] 71	[0.3.2—0.1.10] 131	0.5.0 131	0.1.10 122
	Thame ...	0.8.6 (0.1.10) 22	0.8.4 22	0.2.10 22	0.2.1 6	0.3.0 21	0.5.0—0.2.3 0.8.7 71	0.3.5—0.0.10 0.4.3 11	—	0.2.0—0.0.6 71
	Chadlington ...	0.8.1 (0.2.4) 68	0.5.5 109	0.3.11 59	0.2.10 25	0.1.9 103	0.2.0—0.6.7 0.8.7 139	0.1.6—0.6.0 0.7.6 61	—	0.1.6—0.0.9 0.2.3 54
	Ploughley ...	0.5.1 (0.1.7) 49	0.4.6 59	0.2.6 46	0.2.0 4	0.1.6 17	[0.10.8] 275	—	—	—
	Wootton ...	0.5.2 (0.1.10) 65	0.4.3 114	0.3.10 76	0.2.8 36	0.0.11 108	[0.7.3]	—	—	—
Oxfordshire	For all hundreds together ...	0.7.0 (0.2.2)	0.4.10	0.2.11	0.2.10	0.1.9	0.8.9	0.5.11	0.4.11	0.2.6

In Table 13 a comparison is given of the amounts of free and villein rents, limited to a few sample hundreds. I have quoted the average figures for the *money* rents of freeholders, other small forms of rent not being taken into account.

The table gives the average figures of rent for holdings of various sizes, divided into five basic groups on the basis of their arable areas. I have distinguished holdings of one virgate (from 20 to 40 acres), half a virgate (10 to 20 acres), and quarter of a virgate (5 to 10 acres). Special groups are allotted to holdings over one virgate and to petty holdings of less than 5 acres. For all these categories—free and villein holdings being given separately—I have given the average rent figures, with an indication of the number of cases dealt with in producing the average figure. For villein holdings money rent and the assessment of labour dues are given separately where this can be done, and are placed above the common total of the two. In a number of cases one has to be satisfied with an over-all assessment of rent (labour and money rent—produce rent has not been taken into account, as being on the average quite insignificant). Aid, where it is referred to in the source, has been counted in with money rent.

In view of the considerable variations in size, within the grouping 'over one virgate', I have given, alongside the average *total* rent of these holdings, the *average* rent of one virgate on holdings over one virgate in size (taking the average virgate to be 30 acres). The rent of one virgate is given in brackets.

Figures which have been worked out approximately or hypothetically are given inside square brackets.

Villein holdings of over one virgate are a rarity in the material I have used, and I have not included them in the table. The only instance is *three* villein holdings of over 1 virgate, in the Oxfordshire hundred of Bampton. Their rent on the average is 12s. 4d.

It should be observed that in some cases the average rents of free holdings were affected by a small number of exceptionally high rents, and it might have been more correct to give lower average figures. Thus for the Cambridgeshire hundred of Whittlesford the average figure for the rent of holdings over 1 virgate (5s. 7d.) is caused by *one* case only of high rent. If this case is omitted, the average figure falls to 2s. 6d. The same applies to the hundred of Thriplow in the same county, where the high average figure for the rent of holdings over one virgate is also due to one case alone. If it is left out, the figure falls from 6s. 11d. to 2s. 10d. It is thus possible to speak of extremely low rents for free holdings of over 1 virgate in Cambridgeshire, and of some high rents which appear as exceptions.

between free and villein holdings is most sharply expressed. The difference in amount of rent between villein and free holdings is more considerable in Cambridgeshire, where the rent of villein virgates is almost three times that of free virgates, in Huntingdonshire, where it is more than three times, and in Bedfordshire, where it is almost five-and-a-half times as heavy, than it is in Oxfordshire, where the rent of a free virgate is only about half as much as that of a villein virgate. While there are very considerable differences between the rents of villein holdings in the east and those in the west, we do not see any such difference in the rents of free holdings. The average rents of free holdings in Bedfordshire and Cambridge-shire are lower than those in Oxfordshire, and those in Huntingdonshire are only a little higher (if one does not count the exceptionally high rental of free half-virgates in Huntingdonshire).

From this the conclusion may be drawn that the growth of feudal rent affected free holdings but little, and that so far as villein holdings are concerned it proceeded more rapidly in the east, in connection with the rapid growth of money-commodity relations.

In the case of small holdings the distinctions between free and villein and between east and west, are considerably less marked, though on the whole villein holdings are again some-what more heavily burdened. But averages have only limited significance when obtained from a wide range of figures, as is the case with the rents of free holdings. It is more profitable to study them in all their variety, as set out in Table 14, than in averages.

A glance at this table shows that the smallest rents are owed from the largest holdings (over 1 virgate). These insigni-ficant rents (Group V) are numerically preponderant in all the counties covered, and even (with unimportant exceptions) in the individual hundreds. For holdings of one virgate the most common rents are less than 1s. or between 1s. and 5s. (these, too, represent very insignificant amounts, even at their upper limit averaging only about 2d. per acre). On the whole rents of less than 5s. account for about 60 per cent of the rents of free holdings over one virgate, and almost as high a percent-age of the rents of holdings of 1 virgate. For holdings of half a

TABLE 14

RENT OF FREE HOLDINGS

County	Hundred	Holdings of over 1 virgate					Holdings of 1 virgate					Holdings of ¼ virgate				
		I	II	III	IV	V	I	II	III	IV	V	I	II	III	IV	V
BEDFORDSHIRE	Willey and Stodden	4	3	4	11	22	—	5	14	25	35	—	11	15	112	33
BUCKINGHAMSHIRE	Bunstow, Stodfold, Mursley, Mucha	—	8	7	13	30	—	16	20	36	49	—	18	20	41	66
HUNTINGDONSHIRE	Normancross	5	2	5	6	17	3	13	18	23	14	—	28	8	13	13
CAMBRIDGESHIRE	Stow	1	—	—	4	3	—	1	6	8	5	—	6	15	23	14
	Thriplow	1	1	—	2	—	—	7	10	9	3	—	4	11	13	9
	Chesterton	1	—	—	2	2	—	—	1	6	3	—	3	2	6	6
	Whittlesford	—	2	4	1	8	—	2	3	2	4	—	—	7	21	10
OXFORDSHIRE	Bampton	8	11	14	4	15	—	20	20	35	20	—	7	28	45	27
	Banbury	4	6	6	1	20	2	—	11	12	12	—	—	—	7	9
	Bullington	3	8	1	—	15	4	2	11	12	10	—	—	8	15	8
	Thame	2	—	—	3	6	—	6	7	4	3	1	—	7	6	9
	Chadlington	5	12	14	13	22	1	23	23	32	27	—	6	13	24	17
	Ploughley	3	8	8	11	19	—	8	21	18	12	—	1	6	27	12
	Wootton	7	4	11	17	26	—	22	26	29	36	3	3	18	23	29
TOTALS FOR THE COUNTIES																
Bedfordshire		4	3	4	11	22	—	5	14	25	35	—	11	15	112	33
Buckinghamshire		—	8	7	13	30	—	16	20	36	49	—	18	20	41	66
Huntingdonshire		5	2	5	6	17	3	13	18	23	14	—	28	8	13	13
Cambridgeshire		3	3	4	9	13	—	10	20	25	15	—	13	35	63	39
Oxfordshire		32	49	54	49	123	7	81	119	142	120	4	17	80	147	113
Total for entire material		44	65	75	88	205	10	125	191	251	233	4	87	158	376	204

This table classifies the rents of free holdings grouped according to size. With this object I take in order, holdings of over one virgate (over 40 acres), of one virgate (20 to 40 acres) and of half a virgate (10 to 20 acres). Holdings of a quarter-virgate are too few and provide little real evidence. The analysis of petty holdings and their rents requires a special study. Rents are divided into five groups: I—rents of over 20s. II—rents of 10 to 20 shillings, III—from 5 to 10 shillings, IV—1 to 5 shillings, and V—less than 1 shilling. The rents of this last group are very small, coming even for half-virgates to less than 1d. per acre on the average. This group also includes a number of cases where rent is reduced to nothing but the rendering of forinseca servitia, attendance at the court, or the payment of a symbolic contribution in kind.

virgate rents of 1s. to 5s. predominate, i.e. ½d. and 6d. per acre; but even here the very small rents account for 30 per cent of the total. Furthermore, among these holdings with light rentals many do not pay any rent at all; their obligations to the lord are limited to attendance at court, and the rendering of *forinseca servitia*. In the Bedfordshire surveys, for example, there are 22 holdings of over 1 virgate owing rents under one shilling, but of these 14 paid no rent money at all.

Among the large free holdings, on the other hand, we find a certain number with quite high rents, paying £1 or more. They are not numerous, less than 10 per cent of the total, and may be due to special peculiarities of tenure, indicating the development of leasehold (for terms of years, for life, or at the lord's will). For instance, the only large rent among the large-scale holdings in the Cambridgeshire hundred of Whittlesford (£2 6s. 8d. from 58 acres) is paid by a life-tenant. In other cases high rents are connected with fee farm. Such cases occur occasionally in the Hundred Rolls, but the entries are so summary that it is impossible to establish any consistent connection between high rents and tenure for a limited term. Nevertheless, it is certain that many cases of high rents occur among holdings for life, for terms of years and at the lord's will. In the hundred of Chadlington (Oxfordshire) one virgate held at the lord's will pays 15s. (the average rent of a virgate being 5s. 5d.), virgates held for life pay 13s. 4d. and 13s., while other holdings for life of single virgates in the same hundred pay 6d., or in two cases only 1d. In the hundred of Banbury two holdings for life of 4 virgates each pay 1 lb. of cummin and scutage; but in the same place 2 virgates pay £2 0s. 0d.[1]

THE ORIGINS OF FREE RENTS

It is also possible that in some cases high rents indicate the recent conversion of villein into free holdings. This seems particularly likely when the tenant has also to fulfil some specifically villein obligations. But here, too, the evidence in the Hundred Rolls is too scanty for certain conclusions. Among villein obligations, only labour dues are normally mentioned,

[1] *R.H.*, ii, 707.

and in the case of free holding these are, on the whole, rare and insignificant, amounting only to two or three days' boon work. Labour dues occur most frequently among the small holdings, and are more often linked with low money rents than with high. It has already been noted that labour dues for free holdings occur more frequently in the west (in Oxfordshire and Warwickshire) than in the east, but even there they are very insignificant.[1] The Hundred Rolls do not usually give us any indication of why a particular free holding pays a high or a low rent. Nevertheless, we can establish some of the factors which determine the levels of peasant free rent. Among these we may note:

1. The origin of the free holding; i.e. whether it was an ancient money-rent-paying holding with a rent fixed long ago, or the result of a more recent contract; whether it was formed by the leasing of part of the demesne, by assarting, or out of a villein holding on which the labour dues had been commuted.[2]

2. The terms of tenure; i.e. whether the holding is hereditary, for the holder's life, for a term of years, or at the lord's will. In other words, whether it is free tenure in the strict sense of the word, or what later came to be called leasehold.

3. The conditions obtaining when the holding last changed hands. In a number of cases a specified rent was not fixed once and for all for the holding. When the holding changed hands, the rent might be altered by contract between the old and the new tenant. In some cases the transfer of a holding might really be a sale and purchase, but concealed owing to the usual practice of enfeoffment for rent. In this case the rent might be reduced to the formal payment of a trifling sum annually, the real price of the land having been paid in one sum at the time of alienation. This payment is sometimes given the name *gersuma*. *Gersumae* are also paid when villein holdings are alienated and sometimes, particularly in the fourteenth century, involve quite large amounts. Here the payment undoubtedly represents an important supplement to feudal rent. But in the case of the alienation of a free holding

---

[1] The Hundred Rolls sometimes omit petty labour dues of freeholders.

[2] Vinogradoff notes that a low rent may indicate that tenurial relations arose not from the surrender of land to the lord, but from the voluntary subordination of the holder to the lord, in which case the rent is only *recognitio*—the recognition of dependence on the lord's patronage. Cf. *Villainage*, 347–48.

the payment of *gersuma* often (though not always) indicates the compounding of the obligation to pay rent.

The Hundred Rolls often mention the sale and purchase of holdings. The term used is, *acquisitus*, acquired holdings. In the Statute of *Quia Emptores* (1290), those acquiring free holdings are buyers, *emptores*. In an interesting document from the muniments of the manor of Wotton Underwood in Buckinghamshire, dating from the middle of Edward I's reign,[1] the lord of the manor, who is letting a plot of land (*placea*), even breaks the links binding the alienated land to the manorial organization. For the holding so alienated the fairly high rent of 3s. has to be paid, but in return the holder is freed from all other manorial payments and obligations. A *gersuma* of 36s. 8d., i.e. twelve times as much as the rent, is paid at the time of alienation; but even then, after the payment of *gersuma*, quite a high rent remains. But more often the *gersuma* paid over *prae manibus* is the main consideration, and the rent is reduced to nominal *recognitio*. For instance, Peter Rokele hands over 6¾ acres, scattered over the open fields, in return for a *gersuma* of 10 marks and 10 shillings (£7 3s. 4d.) and an annual rent of 1d. *legalis monetae*.[2] The holding surrendered does not have to carry any other manorial services; evidently they are all compounded for by the high *gersuma* of approximately £1 1s. 1d. per acre. In transactions of this sort *forinseca servitia* might or might not be bought out.

Among the manorial free tenants there are people who make a business of accumulating land. Putting down a more or less high *gersuma*, they pay practically no rent to the lords of the manors. Thus at the end of the '80s or during the '90s of the thirteenth century very active buyers of land appear on the manor of Wotton in the persons of a certain Peter Spillman of Wodeham and his wife, Margery. Eighteen documents have been preserved recording the acquisition by them of small plots of land, for *gersumae* of 10, 20 or 40 shillings. For these acquired plots they paid no rents except various *forinseca servitia*.

Analogous cases are by no means rare in the Hundred Rolls. An example of a considerable property amassed in small

[1] F. M. Powicke, 'Observations concernant le franc tenant anglais au XIIIᵉ siècle', *Receuils de la Société Jean Bodin*, iii (1938), p. 211.
[2] *Ibid.*, p. 226. Compare Vinogradoff, *Villainage*, p. 348.

scraps is provided by the estate of Roger of Willey in Bedfordshire, which is described in part of the Hundred Rolls, but
even more fully in an inquisition *post Mortem*.[1] This estate
consisted of almost 50 holdings, small for the most part, held
under various people on various manors, and comprised more
than 200 acres. The well-known fragmentation of peasant
holdings (and often of the demesne as well) into small strips
made more easy the acquisition of land in small parcels. Thus
a system which was originally intended to ensure the equality
of allotments now facilitated the growth of inequality.

The lord of the manor himself might become a buyer of
free holdings, particularly as he occupied an especially advantageous position for such activities. Thus in Wotton in the
reign of Edward I this was done extensively by the family of
the lords of the manor, the Grenvilles. But while the purchase
of land with *gersuma* paid *prae manibus* created low rents in a
number of cases, transactions which raised the rent of free
holdings were also possible. The purchase of rents is not a
rarity at the end of the thirteenth century. Powicke mentions
such a transaction at Wotton between the lord of the manor,
Richard Grenville, and his freeholder, W. Olive, in which,
in return for a single payment by Richard of 10s., Olive was
bound to pay him 10d. a year on one of his holdings in Wotton.
There are many similar cases in the Hundred Rolls.

These transactions illustrate how the payment of a definite
sum *prae manibus* might influence the amount of free rent. Great
caution must therefore be observed in drawing conclusions
concerning the origin of a rent from its amount. But it is
important in any case to have established that a very considerable percentage of peasant freeholders paid exceptionally low
rents. High rents are exceptional, especially in the upper
categories of peasant holdings, and this suggests that the
more prosperous section of the peasantry used their wealth
to buy out their rent by making a single cash payment.

Among the free holdings on many manors covered by the
Hundred Rolls, Vinogradoff noticed the same symmetry that
characterizes villein holdings.[2] These free holdings are virgates
or half-virgates with identical dues. Against those who attributed this symmetry to the freeing of villein lots, Vinogradoff

[1] C. Ed. I, File 22-2.   [2] *Villainage*, 337.

argued that most of the free holdings involved paid only a low rent (a mere *recognitio*), whereas commutation means the replacement of labour dues by a more or less equivalent money rent. Although a final solution of this problem is not possible on the basis of the material provided by our sources, I am not altogether convinced by Vinogradoff's arguments, which are influenced by his tendency to find everywhere traces of the ancient free community. The transformation of a villein into a free holding might be, and frequently was, accompanied by the buying-out in part or in whole of the landlord's rights, and the object bought out might be not only the unfree character of the holding, but part of the rent. In spite of the fact that at Common Law the villein could not own personal property, and, according to Glanville, could not buy his freedom, among the upper ranks of peasants both accumulation of resources and purchases of freedom took place. The lords, of course, tried to extract from the villeins their accumulated savings, by means of entry fines and aids which were often at the lord's will. It is possible, also, that in some cases they might be compelled to purchase their freedom, as provided for in the famous *ordonnance* of Louis X.[1]

The large sums sometimes paid over as *gersuma* for free holdings compel us to consider how such sums could have been accumulated. Was not some part played here by money accumulated in the towns, either through the buying up of land by townsmen, or, more probably, through credit given by usurers? There is evidence that money accumulated in the towns had already begun to have some influence on the countryside. For example, a certain John of London holds the manor of Bladon from the king.[2] Sometimes the usurer might also be a lord, buying up the rents of free holdings, and the holdings themselves. The lord, it seems, used the feudal rent he received from his tenants to increase this rent further, or to take over land from his tenants.

CONCLUSIONS

In summing up, we must emphasize once again the extremely varied composition of free holdings, even if we limit our view

[1] Cf. H. Sée, *Les Classes Rurales et le Régime Domanial en France* (1901), p. 242.
[2] *R.H.*, ii., 851.

only to holdings of peasant type. This complicated grouping includes holdings with very varied forms of dependence, sometimes coming very close to villeinage. But on the whole there is a sharp distinction between villein and free holdings. This does not preclude, however, a certain 'unfreedom' in the case of a free holding which may vary, as Marx says, 'from serfdom with forced labour to the point of a mere tributary relationship (*Tributspflichtigkeit*).'[1]

The characteristic features which distinguish the free holding from the serf holding, the free tenant from the villein, are:

1. The predominance among free holdings of *money rent*. But money rent also occurs among villein holdings with commuted rents.

2. The predominance of money rent results in a series of characteristic peculiarities in the position of free holdings. 'With the coming of money rent the traditional and customary relation between the landlord and the subject tillers of the soil, who possess and cultivate a part of the land, is turned into a pure money relation fixed by the rules of positive law.'[2] It is the predominance of money rent from which arises the personal freedom of the vast majority of free tenants, their right to leave the manor, the fixed level of their rents, the right of free alienation and bequest, and finally, the protection of free holding in the king's courts. Of course, circumstances determined to what extent any particular free tenant could, in fact, avail himself of these rights. All these 'freedoms' of free holding existed chiefly for the small upper section of the free peasantry, in whom the government saw an important source of support in its administrative, judicial and fiscal activity, and to whom it saw fit to afford patronage.

3. Free holdings present a much more variegated picture than villein holdings so far as size is concerned. The typical peasant holdings of one virgate or half a virgate, which comprise more than 60 per cent of all the villein holdings under consideration, account for only 33 per cent of the free holdings. But small holdings (less than 5 acres), which account for

[1] K. Marx, *Capital*, iii (1909), 918. A more accurate translation would be 'the obligation to pay rent'.
[2] *Ibid.*, p. 634.

29 per cent of villein holdings, come to as much as 46 per cent of free holdings, while very small free holdings (less than 3 acres) are considerably the more numerous (40 per cent). Similarly, among the free holdings the upper crust is much more strongly differentiated. But comparison here is made difficult by the fact that the surveys ignore the question of villein tenements held on lease, while, on the other hand, the large free holdings merge into the manors.

4. Light money rents predominate among free holdings, and the larger a holding is, the lighter they are relatively. On the average a free holding of a virgate or half-virgate pays a rent three or four times as light as that of a comparable villein holding. Furthermore a considerable percentage of free holdings pay only symbolic rent (*recognitio*), or none at all. Labour rent plays an insignificant part among the dues of free holdings. Generally speaking, the bigger a holding, the 'freer' it is in the matter of rent. The very smallest holdings (5 acres and under) often approach villein standards in the level of rent. They also more frequently owe labour dues.

Among the holdings of half a virgate or more (10 to 20 acres) which are entered in Table 14, about a third pay a quite insignificant rent. In the upper division (40 to 120 acres) about half the holdings pay trifling rents. Non-monetary obligations (e.g. attendance at hundred- and county-courts, journeys on the lord's business,) occur sporadically.

5. Among free holdings a process of alienation is evident which on the one hand breaks up the former holdings, while on the other hand it leads to the accumulation of holdings in the hands of the upper ranks of the peasants. This is carried out principally through small acquisitions, accompanied by the payment of *gersuma*, i.e. the full or partial buying-out of rent claims.

6. Very small rents, the weakening of links with the manorial organization, freedom of alienation, protection of tenants' rights by the king's courts—all these factors are bringing a section of the freeholders close to the position of small landowners, in so far as it is possible to speak of 'property' while feudal conceptions of land law still prevail. Given certain conditions, the development of money rent can lead to 'a release of the old possessors from their tributary relationship

by buying themselves free from their landlord, so that they become independent farmers and free owners of the land tilled by them.'[1]

7. Side by side with the beginnings of small-scale property, one can also observe the beginning of tenancy relationships, in the form of the development of limited tenures—for life, for a term of years, at the lord's will, and fee-farm. Many examples occur in the Hundred Rolls; but the information they give is too inexact for general conclusions to be drawn.

8. The commutation of villein dues must have contributed to the growth of free holdings. The villein who pays money rent remains a villein. His holding remains a villein holding, held at the will of the lord and subject to the custom of the manor, even though villeins paying money rent occupied a privileged position compared with villeins rendering labour dues.[2] Nevertheless, some free holdings were probably created out of villein holdings as a result of the buying out of labour dues. Perhaps the high rents of certain free holdings are an indication of their villein origin. But on the whole the development of villein holding pursued its own course, and copyhold preserved many of the characteristic features of the earlier servile tenure. Between freehold and copyhold there remained a sharp distinction, social and political as well as legal.

9. Under the conditions of feudal economy and law, the formation of an upper crust of large freeholders took the form of the creation of small manors, with their own tenants, free and unfree.

10. Among the freeholders the number of peasants insufficiently provided with land increased rapidly. They had no effective defence particularly against the arbitrary actions of the manorial administration and the oppressions of their own prosperous fellow-villagers, and could not dream of seeking protection in the king's courts, which in law they had the formal right to do. Hence, on the whole, the history of the free cottar merges with that of his unfree neighbours.

[1] K. Marx, *Capital*, iii, 634 (= 1909 edition, p. 928).
[2] On this category of holders—*molmen, censuarii,*—see Vinogradoff, *Villainage,* p. 186 ff.

CHAPTER V

SMALL LANDOWNERS IN MEDIEVAL ENGLAND

POLITICAL AND SOCIAL IMPORTANCE OF THE SMALL LAND-OWNERS

The traditional interpretation of the English manor, based on sources derived from the large estates of the great feudal landowners, has concentrated attention on certain problems, such as that of 'villeinage', to the exclusion of others equally important. In particular, historians of agrarian development have ignored that unique social group to which the political historians have paid so much attention—the well-to-do free peasant and the small knights. It was only by gaining the support of this group that royal power could be maintained in the eleventh and twelfth centuries in the face of the separatist ambitions of the barons. And it was primarily for them that the legal reforms of Henry II were designed. For not only were such measures as the possessory assizes chiefly useful to the small manorial lords and richer free tenants, but the same people played, as jurors, a decisive part in their operation, as well as participating increasingly in local government.

The interchangeability of knights and free men in affairs of law and government is very significant. It reflected the indistinct line which was drawn in the land law between military tenure and socage, as well as the fact that even as early as the twelfth and thirteenth centuries the knights were being reinforced by recruits from the upper ranks of the free peasantry. As knight's fees were broken up their specifically military character was lost, while on the other hand the government insisted on the military responsibilities of ordinary free men throughout the twelfth and thirteenth centuries. Finally, the obligation imposed, at the end of the thirteenth century, on free men with a certain property qualification to become knights ensured that the latter should not become a closed estate. These *agrarii milites* (as earlier chronicles had called them) were too important in the conduct of local affairs to be allowed to die out, though the continued shortage of knights for assizes and inquisitions caused the sheriffs to fall back again and again on the services of the more prominent free men.

Economically the group ranged from the knights with an income from land of £10 or £20 a year, to free peasants with incomes of 20s. or more. The knights obviously anticipate the gentry of the future—county notables occupied with farming and local affairs. But the lower reaches of the group might include (from 1285) free tenants who, having an income of 20s. a year, could be called upon to serve as jurors in their own county, or who, if in receipt of 40s. a year, had to serve in other counties. This anticipation of the franchise qualification of 1430 reminds us that the local leaders of these people would be drawn from those lords of small or middle-sized manors, sometimes known as *buzones*, who later played an important part in parliament.

On a number of occasions the great and small feudal lords had acted together in order to ensure that the king, the first baron of England, should not misuse the power they allowed him to wield on their behalf. But in fact the lines of development of the upper and lower ranks of the feudal class were different. The barons, the earls, and the lords spiritual did not attend the hundred courts—did not serve as *milites de comitatu*. Political experience should have taught them that an alliance with the gentry (as well as with the upper classes in the towns) was an essential condition for the control of royal power. The crown fully realized, on the other hand, that this group was the natural counterpoise to the oligarchic tendencies of the barons. This was the political lesson Edward I learned from Simon de Montfort, after he had used the barons to defeat him. The association of the knights with the burgesses in Simon de Montfort's 'parliament' and later was an expression of social fact. In England the division between town and countryside was far from complete; many towns remained semi-agrarian in character. Burgage tenure was a variety of free tenure, and there was no legal distinction between the free tenant and the burgage holder. The same persons often held both town burgages and rural free tenements. England

R

saw little of the conflicts between towns and feudal lords which were so frequent on the continent. Industrial development from the fourteenth century, and perhaps earlier, took place in the countryside, often by-passing the towns. From this point of view, also, the knights were not a closed estate; they were never divided from the bourgeoisie by an insuperable wall.

But what was it that divided the knights from the great barons, and linked them so closely with the upper ranks of the free tenants and the burgesses? Was the difference between them simply a matter of the size of their estates? Or was there some other qualitative distinction in their social and economic positions? The clue is given at a later date, when the labour legislation of Edward III occupied such an important place in parliamentary business. A petition of 1368 contains a complaint of the high price of labour by *la Comune qe vivent par geynerie de lour Terres ou Marchaundie e qe nont seigneurie ne Villeins pur eux servir*.[1] It would be difficult to put more in so few words. The lesser lords and the wealthy townsmen, whose primary need is cheap hired labour, set themselves apart from the great estate owners, with their lordships and their villeins who work for them. Here, in embryonic form in feudal society is the capitalist mode of production, based on the exploitation of hired labour, already seen as the antithesis of the feudal mode of production. Yet less than a century separates the period of labour legislation from the date of compilation of the Hundred Rolls—not a very long time considering the slow rate of development of feudal society. If, therefore, we examine the situation of the knights and the wealthy free tenants at the end of the thirteenth century, we may find an answer to some of the riddles of English social and political history.

The Jurors of 1279

The Hundred Rolls contain useful information on the social and economic position of the knights and free men whom we have been discussing. They contain the names of the jurors, making up the twenty juries which provided the information for the composition of the rolls, and they contain descriptions of the landed estates of these jurors, or most of them. I have

[1] *Rot. Parl.*, ii, 296.

examined the composition of eighteen of these juries, comprising
179 jurors, serving in the hundreds of Bunstow (Bucks.),
Chesterton, Northstow, Staine, Staploe, Thriplow, Wetherley,
Whittlesford (Cambs.), Leightonstone, Toseland (Hunts.),
Bampton, Banbury, Bullington, Ewelme, Langtree, Thame,
Ploughley, and (in part) Chadlington (Oxon.). About thirty-
five jurors named in the lists could not be traced in the pages of
the survey, or the information concerning them was clearly
incomplete. We cannot be sure, either, that in other cases
we have complete information. But a general idea of the
composition of the body of jurors can, it seems to me, be
obtained.

If the procedure followed for the 1279 survey was that
employed when the king's justices arrived on circuit, the first
step would be for the sheriff to call a full county court upon
the arrival of the king's commissioners. Then the bailiffs of
the hundreds would choose four knights from each hundred
and these knights in their turn would choose twelve knights, or
if it were impossible to find knights, they would choose freemen
who would carry out the king's commission in a proper manner.
In actual fact the number of knights among the jurors is inconsiderable. On some juries not a single knight is specifically
named; but it is not certain whether the placing of the title
dominus (sir) before the name of a knight was a normal practice.
In any case, only fifteen men are actually referred to as *dominus*
or *miles*, the property of fourteen of whom is described. It may
be that the information is not quite complete; but it is probably
not far removed from the real facts.

These knights form a fairly homogeneous group. A few
may be described as lords of medium rank; the rest are small
landowners, the size of whose estates is close to the minimum
required for a knight's holding. Not all their domains are
described as being held by military tenure. Thus 'dominus'
W. de la Haye holds one of his two manors by fee-farm (*feodi
firma*) from the Hospitallers for £5 a year. The tenure of the
other manor is not indicated, but it would appear to have been
fee farm also. Clearly we have before us small knights, the
agrarii or *pagenses milites* of the chronicles.

The composition of the juries is extremely varied and includes both knights and cottars, the lords of thousands of

acres and the tenants of plots of two acres. General descriptions and average figures are therefore of little use here, and we shall be obliged to break up our evidence into a number of more or less homogeneous groups. The jurors can be divided into three groups, between which there is, however, no sharp dividing line. These groups are:

(1) The lords of typical manors with a demesne and villeins, and in most cases freehold land as well. There are 53 such individuals in our material. We must note that only a small minority (12) of the manors belonging to this group (Group 1A) are sufficiently provided with villein land, to base their economic organization on villeinage. The vast majority of the manors of the first group (Group 1B) are very badly endowed with villein land.

(2) Fifty-five landowners practically without villeins, whose manors consist of demesne and freehold only. Most of them are very small men, only 22 having over 120 acres of land.

(3) The third and most numerous group is composed of the owners of individual holdings, that is 'demesnes' without tenants. There are 77 men in this group. Their individual 'estates' are in the majority of cases not large. Only 7 of them exceed one carucate (120 acres), 23 are between a carucate and two virgates, 18 are of two to one virgate, and 24 are smaller than one virgate. Six of these last are tiny holdings of five acres or less. It is difficult for us to say whether the income from these small holdings was so small that the inclusion of their owners among the jurors was *contra formam statuti*.[1] Possibly the assessment of income was in some cases based on things other than land held; in other cases it is possible that our fragmentary source does not give us all the relevant information.

Among the jurors, even those with the title *dominus* or *miles*, we find no great lords. We practically never encounter large manors. The larger estates are usually made up of two or more manors. Only one of the manors in question is slightly over 1,000 acres, and falls into the 'large' category; 26 are between 500 and 1,000 acres and so come in the 'medium' class; the rest are all in the 'small' category, being less than

---

[1] Up to 1285 it was not yet *contra formam statuti* to call upon smallholders to do duty as jurors, and, as can be seen from the statute itself, this was sometimes done

500 acres. But almost every manor is surrounded by a variety of odd parcels of land attached to it—the lord's holdings on other manors. Only occasionally can the estate of a juror be described as one manor of simple composition. Sometimes the elements comprising it are scattered, demesne as well as holdings, over several manors, several villages and sometimes over several hundreds. A manor, especially a small one, might be made up of two, three, four, or as many as ten parts.

A typical example is the estate of William, son of Gregory, a juror from the hundred of Toseland in Huntingdonshire. In Beachampstead he holds a windmill, and for the *situs molendini* he pays 4*d.* to Geoffrey Beaufuy and 4*d.* to William Aungevin. In the same place he holds 2 acres from John Engayne for 1 lb. of cummin; two pieces of meadow (3½ and 1¾ acres) he holds from Thomas de Beachampstead for ½*d.* In Southoe he holds 40 acres of arable *in una cultura* by joint tenure with four other individuals for a rent of 20*s.* and the scutage due from one-fiftieth of a knight's fee. In Great Staughton he has one-sixth of a knight's fee, which he holds from Adam Creting for homage and scutage. In this property he has 20 acres of demesne and small free holdings. In the same vill he has half a virgate and a messuage held from the prior of Huntingdon for 6*s.*, a quarter of a virgate held from William Scohisfot for ½*d.*, one virgate held from Adam Creting for homage and scutage, 2 acres held from the same man for 4*d.*, 3½ acres of arable, ½ an acre of woodland and ½ an acre of meadow and pasture held from Thomas de Beachampstead for 1*d.*, and ½ a virgate held from the Prior of Bushmead for 1*d.*

In some cases the estates of a non-manorial type, the holdings of the free tenants, are just as complicated. We have not sufficient data to enable us to distinguish between 'peasants' and 'small landowners' among the jurors, and it may be that one of the most important conclusions to be drawn from our material is precisely the impossibility of making such a distinction. As in the Assize of Arms, we cannot detect just where the free peasants end and the 'nobility'—if this term is applicable at all—begins. From the well-to-do free peasant's holding, almost imperceptible intermediate stages lead up to the small manor, the knight's estate. I am quite arbitrarily counting as manors (1) all complexes which include villein land;

(2) all complexes which include demesne and free land and which amount altogether to more than one carucate; (3) all individual holdings (demesnes) which amount to over one carucate. In the last group the factor which makes a holding into a feudal estate, viz. the appropriation of feudal rent, would not appear to be present at all, but the cultivation of such 'demesnes' was undoubtedly connected with some kind of exploitation of the direct cultivators of the soil, an exploitation which under the conditions of feudal production could not but assume a feudal character, even though it was in the form of wage labour.

SOCIAL STRUCTURE OF JURORS' MANORS

In order to appreciate the significance of the structure of the estates of the period we should note for the purpose of comparison the average proportions between demesne, freehold and villein land in the 1,031 manors of various sizes described in the Hundred Rolls. Here we get a proportion of 32—28—40 per cent. Only twelve of our jurors have manors which approach this average (Group 1A). On the other jurors' manors villein land is either extremely small in amount or else entirely absent. If we exclude Group 1A, then the proportion of demesne to free and villein land on the remaining 63 manors is 45—44—11 per cent. Moreover, the villein allotments on the Group 1B manors for the most part pay money rent, so the villeins played a very small part in the cultivation of the demesne. Where the area of villein land was small, the money revenue it brought in could not be large either. In this group the amount of freehold land is very great, but rent revenue from it is insignificant. It carried mainly *forinseca servitia*, especially payment of scutage. The lord himself got very little. Therefore on these manors feudal rent played a secondary part.

THE ESTATE OF ROBERT DANVERS IN OXFORDSHIRE

Sometimes even large manors brought in practically no rent. The estate of Robert Danvers in Oxfordshire, the largest of all the jurors' estates, provides a good example. It was counted as $3\frac{7}{12}$ knight's fees, and contained about 2,000 acres of arable, spread over 4 manors. The estate is so peculiar that it is worth while pausing to give it special consideration. In Little Bourton (Banbury hundred) Robert held $\frac{3}{4}$ of a knight's fee of Nicholas Segrave, who held of the bishop of Lincoln, who held of the king. For this fee Robert was bound to attend the Banbury hundred court, to perform garrison duty at Banbury castle in time of war for thirty days at his own expense, and to pay scutage. His demesne amounted to $2\frac{1}{2}$ virgates, and free holdings to $14\frac{1}{2}$ virgates and 80 acres. There were no villeins. The income from the free holdings was very small, totalling about £1 in money rent together with small payments in kind. The main obligation of the freeholders[1] was to share in the payment of scutage. Taken altogether they paid 24s.[2] In Swaecliff (in the same hundred) the survey mentions *feodum Roberti Danvers*, consisting of twenty virgates, all in the hands of tenants. This estate counted as five-sixths of a knight's fee. The tenants paid scutage (altogether $2\frac{1}{2}$ marks); this money was received by Robert Danvers and paid over by him to his lord, the bishop of Lincoln. Further, two tenants attended the Banbury hundred court *nomine domini sui*. Some of them also paid small contributions in kind. In Epwell (Dorchester hundred) and elsewhere he has one knight's fee, for which he paid scutage, again to the bishop of Lincoln, for all service. In this fee 18 virgates were in the hands of tenants, who pay scutage, attend Robert Danvers' court, and brought him money to the amount of about £1 4s. 0d. He had yet one more fee at Tetsworth (Thame hundred), again held from the bishop of Lincoln, for attendance at Thame hundred court and payment of scutage. Here we at last have something resembling a manor. Robert has 4 virgates of demesne, one villein with half a virgate of land (the assessment of his labour dues and money rent comes to 5s.), and one cottar, who pays 2s. In addition there is quite a large portion of free land, amounting to $11\frac{1}{2}$ virgates, 6 acres and 1 cottage. The free tenants pay

---

[1] With the exception of the Prior of Chacombe, who holds 80 acres and 1 virgate for 10s., and is free from scutage.

[2] The scutage due from a knight's fee was 40s. (or 30s. for three-quarters of a fee).

scutage, attend Robert's court, and also pay him money rent to the total of 6s. 11d., and small contributions in kind.

TABLE 15

DEMESNE, FREEHOLD AND VILLEIN LAND ON JURORS' ESTATES

Group	No. of land owners	Average size of estate	Demesne	Freehold	Villein land	Total area
1A	12	920	4,245 38%	2,217 20%	4,581 42%	11,043
1B	34	511	6,214 36%	8,611 49%	2,561 15%	17,386
II	22	207	3,019¼ 66%	1,526¼ 34%	—	4,545½
III	7	180	1,263	—	—	1,263
Overall ..	75	—	14,741¼ 43%	12,354¼ 36%	7,142 21%	34,237½

On all these manors of Robert Danvers, there are only 6½ virgates of demesne land, one half-virgate and one cottar's holding of villein land, and a very large area of freehold—64 virgates and 85 acres. But all this free land brings him in only £2 9s. 1d. money rent and small payments in kind. The other payments made by the free tenants are for *forinseca servitia*—the payment of scutage and attendance at hundred assemblies. On two of the fiefs a further obligation of the freeholders is indicated, that of attending Robert's court. It is possible that this obligation was binding on the other free tenants as well—the omission of reference to these obligations is quite common in the rolls. But the court for free tenants can scarcely have yielded much at the end of the thirteenth century. The revenues from the villeins, and their labour dues, are minute. Robert's demesne was not large, but could not of course be worked by the labour dues of one villein.

In his relationship to the majority of his freeholders, Robert appears mainly as the individual responsible for the payment of scutage to the bishop of Lincoln (direct or through an intermediary lord). His own income from his quite extensive estates is very inconsiderable, scarcely more than £10 net, and the estates have little that reminds us of the manorial system. Rather we may use a term which, if archaic, is not infrequently used in our source, though not applied to this given case—the term 'soke'.

It consisted of a group of freeholders paying small, sometimes nominal, rents, linked together only by the jurisdiction of the lord—which had, incidentally, by the end of the thirteenth century lost its previous significance—and with only rudimentary elements of the manor as a serf-worked organization. It had an early-feudal appearance, and had not yet developed into a manor. This is an extreme case. But on the remaining manors of Group 1B the rent revenue was also small. The large size of a number of manors was due to the large area of that kind of land least profitable for the lord—land in free tenure.

THE ESTATE OF JAMES GRIM IN HUNTINGDONSHIRE

Lastly, we meet with yet another type of manorial structure, one which is rare among the larger manors, but becomes commoner and commoner the lower we descend in the scale, namely, the manor where tenants' land is quite insignificant in comparison with the demesne. As an example of this kind of manorial structure we may take the estate of James Grim in the Huntingdonshire hundred of Leightonstone. Its structure is so interesting that I shall dwell on it in some detail.

James Grim's manor lies in two neighbouring villages, Sibthorp and Brampton. In Sibthorp he has two holdings from the abbot of Ramsey; on one there is one carucate of arable, one rood of meadow, and a windmill; on the other, 6 virgates and 2 acres of arable. For the first of these two holdings he pays 10s.; for the second he is bound to visit every three weeks the abbot's free court at Broughton. Actually all the Sibthorp holdings belong to James's mother as her widow's portion (*nomine dotis*), and he holds them from her by *firma*, paying her 10 marks a year for her lifetime. Besides this, 164¼ acres of arable are held from him by freeholders, most of them small men, and 10½ acres are held by tenants at will.

In neighbouring Brampton he has 2 hides of arable, which he holds from the bishop of Lincoln by fee farm for £10, and on them small freeholders who altogether account for about 20 acres of arable. Besides this he holds 14 acres of woodland at Alconbury, and is the patron of a church at Denton. His Sibthorp holding represents one knight's fee when taken together with the holding of Nicholas Grafton (which is small).

Thus James Grim's demesne comprises, to all intents and purposes, 2 hides, 1 carucate, 6 virgates and 2 acres of arable, which is equal to something in the region of 542 acres, or the demesne of a quite considerable manor. Even if we assume that the 195 acres of tenants' land has been counted in with the area which we have treated as demesne (the source can bear this interpretation as well), there are still 347 acres of demesne land. The money rent of the tenants amounts to £3 13s. 10½d., some of the holdings, especially the small ones, being quite heavily burdened. But this rent is insignificant in comparison even with the payments which James himself has to make on account of his estate, which come to £17 3s. 4d. a year. Furthermore, the abbot of Ramsey retains a number of feudal payments from James's tenants in Sibthorp, namely wardship, marriage, relief and escheat. The sum total of labour dues coming to James from his tenants consists of the three days' autumn work performed by one of the Sibthorp tenants at will.

We have before us a manor of a particular type, which is not based on dependent holdings, their payments and labour dues—not based, in fact, on feudal rent in the ordinary sense of that expression. Its main constituent in terms of revenue is its impressive demesne. What kind of labour was used on the demesne is a separate question, which will be dealt with later. For the moment the essential point is the existence of such manors, even among the upper ranks of the jurors. In fact the independent character of the demesne and its decisive importance within the structure of the manor grow greater as we reach the lower categories. The smaller the manor, the more often it has no villein land at all, and even no land in free tenure. In this way the manor gradually merges into the individual free holding.

THE DANVERS AND GRIM ESTATES CONTRASTED

There is an undoubted similarity between the manors of Robert Danvers and James Grim. On both of them feudal

rent occupies an entirely secondary position, and on both of
them villeinage and labour dues play no part at all. Their
'manorial' character is very slight. But there the similarity
ends. The basis of Robert's estate is a vast area of freehold
with an insignificant demesne. The revenue from this freehold does not so much consist of rent in the immediate sense,
which is very small, but is rather derived from feudal jurisdiction. James Grim's manor consists chiefly of a large demesne,
which he holds on lease for £17. Clearly this demesne must
have brought him in a very considerable revenue, if he found
it profitable to exploit it while paying such a high rent. James
has no villeins; and from his freeholders, especially the small
ones, he takes a high rent, which does not, however, play any
conspicuous part in his income. Furthermore he is interested
only in rent in the direct sense, leaving in the hands of the
abbot of Ramsey those payments which originate in the
jurisdictional and personal dependence of the holders.

Whereas on Robert's estates the manor is only just beginning
to crystallize out of a form of soke, and the demesne is still
completely insignificant, on James's estate the demesne has
crushed the holdings, and has pushed feudal rent into the background. We see before us in embryonic form something
between a 'new noble' and a 'capitalist farmer'. That does not
imply that Robert's estates were created long ago, and James's
quite recently. But they represent two morphologically distinct
types, which reflect two characteristic stages in the development of the manor—the incompletely formed manor, and the
manor which is already undergoing reorganization on a new
system.

TABLE 16

COMPOSITION OF VILLEIN HOLDINGS ON MANORS OF GROUPS
1A AND 1B

Group	Virgates	Half-virgates	Fardels	Small holdings	Total
1A ..	79 31%	107 43%	10 4%	55 22%	251
1B ..	16 7%	61 28%	40 18%	104 47%	221
Together	95 20%	168 36%	50 11%	159 33%	472

SUMMARY OF THE PECULIARITIES OF THE JURORS' ESTATES

If we take into consideration that in our material there is a predominance of Oxfordshire manors, on which the percentage of cottars' holdings is on the average low (20 per cent), the peculiarity of the jurors' estates stands out even more sharply. On some juries there is no one to whose estates the name 'manor' is applicable. Others have only very small manors with few or no villeins. For instance, among the jurors of the hundred of Bunstow (Bucks.) there are only two whom it is possible to call lords of manors, and one of these is dubious. None of the jurors of the Cambridgeshire hundred of Chesterton seem to have held manors, but here there are too many gaps in the evidence for a certain conclusion. There are only forty acres of villein land on the estates of the jurors of the Cambridgeshire hundred of Northstow; there is not a single estate resembling a manor in the hundred of Staine (Cambs.), nor in that of Staploe.[1] The jurors of Thriplow hundred have no villeins, and villein land is insignificant in the hundred of Whittlesford (40 acres). Of all the Cambridgeshire hundreds it is only in Wetherley that we can find over 360 acres of villein land in the possession of jurors. Furthermore, if we look at the composition of the villein holdings on the lands of the Cambridgeshire jurors, we shall see that they are for the most part small holdings.

Not all the juries can boast of knights among their members, or even of jurors who ought to have been knights. The vast majority of jurymen of this class is concentrated in the Huntingdonshire and Oxfordshire hundreds. It is not without interest that the information concerning the villeins and their dues had often to be given by individuals who had no connection with the exploitation of those villeins, mainly by free peasants or by small estate-owners who did not exploit villein labour. Was Vinogradoff right in attributing to the jurors' findings definite class tendencies in the interests of the 'gentlemen' or 'owners of landed property'?[2] In a number of cases at least this appears doubtful.

In summarizing the evidence on the 'knights and lawful

---

[1] But there are many lacunae here.
[2] Vinogradoff, *Villainage*, 155.

freemen' serving on the hundred juries, the following points stand out so far as their estates are concerned:

1. There is an absolute predominance of small manors.

2. Only an insignificant minority of jurors have typical serf-worked manors (Group A).

3. On the majority of the manors in the jurors' possession either there is no villein land, or it is inconsiderable in area.

4. Among the villeins, in the majority of cases, small holders are predominant.

5. The jurors' manors are distinguished by their high percentage of demesne land, and by the insignificance of the part played on them by feudal rent.

6. On the majority of these manors the predominant form of rent is money rent.

7. Jurors' estates usually consist of small and scattered parcels held from different lords.

We have before us a peculiar stratum of feudal society, with a number of characteristics that distinguish it (or at least most of it) from the 'typical' feudal lords.

We have now become acquainted with the picture presented by the estates of those knights and lawful free men of whom so much is heard in the political history of England. We have made this acquaintance by examining the estates of the representatives of that stratum who served as jurors. We must now try to extend and generalize our observations over a broader range of material, to make it clear what part the small manor played alongside the large, and to see what other peculiar features this type of manor may have to disclose besides those which have come to light in the material we have dealt with.

The small manor has left no records like those of the large manor of a great lord. On it there was no need of surveys, or annual accounts, or manorial court rolls. The simple forms of accountancy which may have been practised on the small manors would scarcely be the object of careful preservation, and they have been irretrievably lost. Here our only records are still the government surveys, the Hundred Rolls for the thirteenth century, and Domesday Book for the eleventh century.

Nevertheless, knowledge of the small estate is vital for an

understanding of the peculiarities of English feudal development. This can be seen from the fact that, according to my
calculations, 65 per cent at least of the manors in the Hundred
Rolls are small manors of less than 500 acres of arable. Only
13 per cent of the total *number* consists of large manors with
over 1,000 acres of arable. The medium-sized manors, with
arable areas between 1,000 and 500 acres make up 22 per cent.
The small manors comprise something under 30 per cent of
the total arable *area* covered by the Hundred Rolls, while
medium-sized manors cover about the same percentage.
The large manors account for about 40 per cent. Not all small
manors, of course, were in the hands of small landowners.
The involved complexes of estates which were the property
of the great lords, lay and spiritual, included not only large
but medium-sized and small manors as well. But fundamentally, large manors are characteristic of the estates of great
lords, and small manors of those of small landowners. We may
find, in part at least, the key to the difference of class interests
between the great and the small feudal lords in the different
characteristics of the large and the small manor.

FURTHER ANALYSIS OF THE SOCIAL STRUCTURE OF SMALL
    ESTATES

The characteristics of the small lay landowners have been
in part revealed by the material which the lists of jurors
yielded. But this material may seem a little one-sided, since
it relates mainly to Oxfordshire. It needs to be supplemented
from other parts of the kingdom. Since Oxfordshire belongs
to the western group within the counties which the Hundred
Rolls cover, I shall examine the evidence from a county in
the eastern group—Huntingdonshire. I have picked out 40
small or mid-ranking landowners,[1] trying to take only those
who so far as could be seen, had no other estates elsewhere.
Thus our calculations do not include small estates belonging
to large landowners. In regard to these 40 estates I have
worked out: (1) the proportion of demesne to villein land and
free holdings; (2) the ratio of labour rent and money rent in
the villeins' dues; and (3) the composition of the villein hold-

---

[1] Twelve of whom have the title *dominus* or *miles*.

ings, from the point of view of the adequacy of their provision of land. The total area of the forty estates is 13,954 acres of arable, giving an average size of 374 acres. Among them there is a predominance of 'typical' manors with demesne, villeins and freeholders all present. There are only seven without villeins.

The proportion of demesne to villein land and free holdings is as follows: demesne 43 per cent, villein land 27 per cent, free holdings 30 per cent.[1] The character of villein rent on the estates of small landowners comes out very clearly. On 7 manors there are no villeins, and on 2 others it is difficult to determine the proportion of labour to money rent. But on the remaining 31 manors the proportion works out as follows:

1. Labour dues are predominant on 4 manors.

2. Labour dues and money rent are in approximately equal proportions on 2 manors.

3. Money rent predominates on 16 manors (and on 6 of these we find only extremely small labour services).

4. Money rent alone appears on 9 manors.

The predominance of money rent is beyond all doubt. Yet we have already seen that Huntingdonshire was a county marked by a preponderance of serfs and labour dues.

The make-up of the villeins' holdings on the small land-owners' estates is as follows:

Virgaters	10	(3 per cent)
Half-virgaters	197	(50 per cent)
Fardel-holders	26	(6 per cent)
Small holdings (under 5 acres)	164	(41 per cent)

For purposes of comparison I recall the corresponding figures for the whole of the county of Huntingdonshire:

Virgaters	15 per cent
Half-virgaters	45 per cent
Fardel-holders	4 per cent
Small holdings	36 per cent

[1] I.e., 5983½, 3,754¾, 4,215½ acres. These figures vary somewhat from those derived from all the small manors in Huntingdonshire taken together (43–34–23 per cent), and the difference takes the form of a lowering of the percentage of villein land (with a corresponding increase in the area of free holdings).

Thus the ratio between peasants with an adequate provision of land and those without it is for the whole of Huntingdon-shire expressed by the figures 60 : 40 per cent, while for the estates of small landowners it is 53 : 47 per cent.

A further question of interest is whether there is any difference between 'small manors' of various sizes, or between the estates of 'small feudal lords' and 'prosperous peasants', indeterminate as the dividing line is. For this purpose I have arbitrarily divided the manors into two groups—those with over and under 250 acres of arable—with the following results:

	Manors under 250 acres	*Manors over 250 acres*
Demesne ..	1,213½ acres (52%)	4,770 acres (41%)
Villein land ..	563 acres (25%)	3,191¾ acres (28%)
Free holdings..	581½ acres (27%)	3,634 acres (31%)
	2,358 acres	11,595¾ acres
Number of manors	17	23
Average size of manor	138 acres	498 acres

The percentage of villein land does not change as between the two groups. But the percentage of demesne alters perceptibly. It is much higher on the very smallest 'peasant' manors. We find again that tendency towards an increase in the size of the demesne which we have already noticed as we pass from large to middle-sized, and from middle-sized to small manors.

Out of the 17 manors of less than 250 acres, there is only one where labour service predominates in the villeins' obligations, as against 6 where money rents predominate, 5 where there are no labour dues at all, 2 where it is difficult to define the different forms of rent, and 3 where there are no villeins. The predominance of money rent is even clearer than it is for all the small manors taken together. The composition of the villein population on these smallest of small manors is also of a special sort, since only two categories are represented: viz., holders of a half-virgate (of whom there are 40), and smallholders with less than 5 acres, of whom there are 65.

Features distinguishing the Small from the Typical Large Manor

The following characteristic features distinguish the small manor from the 'typical' large manor:

1. The typical large manor coincides, as a rule, with the village. It makes up one whole with the village community, and by virtue of this is also an administrative and fiscal unit. The small manor does not as a rule coincide with the village, or with the village community, but represents either a part of it or sometimes a sum of parts lying within several villages. The characteristic non-coincidence of the vill and the manor is the result of the widespread occurrence of the small manor, in consequence of which a large proportion of the vills are divided between two, three, four and more manors.

The fact that the small manor does not coincide with the village community vitally affects its organization and development. The small manor is without that territorial unity and self-containedness which the large manor acquires from the customary coincidence of its boundaries with the boundaries of the village. Its lands lie split up, alternating with those of other manors, among the ploughed fields of the village; its rights in the commons are intermingled with the rights of other manors. As it constitutes only a part of the village community, its peasants, its assembly or its court are not competent to decide on economic affairs which affect the whole community.[1] The small landowners continue to live together within the framework of one village community, and this fact must have resulted in involved economic, administrative and fiscal relationships.

The organization of the village community, which arose before that of the manor and on which the latter rested, was strengthened and preserved by the manor. The manor turned the community into its servant, used its organization for controlling the servile tenants, and gave it a definite place and definite functions in feudal society. The dispositions of the community formed the inhabitants of the manorialized village into one whole. But the small manor was not based on the

---

[1] In some exceptional cases (when two or more large estates were divided) this led to the disintegration of a village.

S

community. Its inhabitants, among whom the villeins were usually only an inconsiderable part, did not represent any unified communal organization. It tended rather to weaken and break up communal organization. The village community and the manor were divided, and existed separately one from another, so much so that in villages with a complex manorial composition Vinogradoff assumed the existence of a general assembly of the village as well as the manor courts. But the existence of such assemblies in the thirteenth century has not been proved, and it would seem that the small manor was more likely to disintegrate than to preserve communal organization.

Having no unity or self-sufficiency territorially, having no 'natural frontiers', the small manor was bound to be distinguished by impermanence, fluidity, changeability; it was easier for new pieces of land to be added to it, and easier for parts to be detached from it, than in the case of the compact large manor which coincided with a village. The small manor, like land in free tenure, brought further entanglements into the cobweb of feudal connections, as its separate parts belonged to various fees.

2. A second important characteristic of the small manor is the varied nature of its manorial structure. Not all large manors have a 'typical' structure. But these departures from type are more in the nature of exceptions, and we see a procession of symmetrical manors one after another, as Vinogradoff not quite accurately remarked of the 1279 Hundred Rolls as a whole. But amongst the small manors an extreme variety of form reigns. In contrast to the finished symmetry of the large manor, the small manor has as its characteristic features variety, incompleteness and mutability of form, indicating a system either not completely settled or else beginning to disintegrate. The existence of a considerable number of manors either completely without villeins or with an insignificant number of them is outstanding. More than a third of the hundred of Chilford (Cambs.), for instance, is occupied by small manors. On half of these manors there are no villeins at all and on the rest villein land is quite small in area.

3. Another important characteristic of the small manor is to be found in the special relation on it between villein land

and demesne. Over the Hundred Rolls as a whole, the proportion between demesne, villein land and freehold is for the
large manor 25—51—23 per cent, i.e. villein land is on the
average twice as extensive as demesne. For the small manor
this proportion is 41—32—27 per cent. Thus, on the small
manor demesne is more extensive than villein land, standing
to the latter in the ratio of approximately 5 : 4. In fact, this
ratio varies greatly; in some hundreds, such as Chilford,
demesne land is twelve times as extensive as villein land.
On the small manor, then, the demesne was less dependent
on the unfree holdings; the part played by *feudal rent*—the
principal mark of the manor—was smaller than on the large
manor.

4. There is a significant dissimilarity between large and
small manors with regard to the types of villein holding.
The percentage of peasants with a full allocation of land
(virgaters and half-virgaters) is considerably lower on the
small manors, the percentage of cottars considerably higher.
For what we have seen in the case of the jurors' estates can
be generalized and applied more widely to the 15,000 villein
households situated in all the different hundreds taken in by
the Hundred Rolls.[1] As we have seen, on small manors the
villein holdings are as a rule smaller than on large manors.
The smaller a manor is, the higher on the average the percentage of cottars' holdings and fardels, reaching 70 per cent
for manors of sub-group 1A. Furthermore, among the small
manors there are a good many entirely without villein holdings.
The huge percentage of near-landless servile peasants which
strikes us on reading the Hundred Rolls, is largely the consequence of the small manor. The cottar, who plays a completely
secondary part on the large manor, assumes a very prominent
place on the small manor.

5. The small manor is further distinguished from the large
by the greater development of money rent as compared with
labour rent. While the large manor is usually an organization
based not only on serfdom but also on the performance of labour
services, these are much less highly developed on the small
manor.[2] Because the number of villeins was small the labour
services they owed could not play any considerable part in

[1] See the tables on pp. 216 and 219.   [2] See Chapter III, pp. 168-9.

the economy of the small manor. Labour services played only an auxiliary part, just as on the large manor a similar auxiliary role belonged to hired labour.

6. All the features listed above imply the existence on the small manor of a special type of demesne economy, distinct from that which we meet on large manors. The exploitation of the relatively large demesne could not be based on the labour and tools of a servile peasantry. Even carrying services are rare. The cottars, who represent the most important element among the servile peasants of the small manor, had in general little draught stock. The demesne economy had to rely on its own livestock as well as its own implements. The surrender of labour rent and the transition to money rent was therefore easier on the small than on the large manor, since the small manor was far less dependent on the implements provided by the peasants, and its demesne was cultivated for the most part with its own implements and its own stock. The abandonment of labour services at the end of the fourteenth century was a catastrophe for the large manors, which in a number of cases were compelled to abandon cultivation of the demesne and to lease it out on terms not always advantageous to the lessor. But this development had comparatively little effect on the small manor where labour services were few, and where their abolition required no radical alteration of the system of husbandry. When the manor and the village community began to disintegrate into a number of competing economies, the result on the large manor was a temporary victory of the upper layer of the peasants. On the small manor the absence of a well-to-do peasantry determined in advance the lord's victory over the handful of small peasant economies.

7. We must assume that the small manors did not possess the same capacity for economic self-sufficiency as the large manor. While the large manor could exist in a natural economy (which was the basis of feudal production) the small manor could not do without the market. In the first place, this applies to the problems of reproduction.[1] Able to organize the division of labour on a wide scale, the large manor was able to reproduce its economy out of its gross income. Its

---

[1] [Marx defines 'reproduction' in the chapter entitled 'Simple Reproduction' in the first volume of *Capital*.]

monetary expenditure, particularly on reproduction, was negligible. The small manor, on the other hand, had to resort more frequently to the market. Although it had less revenue at its disposal in absolute terms, the demesne economy of a small manor needed to lay out a greater percentage of that revenue on reproduction expenses.

The large estate-owner sold on the market the surplus he had left after meeting consumption needs. He was not particularly concerned if it was sold at a price lower than its real value. But the small estate-owner, who had a comparatively insignificant amount of produce to sell, was much more concerned with questions of price. The problem of productivity, the extraction of the greatest possible amount of revenue by producing for the market, was bound to play a greater part on the small manor than on the large one. We have reason to suppose that the commodity nature of production developed there earlier and more strongly than on the large manor.

8. We must now consider the important question of the place of the manor court and manorial custom on the small manor. The existence of courts even on some very small manors is confirmed by contemporary evidence. But in many cases we can presume the absence of courts, especially where there were no villeins or where the villein population was represented by a few cottars. What was the court of a small manor like? What sort of manorial custom could be evolved among a dozen or so cottars? Was there any custom at all, any tradition capable of opposing the will of the lord, any tradition preserving the rights of the peasant and setting bounds to his exploitation, in so far as that was possible at all in feudal society? One cannot but suspect that custom, tradition and inertia had far less place on the small manor than on the large, the more so since the former was less bound up with that repository of tradition, the village community. Another vital point may be the fact that the small landowner, the man of small means, the local 'master', lived on his own manor and was able to take a direct part, if not in the work itself (as must have happened on the very smallest manors), at any rate in the supervision. The close proximity of the lord, in conjunction with the other weaknesses in the position of the peasant on the small manor, was bound to influence and

reshape customs which had originally been moulded to suit traditional methods of production.

In summarizing our observations on the peculiarities of the small manor, we must note that it was better adapted to the development of capitalism. The small manor was less bound up with feudal rent, and more with the exploitation of what may be called wage labour (taking into account, of course, the specific features proper to wage labour within a feudal society). Many of its unfree labourers were already becoming settled workers. It was closely linked with the market, and on it money rent predominated. Finally, it would appear to have been less bound up with tradition, with custom. These innumerable small manors, unstable in character, were not frozen in the traditional, immobile feudal mould. Belonging to small knights and prosperous freeholders they were a vehicle of bourgeois ferment in the feudal countryside of medieval England. Here, the disintegration of feudal institutions, which had not yet taken their final form, began more easily and proceeded more quickly than on the large 'set' feudal manors. May we not see in these knights and well-to-do freemen the ancestors of the new nobility and gentry who were to be so characteristic an element in the later history of England? The problem of the future development of this group needs study; but for the time being we may dwell briefly on its origins.

PRE-CONQUEST FORMATION OF SMALL MANORS

A comparison between Domesday Book and the Hundred Rolls has shown us[1] that the distinction between irregular small manors and uniform large manors was characteristic of the country in both the eleventh and the thirteenth centuries. The question naturally arises: in what relation do the large and small manors of Domesday Book stand to the large and small manors of the Hundred Rolls? Small manors sometimes resulted from the break-up of a large manor, as we have seen. Sometimes a complex of holdings of manorial type might arise in consequence of the buying up of lands and their leasing out at rent. In this way 'manors' with free tenants only might easily arise, though the acquisition of villein holdings was also

[1] *Supra*, pp. 145–51.

possible. As I have already stated, every holding of any considerable size was bound, under feudal conditions, to develop dependent holdings paying rent, and thus to take on the appearance of a feudal manor.

But while the small manor sometimes appears as a new formation, it would seem that even more often it was a survival of an incompleted process of manorialization. As we saw earlier, the distribution of large and small manors throughout the hundreds and vills had not altered in any essential way between 1086 and 1279. The considerable structural differences between large and small manors at the time of Domesday Book, may be explained by the differing historical origins of the two types.[1] In Gurevich's opinion the large manors, especially the large church manors, were in the main the result of royal grants of rights of *bocland*. The essence of grants of *bocland* was, of course, the alienation by the king, in favour of the church or of some layman, of the right to collect the taxes, which had previously been paid to the king by the free population. This led to the tax being transformed into rent and free peasants into dependants. Since the right to collect the profits of justice as well, and even to sit in judgment on the inhabitants of the *bocland*, was sometimes also granted, the result was the superimposition on the previous free rural communities of a manorial organization with a demesne and labour services. The free community was transformed into the manor. In this way the transfer by the king to churches or lay nobles of his own fiscal and judicial rights over free peasant land led to the usurpation of peasant property and the establishment of feudal property.

But there was another way in which manors might be formed—namely, by the decomposition of the ancient rural community from within. The break-up of tribal organization and the emergence of private property in land led to differentiation within the village community, to the impoverishment of some of its members, to the advance of the bigger landowners and the subordination of the impoverished peasants. The member of the village community who prospered gradually turned into a lord of the manor. This is the typical way in

---

[1] Cf. the unpublished thesis of my pupil, A. Y. Gurevich, *The Peasantry of South-Western England in the Pre-Norman Period*.

which the small manor was formed. The embryo of the small manor was the large holding of the English *ceorl*, who was already to some extent exploiting slaves and letting some of his land to smallholders.

Of course, the formation of small manors by grants of *bocland*, and of a large manor by the disintegration of the communal order were possibilities, but the lines indicated were the typical ones. The differing origin of the two types of manor explains their structural peculiarities, which exist from the very beginning. The manor which arose in the process of disintegration of the communal order is distinguished by the scattered nature of its lands, which often lie in different settlements, interspersed with the lands of other property-owners, and are distinguished by the small size of the subordinate peasant holdings. Similarly, the allotments granted to the landless peasants settled upon its territory are small in size. But as it had developed out of the comparatively large property of the successful villager, this kind of manor is marked on the other hand by a considerable demesne. According to Gurevich's calculations, in Domesday Book the lords' demesne amounted to 39 per cent of the total area on the small manors studied, and 26 per cent on the large manors. If we compare his figures with those which we obtained from the 1279 Hundred Rolls, we find that they coincide almost completely.[1] Not having at their disposal a sufficient quantity of peasant labour, the lords of this type of manor made wide use of the labour of slaves, which played a considerable part in Anglo-Saxon society from the time of the Conquest.

The characteristics of the manor which had grown out of *bocland* were different. Usually it was large, taking in a whole village or several neighbouring villages. The holdings of the peasants were of various sizes, small, medium and comparatively large, for the grant gave the new lord rights over a community where the process of disintegration was far from complete. The resistance of the peasants, who were organized as a community, and in part even the interests of the lord himself, who needed a peasantry adequately provided with

[1] However, the principles followed by myself and by Gurevich in selecting our large and small manors were not the same, nor is the territorial scope of our investigation. According to my calculations the demesne came to 26 per cent of the total arable on large manors and 41 per cent on small.

land, stock and implements, to some extent held back further differentiation. On such manors the demesne, being a late formation, was not large in comparison with the holdings. Containing whole village communities, this type of manor did not destroy communal organization, but conserved it and employed it for its own ends.

The principal feature distinguishing the manor of the Anglo-Saxon (and of the Norman) period from the small manor of the thirteenth century was the presence, on the small manor of earlier times, of a considerable number of slaves. Gurevich has calculated, from Domesday Book, the number of slaves on small and on large manors. On 140 small manors which he studied, the ratio of slaves to ploughs was 7 : 10, while on the large manors this ratio was 4 : 10. In the thirteenth century surveys we no longer find slaves, who by that time had merged with the rest of the unfree population, and swelled the numbers of poorly-provided bordars, the unfree cottars whose importance in the thirteenth century we have already seen. Thus a number of the characteristic features of small and large manors in the thirteenth century had already taken shape during the feudalization of Anglo-Saxon society.[1]

We have sufficient grounds for thinking that small manors were largely of ancient origin, and that the process of concentration was less successful than Vinogradoff thought. Most large manors seem to have taken shape as early as the eleventh century, while the unformed chaos of small manors remains even in the thirteenth century approximately where it was at the time of Domesday. Of course, within this 'chaos' very considerable rearrangements had taken place in the intervening period, and while we can often identify particular large manors of the thirteenth century with those of the eleventh century, it is only very rarely that we can do the same with certainty in the case of small manors. It would seem that the special peculiarities of the small manor at the close of the thirteenth century result from a combination of incomplete feudalization (or manorialization) and of the already advancing process of the disintegration within feudal society.

[1] Gurevich considers the decisive period in this process to have been the eighth to ninth centuries.

I have already emphasized more than once, as a characteristic feature of English feudalism, its incompleteness, the tenacity of the pre-feudal elements within it, and the early disintegration of the feudal structure itself. It is always in precisely those spheres in which feudalism had not had time to settle down and grow strong that the process of disintegration first begins. The analysis of the small manor once more underlines these special features of English feudalism.

CHAPTER VI

THE SUPPLY OF LABOUR ON THE ENGLISH MANOR IN THE THIRTEENTH CENTURY

THE 'CLASSICAL' THEORY

The problem of the supply of labour in the demesne economy did not present any special difficulty to the leading historians of the English manor. For them, the demesne economy was, fundamentally, based on the labour services of the villeins, particularly of the virgaters and half-virgaters who worked with their own stock. The analysis, or more correctly the description, of this forced labour forms the main content of the appropriate sections in the classical works of research. Alongside the work of these servile peasants, they noted the work of the permanent farm servants, who were also of servile origin, and who worked with the lord's stock. Finally, at busy times a certain number of workmen would be hired, and they were drawn from among the near-landless peasants (cottars). But in the main the demesne economy was served by the forced labour of the villeins. This was seen as the essential feature of the manorial system.

The manorial system is defined as the cultivation of the demesne by the serfs. The process of commutation gradually undermined this system and compelled the demesne economy to go over increasingly to hired labour. But whatever may have been the views of different historians on the advance of commutation in the fourteenth century, the thirteenth century, the classical epoch of the manorial order, was accounted a period in which forced labour reigned supreme.

The results of our investigations oblige us to submit this familiar picture to review. We have seen that on a number of manors there were no villeins at all, or very few of them; that even by the thirteenth century money rent had become quantitatively predominant, while in the majority of counties the labour dues of villeins were playing only a secondary part.

A significant differentiation among the peasantry was already observable, with the formation of a very numerous stratum of near-landless peasants whom their own plots of land could not support, alongside the emergence of an upper stratum of peasants who could not get along without the labour of others. We have seen that servile virgate and half-virgate holders composed only about one-third of the peasantry. We have noted the entirely secondary part played by labour rent in the small manor. For the most part it was only the large manor (and that not in every case) which could be based on labour rent. In thirteenth-century England there was a large area of demesne land the needs of which were not covered, or only inadequately covered, by the labour services of villeins. Nor must we forget the rich peasant holdings (especially the free holdings) which could not do without additional labour. Our sources do not enable us to work out the needs of the manors, still less of the prosperous peasants, for supplementary, non-obligatory labour. But we can nevertheless give some suggestive statistical data.

Supply of Villein Labour Estimated from Ratio of Demesne and Villein Land

It is difficult to decide what is the right proportion between demesne and villein land to ensure that the demesne was fully provided for by villein labour. But we can take as our starting-point the proportion obtaining on the large manors which were best provided with obligatory labour. Here the area of villein land was, on the average, roughly twice as great as that of demesne (we are speaking, of course, of arable land only). Hence, on a manor of medium size, where the demesne was only slightly less than the area of villein land, there would already be a discrepancy between the villein works due and the full requirements of the demesne, and this would be all the greater on the small manor, where the demesne was considerably greater in area than the villein land. But even large manors did not always have enough villein land. The manors of the Cistercian monasteries are a good example of this.

In the table given below I have made an attempt to establish the approximate area of demesne land which was quite unprovided for by forced villein labour or on which this labour was negligible. I have not made all-embracing calculations, but I have covered more than half the hundreds dealt with in the Hundred Rolls for which the area of demesne land can be worked out (15 hundreds out of 28), comprising more than 60 per cent of the total number of manors. I have distinguished (1) the demesnes of those manors which have no villeins (or on which villein land is so small as to be negligible); (2) the demesnes of those manors where there is villein land, but where the villeins do not perform any labour services, or where such services are a negligible factor; (3) the demesnes of those manors where there are villeins and labour services, but on a scale clearly insufficient for the cultivation of the demesne. According to my calculations, these categories account for 46 per cent, or almost half of the demesne land in question. The relation of the demesne land covered by these figures to the total area of demesne in each hundred is given in the 'percentage' column.

The table calls for explanation. We see that in Huntingdon-shire, a county of villeinage and labour dues, more than half the manors and more than 40 per cent of the demesne land is not provided for, or is ill provided for, by villein labour dues; in Cambridgeshire 68 per cent of the manors and 55 per cent of the demesne, and in Warwickshire half the manors and 70 per cent of the demesne land, are similarly unprovided for. In individual hundreds the percentage of demesne land un-provided for by labour dues is even higher; it reaches 57 per cent in the Huntingdonshire hundred of Normancross, 66 per cent in the Cambridgeshire hundred of Chilford; and 79 per cent in the Warwickshire hundred of Stoneleigh. But this does not mean that the remaining manors were suffici-ently provided for by villein labour dues. The table does not show that the demand for villein labour was satisfied, but that there was a considerable proportion of manors where the demand was ill-satisfied. How great this proportion was in the different regions depends not only on the stage of development of the labour dues system in the region, but on the differing forms of rent on individual manors. The figures for Oxfordshire illustrate this point. Here the labour dues system was less well developed than in Huntingdonshire and Cambridgeshire, but the existing labour services were more or less evenly distributed between the manors. In the latter two counties, however, we find a sharp distinction between the labour rent manors—mostly large—and the money rent manors—mostly small. In Oxfordshire only 27 per cent of demesne land was ill provided for by villein labour. But over the remaining 73 per cent there was rarely a full provision.[1]

If rather less than half the total area of demesne land had no provision, or a totally inadequate supply of villein labour services, that does not mean that the remainder had enough. Even approximately accurate evidence is difficult to obtain, but we have every ground for supposing that the greater part of the demand for working hands for the demesne could not be satisfied by means of obligatory villein labour.

From what has already been said about the respective characteristics of the small and the large manor, it is quite clear that the demand for non-obligatory labour was much higher on the small manor with its comparatively high percentage of demesne arable, its lower provision of villein land, its considerable predominance of money rent, and the special features of its villein population. While the economy of the large manor could in the main be based on the obligatory labour of villeins, other types of labour being used only as a supplementary resource, on the small manor as a rule this was impossible. The very low figures for the average size of the demesne on the manors dealt with in our table confirm that it was precisely the small manors that had little villein labour. The average area of demesne unprovided for by villein labour services comes out in our table at 170 acres, which is about half-way between the average area of the demesne on a medium-sized manor and the average on a small manor.

[1] Formally, there is an approximate equilibrium between the labour rent and the money-rent system, with a frequent occurrence of the alternative system under which the choice between labour services and money rent was at the lord's will. We must bear in mind that the same kind of alternative, in the form of the practice of *venditio operum*, existed even in places where the evidence seems to indicate the undisputed rule of the labour service system.

County and Hundred	Demesne land without villeins			Demesne land without labour dues			Demesne land with negligible labour dues			Totals		
	No. of manors	Demesne in acres	Percentage	No. of manors	Demesne in acres	Percentage	No. of manors	Demesne in acres	Percentage	No. of manors	Demesne in acres	Percentage
HUNTINGDONSHIRE												
Normancross	9	2,545	30	5	770	9	9	1,437	17	23	4,752	57
Leightonstone	7	1,138	12	11	1,193	12	7	2,045	20	25	4,376	44
Toseland	6	1,016	13	3	708	9	8	1,200	15	17	2,924	37
Hirstingstone	1	192	—	2	124	—	1	80	—	4	396	9
	23	4,891	16	21	2,795	9	25	4,762	16	69	12,448	41
CAMBRIDGESHIRE												
Chilford	12	1,917	28	—	—	—	9	2,540	38	21	4,457	66
Papworth	7	295	14	2	60	3	5	449	21	14	804	39
Longstow	9	1,227	20	7	526	8	8	1,162	18	24	2,915	45
Whittlesford	3	215	7	2	81	3	10	1,558	48	15	1,854	57
	31	3,654	20	11	667	4	32	5,709	32	74	10,030	55
OXFORDSHIRE (demesne given in virgates)												
Banbury	3	12½	8	3	18	13	4	12½	8	10	43	30
Ploughley	8	27½	6	9	69½	15	1	6	1	18	103	22
Lewknor	—	—	—	4	39¼	25	3	16½	10	7	55¾	35
Wootton	2	36	7	9	39	8	3	16	3	14	91	19
Ewelme	7	53	28	3	22	12	8	36½	18	18	111½	58
(in virgates)	20	129	8	28	187¾	13	19	87½	6	67	404¼	27
(in acres)	—	3,225	—	—	4,697½	—	—	2,175	—	—	10,095½	—
WARWICKSHIRE												
Stoneleigh	18	4,698	58	8	889	11	11	1,897	24	37	7,484	79
Kineton	9	1,380	9	20	4,215	28	16	4,050	27	45	9,645	65
	27	6,078	26	28	5,104	23	27	5,947	25	82	17,129	70
For all hundreds taken together	101	17,848	16	88	13,263	12	103	18,593	18	293	49,729	46
Average area of demesne		177			151			180			170	

SUPPLY OF VILLEIN LABOUR ESTIMATED FROM RATIO OF LABOUR RENT AND DEMESNE AREA

There is another method of approach which permits us to extend our observations over practically the whole country. The extent to which the demesne economy was run by villein labour services and the extent to which it required further supplementary labour can partly be answered by comparing the amount of labour rent on each manor with the size of the demesne arable. The amount of labour services (assessed in money) to one acre of demesne, in other words, the over-all assessment of labour services divided by the number of acres under demesne arable, can serve as an approximate index of the degree to which the supply of villein labour for the demesne was enough. Here, however, we are faced with a number of difficulties. First of all, by what measure are we to reckon the degree to which the demand for villein labour is satisfied? What quantity of obligatory labour (expressed in pence) per acre of demesne arable, entitles us to assume that the demesne's need of villein labour was fully satisfied? According to Walter of Henley, every acre of arable required the following works: three ploughings (each of which was assessed at 6d. on the average); harrowing (1d.); weeding (1d.); reaping (5d.); and carting (1d.). Threshing was rarely carried out by labour services. Thus one acre needs services to the value of 2s. 2d. This is, of course, a very high assessment. We must first of all make allowance for the two- or three-field system, under which one-half or one-third of the arable would be lying fallow. Secondly, although an acre of arable was ploughed three times (or sometimes only twice) under winter corn, under spring corn it was ploughed only once. Furthermore, the assessment of ploughing at 6d. is very high; the Hundred Rolls give 4d. to 6d. Equally high is the assessment for reaping, which in the rolls is estimated at 3d. to 4d. Walter of Henley gives no assessment for sowing, which was not usually entrusted to those performing labour service. All these factors allow us to lower Walter of Henley's assessment by a half, and to estimate the value of works at about 12d. If we remember that a considerable part of the ploughing was done by farm servants—*carucarii, akermanni*—, with the lord's stock, we should lower the figure a little further still. On the other hand, we must remember that the villein's labour services were not confined to work on the lord's fields; he had to cut and cart the hay, shear the sheep, perform a number of carrying services which are sometimes assessed at quite a high figure, dig ditches and repair buildings. All these works together must have come to a considerable figure. If we keep the figure of 12d. as the control figure, we shall hardly be making any substantial error.[1] And in fact there are manors on which this, or higher, figures obtain, showing a sufficient provision of villein labour for the needs of the demesne economy. Thus for the Earl of Gloucester's manor of Rothwell (Northants), the figure is 10d., on the manor of Bliburgh (Suffolk) it is 23¼d.; on the manor of Sheringham (Norfolk) it is 31½d. These figures are taken from the inquisitions *post Mortem* and the last two represent rare and exceptional cases. Usually the figure is lower, often much lower, than 12d.

We must not, of course, lose sight of the fact that these are arbitrary figures, which merely provide us with a rough basis for calculation, and consequently I do not wish to attribute great significance to the figures in Table 18. But they do, it seems to me, provide clear-cut evidence of one thing, namely, that demesne economy in England was quite insufficiently provided for by the obligatory labour of villeins. Furthermore, this is the case in all counties. The fullest provision of villein labour is seen in the eastern group of counties, where, incidentally, we also have the highest average figure for areas of demesne arable. But even in this group the index of the adequacy of this provision is still very low. The highest indices are given by the counties of Huntingdonshire, Northamptonshire and Norfolk, but even here they are much lower than the control figure of 12d.

It should be noted that the comparatively high figure for Northamptonshire is due to a single manor, the Earl of Gloucester's manor of Rothwell, which has considerable labour services. If this manor is left out of account, the average figure for Northamptonshire falls to 2½d. This strengthens our previous impression of the extremely uneven distribution of villein labour among different manors in the majority of

---

[1] I am here discarding the figure which I adopted in *The English Village in the Thirteenth Century*.

T

TABLE 18

PROVISION OF LABOUR DUES FOR THE DEMESNE

Counties	Average area of demesne arable per manor (in acres)	Average provision of labour dues (in pence) per demesne acre
EASTERN GROUP		
Essex	292	$2\frac{1}{3}$
Suffolk	385	$4\frac{3}{5}$
Norfolk	152	$6\frac{2}{3}$
Cambridgeshire	305	$2\frac{1}{5}$
Hertfordshire	351	$2\frac{3}{5}$
Huntingdonshire	344	$6\frac{3}{8}$
Northamptonshire	(201)	8
Middlesex	597	$2\frac{2}{3}$
Lincolnshire	164	$4\frac{1}{2}$
	300	$4\frac{1}{2}$
SOUTH MIDLANDS		
Bedfordshire	245	$1\frac{3}{4}$
Buckinghamshire	184	4
Berkshire	402	$1\frac{1}{2}$
Oxfordshire	227	$3\frac{1}{4}$
Warwickshire	243	$2\frac{1}{3}$
	262	$2\frac{1}{2}$
NORTH MIDLANDS		
Rutland	(268)	
Leicestershire	(291)	Labour rents
Nottinghamshire	(207)	are not
Derbyshire	(103)	defined
	217	
SOUTHERN GROUP		
Surrey	190	$4\frac{3}{4}$
Sussex	325	$3\frac{5}{6}$
Hampshire	209	$1\frac{5}{6}$
Dorset	(196)	($1\frac{1}{3}$)
Wiltshire	(210)	($3\frac{3}{8}$)
Somersetshire	(229)	($3\frac{3}{4}$)
Gloucestershire	(276)	(2)
Devonshire	(188)	(2)
	(228)	($2\frac{7}{8}$)
WESTERN GROUP		
Herefordshire	221	($3\frac{3}{8}$)
Worcestershire	(132)	($1\frac{3}{4}$)
Shropshire	(116)	($1\frac{1}{3}$)
Cheshire	(198)	($1\frac{4}{5}$)
	(167)	($2\frac{1}{4}$)
Northumbria	220	3
Yorkshire	134	$3\frac{1}{4}$
Kent	201	$1\frac{1}{4}$

Table 18 follows on from Table 8, and is based on the same material. It gives the average area of manorial demesnes for the different counties, and the valuation in pence of labour dues which can on the average be set against one acre of demesne.

I have kept the same division of the counties into groups as was followed in Chapter IV.

Figures based on an insufficient number of cases are enclosed in brackets.

counties. But it is quite clear that the more uneven the distribution of labour dues among the manors, the smaller is the part played by them in demesne economy as a whole, since an excess of labour dues on one manor cannot make up for a shortage on another, although it influences the average figures obtained.

The figures are very low even in counties where labour services were prominent among villein obligations. Cambridgeshire is one of the most 'laborious' counties, if one considers only the dues of the villeins; but it nevertheless contains a considerable area of demesne which is not, or only very poorly, provided with villeins.

Comparative figures from the Hundred Rolls give similar results to those from the inquisitions. In particular, the Hundred Rolls for Cambridgeshire yield the same index, $2\frac{1}{2}d$. Indices for the Oxfordshire hundreds[1] do not conflict with the average figure for Oxfordshire from the inquisitions—$3\frac{3}{4}d$. For the Warwickshire hundred of Stoneleigh the Hundred Rolls give the very low index of $1\frac{1}{2}d$., but in the other hundred, Kineton, the provision of villein labour for the demesne is higher, so that the average figure of $2\frac{1}{3}d$. for Warwickshire does not show a discrepancy. The very low index for Bedfordshire is not unexpected, since the Hundred Rolls, though they do not give details of labour dues for the county, reveal a very low percentage of villein land.

Villein labour services, then, were inadequate for the demesne economy. But the demand for non-obligatory labour was not limited to the 'demesne' in the strict sense of the word. A large peasant holding also would undoubtedly require farm labourers. It is difficult to calculate the demand for working hands put forward by the top layer of the peasants, both villein and free, who had either no servile labour power at all at their disposal, or only a tiny amount of it; but we cannot disregard this demand.

How, then, was the demand for labour power in the village and, above all, on the demesne satisfied? What were the sources of labour power? Quantitative comparisons are hard to make, but we must make a concession to the commonly accepted view and put in the first place the obligatory labour of the

[1] Bampton—$4\frac{1}{2}d$., Chadlington—$3\frac{3}{4}d$., Banbury—$3d$., Thame—$1d$.

villeins.[1] We must, however, again emphasize that these dues were very unevenly distributed, that they could, in part, be replaced by money payments (*venditio operum*), and were an inconstant quantity changing from year to year.

ALTERNATIVE SOURCES OF LABOUR POWER

Slaves (*servi*), who are so numerous in Domesday Book, the permanent unfree workers of house and farm, usually with no holding of their own, do not stand out so clearly in the surveys and account rolls of the thirteenth century. The term *servi* becomes equivalent to the term *villani* (*isti sunt servi de sanguine suo emendo*). But on the lord's farm we usually find a small 'staff' of permanent workers, who possibly may, in part at least, be descendants of the slaves.[2] On almost every manor one can find several ploughmen (*akermanni, carucarii*), a carter, some shepherds, a dairymaid (*daya*). On the Earl of Norfolk's manor of Forncett there were in the thirteenth century 8 or 9 permanent farm workers: 4 ploughmen, a carter, a cowherd, a swineherd, and a dairymaid; for three or four months in the year a workman was hired to do the harrowing. At times other workmen would appear: the *grangiarius*, the *warenner*, and the cook who prepared the labourer's food. At one time a miller was numbered among the servants, but he did not live on the premises.[3] It is hard to define exactly the personal rank or condition of the farm workers of Forncett. They lived in the *domus famulorum*, and their food was prepared for them by a woman appointed specially for that purpose. The famous *Scriptum Quoddam* of Gloucester Abbey depicts the recruitment of farm servants from the ranks of the villeins (*nativi*); evidently from among those members of the villeins' families who were not fully burdened with labour dues.[4]

In the description of the dues of the villeins on one Oxfordshire manor we read: *Item veniet ad curiam Sancti Michaelis cum filiis suis, si quos habuerit, qui panem suum lucrari potuerint; de quibus*

[1] In order to avoid misunderstandings, I must qualify this statement by saying that by 'obligatory labour' here is meant the 'customary' regular labour services of villeins, chiefly tenants of virgates and half-virgates, services which are recorded in the manorial accounts, and in the government surveys which were modelled upon them.

[2] Cf. Ashley, *An Introduction to English Economic History and Theory*, i, 32, 61.

[3] Davenport, *The Economic Development of a Norfolk Manor*, 24.

[4] C. Glouc. iii, 213.

dictus W. de Spina (the villein) *unum eligere poterit, ut sibi serviat; et alii, si dominus indigeat, si servire voluerint, domino deserviunt secundum consuetudinem manerii, scilicet per liberationem et stipendium per annum, sicut ceteri famuli.*[1] One of a villein's sons (to be chosen by the villein) is bound to enter the house or farm service of the lord. The other sons can enter the service of their own will (*si servire voluerint*), if their master happens to need men to work for him. But this service, too, is 'according to the custom of the manor', and they receive the same allowances and pay as the other *famuli*. Apart from their own particular line of work these farm servants had to perform miscellaneous duties on the lord's farm. The Gloucester Abbey instruction gives particular advice that servants are not to be left without work, and are promptly to be given another job if they have finished one. They had the main burden of work at ploughing, sowing and threshing time.

It is not easy to estimate the part played by the unfree farm servants in the working of the land. It would appear that they could occupy a prominent position only in the economy of fairly large manors which disposed of a considerable number of villeins. They could hardly play any conspicuous part in the economy of a small manor, and it was there, as we have seen, that there was particular need of working hands apart from labour services. We should regard the labour of unfree farm servants as closely connected with the system of villein services, representing a particular variety of labour service, one which made use of those members of the villeins' families who were not occupied in the usual unpaid labour.

Large demesnes without villein labour are met with on the manors of Cistercian monasteries. But there the question of labour supply was solved in a special way, namely by the recruitment of 'lay brothers' or *conversi*, who received from the monastery lodging, food and clothing, and were bound to do all the farm work. In addition the Cistercians also used *mercenarii*, who lived outside the monastery walls and were not bound by vows. They were granted plots of land, and rented additional plots as well. They were not tied to the land, but could go away, although in practice they were held down by arrears in rent and seem to have had little to distinguish them

[1] *R.H.*, ii, 768.

from serfs.[1] On the small manor of semi-peasant type a certain part must have been played also by the personal labour of the master and his family, and it is even possible that some small knights were sometimes obliged to put their hand to the plough. Finally, there was one further well-known source of labour; the near-landless peasantry, or the cottars. The growing importance of this class in succeeding centuries has been generally admitted, but its part in feudal times has not, in my view, been estimated at its true value.

To appreciate the role of the cottars we must recall a few figures. We have seen that small villein holdings (5 acres and under) make up 29 per cent of all the villein tenements mentioned in the Hundred Rolls; together with fardel holdings they amount to 38 per cent of all villein holdings. In the eastern area (Huntingdonshire, Cambridgeshire, Bedfordshire, Buckinghamshire) the small holdings and the fardels together account for 50 per cent of all villein households; in Buckinghamshire alone they are 53 per cent, and in Cambridgeshire 57 per cent. While they play a comparatively modest part on the large manors, on the small manors they account for more than half the villein households.

The figures for small free holdings are even more striking. In this case small holdings of 5 acres and under amount to 47 per cent of all the peasant free holdings, and if we include fardels as well the figure rises to 59 per cent. The greater part of these are holdings of 3 acres or less, which make up 37 per cent of all free holdings. In Buckinghamshire the holders of small plots and of fardels account for 60 per cent, in Bedfordshire for 66 per cent, and in Cambridgeshire for 80 per cent[2] of all peasant free holdings.

We must remember, also, that surveys do not mention the completely landless, those who had not even a hovel of their own, and who lived in the houses of others as hired labourers. Of their existence we learn only from chance remarks in our sources, but they help to swell the category of workers not

[1] Cf. J. W. Thomson, *Economic and Social History of the Middle Ages*, 612–19. Hoffman, E., 'Die Entwicklung der Wirtschaftsprinzipien im Zisterzienzer Orden,' *Historisches Jahrbuch*, xxxi (1910). Dolberg, 'Zisterzienzer Mönche und Konversen als Landwirte und Arbeiter,' *Studien und Mitteil aus d. Bened. und Zist. Orden*, xiii (1892). Arbois de Joubainville, *Les abbayes Cisterciennes* (1868).
[2] See also Table 12.

performing labour services. Furthermore it was not only the cottars and the holders of fardels who were obliged to hire themselves out to work, but at times the holders of virgates and half-virgates. In the Ramsey cartulary[1] a case is quoted of a villein virgate-holder hiring himself out to his lord at a busy season *propter indigentiam*. A further source of labour power was represented by members of the land-holding peasant families, both serf and free. Part of the serf's family might have to work for the lord as farm servants, but others could hire themselves out elsewhere. A villein had to pay a small levy to his lord if his son worked away from home.[2] The supply of labour was further increased by town workers going to the country at harvest time. In the same way the inhabitants of the northern regions, and of those bordering on Wales, where stock-breeding was the prevalent form of farming, used to go off in the autumn to earn money in the agricultural areas.[3]

These facts point to two important conclusions. In the first place, the obligatory labour of villeins probably covered less than half the requirements of the demesnes for labour power, quite apart from those of the large peasant holdings. In the second place, numerous sections of the population were not supported by their own land and were dependent, in whole or in part, on wages. It is evident that wage labour played in the thirteenth century countryside a very important part, far more important than the sources would indicate and that historians have allowed.[4]

But if wage labour played such an important part in the thirteenth century, why has this fact not found adequate expression in the sources, in particular in ministers' accounts, where every penny and every bushel of grain is accounted for? Everyone who has studied these sources knows that expenditure on wages did not play a conspicuous part in the budget of a

[1] i, 473.

[2] *Et si filius suus servierit alicui extraneo, dabit domino suo duos capones per annum ad recognitionem domini*; R.H., ii, 463.

[3] As set down in the famous statute of the twenty-fifth year of Edward III's reign. This document is later in date, and its appearance was due to special circumstances, but it appeals to ancient custom; the people of these parts *puissent venir en temps Daust de laborer en autres Countes et salvement retourner come ils soleient faire avant ses heures.* Stats. i, 312.

[4] I use the expression 'wage labour' in a conditional sense; its real meaning still requires analysis.

manor, and that under this heading we find mainly the keep and pay of the permanent farm servants, a considerable proportion of whom were serving under compulsion. Miss Levett came to the conclusion that on the bishop of Winchester's manors just before the Black Death comparatively little was paid out in wages, especially wages in money, and that the rates of pay for regular workers were traditional and altered little. Payment was made in kind, and also in land, by remissions from rents. Miss Levett formed the impression that the bishop could have doubled or trebled his expenditure on wages without noticeable diminution of his revenue.[1] The same thing is noted by Maitland: 'Wages are a comparatively trifling item in his (the lord's) accounts'.[2]

But it is not surprising that manorial sources, particularly the ministers' accounts, which reflect the organization of large manors, mostly belonging to the church, should give little information about hired labourers and wages. The large manor was better provided with the forced labour of villeins, and the place where hired labour was needed most of all was the small manor, which has left practically no traces in the form of manorial documents. We cannot hope to find direct evidence here. Our conclusions are therefore bound to be indirect.

THE SMALLHOLDERS

The main source of hired labour power was, beyond doubt, the smallholders, the cottars and the holders of fardels, *pauperes cotarii qui de labore manuum victus perquirunt*.[3] They have long troubled historians of the English village, but they have never been studied in detail, because, like the small manor, they have left few traces in the sources. The manorial surveys become summary and careless when they reach the smallholders, since tenants of small holdings with small rents played an insignificant part in the system of feudal holdings and rents which was the main object of interest for those compiling manorial and analogous government surveys.

In his main work, *Villainage in England*, Vinogradoff hardly touched the question of the hired labourer, just as he did not

[1] Levett, *O.S.S.L.H.*, v, 35–6; cf. also *Studies in Manorial History*, 60–2.
[2] *E.H.R.*, ix, 422.
[3] *Nonarum Inquisitiones*, Record Commission (1807), 15.

touch the question of the market. For him the labour power for the demesne came mainly from the serfs who owed labour services. When he speaks of the 'staff' serving the demesne he has in mind the *ministeriales*, including the ploughmen and carters. But these are farm servants drawn from the ranks of the serfs, and Vinogradoff has in mind not serf cottars but the younger or older members of a villein family, who are not occupied on labour service ('elder or younger brothers as it might be'). The hired labourers in the more direct sense of the word have not more than half a page devoted to them. He concedes that in thirteenth-century agricultural treatises and ministers' accounts, there are references to the existence of hired labour, but considers this exceptional and a new departure. He does not connect the question of hired labour with the cottars. For Vinogradoff the hired labourers are strangers to the manor, 'outsiders'.[1]

Vinogradoff pays far more attention in his later work, *The Growth of the Manor*, to the bordars and cottars and their role in manorial economy.[2] He speaks of the 'remarkable history of the small tenants', and adds that it is 'hardly appreciated rightly by modern scholars'. In his view the bordars played an important part in the economy of the manor, since they provided the main body of agricultural workers, as well as working on their own plots of land. They were, to a large extent, outside the organization of the village community and their labour services were commuted early. Vinogradoff points out how superfluous members of the more prosperous villein families were settled on cottars' holdings, and how the latter then provided the hands needed on both the bigger holdings and the demesne. Cross-currents were thus created which found no reflection in the surveys but which evidently produced results that cannot be explained in any other way.

Granat paid much attention to this question, and stressed the numerical strength of this class in feudal England, and its role as a 'proletariat', or as 'wage labourers'. But he considered the cottar chiefly as a labourer on the virgater's land, paying little attention to his part in the manorial economy. He failed to perceive the extent of the need for hired hands in the demesne economy, accepting the traditional view of the

[1] *Villainage*, 321.   [2] Pp. 352 sqq.

predominance of servile labour. Furthermore, he was interested primarily in the peculiarities of the cottars as a 'proletarian' reserve ready to be transferred from agriculture to industry, and therefore did not examine in detail the place of the cottar within the feudal agrarian system.[1]

What did the cottar live on? In the first place there was the cottar's holding, that 'natural wage' of the direct producers of feudal society, however small a plot it may have been. Although we may assume the existence of a stratum of completely landless labourers who hired themselves out by the year (*locati per annos*), the typical agricultural worker was still the near-landless peasant with his own yard and kitchen garden, with his own small plot of arable land, with certain common rights, and with a certain amount, usually small, of livestock of his own. Some of the needs of the cottar and his family were met by the income derived from his land, and this was all the more true in the case of the fardel-holder. We know very little of the economy of a cottar, apart from the area of his land, and the area of his arable land might not account for all the income from his holding. A considerable part might be played in a peasant's economy, especially in that of a small peasant, by the grazing of beasts on the common pasture. Fishing, hunting, the use of woodland, and the cutting of peat are other possible supplementary means of existence for the small peasant. The drive by the lords against the common rights of the peasants, already under way in the thirteenth century, the seizure of exclusive rights of hunting and fishing over forests and waste lands, must have dealt a heavy blow to the small peasantry, making it more and more difficult for them to exist without earning extra money, if, indeed, this had ever been possible.

The occupation of the commons by the feudal lords with support from the government, which met with the strongest opposition from the peasantry, must have increasingly undermined the importance of his holding as the economic base of a cottar's life. Not that the cottar always had rights in the commons. Such rights were connected with holdings in the

[1] Some attention to the fortunes of the cottar is paid by Lipson, *The Economic History of England*, i (1937), 46–9. Among recent historians of the English medieval village Bennett (*op. cit.*, 63 sqq.) more than anyone else has stressed the importance of the cottars.

arable fields, and the cottars in nine cases out of ten had no holdings in the arable fields of the village. Their holdings originated in small clearings (*assarta*) from forest and waste, or in the leasing out by the lord to newcomers of small, inconveniently situated scraps of demesne land, for low rents.[1] They stood to a large extent outside the organization of the village community, outside the usual routine of the community's economic life, and partially outside the community itself. Bennett is inclined to see this as advantageous to the cottar, as giving him greater freedom by comparison with the virgater, who was better off, but was burdened with heavy dues. The dissociation of the cottar from the village community, he suggests, may have enabled the cottar to improve his methods of cultivation, something which was impossible for the virgaters who were bound by the compulsory crop-rotation. Thus, in Bennett's view, the presence of the cottars worked in favour of the liberation of the servile village; if there had been no comparatively free working hands, commutation would have been hindered.

But if it is true that the cottar stood to a great extent outside the manorial organization, one may ask whether this was all pure gain. The cottar had little chance of carrying out agricultural improvements on his small scrap of land. He hardly stood to gain in cases where he had no rights to common pasture and woodlands. In the manor court, too, his voice would not have the same weight as that of the peasant with a full holding. It has long been known that the village community was not egalitarian, and that holdings had become the private preserves of definite families. This differentiation affected the manor court. The jurors were usually chosen from the ranks of the prosperous, and so were the manorial officials whose election was the court's business, the reeve (*prepositus*) and his assistant (*messor*). Together they formed a leading group in the hallmote and backed one another up. The interests of the well-to-do peasants and of the small peasants were already distinct, and it is not hard to guess whose interests suffered in the clash. We may recall the case of Michael the reeve, supported by his own party in the hallmote, who

[1] Bennett, *op. cit.*, 70, may again be referred to as a useful summary of the special types of labour service owed by cottars.

oppressed the peasants by making them work for him, and lease or even sell their land to him at a low rate. Whatever opinion we may hold concerning the extent to which the manor court and manorial custom safeguarded the personal and property rights of the servile peasantry, it is obvious that they were a poor safeguard to the rights of the cottars.

The vagueness of the line between free and servile small-holders has already been noted. Recent writings tend to ignore the distinction between villein and free peasant, which for lawyer-historians of the older generation was the keystone of their theories. Nevertheless between free peasant and villein, and between free and villein holding, there is a very con-spicuous difference; but it becomes more and more obliterated as one passes from the peasants with adequate holdings to the cottars. It should be noted that the manorial and government surveys often separate the cottars as a special group, distinct from both villeins and freeholders.[1]

This may appear to be an inconsistent application of two different principles of division: the one according to personal status (or character of holding), the other, according to size of holding. In actual fact free tenants, villeins, and cottars all had different parts to play in the manorial system, and from this point of view there was no essential difference between the free and the unfree cottar, or between their holdings. The villein cottars bore a number of labour dues, but usually the greater part of their rent was in money. But the free cottar very frequently performed labour service, mostly in the form of boon-works, as well as paying money rent. So far as his rent was concerned there was little to distinguish the free from the villein cottar. Furthermore, the free cottar was in practice deprived of the chief privilege of freeholders—the ability to uphold his rights in the king's courts. In this respect he was equated with the villein. He was not precluded from suing, but the fact that a lawsuit had to be paid for made it unattainable for the poor free peasants. He was also deprived of certain political rights, although this was given the appear-ance of release from political duties, for example the property

---

[1] The statute known as *Extenta Manerii* distinguishes cottars from other cate-gories of peasant: *Item de libere tenentibus . . . item inquirendum est de custumariis . . . item inquirendum est de coterellis qui cotagia et curtilagia teneant.*

qualification for jurors established in 1285. So far as we can picture this world of poor peasants that has left so few traces in the sources, they were a needy and defenceless mass, much more defenceless than the middle rank of servile villeins; personal freedom and free holding brought with them no effective legal protection or advantage.

THE TWO ASPECTS OF THE LABOUR OF THE COTTAR

There are two aspects to the cottar's position. On the one hand, he is the object of feudal exploitation. He holds his land from a lord, he pays rent for it, he owes various dues. On the other hand, at the same time he hires himself out to work and receives wages. Which of these two aspects is the dominant one? According to Rogers, the earnings of the higher paid worker, in kind and in money, amounted to approximately £2 7s. 10d. a year, assuming that his wife and boy worked as well. This is a very high estimate, which presupposes that he is hired for a whole year. A freeholder with 20 acres of land, by Rogers' calculations, might earn an extra £1 during busy seasons. The average assessment of an unfree cottar's rent in the Hundred Rolls, is 2s. 1d. (1s. 4d. in money and 9d. in labour dues). If we take Rogers' figure to be somewhat exaggerated, and the rent figure given above as considerably below reality, in view of various supplementary payments not included,[1] comparison of the two figures still leaves no doubt that the cottar was far more a 'wage labourer' than a feudally exploited peasant. On the other hand, it may be that the exploitation of the cottar as a wage-labourer had a considerable element in it of coercive feudal exploitation based on non-economic pressure.

We must distinguish between the exploitation of the cottar by the administration of the manor to which he belonged, and the work he did elsewhere. The latter might, with some qualifications, be called wage labour. But in the case of a cottar earning wages on his own manor, a prominent place must be given to non-economic factors. It is hard to imagine a cottar—and the freeman in this instance differs little from the serf—as a worker 'freely' selling his labour-power. The

[1] See Chapter III. Rogers' figures relate to the period immediately before the Black Death.

manorial administration always had power to detain him within the manor. Like other serfs, he could leave only with the lord's permission. This power was recognized by the state, and was only partially limited by the labour legislation of Edward III. The manorial administration could, therefore, always retain within the manor the necessary number of cottars or other men not engaged on labour services (sons and older or younger brothers of villeins), and force them in this way to work on the demesne. Meanwhile neither the work they were to do nor the reward they were to receive for it was defined by custom, nor was it recorded in any survey. Can one apply to conditions of this sort the appellation of 'wage labour', or does this term denote in this case an altered form of obligatory labour,—worse, in fact, than ever, since it allowed greater impositions than the traditionally regulated *consuetudines*? The main difference lies in the fact that the performer of labour services received in return for his work a 'natural wage' in the form of his land, while the exploited cottar received his pay partly in land, partly in allowances in kind, and partly in money. Part of the work of the exploited cottar on the manor is labour service in the direct sense, the labour rent fixed by custom as payment for his plot of land. But the rest of it? He is in a position not far off that of the unfree farm servant, with this difference, that he lives on his own bit of land, working for part of the year (and receiving payment for only part of the time), but only when the manorial administration has need of him. The 'wages' of the exploited cottar look like the *liberationes* and *stipendia* received by the farm servants. Thus the cottar working on the manor to which he belongs, can be considered as something midway between a feudally dependent peasant and an unfree farm worker. Among farm workers it is very difficult for us to distinguish free and unfree, those working there by virtue of villein service and those 'hired'. The position of both groups, so far as board and payment are concerned, is essentially the same.

The cottar working on his lord's manor was at the same time paying rent for his piece of land, and receiving 'wages' for his work. Such a contradiction presented no difficulties at all to the manorial administration, and was common in manorial practice. Peasants who rendered labour services and paid money rents for their land were often set to other work which did not enter into their customary service, and in return for it corresponding remissions from their rent would be made. Remissions of this kind are met with in practically every account roll. On the bishop of Winchester's manors, the reeve in return for work done had a remission from his rent of 5s.; a ploughman, a shepherd, a smith and a forester had remissions of from 2s. to 5s. Remissions of labour service were also made. Systems of labour service which were more or less regulated by custom, and of completely unregulated coerced 'hired' labour existed side by side on the manor, mutually interrelated and forming flexible combinations which afforded the manorial administration wide facilities for manœuvre.

OTHER FORMS OF COMPULSORY HIRED LABOUR

Hired labour which was really coerced was not only done by cottars. Peasant householders who had bought themselves off from their labour services were also sometimes bound to hire themselves out to their lord if he required it. The abandonment of the labour service system did not always mean the disappearance of obligatory labour, but rather that the latter took on another form. On the bishop of Winchester's manor of Waltham, after a general commutation of dues, the lord retained the right to certain services from the villeins, but against payment: *Dominus habebit huiusmodi operarios ad liberationem et stipendia sua dum sibi placuerit.*[1] A form of paid obligatory labour combined with labour rent can be seen in the system of works with food provided, or works with a feast afterwards, which played a prominent part on many manors. The food was not infrequently commuted and replaced by a money payment, or sometimes payment was made in kind (hay, a sheep, etc.).[2] Six villein virgaters receive 15d. between them at hay-mowing time, 6d. at harvest time.[3] At Stanton (Cambs.) twelve tenants of 5-acre holdings owe quite heavy labour dues, but the works are not unpaid. They receive in return for them a quarter of wheat, a sheep (price 12d.) and

---

[1] Cf. Levett, *O.S.S.L.H.*, v, 20, 33.
[2] *Metet 4 acras pro precariis et habebit pro cibo precarium* 8d. *R.H.*, ii, 544.
[3] *R.H.*, ii, 788.

half an acre of meadow. The payment for such works was sometimes quite high and, in fact, was not distinguishable in amount from real wages: villeins at Piddington (Oxon.) are bound to mow the lord's meadow within one day, and they receive the so-called *medsipe*, 40*d. de bursa domini*.[1] This is, in fact, practically the full wages of twenty-five men. The manorial accounting system sometimes reckons the food provided or the money paid as the full equivalent of the works done, and so does not include the latter in the general assessment of rents (*nihil operabitur nisi ad cibum domini*) and similar expressions). Work with food thrown in is sometimes reckoned *nullius pretii* and does not count when *venditio operum* is being carried out or commutation arranged. *Arure de precariis* at Peasenhall (Suffolk) *non appreciantur quia nihil dant*.[2] Many cases occur where the value of the food exceeds the assessment value of the work,[3] so that the manorial administration renounces the works, as they are considered uneconomic.

This whole category of works thus comes very close to compulsory labour for hire, though in origin it is connected, not with hired labour, but rather with the pre-feudal mutual assistance of free peasant neighbours. It is interesting that an obligation on the part of the lord to provide food during any labour service was held to be a proof that the labour service in question was not villein in character.[4]

On the other hand cottars could be brought into the system of labour services in place of a peasant with a full holding. Here we see a very remarkable combination of obligatory and hired labour. The virgater, and even the half-virgater, often needed labourers. Lack of family help on such a peasant's holding would, if he was overloaded with labour services for the lord, make it necessary to recruit supplementary labour-power not only to work on the peasant's own land, but to replace him on the lord's demesne as well. Sometimes a peasant rendering labour services would be instructed to appear for work 'with one, two or three men'; sometimes he would be required 'to find a man' for the execution of this or

[1] *R.H.*, ii, 717. [2] M.A. 1003-13, 11 Ed. I.
[3] Petrushevsky, *op. cit.*, ii, 1st ed., 87–88, note 4: *Sic saepe cibus illarum extendit valorem operis . . . Sic valet cibus plus quam profectus operis per extentem, ideo nihil inde exegitur.* These examples are taken from ministers' accounts.
[4] See examples given by Vinogradoff, *Collected Papers*, i, 125.

that piece of work (*inveniet unum hominem, duos homines etc.*). Thus the labourer whom the peasant paid to work, who was most probably a cottar belonging to the same manor, replaced his employer on labour service. The payment of a substitute by the peasant is sometimes directly provided for: *et inveniet unum hominem ad bondbederipa, proprio custu.*[1] The villeins at Kingston had to find *operarios* for autumn work at Foxton.[2] In the list of services owed by a villein woman, Joan the widow, it is stated that she must provide *ad magnam precariam duos homines, ultra quos ibit dicta Johanna ad videndum quod bene operentur.*[3] Sometimes the sub-tenants (*undersets*) of the villeins had to perform service.[4] Sometimes even free tenants had to appear with their labourers to do boon work. Thus, at Burcot (Oxon.) a certain Hugh Frankeleyn, tenant of 3 virgates, had to pay his lord (the bishop of Lincoln) 17s. and do labour services. Among others he had to find. *omnes servientes suos locatos per annum excepta uxore sua et nutrice et pastore in autumno ad duas precarias.*[5] In this way, without commutation taking place and with the system of obligatory works preserved, the labour of the peasants liable for labour rent was partially replaced by the labour of cottar workmen.

'FREE' WAGE LABOUR

Lastly, we also find hired labourers in the proper sense of the word. These are the *extranei* or *vagantes*, as the sources call them; people from other parts who hire themselves out for the season. We have no grounds for supposing this group to have been numerous, although it includes both the seasonal workers from the West and North and the town-workers who came to the country for seasonal work. Since there is no exact correspondence in any region between the demand for labour on the demesnes (so far as we can judge what this was) and the supply provided by cottars and other smallholders, we must suppose a certain mobility of labour, even if only at harvest time. This is why among the labourers on particular manors we find *extranei conducti* who get their keep on the same

---

[1] See D. M. Petrushevsky, *op. cit.*, 4th ed. 436, note 33.
[2] *R.H.*, ii, 515.   [3] *R.H.*, ii, 765.
[4] Cf. Granat, *op. cit.*, 59.   [5] *R.H.*, ii, 748.

basis as labourers from the home manor who are working on the lord's demesne.[1]

Lenin saw the development of the mobility of agricultural workers (that is, in the majority of cases of near-landless peasants) as a progressive phenomenon, which destroyed feudal, servile forms of hire and labour,[2] and promoted the development of capitalist relations. But in thirteenth-century England this development was only beginning. If we make so bold as to call these *extranei conducti* wage labourers, a number of qualifications must be attached, since the social characteristics of a 'wage labourer' at this epoch were determined by the dominance of production-relations of a feudal type. The thirteenth-century agricultural labourer was often not a free man, or if he was free the distinction between him and the unfree was not great. He had not broken his link with the land; as a rule he was a near-landless cottar. He was burdened with dues of feudal character; he usually rendered some small labour services, and handed over to his lord part of his wages, in the form of rent. And within the economy of his employer, who was most often a feudal lord, there was little to distinguish him from the unfree farm servant; they both received the same payment. Wage labour in the proper sense of the term was only beginning to come into being. At this time it still constituted only one element in the feudal mode of production.

THE ECONOMIC POSITION OF THIRTEENTH-CENTURY AGRICULTURAL WAGE WORKERS

Rogers took a very optimistic view of the position of a wage labourer in the thirteenth century. The money earnings of a worker in the higher categories—e.g. a ploughman, or a carter—before the Black Death, amounted on his calculation to 7s. 6d. a year. Further, such a worker received allowances of grain to the value of £1 4s. 8d. with a certain amount extra at harvest time. Besides all this, his wife and son worked as well. In this way a workman's family could earn £2 7s. 10d. a year, which by thirteenth and fourteenth-century standards was not at all bad. To this must be added the fact that the

---

[1] Cf. *C. Ram.*, i, 473–74.
[2] *The Development of Capitalism in Russia*, Chap. III, s. 10 (partially translated into English in *SW*, i).

workman had a plot of land at a low rent, and that he enjoyed common rights.[1] But Rogers intentionally took the better-paid workers, and assumed that their earnings were regular. But the position of workers who only received wages and food for the limited periods when they were at work, was evidently quite different.

According to Rogers there was a rise in wages towards the end of the thirteenth century. He saw the reasons for this in a general improvement of the peasants' situation; in commutation; in the growth of peasant property; and to some extent in the spread of manufacture. Wages were higher in the east of the country and around London than in the other parts of England. Whether there was general improvement in the position of the peasantry is another question. If there really was an increase in wages, as Rogers thinks, it is to be explained rather as a consequence of the rise in food prices.

If we have grounds for doubting the prosperity of peasants who had an adequate allowance of land, even greater doubts are aroused by the optimistic picture drawn by Rogers of the position of the cottar. Their ownership of small patches of land scarcely did much towards ensuring their prosperity,[2] and the leasing out of land through inability to cultivate it was apparently a widespread phenomenon among English thirteenth-century cottars. If we remember that the cottar was the most defenceless element in the countryside, the one most bereft of rights; that it was on his head that all the evils of contemporary life fell first, especially those of oppression by the manorial administration; that his earnings depended upon a lord who was free to let him depart or not as he saw fit; that he was, when all was said and done, the object of non-economic coercion; that the village community, the manor court and the custom of the manor scarcely afforded him any protection, while protection from the king's courts was even more inaccessible,—then we shall begin to see a somewhat cheerless

[1] Rogers, *op. cit.*, i, 253 sqq.
[2] We may recall here the picture which Lenin drew of the position of the 'wage labourers possessing allotments'. 'The insignificant dimensions of the farm on a small patch of land, and, moreover a farm in a state of ruin (this is particularly evidenced by the letting of land), the inability to exist without selling labour power . . . an extremely low standard of living, probably lower than that of the labourer without an allotment—these are the distinguishing features of this type.'

picture taking shape. Given the large numbers of near-landless peasants, given the sporadic and unreliable nature of the demand for working hands in agriculture, given the general insecurity of life, the cottar could hardly survive without getting into debt, which was bound to create further dependence on the lord's household or on a prosperous fellow-villager, and thus became a source of new 'labour dues' which he had to work off. All in all, it would appear that the cottar had to do a lot of work, and received very little in return.

In contrast to the familiar picture of the servile village, where the members of the village community are more or less adequately provided with land, render fixed labour dues, enjoy the protection of custom and of the court, and have certain possibilities of accumulation open to them, we begin to see sketched a quite different village, where practically half the population is deprived of any protection whatso-ever, whose work is not defined or regulated, and who live not on the border-line of poverty, but in very real poverty. The sale of works and the substitution of cottars for the peasants owing labour services, suggest that the parts played by regulated labour services on the one hand, and the unregulated labour of cottars on the other, were not such as is usually supposed.

POSSIBLE COMBINATIONS OF LABOUR SUPPLY

On thirteenth-century manors we usually find a combination of several forms of labour—fundamentally non-voluntary labour.

1. First, there is the system of labour services which are to a greater or lesser degree fixed by custom, and which are done mainly by the peasants with full holdings, the virgaters and half-virgaters. Under this system not only the labour but the stock of the dependent peasants is exploited. This system prevails first and foremost on the oldest manors, lay and ecclesiastical, of the great feudal lords. Part of their feudal rent is rendered by the dependent peasants in the form of contributions in kind or in money; part of the works are 'sold' every year, i.e. replaced by money payments.

2. A second system, closely connected, is the farm servant

system. It would seem that here the workers are mostly drawn from the families of villeins, and hired temporarily (for the year), but probably there are also a certain number of permanent servants. Here the work is done with the lord's stock, the workers live on the lord's farm and there get their board, allowances in kind (*liberationes*), and payment in money (*stipendia*). This system, too, was apparently practised mainly on the large manors, which had at their disposal a considerable number of villeins.

3. The system of non-voluntary hiring, which chiefly involved the cottars. We presume that it was most widespread on the small manors, where there were no villeins with full holdings, or very few of them, or where labour services were either absent or insignificant. But even on the large manors, where labour services were prominent, the part played by this system was much more considerable than one might conclude from manorial and governmental surveys.

4. Lastly, one cannot ignore the beginnings of the development of wage labour in the real sense, a development which got under way under the prevailing conditions of the feudal mode of production, but which already contained within it elements of capitalist exploitation.

None of these systems appeared in the thirteenth century in its pure form, but always in some more or less flexible combination. The system of fixed labour services, which at first sight appears to be an immobile and hide-bound system, in actual fact was capable of considerable flexibility, owing to the practice of *venditio operum*, and to the possibility of replacing servile labour by wage labour (in its qualified sense) in whatever proportion was required—agricultural labourers *quandoque accrescunt et quandoque decrescunt*.[1]

The agricultural treatises of the thirteenth century noted this coexistence of several systems of labour organization. Walter of Henley speaks mainly of the labour of villeins rendering labour services, and of regular farm servants—it is not clear whether they are villein or free,—but the anonymous treatise called the 'Husbandry' gives special attention to the question of hired workers who have to be paid wages in money, and compares the systems of piece-work at a daily rate. A Paris

[1] Neilson, *O.S.S.L.H.*, ii, 174.

manuscript published by Lacour[1] speaks of hiring (for the year) from outside, regular workers who are expected to provide a recommendation and surety.

SMALLHOLDERS IN DOMESDAY BOOK AND EARLIER

It was not only in the thirteenth century that the cottars began to play a large part in manorial economy. Already in Domesday Book, compared with about 108,500 villeins, there are about 82,000 bordars, 6,800 cottars, and 25,000 slaves (*servi*), as well as approximately 23,000 sokemen, and about 12,000 *liberi homines*. The bordars and cottars, the near-landless peasants, thus make up more than one-third of the whole agricultural population. Even if the figures of bordars and cottars may include a certain number of craftsmen, fishermen and the like, the proportion is still eloquent.

What changes can be discovered between the eleventh and the thirteenth centuries? We may compare, county by county, the figures of Domesday Book and the Hundred Rolls, even though such comparisons, as has already been said, are beset with many difficulties. First of all, the terminology of the two sources is different. The meaning of the term 'villein' in the eleventh century was quite different from that in the thirteenth century, and in the villeins of Domesday we may descry the ancestors not only of the villeins of the thirteenth century, but of many of its free tenants. Furthermore, persons of the same status were in one place put in the category of sokemen, while in another they were in that of villeins. The term *bordarii* disappears in later sources, as does that of *servi*, in the sense in which the latter was used in Domesday Book. Nevertheless, an approximate comparison is possible. Table 19 gives the Domesday figures for the most important categories of the population, for the counties covered by the Hundred Rolls, and should be compared with the analogous table for the thirteenth century (Table 12).[2] We shall probably not be far wrong if we equate the villeins, sokemen and *liberi homines* of Domesday with peasants with full holdings, and the bordars and cottars with near-landless peasants. It is, however, not known where the compilers of the great census of the eleventh

[1] 'Traité d'économie rurale,' *Bibl. de l'Ecole des Chartes*, ii, 4me série (1856).
[2] Cf. above, p. 228.

century drew the line in this respect, and we may assume that bordars may have included holders of fardels and even of half-virgates.[1] And what about the *servi*? If the slaves (*theows, esnes*) of the Anglo-Saxon period had already became to a large extent settled peasants by the time of Domesday Book, that process had apparently been completed between the eleventh and the thirteenth centuries. They must have gone to swell the ranks of the cottars.

TABLE 19

County	Villeins	Sokemen and liberi homines	Bordarii	Cottarii	Servi
Cambridgeshire	1,907	213	1,428	736	548
%	39	5	29	15	12
Huntingdonshire	1,933	22	490		
%	79	1	20		
Bedfordshire ..	1,829	107	1,132		474
%	52	3	32		13
Buckinghamshire	2,893	20	1,651	1,326	833
%	43		25	20	11
Oxfordshire ..	3,545	26	1,849		963
%	55		29		15
Warwickshire	3,500	19	1,775		845
%	57		29		14
All together ..	15,607	407	8,365	2,062	3,363
Percentage	52	1	28	7	12

The most important conclusion to which the above table points is the appearance, as early as the eleventh century, of a near-landless peasantry. It evidently progressed considerably between the eleventh and the thirteenth centuries in the eastern counties (Cambridgeshire, Huntingdonshire). Particular note should be taken of the fact that even in the eleventh century the percentage of cottars, bordars and slaves is considerably higher on small manors than on large.[2]

In any case we have here a fact of cardinal importance

[1] My pupil, M. A. Barg, has been working on the question of the composition of the bordars in Cambridgeshire at the time of Domesday Book. According to his calculations, the bordars included quite a number of peasants whose holdings were up to half a virgate in size.

[2] In saying this I am supported by the calculations made by A. Y. Gurevich.

for the whole problem of the history of the feudal mode of production in England. As early as the eleventh century, and apparently for a considerable time before that, there existed in England a very considerable stratum of near-landless peasants who were obliged to make a living by working on other men's land. This is a fact which has long been known, but from which all the possible conclusions have not been drawn. Even Granat, who occupied himself particularly with this question, considered it predominantly as evidence of an 'immemorial' division within the peasantry and of the development of a 'proletariat'. But the problem should be posed differently. The English manor was established and developed at a time when a numerous near-landless element in the peasantry existed and was, in fact, growing more numerous, providing a constant and ever-growing source of man-power. It is hard to believe that the presence of this numerous near-landless peasantry was without influence on the way in which the manor developed.

We have already touched on the problem of the origin of land shortage among the peasants. We saw that this shortage cannot be regarded merely as a result of the disintegration of the village under the influence of developing money and commodity relationships. No doubt this development considerably hastened the process of the stratification of the village community, but the near-landless as a separate stratum had in the main taken shape as early as the eleventh century in England, i.e. at a period when the feudal order, far from disintegrating, is commonly thought not yet to have been fully formed. In fact, small holdings, as we have seen, arose in the process of manorial development, when the manor, to ensure the proper functioning of labour services, required a certain number of peasant households equipped with a sufficient supply of land and stock. But the inherent difficulty of providing sufficient land led to an extremely slow increase in the number of households of normal type, and favoured the formation of a surplus population on the manor, provided with small holdings with an insignificant amount of stock. Another influence working in the same direction must have been the fragmentation of free land as the result of divisions and alienations.

The problem of the origin of small holdings in England

leads us back, however, to a period before the prevalence of the feudal mode of production, and is in part connected with pre-feudal relations. The disintegration of the primitive communal order could lead not only to the growth of large land-owning, but to the rise of small property in land, to the fragmentation of a holding. Men who had 'failed' and become nearly or completely landless, are found early. Peasants settled on new lands were not always given a suitable provision of stock. Small holdings could arise as the result of assarts. Finally, the near-landless peasantry may have derived in part from patriarchal slavery of a pre-feudal type. From Tacitus' time slaves had been settled on the land;[1] even though mainly employed in the demesne economy, they could have their own small holdings. Later these slaves might swell the ranks of the unfree cottars, while continuing to be exploited in the demesne economy as wage labour under coercion.[2]

INFLUENCE OF LABOUR SUPPLY ON MANORIAL ORGANIZATION

How was the formation of the English manor influenced by this numerous stratum of near-landless peasants, and therefore by the availability of working hands among the bordars and cottars, in addition to the slave farm-servants and those serfs who had land? It may be that this possibility in certain cases retarded the development of the labour service system. In a number of cases the exploitation of the cottars' labour may have been more advantageous for the feudal lord than the organiza-tion of a manor worked by labour services, or the labour of household slaves.

This apparently was the situation in Kent, where we can confirm both the early development of near-landlessness and the practically complete absence of labour rents and villeinage. In a number of other counties the same factors were at work, but more sporadically and not so clearly. However, the adop-tion of any particular system, or more accurately of a particular

---

[1] *Germania* (ed. J. G. C. Anderson), § 25.
[2] Kovalevsky supposes the *cotarii* to have been 'slaves settled on the landlords' land'. *Ekonomicheskii Rost Evropy do Bozniknoveniya Kapitalisticheskayu Khozyaistva* (3 vols., Moscow, 1898–1900), ii, 81. This is confirmed by the considerable percentage of slaves on the small manor observable in Domesday Book in places where in the thirteenth century we find a predominance of cottars among the tenants.

combination of three (or even more) systems, often depended not on considerations of profit or rational farming, but on the existing historical circumstances. For instance, the organization of a manor worked by labour services presupposed a plentiful allocation of land to the peasants performing them. On manors of this type, the villeins' land was commonly twice as large in area as the demesne. For a great feudal lord whose power extended over whole communities, it was easy to take as a starting-point in the organization of his manor the existing organization of the peasant village and make it liable for the performance of labour services. The labour service system required a complicated system of administration, supervision, the delegation of powers to manorial officials, and the use of the organization of the village-community for the supervision of work and view of frankpledge. It required particularly severe forms of compulsion. The same thing applies, to a large extent, to the organization of the labour of unfree farm servants, which was closely bound up with the manorial organization of servile labour rent.

The small landowner must have found himself in a very different position, for he had at his disposal only a limited amount of property, and he was greatly hampered in the disposal of common rights, since his rights in the commons were interwoven with the rights of other landowners. He was not able to offer his peasants full holdings, and naturally tried to carve out as large a demesne for himself as possible, by limiting the area of tenants' lands. He could not set up an expensive machinery of coercion and control. In fact the power over the population of a small landowner, especially at a time when he could not place much reliance on the support of the state, could hardly be compared with the power of a mighty lay or ecclesiastical lord. He could, of course, exercise coercion and control in person; but no doubt it was easier to deal with cowed and unorganized cottars than with the 'solid' peasant members of a village community.

The cottar's labour was profitable for the feudal lord for the further reason that it did not have to be paid for all the year round like the labour of a farm servant, but only during the time he was working. The cottars' holdings yielded the lord rent for poor and inconveniently situated portions of the demesne, and for small assarts. And the rent of a small holding was relatively high; a thirty-acre virgate in the hands of one peasant brought in much less rent than ten cottars' holdings of three acres each. If we take the average figures,[1] a villein virgate carries dues to the value of 10s. 8d., while ten cottars' holdings owe dues worth £1 0s. 10d. Furthermore, much more work will be got out of ten cottars than out of one virgater. The presence of a considerable number of near-landless peasants in the English medieval village, therefore, made it possible for the demesne economy to do without the labour services of villeins, or to employ the latter only on a limited scale. In places where, at the end of the thirteenth century, labour rent is not found, or is insignificant, and where money rent predominates, there is no need to assume that a previously existing labour rent had been commuted. It is just as likely that on a number of manors labour rent was not developed at all, or was not fully developed, but was always combined with the labour of cottars. This does not imply in any way the development of capitalist relations, and the cottar's labour can be described as non-voluntary labour. The growth, then, of the demesne and of a demesne economy was possible apart from, or at any rate not in direct connection with, the growth of labour services.

It was, perhaps, this fact which in England enabled a considerable stratum of free peasants to survive who knew no labour dues and passed straight from light contributions in kind, to money rent.[2] Perhaps for the same reason not all villeins everywhere passed through the stage of heavy labour services. And the same factor explains why commutation came easily, in cases where labour dues were commuted.

TRANSITIONAL CHARACTER OF COTTAR LABOUR

The exploitation of the cottars, although not capitalist exploitation, was much more easily transformed into such than that of the feudally dependent peasant, who had first to be deprived of his land before he could be turned into a proletarian. The cottar was already partly divorced from the means of production; he was obliged to 'sell' his labour power. For the

[1] From Table 13.   [2] I am not speaking of boon-works here.

time being this 'sale' took place under feudal conditions, but it could easily be transformed into capitalist exploitation; *stipendia* and *liberationes* could become wages, and the cottar could become a 'settled worker', a 'worker with a plot of land', and then a worker without a plot of land, because it was easy to drive him off the land. All that was needed to bring this about was, fundamentally, the breaking of the non-economic link between the cottar and the lord of the manor who was at the same time his 'employer'. And though semi-feudal links between the employer and the 'settled worker' survived for a long time in the rural world, the link broke early in the case of the *extranei* or *vagantes*, the wandering or transitory workers. A similar 'anti-feudal' tendency on a wider scale is, perhaps, evident in the labour legislation of the fourteenth century, when it limits the rights of the lord of the manor over the cottar or, more exactly, over every peasant with an inadequate allowance of land.[1] But Petrushevsky exaggerated the anti-feudal tendency in this directive, which is not repeated in later labour legislation. The paragraph in question introduced nothing essentially new, and had as its object the strengthening of the existing order and, first of all, the defence of the rights of the lord. The release of superfluous men to go and work elsewhere had been customary much earlier. It is also hard to agree with the statement that the conditions which this ordinance and the statutes created for the workmen meant in essence depriving them of all human rights.[2] The workmen had very few 'human rights' even before this legislation, and the whole of this incorrect interpretation is connected with Petrushevsky's exaggeration of the previous freedom enjoyed by both the villein and the small tenant.

This labour legislation, with its inveterate hostility to the working class, shows how labour services were being displaced by wage labour and by the increasing development of capitalist relations. As this took place the 'employer' tried to enslave the 'worker' by subjecting him to 'non-economic' as well as economic pressure, using the authority of the state, which by this time had become very powerful. As noted earlier, the

---

[1] *Domini preferantur aliis in nativis seu terram suam nativam tenentibus sic in servicio suo retinendis ita tamen quod huiusmodi domini sic retineant tot quot sibi fuerint necessarii et non plures.* Ordinance of June 18th, 1349, *Stats.* i, 307–08.

[2] D. Petrushevsky, *op. cit.* (4th ed.), 303.

demand for labour legislation and for increasingly stern measures came from the House of Commons, which sometimes set itself up in opposition on these matters to the Lords. It was precisely on the small manor, where the labour service system had not been developed, that the early development of capitalist relationships took place.

We must reckon as one of the causes of the early development of capitalism in English agriculture, the fact that at a very early stage, even before the full development of feudalism, there existed a considerable stratum of near-landless peasants, who worked on the fields of the lords—mainly the smaller lords—and of the prosperous peasants, receiving in return their food and some payment in money, and who were not subject to the routine of labour dues and of manorial custom.

The cottars of the feudal period have left few traces of their life, their feelings, their ideas. It is hard to pick them out in the wider context of peasant movements. But we can, I think, find traces of them, partly in the works of the serf-owner Gower, and partly in Langland's poem, where he speaks of the workers from the point of view of the benevolent employer. I am not thinking of the famous passage in which he mocks at the worker who does not want to eat old vegetables and a cold dinner, but rather of such expressions as: 'He can only be hired for high wages, otherwise he will rail and bewail the day when he became a workman.' But 'bewailing' is not all. 'He grieveth him against God and groucheth against reason and then curseth the king and all his council that they enforce such laws'.[1] This has an ominous sound. The workmen hate not only the lords and those who preach, from the Gospel and from Cato, patience in bearing the burden of poverty, but the king and his council, and the laws which oppress the workers.

In the Peasants' Revolt, also, it is possible to distinguish the ideology of the near-landless cottar from that of the servile peasant who is adequately provided with land. The former is turning into a hired labourer and is the foremost sufferer from lack of land and from the labour legislation; the latter into a commodity producer, and is hindered most of all by serfdom and by feudal rent. At the centre of the rising are two counties, with differing social structures, with different programmes, and with

[1] See W. Langland's *Vision of Piers Plowman* ed. Skeat, i, 222-3.

different tactics; serf Essex and 'free' Kent. It was Kent, where there were few villeins but many near-landless peasants, that put forward the most radical programme of social and political reform. It was here that the doctrine of John Ball was popular, who preached the destruction of the feudal lords, the establishment of universal equality, and community of property.[1]

[1] See my essay in *Srednie Veka*, i.

CHAPTER VII

THE STRUGGLE FOR RENT IN THIRTEENTH-CENTURY ENGLAND

FACTORS IN ENGLISH SOCIAL AND ECONOMIC DEVELOPMENT

Among the peculiarities of English history the one which is most striking in the field of social and economic relations is the classical and finished development which capitalism attained in that country earlier than in the other countries in Europe. England was not the first country to start out on the road of capitalist development; but she quickly overtook the countries which had taken that road before her. She was the first country to carry through a bourgeois revolution of European importance, emerged first as a colonial power, was the first country to carry through an agrarian and industrial revolution, and for a long time was almost a monopolist in the field of capitalist industry. England was the first country to provide material for the generalizations made by the classical political economists, and it was on the basis of English material that Marx and Engels discovered the law of motion of the capitalist mode of production.

How are we to explain this all-conquering growth of capitalism in a country which apparently occupied a very modest place in the economic life of medieval Europe? Some historians connect it with the shift of trade routes resulting from the great geographical discoveries. One need only glance at the map to see the great difference that the discoveries made. Medieval England, according to one historian, was on the edge of the European world; from the sixteenth century onwards she lay at the centre of the world trade.[1]

The importance of the changes brought about in the economic life of Europe and of England by the great discoveries should not be minimized, nor the role of the latter in the history of European and English capitalism. Marx did not do so, as is evident in the *Communist Manifesto*, and in Chapter 20 of the

[1] See Trevelyan's *History of England* (1943), xix.

third volume of *Capital*. But Marx also pointed out the danger, in such explanations of the capitalist development of Europe, of neglecting earlier developments. The capitalist mode of production in its initial stages developed only in those places where appropriate conditions had already been created during the Middle Ages.[1] The rapid extension of trade and the creation of a world market in the sixteenth and seventeenth centuries were based on a development of the capitalist mode of production, which had already begun. It seems to me that the economic history of England serves as an outstanding proof of Marx's argument. The rapid development of English capitalism had begun before the great geographical discoveries were made; it made great strides forward at the time when the discoveries had not yet exerted any noticeable influence on English economic conditions; the entrance of England into the world market and her lightning successes were the result of this earlier development, and in their turn conditioned the rapid capitalist transformation of the English social order.

The process of primitive accumulation began in England prior to the shift of trade routes to the ocean. The first Enclosure Acts, provoked by the eviction of peasants from their land and the conversion of arable land into pasture, belong to the eighties of the fifteenth century. They bear witness to the fact that this process had already advanced quite a long way. As early as the end of the fourteenth century England was changing from a country that exported wool into one that exported cloth—cloth produced by methods which, as time went on, more and more assumed the characteristics of 'manufacture'.[2] As early as 1436 the *Libelle of Englyshe Polycye* proclaimed that the future of England was in sea trade.

In England deep-seated changes had long been ripening, but they had been ripening gradually and unnoticeably. The advance of English industry had been overshadowed by the industrial growth of Italy and Flanders. The stuffs of Flanders and of Florence gained fame at the fairs of Europe and in the Near East, but a considerable part of these cloths was made of

---

[1] *Capital*, iii, cap. 20, p. 264 (1909 ed., pp. 391–2).

[2] [For 'manufacture' as a stage in the history of industrial organization, cf. Marx, *Capital*, vol. i, chap. xii.]

English wool, or even woven in England and merely finished in the workshops of Flanders and Florence. But even less observed than England's early industrial development are the changes which were taking place in agrarian relations.

Trevelyan is unjust when he depicts medieval England as an island on the edge of the European world. Actually her south-eastern corner, with London and Kent and its many harbours, extended into its very heart; London is closer to the coast of France than to Bristol, closer to Flanders than to Yorkshire, closer to Paris than to Durham. The Channel does not divide England from the continent so much as connect her with it. The sea route was in many respects more convenient than those by land, and in any case it was incomparably easier than the Alpine passes which the main European trade routes had to cross. The south-east of England lay at a great cross-roads where the trade routes from Scandinavia, the Baltic, the North Sea, the Atlantic coast and the Mediterranean all met, as well as the great river-ways of the Rhine, the Meuse, the Scheldt, and the Seine. Lastly, England was politically united with the continent: first as part of the Norman realm of the Conqueror and his successors, and then as part of the 'empire' of the Plantagenets. This empire shrank considerably in the thirteenth century, but questions of continental politics, of the defence and acquisition of territory and spheres of influence, continued to play a very great part. From the twelfth century onwards England had commercial and political interests in the Mediterranean. Nor should we forget that England was one of the leading countries of Europe in cultural life, that out of her came a number of scholars and thinkers of the greatest stature. It was here that in the doctrine of Wycliffe the first clear formulation was given to those demands for Church reform which were to echo through Europe for centuries; it was here, a hundred and fifty years before the Peasants' War in Germany, that the clear-cut demands of a peasant revolution were first put forward. We shall not understand the history of England, in particular its economic history, if we consider it in isolation from the history of Europe.

Medieval England might appear to be an economically backward country because the most important upheavals took place not so much in full view, in the towns, as in the less obvious sphere of agriculture and agrarian relations. They went all the deeper for this, since they were making changes in the very foundation of the feudal mode of production. The separation of town from countryside and the development of a market for agricultural products, as we have seen, took an unusual course in England. The country was only slowly separated from the town, and the division remained incomplete for a long time. The towns long retained a semi-agrarian character; the country clung stubbornly to its home industries. English trade and industry, particularly the trade in wool and the cloth industry, to a large extent by-passed the towns. In both home and foreign trade a most important part was played by the fairs. Among these, the three-day fair at Stourbridge, near Cambridge, was of European importance. To it with their wares came the Lombard bankers, merchants from Venice and Genoa, from the Hanseatic towns, from Spain and from France. Industry, too, was not fitted into an urban framework. Spinning and weaving were usually done by craftsmen in the villages, the cloth being finished in the towns. Even when the cloth industry began to move into the towns, the countryside continued to produce unfinished cloths which found a good market both at home and later abroad, as semi-finished goods. The merchant, in contact with a wide market, appears as the organizer of this village industry. Thus the English towns, apart from London which had long attained the standing of a national and international market, did not play the important part they played on the continent. Urban industry in England lagged behind that of Flanders, Italy, northern France and the Rhineland. The political history of the English towns is dim compared with that of the towns of the continent, not only because in England a strong central power was established early.

Nevertheless, by the middle of the thirteenth century the process of separation of town from country had made considerable progress. The number of towns, which at the time of Domesday amounted to 80, had grown greatly by the thirteenth century. If in 1086 the town population at a conservative estimate was 5 per cent of the total population, and about 12 per cent by 1377, in the middle of the thirteenth century the percentage was to all appearances nearer to the second figure than to the first. London in 1377 could boast of up to 40,000 inhabitants, and the average for the other towns was not less than 5,000. These figures should probably be reduced somewhat for the mid-thirteenth century, but even so they give a picture of a market for agricultural produce which was steady if not very large, and which was more or less evenly spread over the whole country, though with some concentration in the south-east. The distances between towns, in most parts of England at any rate, were not great. Bücher's description of medieval Germany is fully applicable to England: almost anywhere in the country a peasant, even from an outlying village, could reach a town market within the day and return home by evening. England was thickly covered with small market towns; and the town markets were closely connected with the countryside by the cornmongers[1] and woolmongers, who might have come from the ranks of the peasantry.

THE GROWTH OF THE MARKET

Gras distinguishes three periods. First there is the period up to 1100 which he considers as 'pre-market'; that is the surplus corn then remained unsold; secondly, the period between 1100 and 1250, the time of the development of manorial trade, during which an active part was played by the estates of the lords which had adapted themselves to the market; finally, the period after 1250, the epoch of the development of the local market served mainly by the peasant—a development connected with the disintegration of the manorial system.[2] But it is doubtful how far this periodization is correct. In my view, from the earliest stages, both peasant and seigniorial economies served the towns, but while the peasants served mainly the nearest market, the lords, taking advantage of their claims on the transport facilities of the servile peasantry, had a wider range. We know little of peasants trading with the towns, but we are well acquainted with the bishop of Winchester's trade with London, and with the far-flung net cast over south-eastern England by the system of carrying-services organized by Ramsey Abbey.[3]

---

[1] Gras, *The Evolution of the English Corn Market*, 19.   [2] *Op. cit.*, 30.
[3] On the Ramsey estate we find *averagia* to Huntingdon, St. Ives, Cambridge, Ipswich, Bury St. Edmunds, Colchester, St. Albans, London and Canterbury. *C. Ram.* i, 462, 476, 477; iii, 243, 282, 302. Cf. *Rent. et Cust. Glaston.* 165; *debet cariare lanam domini per viginti leucas et habebit cibum suum de mercatoribus.*

The economic activity of the English countryside in the twelfth and thirteenth centuries was not confined to the local market. The villages were linked with more distant markets and in this long-distance trade the lords played the leading part. In south-eastern England, the part best known to us, the trade took the form of supply to the great centres of consumption, first of all London; to those regions which did not produce corn in sufficient quantity (mainly the northern stock-breeding areas); and to the continental markets.

As early as the second half of the eleventh century, English wool occupied a prominent position in continental markets, and its importance grew during the succeeding two centuries.[1] The export of corn, though occurring sporadically in the twelfth century, had not at that time begun to exert any noticeable influence on the agrarian economy. Even so, the corn trade was not confined to local markets, though we may agree with Gras that the local market predominated. In the south and west of England, and especially the east, trade with distant English, and to some extent with foreign, markets influenced the course of economic development. This is clear from a study of the well-known Pipe Rolls of the See of Winchester for the years 1208–1209. On 17 manors belonging to the see more than half the harvest of wheat was sold that year, and on some manors the percentage sold was as high as 86 (Woodhay), 88 (E. Meon) and 92 per cent (Crawley).[2] From the total production of 32 manors (3,679 quarters) 1,767½ quarters were sold, or 48 per cent. At the same time 44 per cent went on the re-sowing of the fields, so that only 8 per cent was consumed within the episcopal economy. Wheat was predominantly a market crop. But a large percentage of other kinds of grain was put on the market as well (barley 28, mancorn 39, oats 17, peas, beans and lentils 38 per cent). The wool was almost all sold. However, from the estate as a whole, the revenue in money from the sale of produce was less than the amount of money rent paid by the peasants. If we assume further that not all the money realized by the peasants from the sale of their produce was swallowed up by feudal rent,

---

[1] E. E. Power, *The Medieval English Wool Trade* (1941), 41 sq.

[2] Tokarev, 'The trade of the English Manor in the Thirteenth and the first half of the Fourteenth Century', in *Uchenie Zapiski Instituta Istorii R.A.N.I.O.N.* vii, 53.

we may conclude that on the whole the peasants of the episcopal manors put more produce on the market than came from the demesnes. By the end of the thirteenth century (1299–1300) the percentage of the total production which was sold rose even higher (70 for wheat, 39.5 for barley, 34 for oats, 67 for rye and 47 for mancorn). Furthermore, the yield of the main market crop, wheat, increased greatly, a result which was probably achieved by an improvement of technique in spite of a slight decrease in the area sown. On the Earl of Norfolk's manor of Forncett the major portion of the corn produced was sold, and the wheat was practically all sold except the amount strictly necessary for sowing.[1] It is, of course, a question how far the figures of 'sales' (*venditiones*) in ministers' accounts really denote exploitation of the demesne economy for the market. Just as the term *venditio operum* may denote the replacement of labour dues by money payments, so the 'sale' of produce received from the peasants as multure or churchscot may often simply imply the commutation of these charges. The sale of corn does not always mean that it went outside the bounds of the manor. At Wistow corn is 'sold' to the workmen on the lord's farm (evidently a corresponding reduction is made in their money wages), and 'sales' to the cellarer are spoken of.[2] The accounts of the same manor, Wistow, refer to 'sales' to persons belonging to the manor.[3] At Holway and Poundisford, manors of the bishop of Winchester, a considerable part of the grain was sold to the villeins of those manors.[4] A 'sale' might often represent merely an accountant's device, the transference of a particular sum from one account to another. Sometimes in ministers' accounts produce supplied to the lord is entered as 'sold'.[5]

Nevertheless, the considerable connections between the demesne economy of the large manors in the south and east of England and the market in corn are beyond doubt. As early as the Articles of the Barons of 1215 we find the demand for a reform of measures, including those of corn. Under the provisions of Clause 35 of Magna Carta there was to be introduced throughout the whole kingdom *una mensura bladi*,

---

[1] F. Davenport, *Norfolk Manor*, 30–31.   [2] Neilson, *Ramsey Manors*, Appendix.
[3] Cf. Tokarev, *op. cit.*, 70–71.   [4] Cf. Levett, *O.S.S.L.H.*, v, 29.
[5] Davenport, *Norfolk Manor*, 43.

scilicet quarterium Londoniense. And it is in connection with seigniorial agriculture that we should note the important corn exports from East Anglia. The figures are very small. But we have every reason to believe that they are much lower than the actual exports, since many cargoes were not registered, or were not registered in full, in the customs and port books. It is quite clear that the sea trade passed exclusively through King's Lynn, Sandwich, Hull and London, that is from the east coast of England. From King's Lynn, the chief export port,[1] corn was shipped to Norway, Holland and Zeeland, Flanders, and Gascony.[2] For the home trade in corn in England the most important route ran coastwise from Lynn to Newcastle.

Nevertheless, for grain production the local market was undoubtedly predominant. On the local market the seigniorial and the peasant economy met, but the latter on the whole was the more important. This is vouched for first and foremost by the predominance of money rent. Yet the production of corn as a commodity within the seigniorial economy, a production linked with distant markets, played a considerable part in different regions especially in the east. And although the increase of labour services was a partial consequence of this production for the market, it also had the result that money rent developed as it did.

INCREASED PRESSURE ON THE PEASANTRY AS A CONSEQUENCE OF INCREASED COMMODITY PRODUCTION

We know very little of the expenditure of the large feudal landowners, in particular of their money expenditure. In manorial accounts we find only small money payments, the major monetary expenditure being on wages. Purchases consist mainly of articles necessary for the reproduction of the manorial economy. The greater part of the money income goes to the lord. How the lord spent it we do not know very well, but the general rise in living standards and in the cultural level of the ruling classes in the thirteenth century impels us

---

[1] On the corn trade through Lynn and its importance for Cambridgeshire, Huntingdonshire and Lincolnshire, see *C. Ram.*, iii, 141–57.

[2] Gras, *op. cit.*, 172; Schanz, *Englische Handelspolitik gegen Ende des Mittelalters*, i, 247.

to assume heavy non-productive expenditure. The import of luxury articles into England increases greatly in the twelfth and thirteenth centuries, and local industry is developing also. All had to be paid for by the peasant, in the form of money or labour rent. We may assume that at this time the pressure on the peasantry, with the object of increasing the profitability of the manorial economy, must have been increasing, and that on this ground the class struggle in the countryside must have been intensified. Much attention has been given to the 'feudal reaction' which set in after the Black Death and was one of the causes leading to the rising of 1381.[1] Savine was certainly right to point out that this development was not new and characteristic only of that period, but was also in evidence earlier on.[2] It is not proposed to discuss the question of the 'feudal reaction' in the second half of the fourteenth century, but it must be noted that there is evidence for an intensification of feudal oppression in a number of thirteenth-century sources; and there are grounds for dating the beginning of this process back to the middle of the preceding century at least, if not earlier.

Vinogradoff, and the majority of succeeding historians, view the twelfth and thirteenth centuries as the epoch in which the manor finally took shape as an estate worked by serf labour, and in which, therefore, there was a general worsening in the position of the villeins, who up to that time had preserved many relics of their former freedom. But Vinogradoff does not explain the causes of this worsening and does not connect it with the development of money-commodity relations. For in his view the latter led to commutation and to the distintegration of the manorial economy.

On the other hand, more recent investigators, noting the growth of labour rent in the thirteenth century, have linked it with the rapid growth of seigniorial trade.[3] The prosperous state of seigniorial trade and seigniorial revenues must have had dire effects upon the peasants, especially in the eastern

---

[1] The most thorough presentation of the facts indicating such a reaction in the second half of the fourteenth century is that of Petrushevsky, *Wat Tyler's Rising* (4th ed.), 316, 351.

[2] In his review of the first edition of Petrushevsky's book, *E.H.R.*, xvii (1902).

[3] To this they often apply the term 'boom', which is taken from another economic milieu and in any case certainly exaggerates; cf. Postan, 'The Chronology of Labour services', *T.R.H.S*, 4th series, xx (1937); N. Neilson, *Camb. Econ. Hist.*, i, vii, § 7.

regions of England, where the prosperity was most marked. Undoubtedly it must have led to an intensification and exacerbation of the class struggle.

Already the Norman Conquest had produced a general worsening in the situation of the peasantry and an intensification of their exploitation. This was not only because it had a depressing effect on the varied social relationships of the English countryside, reducing them to one uniform feudal level, but also because it strengthened the main instrument of class oppression, the feudal state. We cannot accept the traditional view of English political history according to which the royal power joined forces with the people against the feudal lords. When they speak of 'the people' the historians who maintain this view have in mind a considerable and influential body composed of the lower and middle ranks of the knights and of the prosperous freeholders. In their conception of 'the people' there is no place for the basic mass of working people—the unfree peasantry. It was this class which had to bear the burden of the state created by the Norman conquerors, of the reforms of Henry II, of the growth of the Common Law, of the political struggle of the thirteenth century, and of the establishment of parliament. Each new step in the strengthening of 'the rule of the state and of law' meant a further stage in the worsening of the position of the villeins.

THE ROLE OF THE STATE AND THE COMMON LAW IN THE DEPRESSION OF THE VILLEIN

Some historians have put forward the view that the English feudal lords, being deprived of political power through the early development of a centralized state, turned all their energies to economic activity, and embarked upon the intensive development of their manorial resources.[1] Our conception of the connection between the development of the state and that of manorial economy in England is different. The desire of the feudal lords to extract the greatest possible revenues from

[1] E.g. Brodnitz, *Engl. Wirtschaftsgeschichte*, 57. A satirist of the thirteenth century says of the lords of south-west Germany that they think of how to get a bigger milk-yield from their cow, worry about the harvest, do not drink wine themselves but sell it at a profit; they concern themselves with eggs, cheese, and the price of wheat, and occupy themselves more with husbandry and profits than with fighting (Dopsch, *Naturalwirtschaft und Geldwirtschaft*, 179).

their manors obliged them to consolidate their ranks and to strengthen the state as an instrument of class rule. The towns and the upper section of the free peasantry supported this order of things. But the greater part of the peasantry handed increased rents over to their lords, rendered extra days of labour services, and so paid the costs of government for those who oppressed them. The period of internal strife after the death of Henry I showed the ruling class as a whole that solidarity and organization were in its own interests. Internal struggles had the effect of disorganizing manorial economy; and for this reason, the Treaty of Wallingford in 1153 promised the restoration of devastated manors. The feudal lords pinned their hopes on the king: *rex colonos praedibus assignabit, aedificia combusta renovabit, replebit pascus armentis, decorabit ovibus montana.*[1]

Henry II carried out these promises. His reign marks a new step on the road towards the consolidation and organization of the feudal state and the oppression of the servile peasantry. The judicial reforms of Henry II were undoubtedly a most important step towards the strengthening of royal power; they brought into general use new procedures which hitherto had been a royal prerogative; they created more reliable guarantees of redress, where rights had been infringed, than had existed in the county and hundred or in the feudal courts. But the blessings of the legal reforms were not shed upon the whole population; the bulk of the people were prohibited from enjoying them. The rule of *exceptio villenagii* made the royal courts useless for the villeins. Heavy lawyers' fees and payments for royal writs made the new courts open only to the more well-to-do. The class character of the reform is quite clear. The assize of novel disseisin represented an enormous step forward in the development of land law, but most of the population, the villeins and the poor, were set outside that law. *Exceptio villenagii* not only put the majority of the working population outside the protection of the king's courts; it created pretexts for the reduction to serfdom of sections of the working population which hitherto had still been accounted free. The sharp line which Henry II's reforms drew between free men and serfs led to a new levelling down of the peasantry, to the

---

[1] W. Stubbs, *Constitutional History of England*, 6th Edn., i, 361, n. 2, quoting Ralph de Diceto, i, 296-7.

enserfment of considerable sections of the people whose status was still undefined.[1]

The distinction between free and serf was extremely vague, even to the judges, who made little haste to define it, since its very vagueness was advantageous to the ruling class. Undoubtedly services which were undefined, and at the lord's will, were one of the basic marks of the villein. But it was not always clear which particular services should be accounted as being at the lord's will. Other distinguishing marks were equally unreliable. The judges, in the interests of the manorial economy, were inclined to consider the chief mark of villeinage to be labour rent, a form of rent which required for its exaction that the peasant should have as few civil rights as possible. In other words, the courts deprived of protection that part of the peasantry which was to be subjected to the most severe exploitation. For the tendency which becomes apparent at this time is to increase labour dues on the large manors, both lay and ecclesiastical. In the manor court, even in the hundred and county courts, the serf often stood on a par with the freemen. In the king's court there is no place for him; civil suits by villeins against third persons were rare exceptions and could only occur, for the most part, amongst the wealthy peasants. The 'artificial crystallization of the law'[2] which was the result of the activity of the royal courts undoubtedly led to a worsening in the position of the broad masses of the working people, to a high wall being raised between them and the minority endowed with full civil rights.

The legal theory of the English judges of the twelfth and thirteenth centuries is sharply hostile to the villeins. Glanville denies their right to hold property, in consequence of which a villein could not buy his freedom with his own money.[3] The *Dialogus de Scaccario* treats the villeins as the property of their master, and speaks of them with the utmost contempt.[4] Bracton equates the villein to the Roman slave. This direct

[1] In Bracton's *Note Book* we find cases in which by way of defence against the assize of novel disseisin the defendant tries to represent the plaintiff as his own villein; e.g. No. 1812.'

[2] Vinogradoff, *Villainage*, 130.

[3] *Posset enim a domino suo secundum ius et consuetudinem regni ad villenagium revocari, quia omnia catalla cuiuslibet nativi ita intelliguntur esse in potestate domini sui.* Glanville, *De Legibus Angliae*, v, 5.

[4] Vinogradoff, *Villainage*, 135.

application of the categories of Roman law to the complicated reality of feudalism has struck historians as evidence of the divorce of legal theory from life. But why should the jurists of the twelfth and thirteenth centuries have put forward such a theory? They were much closer to life than is commonly assumed. In equating the villein to the Roman slave, in declaring him and his belongings to be the property of his lord, in denying him the right to proceed in law against his lord, the king's judges were expressing quite definite class interests. The age of Glanville, and still more the age of Bracton, was a time of intensified pressure on the servile peasantry by the great landowning interests, with the object of increasing feudal rent. For a lord who was developing his manorial economy it was necessary that the peasantry should have no rights, just as the denial of the villeins' rights over the land was necessary for the lord who was seizing the common lands for his own exclusive use or in order to lease them out for money rent. The Statute of Merton gave the lords extensive rights in the enclosure of common lands, only protecting the rights of freeholders. Nothing is said about villeins; here, too, *exceptio villenagii* holds good.

INSUFFICIENT PROTECTION BY MANORIAL CUSTOM

We cannot treat the denial of villein's rights as an abstract legal theory, since the king's courts applied it in practice. The villein could find protection for his rights only in the manor courts. But there the lord was not only an interested party; he was the judge as well. The effectiveness of the manor court and of manorial custom as organs for the defence of the villeins' rights has been highly exaggerated. The decisions of the manor court and the precedents of local custom might be binding on the peasants, but only bound the lord within narrow limits. Vinogradoff supposed that in practice customary law limited the rights of the lord, and that cases of the lord infringing such rights of the peasants as were sanctioned by custom were rare exceptions. But he concedes that these limitations had no legal force, and that their only sanctions were, on the one hand, the fear of causing the peasants to revolt or to take refuge in flight, and, on the other hand, the force of the prevalent moral code. Petrushevsky, on the other hand, after investigating the administration of justice in the manor courts of the Duchy of Lancaster, came to the conclusion that manorial custom expressed real legal rulings, and that it was not the will of the lord but the process of law which regulated relations within the manor. In his view manorial custom gave the villein a protection of his property rights in no way inferior to that enjoyed by the free man in the king's courts. This protection was effective against all under the jurisdiction of the court, and indirectly against the lord himself. Hence Petrushevsky concludes that official legal theory 'construed entirely incorrectly the whole order of life on the manor, and in its urge to reduce everything to the simplest possible categories completely ignored all that was most characteristic of that order.'[1] Maitland held a different view. In his opinion the distinguishing mark of villein holding was vagueness of dues. In this respect manorial custom gave the villein no firm guarantees, but rather created wide opportunities for arbitrary action. Ethical considerations, in Maitland's opinion, could not have played the part attributed to them by Vinogradoff; the religious beliefs of the period put no obstacles in the way of exploitation of the villeins.[2]

Even more unequivocal is the opinion expressed by Coulton, who notes the weakness of the protection that custom offered the villein. The dues of the villein were rarely fixed by record, and a considerable proportion of the levies imposed by the lords (fines, monopoly charges, duties, and other *consuetudines non taxatae*) could not be precisely defined. Manorial custom was extremely elastic and left room enough for arbitrary action by the lord. Coulton stresses the miserable and unprotected position of the medieval peasantry.[3] Maitland's conception of the nature of manorial justice—that it represented one of the most important forms of revenue of the lord—was later developed by Zvavich.[4] The landowner, he argues, was the monopolist vendor of the commodity called manorial justice. After analysing the court rolls of a number of manor courts,

---

[1] Petrushevsky, *op. cit.*, 3rd edition, 131.
[2] Pollock and Maitland, i, 371, 376, 379.
[3] Coulton, *The Mediaeval Village* (1925).
[4] I. S. Zvavich, 'The class nature of manorial justice', *Uch. Zap. Inst. Ist. R.A.N.I.O.N.* iii (1929).

his conclusion is that the protection afforded by customary law to the serf population in the English village of the thirteenth and fourteenth centuries was far from complete, and that it allowed wide openings for arbitrary action by the landowner. Zvavich supposes that by this time there had already begun that process of the disintegration of the feudal estate which sharpened the struggle between lord and peasantry and destroyed the 'constitutional order' which had been built up on the basis of customary law. The practice of the manorial courts at the end of the thirteenth and the beginning of the fourteenth centuries was beginning to follow the road fore-shadowed by earlier legal theorists, and the resistance of the villeins was not supported by the state or by the law. Half a century later this resistance took the form of revolts and the destruction of manorial documents. In the sixteenth century, also, according to Savine, manorial custom generally worked out to the disadvantage of the tenants, since it arose 'at a time of the predominance of a fighting and ruling minority which was long able to impose its will on the badly organized working majority'. The legal grounds for the eviction of copyholders were established by social relations in the twelfth and thirteenth centuries.[1]

Petrushevsky's conception of 'economic harmony' between the lord and the peasant community is unacceptable. The class struggle grew sharper as the commodity nature of agriculture developed, but it is also clear that the class struggle is inseparable from feudal production as such. It is quite obvious, as Marx observed, that the slow growth of productive forces in feudal society caused tradition and custom to predominate. But this custom was built up on the whole in a spirit unfavourable to the exploited 'working majority', and protected first and foremost the interests of the 'ruling minority'. In view, however, of the continued worsening of the position of the labouring classes, custom, in so far as it recorded an earlier and less severe degree of exploitation might, to a certain extent, serve as a defence against attempts to intensify exploitation. A certain degree of protection for the rights of the peasant was thus inevitable under the rule of feudal production. The peasant must live on his holding and have a necessary

[1] A. N. Savine, *The English Village in the time of the Tudors* (Russian), 207 sqq.

minimum of stock; he must be assured the conditions of economic reproduction, if the most was to be got out of him. Manorial custom, therefore, established a regulated and ordered form of exploitation, taking traditional and little-changing production-relations as its starting-point. 'It is evident that tradition must play a very powerful role in the primitive and undeveloped circumstances, upon which this relation in social production and the corresponding mode of production are based. It is furthermore clear that here as everywhere else it is in the interest of the ruling section of society to sanction the existing order as a law and to perpetuate its habitually and traditionally fixed limits as legal ones. Aside from all other matters, this comes about of itself in proportion as the continuous reproduction of the foundation of the existing order and of the relations corresponding to it gradually assume a regulated and orderly form. And such regulation and order are themselves indispensable elements of any mode of production, provided that it is to assume social firmness and an independence from mere accident and arbitrariness.'[1]

It is obvious that the social relations in a natural economy established certain limitations on the exploitation of the peasants. But neither the rule of tradition and custom nor the regulation of the reproduction process of the feudal economy created insuperable barriers to the increase of exploitation. Manorial custom regulated the exploitation of the villeins, preserved order and discipline within the serf community, and assured the uninterrupted flow of feudal rent. But it did very little to hamper the *voluntas domini*, under whose regulating control the custom itself had taken shape. First of all, as has often been observed, it left very wide margins for the increase of feudal rent. The exact amounts of a number of very important dues remained assessable at the lord's will. Such burdensome obligations as carrying services were very often at the lord's will in thirteenth-century England, just as they had been in the Frankish state of the ninth century. But even the other labour rents were not always fixed.

Money rents were even less fixed. While *redditus assisae* was a more or less unchanging quantity, *auxilium* was more often

[1] *Capital*, iii, 629 (1909 ed. 921).

at the lord's will; so also were heriot and entry-fines. But even
the fixed dues which were recorded in extents, on the evidence
given by the oldest and most experienced peasants, not
infrequently increased in the course of time, as we see, for
instance, from a comparison of the different amounts of week-
work given in the Ramsay cartulary between the twelfth and
the thirteenth centuries.[1] It is very probable that on this issue
a struggle was carried on within the manor court, that the
peasants tried to appeal to the custom of the manor. But—and
this is the essential point—manorial custom was not binding
on the lord, or was binding only so far as suited him. The
manor court has no legal sanctions at its disposal by which to
compel the lord to submit to its decisions. Maitland's view that
religious and ethical considerations did not prevent a lord
from raising feudal rent was correct. All that remained in the
last resort was flight and direct opposition. Cases of these were
not rare, so far as can be judged, but subsequently the state
abandoned its policy of non-intervention between villeins and
lords, and gave all possible help to the latter.[2]

LEGAL DOCTRINE IN THE SERVICE OF THE LANDOWNERS

Were the legal doctrines of the twelfth and thirteenth
centuries, then, merely a development of legal principles in
contradiction to reality?[3] It would be more correct to describe
these doctrines as an attempt to change reality to accord with
class interests. The theoretical counterpart of the general
offensive against the peasantry was the proclamation by the
lawyers of the slavery of the villein and the vesting of rightful
ownership of his goods in the lord. And this did not remain
theory only. It was applied in the practice of the courts, which
kept the villein strictly separate from the freeman. It is true
that the villein enjoyed a certain protection in law,—but in
the last years of the Roman Empire so did the slave. The
attempt to make slaves of the villeins was serious; it was carried
through in reliance on the backing of the power of the state,
on the king's courts, and on the doctrines of those learned in
Roman law. Glanville and Bracton are too close to life, too

---

[1] N. Neilson, *Ramsey Abbey Manors*, 39 sqq.
[2] Many examples occur in *Placitorum Abbreviatio*, (Record Commission) (1811),
see below, pp. 339–52.   [3] Vinogradoff, *Collected Papers*, i, 125.

close to legal practice, for us to accuse them of being divorced from reality. The legal theory of villeinage was the outcome of a new stage in the development of feudal exploitation, connected with the development of the organization of the feudal state. Roman law here plays the part it played everywhere in medieval Europe. 'Roman law, the first world law of a commodity-producing society, with its insurpassably acute elaboration of all the essential legal relations of simple commodity-owners (of buyers and sellers, debtors and creditors, contracts, and obligations)',[1] not only gave Europe a new legal system, corresponding to the development of commodity production, but also provided political doctrines which corresponded to the new stage in the development of the state, and a new ideological weapon for intensifying the exploitation of the labouring classes.

The following are characteristic pronouncements of the king's courts: 'villein service is when a man does not know in the evening what he may be ordered to do in the morning'; 'everything a villein has belongs to his lord'; 'to hold in villeinage is nothing else but to say that one holds at the will of the lord'.[2] Manorial custom carried no weight in the eyes of the king's court, until the increasing numbers of landless peasants caused the government in the fifteenth and sixteenth centuries to have fears for the very basis of feudal production, fears which were to no small extent crystallized by the growing discontent and disturbances among the peasantry. Then the courts—first the courts of Equity, then the courts of Common Law—took upon themselves the protection of manorial custom. But this custom did so little to protect the interests of the peasants, and the courts were so permeated with class bias, that their activity brought no relief to the peasantry.

Manorial custom did not, and could not, become the shield of the peasants. The manor court was to a far greater extent an apparatus for the maintenance of servile discipline among the peasants and for the extraction of additional rent, than an organ for protecting their personal and property rights. With the development of the king's justice it became more and more a purely villein court.[3] Well-to-do freeholders were able

---

[1] F. Engels, *Ludwig Feuerbach*, in Karl Marx, *Selected Works*, i, 463.
[2] Vinogradoff, *Collected Papers*, i, 126.
[3] Cf. Pollock and Maitland, i, 586.

to appeal to the protection of the king's courts; some lords also introduced special courts for their freeholders. The Statute of Marlborough in 1267 established the rule that no freeholder was bound to attend his lord's court unless attendance was a specific condition of his holding, and not then if it had been waived since before 1230.[1] Freeholders avoided attendance, which brought them no benefits, and considered that in general it should not be demanded of free men.[2]

While abandoning the villeins to the lord's will, the state nevertheless did not cease to exploit them for its own ends. In the allocation of taxes the property of villeins was assessed and taxed by the state individually, in spite of the fact that legal theory made that property actually the property of the lord. A considerable part of the taxation was collected from the villeins by royal officials, not those of the lord. It was for this reason that the state gave a certain protection to the villein, forbidding the lord to kill or maim him or ruin him by depriving him of the essential means of production (*waynagium*).

In spite of the levelling action of the Norman Conquest and of a hundred years' work by the king's courts, by the end of the thirteenth century the line between villein and freeman was still not clear. Between the two came a stratum of freemen holding villein land, who might easily end up as villeins,[3] and all sorts of 'sokemen'. Villeinage continued to increase; no element of prescription was needed for villein tenure such as was later required for copyhold. The lord could create new villein holdings by splitting off pieces of the demesne, or by letting out on villein conditions holdings which had previously been free. Villeinage increased even on the ancient demesne of the crown, the ranks of the villeins being swelled by arrivals from outside (*adventitii*). On many manors there were groups of peasants of whom it is hard to say whether they were free or villein, and who continued to consider themselves free men

---

[1] Maitland, 'Select Pleas in Manorial and other Seigneurial Courts', *S.S.* ii, xlviii-l.

[2] Vinogradoff, *Villainage*, 385–6.

[3] The theory that a contract with the lord assured the freedom of the other contracting party is refuted by the practice of the abbey of St. Albans, where newcomers who took villein land were reduced to bondage by a document over the tenant's seal in which they promised to submit to the abbot's will and to be in respect of their persons and property the same as the other villeins. Cf. Levett, *Studies in Manorial History*, 192, and 'The Courts and Court Rolls of St. Albans Abbey', *T.R.H.S.*, 4th series, vii, 69, 75.

Y

until the manorial administration proved the contrary. On the manors of the abbey of St. Albans the position of the villeins in the thirteenth century had many of the features of freedom, and the status of many was not always clear. In the fourteenth century they demanded the restoration of the status they had held under Henry III. They considered that their status was being depressed, and the documents show that they were right.[1]

CLASHES BETWEEN PEASANTS AND LORDS IN THE THIRTEENTH CENTURY

In the thirteenth century many free peasants were turned into villeins. On this issue there were continuous clashes between lords and peasants; the latter considered themselves free; the lord insisted on their villeinage. Such cases frequently reached the courts. Where the peasants owed labour services, they found it hard to prove their free status and to defend successfully their right to the protection of the court. Vinogradoff notes that in the thirteenth century the courts were in the main against allowing those holdings to be free which were burdened with labour rents.[2] And even comparatively insignificant labour rents were enough to get a holding accounted a villein holding. In Bracton's Note Book[3] a case is cited in which a tenant admits that he is bound, besides paying money rent, to do three days' ploughing and three days' harvesting. The court found this to be a villein holding, *quia illa sunt servilia et ad villenagium spectantia et non ad liberum tenementum.* Yet dues of this kind were attached not only to many sokemen's holdings, but to many free holdings as well. The line adopted by the courts may be put this way: a lord has the right to raise without limits the rent of those peasants who perform works. The process of turning sokemen into villeins—that is, the process by which fixed dues were replaced by arbitrary ones—can be observed at work in the Hundred Rolls, at Swaffham Prior, a manor belonging to Ely, where the prior converts the fixed rate of heriot and merchet owed by the free sokemen of this manor into an arbitrary imposition.[4] Custom offers no obstacle to the change-over.

The attempt to make sokemen, peasants with rents fixed by

[1] Levett, *T.R.H.S.*, 4th series, vii, p. 69 n.   [2] *Collected Papers*, i, 122.
[3] No. 1819.   [4] *R.H.*, ii, 485.

custom and protected by law, into villeins, with undefined rents dependent on the lord's will, is not infrequently encountered. In 1268, for example, James Painton is brought before a court by the tenants of the manor of Grendon in Northamptonshire; they and their forebears held their lands on the manor for defined rents (*certas consuetudines*), and James had driven them off their holdings (*de terris suis eiecit*). They consider themselves *liberi sochemanni* holding for a definite rent (*certum servicium*). This rent comprised (for the virgate) 44*d*., and two ploughings—one of which, in autumn, is with food provided by the lord, while the other is without—and one working day of harvesting and haycutting from two virgates. They were able to leave their wives enough to live on (*dotare*), and to alienate their lands as they wished. But James had compelled them to render new dues, and deprived them of their right to dispose freely of their holdings. James declared that they held the land *per villenagium*. No steps, apparently, were taken to check this declaration, and the plea was left undetermined. The fact that the plaintiffs rendered some small labour dues may have served as a pretext for their being declared villeins. However, sometimes peasants succeeded in fighting off attempts upon their freedom by the lords. Thus in 1261 two tenants from Mears Ashby (Northants) on their own behalf and on that of other tenants of the same vill, fought a lawsuit with Sybill Mares. According to the jurors' findings Sybill's late husband had for seven years required no dues of the tenants beyond the normal (*debita et consueta*), but then he had compelled them to pay an arbitrary tallage, and levied this for two years *ad plus et ad minus*. The tenants filed a suit against him at Westminster and insisted that the tallage should be reduced to 21*d*. The same lord fined tenants arbitrarily, by-passing the manor court (*non per pares suos*). Yet the tenants were free men and able freely to alienate their holdings. Here we see how the tenants' obligation to pay tallage is made the point of departure for the lord's attempt at enserfment.[1]

PEASANT ATTEMPTS TO MAINTAIN ANCIENT DEMESNE STATUS

The extension of serfdom among the peasants continued throughout the twelfth and thirteenth centuries, and the

[1] *Pl. Abbr.*, 177 and 150.

extreme vagueness of the line between bond and free status
worked in its favour. The privileged position which had been
enjoyed by the peasants on many royal manors was revoked
when these manors passed into the hands of private lords.
Thus at the end of Henry III's reign the manor of Withcote
in Leicestershire was put in the custody of Peter Neville. He
declared that the tenants of the manor were not the king's
sokemen but villeins, drove them from their homes (*ipsos a
domibus suis eiecit*) and seized their property. Besides this, he
compelled them to bear dues (*consuetudines et servitia*), doubtless
including labour dues which according to custom had not
been borne either by them or their forebears. The jurors
found that these tenants had been the villeins of one Reginald
Norton, and that in King John's time the manor had, through
exchange, come into the king's hands (which meant that it
was not the ancient demesne of the crown). Under the king
they had paid only 4s. a virgate, and tallage when the king
exacted the same from all his manors. But they were not
sokemen, but the king's villeins, and were therefore bound to
bear villeins' dues. Their plea thus failed, but a warning was
issued to Peter Neville that he was not to reduce them to ruin
during the period of his custody.[1]

An analogous case is given in Bracton's Note Book. The
peasants sue their lord for requiring of them 'other dues than
those they are bound to bear and commonly did bear at the
time when the manor was in the hands of the forebears of the
present king' (Henry III). The court found that the plaintiffs
were villeins, and that they had rendered villein obligations and
paid compulsory tallage from as early as the reign of Henry I.
Therefore they were adjured to render villein dues for the future
as well, and the sheriff was ordered to see that they did so.
This case was heard in 1237–38.[2]

In 1279 the men of the manor of Clandon (Surrey) sued their
lord, John Attewater, for requiring of them other dues than
those they had always rendered in other reigns, when the
manor was in the king's hands. But the court found for John,
and an order was given to the sheriff *quod permittat eum distringere
villanos suos ad faciendum ei consuetudines et servicia sibi debita.*[3]

In the same year various tenants of Halvergate and Wick-

[1] *Pl. Abbr.*, 161.   [2] *N.B.*, No. 1230.   [3] *Pl. Abbr.*, 270.

hampton sued Roger Bigod, Earl of Norfolk and Marshall of England, for devastating their homes and felling their woods. Roger declared that this was not the first time they had made complaint against him; they had already lodged a plea that he was demanding of them other dues than those they used to render previously when the manors were in the king's hands. They considered themselves the king's sokemen, but the lord averred that they were no longer such, and the plea failed.[1]

Only a few episodes have survived of this struggle, in which the peasants were defending their ancient rights. Chief among these rights was the fixed nature of their dues. Hence they resisted the lord's attempts to make those dues arbitrary and dependent entirely upon his will. The rule which forbade a villein to sue his lord prevented the majority of these cases from reaching the courts. But in cases where the peasants linked their pleas with pretensions to 'privileged villeinage', i.e. holding on the ancient demesne of the crown, the disputes reach the courts and so were recorded.[2]

Everywhere we find that the case was started because of the increase of rents and services by the lord. Almost always the court takes the lord's side. In 1276 the tenants of the manor of *Suthamton* in Devonshire sued their lord, Richard Pultimor, for increasing their dues, and stated their claim to belong to the ancient demesne. The court decided the case in the lord's favour.[3] In 1277 the tenants of the manor of Headington in Oxfordshire sued Hugh de Plesset for demanding new dues of them, again claiming to belong to the ancient demesne.[4] About the same time a very interesting case took place between the tenants of the manor of Tavistock (Devonshire) and Geoffrey de Caunville, over the same trouble—*quod exigebat alia servicia quam debita*. In this case the manor really did belong to the ancient demesne of the crown. But the court had already twice rejected the plea on the grounds that: (1) In Domesday Book there was no indication that there were sokemen on the manor as well as *servi* and *villani* (a quite fantastic requirement); and (2) the plaintiffs are not the descendants of the original tenants of the manor, but of

---

[1] *Ibid.*
[2] Petrushevsky, *op. cit.* (3rd ed.), 275 sqq.; Vinogradoff, *'Studies'*, (Russian), 98, *Villainage*, 89–126; Pollock and Maitland, i, 378.
[3] *Pl. Abbr.* 190, 211, 212.   [4] *Ibid.*, 267.

newcomers (*adventitii*), as had been established by investigation, and as such they were of servile condition and rendered arbitrary dues (*fuerint servilis condicionis faciendo incerta servicia*). Their holdings were at the lord's will. The first suit had been begun against the previous lord, Henry de Tracy, a long time ago, so that all the judges involved had since died. Now the court, for the third time, rejected the plaintiffs' case and laid it down that their holdings were villein holdings (*quod . . . teneant predicta in predicto manerio per servilia servicia*), although they personally were allowed to be freemen (*salvo statu corporum suorum*) and were given the choice of taking up the holdings or not. In future they were not to lay claim to fixed dues (*certum statum*). Geoffrey obtained a writ to the sheriff instructing him to compel the tenants to render villein and servile dues (*villanas consuetudines et servilia servicia*), whenever they showed resistance (*quociens fuerint rebelles*).[1] In the same year the tenants of the abbot of Reading at Blewbury (Berks.) began a lawsuit against their lord, asserting that they belonged to the ancient demesne of the crown. The court rejected the plea, even without consulting Domesday Book, on the ground of an error in formulation; according to the plaintiffs the manor had belonged to Henry II, but the abbot produced a grant in the name of the Empress Matilda.[2]

In 1280 a long lawsuit was in progress between the tenants of the manor of Steventon, which belonged to the ancient demesne, and the abbot of Bec—again over the demand for new dues (*servicia non consueta*). The jurors made a deposition about the dues, and the tenants were compelled to render them.[3] In a suit of the same kind brought by the tenants of the manor of Havant against the prior of St. Swithun's at Winchester, Domesday Book was consulted; and it was decided that the manor was not the ancient demesne of the crown.[4] In 1281 a court, after consulting Domesday Book, brought in judgment against the tenants of the manor of Cotham in Nottinghamshire. They had claimed to belong to the ancient demesne, but the sheriff was instructed to compel them to render such dues as the lord demanded of them.[5] In the suit of the tenants of the manor of Messing in Essex against the abbot

---

[1] *Pl. Abbr.*, 270–71.   [2] *Ibid.*, 197.   [3] *Ibid.*, 198–99, cf. also 200, 205.
[4] *Ibid.*,185.   [5] *Ibid.*, 201.

of Walthamstow in 1285 recourse to Domesday again showed the incorrectness of the peasants' pretension to belong to the ancient demesne, and they acknowledged themselves the villeins of the abbot.[1]

References in Domesday Book were sometimes deliberately falsified, to the detriment of the peasants. In this connection the case between the abbot of Bec and the tenants of the manor of Ogbourne (Wilts.) in 1277 is interesting. The case was before the court for the second time, and again was decided against the plaintiffs. The abbot asserted that the plaintiffs were his villeins and that he was not obliged to answer. The position in Domesday Book was that two manors appeared with the name 'Okeburn'—one, Ogbourne Regis, belonging to the king, and the other belonging to Miles Crispin. It was decided that the manor in question was the one which had belonged to Miles, which was plainly incorrect.[2] In exactly the same way a case was lost by the tenants of the abbey of Bittlesden at Boycott in Buckinghamshire, in 1277; by the tenants of the manor of Langar in Nottinghamshire in 1279;[3] by the tenants of the manor of Chollington in Sussex in 1344;[4] by the tenants of the prior of Merton at Shellwood (Surrey) in 1317;[5] by the tenants of the manor of South Walsham in Norfolk in 1324;[6] by the tenants of the manor of Bozeat in Northamptonshire, to the abbot of St. James in Northampton, in 1316.[7]

Cases in which tenants were successful are extremely rare, either because their legal position was dubious, or because the court maintained the class interests of the lords. A rare case of a suit not being decided in the lord's favour occurred in 1276, when the tenants of the Wiltshire manor of Allington sued the prior of Farley for demanding new dues. Here the court established that Allington was part of the ancient demesne of the crown, and brought judgment in favour of the tenants. The jurors established a list of customary dues.[8] In rare cases, too, such lawsuits resulted in an agreement between the lords and the tenants.[9] The *Placitorum Abbreviatio* contains

[1] *Ibid.*, 207.   [2] *Ibid.*, 313, 192.   [3] *Ibid.*, 197.   [4] *Ibid.*, 198.
[5] *Ibid.*, 325.   [6] *Ibid.*, 346.   [7] *Ibid.*, 323.   [8] *Ibid.*, 189–90.
[9] For instance, between 15 tenants and the lords of the manor of Sherfield in Hampshire, in 1274 (*ibid.*, 263); and between the lord and the tenants of the manor of Headington in Oxfordshire, in 1277 (*ibid.*, 193).

a number of other suits, brought by tenants against lords who had raised their dues, in which the plaintiffs sought to establish their rights as part of the ancient demesne. Such were the suit of the tenants of the manor of Hayling in Hampshire in 1316;[1] that of the tenants of the manor of Leighton Buzzard in Bedfordshire, in 1290, against the abbess of Fontevrault and the prior of Grove, in which the plaintiffs complained that they were being compelled to render dues other than those rendered in the reigns of Henry II and Richard I;[2] and the suit of the tenants of the manor of Weedon Beck (Northants) against the prior of Ogbourne in 1297.[3]

ATTEMPTED DEFENCE WITHOUT APPEAL TO ANCIENT DEMESNE

In other instances the peasants began their suits without appealing to their right under ancient demesne. Evidently they either did not consider themselves villeins or were naïvely expecting protection of their rights from the king's justices. Vinogradoff cites such a case from the *Placita coram Rege* in 1274–76. The villeins plead that the lord had increased their dues and limited their use of the common lands. They say they are ready to render all dues which were rendered by their forebears, but that the present lord had laid on them intolerable services and customs (*intolerabiles servitutes et consuetudines*). But the lord's declaration that the plaintiffs were his villeins decided the issue.[4] In 1279 the lord of the manor of Garthorpe in Leicestershire, and his wife, were brought before the court by three tenants of that manor, on an accusation of increasing dues. The defendants replied that the persons concerned were their villeins.[5] Pleas of this kind occur in a steady stream throughout the *Placitorum Abbreviatio*,—between the abbot of Titchfield and his tenants in South Titchfield in 1285–86; between the abbess of Tarrant and the tenants of the manor of Hurstbourne in Hampshire in 1297; between Master Ralph Germayne and the tenants of the manor of Bampton in Oxfordshire in 1307.[6] Complaints of increased rents occur in the Hundred Rolls too; thus the jurors noted that on the manor of Draycott in Oxfordshire the villeins were

---

[1] *Pl. Abbr.*, 325.   [2] *Ibid.*, 283.   [3] *Ibid.*, 293.
[4] Vinogradoff, *Villainage*, 46, note 1.   [5] *Pl. Abbr.*, 196.
[6] *Ibid.*, 209, 237, 300, and many others.

bound to pay 8s. per virgate and work 6 days at hay-time and harvest-time, but that these dues had been wrongfully increased by the farmer, John de Tywa, who had held the manor in the time of the present lord's grandfather. The jurors included this complaint in the rolls; a court would have considered it unfounded.[1]

We should remember that we possess only fragmentary evidence of the struggle of the English peasantry for fixed rents. Although he holds that many of the peasants' complaints were exaggerated, Vinogradoff nevertheless admits that they are very inadequately reflected in the sources.[2] With the support of the state, in the person of the judges, the lords were making a concerted attack on the mass of the working people, not merely in theory, but by practical application of the legal doctrine that it was their right to impose rent arbitrarily upon the peasant. It was only very rarely that disputes of this kind reached the courts, and I have here used only a small proportion of the court cases of the period. Nevertheless, the activity of the king's courts must have hastened the reduction to serfdom of the still considerable intermediate groupings of semi-villeins, and finally turned them into villeins without rights in the eyes of the law. With increasing consistency the theory was put into effect that the essence of villein status is complete subordination to the will of the lord, in respect of both dues and rights over the land. And the most important proof of villeinage is the rendering of labour services. The ruling class, with the help of the state, finally reduced to serfdom those sections of the peasantry which were liable to labour rent.

ATTEMPTS TO INCREASE MONEY RENTS

It would, however, be a mistake to think that only labour dues were affected. Although in the majority of cases the legal documents are too summary and formal for us to see the full burden of the peasants' complaints, we can at times define exactly which rents have been raised by the lord, and by how much. Cases of the raising of money rents are not infrequent. For example, in 1242 the tenants of the Staffordshire manor

[1] *R.H.*, ii, 757.   [2] Vinogradoff, *Villainage*, 205.

of Whitmore sued their lord, William le Burgvillain. Appealing
to their right as tenants on the ancient demesne, they asserted
that each virgate was bound to pay only 4s., and bore no
further dues. But the lord of the manor was demanding 12s.
from every virgate, and the payment of tallage, merchet,
heriot and other villein dues besides.[1] In the case mentioned
above when the tenants of the manor of Mears Ashby in
Northamptonshire sued their lady, Sybill Mares, it was for
increasing their tallage from 21d. to 5s. a virgate, whereas
the manor was of the ancient demesne and they held their
land for fixed dues.[1] In 1277 the tenants of the manor of
Pamber in Hampshire, which was considered to be of ancient
demesne, agreed to pay their lord 8s. a year over and above
their former dues.

In the Hundred Rolls we find further cases of the raising
of money rents. Thus, at Draycott (Oxon.) the villeins complained that, whereas formerly each virgate had to pay 8s. and
work 6 days (mowing and reaping), these rents had been
unjustly increased by a farmer. The labour dues remained
the same as before, but the money rent had been increased
to 12s. The money rents of the cottars had also been increased,
and these tenants had been compelled to render 6 days' labour
dues, from which they had previously been free.[3] Usually
it is not the basic element of the money rent, the *redditus
assisae*, which is increased, but such things as tallage and
entry fines. The effort of the lords is to replace fixed payments
by payments 'at will'. In 1276, for example, the tenants of the
manor of Harmondsworth (Midd.) sued the abbot of Holy
Trinity, Rouen, who had imposed tallage at will upon them.
They claimed to belong to the ancient demesne, but the court
gave judgment in favour of the abbot.[4]

The considerable increase in money rents on the manors
of the bishop of Winchester in the thirteenth and at the beginning of the fourteenth centuries was noted by Miss Levett.
The increase was very considerable between 1280 and 1346,
but thereafter they remain static and hardly change at all
until 1455. It would appear that the increase in the *redditus
assisae* was connected chiefly with the intensive drive to bring
the common lands into cultivation, and with the leasing out

[1] *Pl. Abbr.*, 119.   [2] *Ibid.*, 152.   [3] *R.H.*, ii, 757.   [4] *Pl. Abbr.*, 188.

of these to the bishop's tenants. Thus the increase in rent was compensated by additional parcels of land—land which, however, had partly been acquired by robbing the same tenants. But the arbitrary nature of entry-fines, sometimes as high as £6 to £8 for a virgate or even a half-virgate, in practice meant an increase in money rent; cases of high entry charges are not rare even in the thirteenth century, and are still more frequent in the fourteenth.[1]

The same part was played by arbitrary tallage and by the growth of monopoly charges, which were in part levied in money. It was thus possible to raise money rents indirectly without any breach of custom. But we have already noted the lords' attempt to increase *redditus assisae*, which was fixed by custom, and to replace fixed tallage by tallage at will, which undoubtedly was an infringement of custom. The considerable growth of assarts in the thirteenth and fourteenth centuries, which has been noted by all those who have studied this period, contributed mainly to the increase in money rent, since the leasing of these lands to tenants for a money rent was the commonest way of exploiting them.

ATTEMPTS TO INCREASE LABOUR SERVICES

But while money rents were still distinguished by a certain degree of immutability, and represented, so far as the basic *redditus assisae* was concerned, a fixed quantity (*certum, certitudo*), the lord had far greater liberty to make his own dispositions in the case of labour rent. Apart from the fact that many labour dues were 'at the lord's will', the thirteenth century saw an increase even of those labour dues which were fixed by tradition. For a number of manors, even for a number of regions, the thirteenth century is the period of the growth of labour dues, the period of the growth of the classical manor. We find this phenomenon both in backward Northumbria,[2] where during this period the serf-worked manor begins to take shape on the large ecclesiastical estates, and in the advanced districts of East Anglia. The Ely Registers permit us in a number of cases to note the growth of week-works on the

[1] Levett, *O.S.S.L.H.*, v, 43–54.
[2] Jolliffe, *op. cit.* The heavy week-works which arise round Durham are a late phenomenon.

manors of the See of Ely;[1] and Douglas has noted the same phenomenon for East Anglia.[2]

The growth of labour dues is noted by Miss Neilson for the manors of Ramsey Abbey. In 1252 a villein works more days per week than in Henry I's reign. Even more noticeable is the growth of boon-works. In general the system of boon-works, which in the twelfth century is only in its embryonic state, attains its full development in the thirteenth.[3] In the court cases of the period also indications have been preserved of the growth of labour dues; sometimes labour dues are being introduced where they did not exist before, or where they had previously been settled by money payments. In 1207, for example, a suit occurred between the lord of the manor of Heckingham and a tenant. This tenant was one of the *hundredarii*, whose service consisted of attendances at the hundred and county courts and who enjoyed a number of privileges.[4] Yet the lord was now demanding of him one day's ploughing, carrying services to a distance of 16 leagues, villein aid and merchet. The tenant declared that he had always paid only 9*d.* a year, done half the *secta comitatus et hundredi*, and paid 1*d.* when the hundred was assessed at £4.[5] In 1206 William Pinkeney took court action to get from Ralph the Merchant labour dues in the form of three days' ploughing on account of a pasture which the defendant held from him. In the hearing it was brought to light that the demand was unjustified.[6] In this case the plaintiff was trying to fasten labour dues upon a freeholder, which in the future might have provided an excuse for declaring him a villein.

We find some interesting cases in Bracton's Note Book. For example, a group of persons complains that their lord is demanding not only the 10*s.* per virgate which they had hitherto paid *pro omnibus serviciis*, but also labour dues. The tenants considered both themselves and their holdings to be free, while the lord declared they were his villeins.[7] Here the imposition of labour dues is connected with the attempt to reduce free men to serfdom. Even in the Hundred Rolls, where such matters fell outside the scope of the survey, cases occur of

[1] Maitland, *Collected Papers*, ii, 369.   [2] *O.S.S.L.H.*, ix, 112.
[3] Neilson, *Ramsey Abbey Manors*, 50, 51.   [4] Vinogradoff, *Villainage*, 188 sqq.
[5] *Pl. Abbr.*, 57.   [6] *Ibid.*, 53.   [7] *N.B.* No. 1062.

labour dues being increased. Complaints came from the free sokemen of the prior of Ely's manor of Swaffham, that they were being made to harvest half an acre of spring corn[1] 'unjustly', i.e. contrary to custom. In all these cases the complaints are made by men personally free, or else by the privileged section of the villeins. The complaints of ordinary villeins never reached the courts, and the lord's right to increase villeins' labour dues was never in doubt. It is characteristic, in certain of the returns to the Hundred Rolls for Oxfordshire, that the exact amount of labour dues is not given, but that instead they are recorded as being at the lord's will. It would seem that the lords wished to reserve the right to increase labour rent at will, and were, perhaps, nervous of recording any definite amounts in an official document.

In the Hundred Rolls we find cases where the lord converts works with food provided—that is paid or partially paid works—into ordinary unpaid services.[2] This was a means of increasing labour dues without reference to money rent. But we also find cases in which commuted labour dues were restored to their old form. Thus Bracton's Note Book cites the plea of the men of St. Swithun's Priory against an increase in their dues, and reveals that for 40 years, during which the Priory manors were in the hands of farmers, certain dues were commuted. At one time the manors were leased to the peasants themselves, and they took advantage of this to reduce their own rents (*redditus detinuerunt et subtraxerunt*). Now the priory is demanding the restoration of the old dues.[3] Here we see both the gradual slackening of servile restrictions on the peasants on manors not under the direct control of the lord, and the 'feudal reaction' taking place when the lord takes the manors into his own hands again.

Not only the quantity of labour dues increases but also the numbers of holdings owing labour rent. On the manors of Ramsey Abbey Miss Neilson has noted an increase in the land *ad opus* in the thirteenth as compared with the twelfth century, and this increase is often at the expense of the land *ad censum*. At Stukely, in the twelfth century, out of 28 virgates 9 were *ad opus*, in the thirteenth century 12½ out of 26½. At Shillington the number of virgates *ad opus* grew from 32½ to 47, with a

---

[1] *R.H.*, ii, 484.   [2] *R.H.*, ii, 471.   [3] *N.B.* No. 1237.

probable reduction in free holdings or in villein tenements held for rent. At Wistow the land held in return for labour services increased from 27 virgates to 30½, at Broughton from 28 to 30, and at Ellington from 24 to 27½. At Houghton and Witton the area of land paying money rent appears to have decreased by 3 virgates. On other manors we notice some increase in the land *ad censum*, partly as the result of the leasing of parts of the demesne, but partly as the result of commutation. But on the whole the total area of land held for labour rent increases between the twelfth and the thirteenth centuries. The increase in the amount of land held for money rent mainly takes the form of an increase in small holdings, probably the result of the assarting of waste lands. After 1252, however, a slow decrease in land held in return for labour services is observable.[1]

LIMITATIONS ON PEASANTS' RIGHTS OF COMMON

The worsening of the position of the greater part of the peasantry continued. In the thirteenth century, dues increased; in a number of cases labour rent increased. The intermediate sections of the peasantry, and sometimes even freeholders, were reduced to serfdom, and dues fixed by custom were replaced by arbitrary ones. At the same time, the lords made a determined attack on the common lands. The provisions of the Statute of Merton and of the second Statute of Westminster are too well known to need emphasis here. We need only stress the fact that both these statutes were the result of a stubborn struggle between the lords and the tenants, and that in return for making vague concessions to the freeholders, the lords received from the state a confirmation of their right to disregard the interests of the villeins. Indicative of the position is the provision of the second Statute of Westminster, which lays down that if a fence or ditch surrounding waste land which a lord has taken for private use is secretly destroyed, and it is impossible to discover by inquest who has done it, and the inhabitants of the neighbouring villages will not name the offenders, then these villages shall be bound to construct a new fence or ditch at their own expense, and to compensate the victim.

[1] Neilson, *Ramsey Abbey Manors*, 26–28, 68.

The destruction of fences and ditches was, however, not always done in secret. The legal documents of the period continually mention attempts by peasants to defend their rights by force. While free tenants could bring lawsuits against lords who seized their vital common lands, the only course open to villeins was to rebel. In such cases the destruction of fences was almost always the work of a crowd, and a number of persons (*multi*, *plurimi*), sometimes more than a hundred, appear as defendants. Sometimes the tenants attempted to recover their rights by armed force. The pages of the *Placitorum Abbrevatio* are studded with such cases. An ecclesiastical lord sues his tenants in Shropshire for having violently and with the use of arms let their cattle out to pasture on his enclosed pasture ground.[1] More than one hundred men in Yorkshire, declaring that they have common rights there (*debent ibidem communicare*), have trampled an assart (*sartum*) of their lord's.[2] In Northamptonshire several men (*diversi homines*) are accused of having entered on a private pasture belonging to the prior of St. John's Hospital at Brackley, where they laid claim to common pasture rights.[3] A great feudal lord, William de Beauchamp, accuses several persons (*plurimos*) of having entered his rabbit warren at Yardley (Worcs.).[4] Master Henry of Bray and W. Le May sue 21 men for having prevented the tillage (*innokare*) of certain lands, on which the accused claimed common rights (Northants).[5] In Somersetshire the abbot of Flaxley sues 9 men for having pastured their cattle on his enclosed pasture.[6] In Nottinghamshire 16 men have destroyed a ditch, declaring that they have right of common pasture on the land in question.[7] In the same place, on the pretext of common pasture rights, two men have destroyed a fence set up around a wood.[8] In Warwickshire 14 men have destroyed fences and trampled down crops, declaring their rights to common pasture there.[9] In Yorkshire 20 men have felled trees in a wood, appealing to their common rights.[10] In Cumberland 21 men have destroyed a fence set up by the lord round additions to his park.[11] The jurors found against them, holding that they had sufficient common apart from

[1] *Pl. Abbr.*, 180.   [2] *Ibid.*, 196.   [3] *Ibid.*, 197.   [4] *Ibid.*, 197.
[5] *Ibid.*, 202.   [6] *Ibid.*, 202.   [7] *Ibid.*, 216.   [8] *Ibid.*, 217.
[9] *Ibid.*, 218.   [10] *Ibid.*, 218.   [11] *Ibid.*, 223.

this enclosure. In Lincolnshire 20 men have seized 14 acres
of waste land previously in common use which had been
appropriated by the lord of the manor and uprooted the fruit
trees planted there.[1] John Grey accuses 20 men in Buckinghamshire of having destroyed a ditch and felled trees. It
transpired that they had not enjoyed common rights to this
land for years past.[2] A multitude of analogous cases might be
compiled. Eight men felled trees on the new assarts of their
lord (Lincs.); 12 men destroyed a ditch (same county);[3]
10 men trampled an enclosed meadow after first carting away
the hay (Leics.).[4] In Lincolnshire more than 40 men destroyed
a wall which cut across a common road.[5] In Northamptonshire
16 men were summoned for pasturing cattle on an enclosed
pasture; they declared that they had common rights there.[6]
In Derbyshire 8 men were taken to court for felling wood;
they appealed to their common rights (*rationabile estoverium*).[7]
In Nottinghamshire 11 men were sued for having filled in a
ditch on waste land.[8] In Suffolk more than a hundred men
were accused of trampling down an enclosed pasture; they
laid claim to common rights.[9] The abbot of St. Albans
summoned a number of persons (*multos*) who justified themselves by appealing to their common rights, to answer for
having burnt down fences.[10] The abbot of Reading came to
court with a plea that his ditch has been destroyed and assault
and battery committed on his men (Berks.).[11] In Dorset *plurimi*
were summoned for the same offence.[12] All these cases belong
to the reign of Edward I, and more could be cited. But they
represent, of course, only a fragment of what actually occurred,
for cases of this kind rarely got as far as the courts. Damage to
crops is the most frequent offence against the lord's rights
in the rolls of manor courts. These tramplings of crops and
the fines imposed for them are the expression of the stubborn
struggle between lord and peasant over the common lands.

DIFFERING EFFECTS OF COMMUTATION ON THE VARIOUS SECTIONS OF THE PEASANTRY

The lords' desire to increase the returns from their manors
gave rise to an intensification of pressure upon the peasantry.

[1] *Pl. Abbr.*, 257.   [2] *Ibid.*, 258.   [3] *Ibid.*, 259.   [4] *Ibid.*, 259.
[5] *Ibid.*, 259.   [6] *Ibid.*, 260.   [7] *Ibid.*, 260.   [8] *Ibid.*, 261.
[9] *Ibid.*, 281.   [10] *Ibid.*, 282.   [11] *Ibid.*, 287.   [12] *Ibid.*, 296.

On the other hand, the thirteenth and even the twelfth century saw not only the growth of labour dues, but the beginning of commutation—i.e., the substitution of money payments for labour dues—and as a rule this later led to an improvement in the legal position of the peasantry. Alongside the seizure of common lands by the lord there was intensified assarting of waste lands by the peasants, and a considerable part of the lands taken over from pasture and woodland was not exploited directly by the lord, but usually leased out to the peasants in return for a money rent. There is nothing remarkable in this especially when we consider the decisive role played by money rent in medieval England. But it must again be emphasized that not every money rent is the result of commutation, that some money-rents of the thirteenth century may have grown out of the money payments (*gafol*, *gabulum*) which existed even in pre-Norman times, and that many money rents were the result of the commutation not of labour dues but of produce rents. Such dues as aid and tallage were, perhaps, money payments from the start; and the same may be assumed of certain other rents also. Nevertheless it is beyond doubt that a certain proportion of money rents came into being through the commutation of labour dues, and this trend had assumed considerable proportions as early as the twelfth century. Undoubtedly commutation represented an important step towards the weakening of manorial discipline and towards the liberation of the peasantry, but one may have grave doubts whether commutation was always advantageous to the peasantry and whether its development resulted in a lessening of the class struggle in the English countryside.[1]

The stratification of the peasantry had already gone a considerable way when labour (or produce) rents were still predominant. At this time, although the medium-sized peasant holding was the rule, a small upper layer of richer peasants had made its appearance, and as a counterpart a rather more numerous body of poor at the bottom of the scale. The

[1] For the problems of the class struggle in the thirteenth-century English countryside, cf. R. H. Hilton, 'Peasant Movements in England before 1381', *Ec. H. R.*, 2nd ser., ii. Using the court cases and the records of manor courts, the author has shown how important a part was played by the class struggle between the feudal lords and the peasants at a period which has been depicted by many historians as one of 'social peace' and of the 'harmony' of class interests.

subsequent development of money rent caused an intensification of this process of social differentiation.

As Marx has pointed out, one of the necessary conditions
for an increase in the productivity of peasant labour, and hence
for accumulation, was that the peasant should be able to
devote all his labour, in security, to the cultivation of his own
holding. While labour rent presupposed close control by the
lord's official over the economic activity of the peasant, over
the size of his holding, and indirectly therefore over the amount
of his income, money rent gave the peasant economy considerable independence of the lord's control. The productivity of the peasant's labour was further developed as the
market for the produce of peasant holdings extended. This
market made its appearance while natural forms of rent were
still predominant, and led at first to a partial replacement of
natural rent by money rent. As peasant accumulation and
social differentiation developed, so did the conditions under
which some peasants could exploit the labour of others.[1] The
increased prevalence of money rent speeded up the process of
differentiation, just as the predominance of labour rent tended
to keep peasant property at a uniform level. The rich peasants'
surplus, being unconsumed, could be accumulated and used
for extending the scale of his productive activities.

DIFFICULTIES OF THE MIDDLE PEASANT

The payment of money rent was an advantage only to
certain sections of the peasantry. The rich peasant with his
surplus, producing for the market, certainly found it an
advantage. The poor man who paid a small rent and part of
whose income was in money wages did not find it inconvenient.
But the largely self-subsistent peasants who had few links
with the market experienced great hardship in the transition
to money rents.[2] Since the middle peasant had to give up all
his surplus labour as rent, it was easier for him to give it

---

[1] *Capital*, iii, 631 (1909 ed. 924).

[2] Cf. Lenin's analysis of those sections of the Russian peasantry whose income
was mostly in money—those who possessed no horses on the one hand, and on the
other hand those with several; 'both groups live mainly by the sale of commodities, only in the one case the commodity is labour power and in the other it
is produce, grown for sale, considerable use being made of hired labour.'
Development of Capitalism in Russia, ii, s. 12 (summarized in Vol. I of *Selected Works*,
English edition).

in the form of labour than as money. When he had to sell his produce in order to obtain money for rent, he was at the mercy not only of natural fluctuations in the quality of the harvest, but also of fluctuations in prices on the market. In order to pay his rent in time he often had to sell his produce under unfavourable conditions, for without reserves he could not afford to wait for prices to rise. At this period, harvests were very uncertain, but money rent was fixed, not proportionate to the yield of the harvest. Nor can it be assumed that a bad yield on one holding would be compensated by a general rise in prices. And even if as a result of high or low yields all round, the price of grain did fall or rise, the middle peasant had little advantage. In a good year he sold his grain at low prices, but in a bad year his crop would be too small for him to take advantage of the favourable situation. Under these conditions, the rent regularly encroached on the essential product.[1] The need to pay a fixed money rent must often have been a heavy blow for a peasant with no savings. He easily fell a prey to the usurer from the town or to a well-off villager; and under conditions still close to a natural economy, indebtedness often led to virtual slavery.

The holding of the middle peasant, in the era when labour rent was predominant, was usually of a size sufficient only for the application to it of the amount of labour requisite for the subsistence of the peasant family. When labour rent was replaced either by produce rent or money rent, the rent had to be subtracted from a total of produce sufficient only for subsistence. The labour power which had previously gone as labour rent, when now devoted to the peasant holding, could not result in any appreciable increase in the final product of the holding so long as its size remained the same and the traditional techniques of husbandry were unchanged. Holdings which were large enough when the rent for them was given in labour no longer sufficed when money rent was demanded. But the peasant whose holding was larger than was required for subsistence gained when his labour was freed from service on the demesne, especially since it was the small number of rich peasants who took demesne land on lease.

[1] [That is, that part of the holding's total product which was necessary for the subsistence of the peasant family and for carrying on agricultural operations.]

z*

As a producer for the market, the peasant found that the lord took advantage of him not only by demanding rent in money. The lord could still appear as the peasant's competitor on the market, his position strengthened by the exercise of his seigniorial rights. The lords laid tolls on peasant trade as well as restricting it by prohibiting the sale of certain classes of goods and the cultivation of certain marketable crops. The peasant could only take his goods to market after those of the lord had been sent by means of the peasant's own transport. And finally the time at which the money rent itself was required put the peasant at a disadvantage.

However, money rent, in enabling the peasant economy to achieve a certain degree of independence, and in bringing a contractual element into the relations between lords and peasants, aided the emancipation of the serfs. In addition to commuting labour services and produce rents for money, the peasant could also buy his personal freedom. Personal freedom guaranteed the richer peasants against seizure by the lords of land they had acquired and money they had saved, although forced purchases of emancipation could considerably embarrass poorer peasants and bring them into bondage to the usurer. Here again, the buying of freedom could stimulate the process of class differentiation among the peasants.

Emancipation did not bring about the abolition of feudal rent. As the lord's tenant, the peasant was still responsible for the obligations previously attached to the land, and often still owed some labour services and rents in kind as well as money rent. He was no longer legally bound to the land and to his lord, but as he and his heirs were tied to the holding by necessity, feudal rent still lay heavy on him.

The Wage Workers

The village poor, who had been an important reserve of labour when labour rent predominated, continued to play an essential part in feudal production when money rent replaced labour rent. They worked for the richer peasants, as well as for those lords who continued to cultivate their demesne and needed a replacement for commuted labour services. The exploitation of wage labour began within the framework of the feudal mode of production, although this element of the new mode of production was still in its embryonic stage. For the hired labourer was still tied by feudal conditions. He was often unfree, tied to the manor and subject to non-economic compulsion. He also held a small quantity of land, and this holding (for which he paid a rent), being one of the sources of his livelihood, affected the level of his wages. With regard to the lord his position was sometimes that of a feudally dependent peasant, sometimes that of a hired labourer.

The labour legislation of the fourteenth century well illustrates the conflicting feudal and capitalist elements in the countryside. The exploitation of the almost landless peasant as an agricultural worker increased (as we have shown) with the development of money rent. And this brought the new problem of wages to the medieval village. Those lords who had given up the exaction of labour rent but had not yet abandoned demesne production were faced with the problems of the supply of manpower. But there existed certain factors which created favourable market conditions for the workers who supplied the necessary labour power for the demesnes. These factors included the existence of small holdings which partially provided the worker with a livelihood, and of a growing rural home industry producing more and more for the market—all making for local shortages of agricultural labour. Consequently the lords had to resort to compulsion in dealing with these rural semi-proletarians, particularly when wars and epidemics caused acute crises on the labour market. The fall in the supply of workers as a result of the Black Death, and the resulting rise in wages, led to labour legislation by which the landlords aimed at reducing wages and subordinating all the landless and near-landless peasants to their employers.

The Importance of State Power and of Peasant Revolt in the Economic History of the Later Middle Ages

The part played by organized force at the disposal of the feudal state is of great importance in the economic development of this whole period. State power grew as trade increased and as the conflict between classes sharpened. We have already seen that the increasing scope of royal as opposed to seigniorial justice emphasized the cleavage between the free peasants and the unfree majority in affording legal protection only to the former. The lords were enabled, through the state, to acquire rights which restricted peasant access to the commons. State power aided the lords to overcome peasant resistance to rent increases. State taxes—in money—promoted the development of money rent, as the lords, who were often responsible for their collection, were able, in whole or in part, to transform them into feudal rent. On the other hand, the church with its tithes tended to conserve produce rent. It is very difficult to draw the line between state taxes and ecclesiastical dues and rents in the strict sense of the word. Both categories continually merged into one another or had never been completely separated. Nevertheless, payments to state and church must be included in the total burden of rent, especially since, while rent payments to the immediate lord may in some cases have remained static, payments to the governing class as a whole increased with the growth of commodity relationships.

Lastly, a most important factor determining the form of development of feudal rent was the resistance which the demands of the lords met with among the peasants. The fourteenth, fifteenth and sixteenth centuries are the classical period of peasant risings, which previously had been confined to isolated flare-ups. 'Resistance' did not only mean actual risings, but also individual cases of 'trouble', and in general the whole atmosphere of active and passive resistance to the lords' demands. The presence of such resistance in the thirteenth-century village is sufficiently clearly indicated by the court cases which were quoted at the beginning of this chapter. The level of feudal rent is to a large extent the result of the conflict between the demands of the feudal lords, backed up by 'non-economic pressure', and the strength of the peasants' resistance. Peasant resistance also influenced the changes from one form of rent to another.

In spite of social differentiation, the peasantry was still a single class, and the rising of 1381 was a single anti-feudal movement. But differentiation made itself felt and found expression in both the course and in the outcome of the rising, in particular in the two programmes, that of Mile End and that of Smithfield. Of these, the Mile End programme is that of the upper and middle ranks of the peasantry, men who were turning into petty commodity producers. Their demands were the abolition of serfdom, the abolition of the labour-rent system, a low money rent, and freedom for peasant trade. This is a programme for the bourgeois transformation of the village. The Smithfield programme was the programme of the poor peasants. Here the main demands were for the confiscation and division of the lands of the church, the return to the peasants of the common rights that had been usurped, and the abolition of all laws, first and foremost the abolition of the savage legislation against workers. Here broader objectives were included as well—the equality of all estates, which in fact meant the liquidation of the whole political system of feudalism.

The peasant rising of 1381 met with defeat, like all peasant risings in the Middle Ages. But the struggle went on. And if in the course of the late fourteenth and fifteenth centuries the Mile End programme was actually put into force, if villeinage practically disappeared in England, if the system of money rents (fixed at a comparatively low rate) finally triumphed, it was the result of the stubborn struggle of the English peasantry, which had suffered defeat but had not lost the will to resist. Some historians consider the fifteenth century to be the golden age of the English agricultural worker. On many large manors, church and lay, the demesne was abandoned and the lands once usurped from the peasants returned into their hands. But they passed into the hands not of those who lacked land, but of the rich, thus hastening the further differentiation of the peasants. Already the bourgeois transformation of the village was under way; a new grouping of class forces was beginning to take shape there, which would find its full expression in the period of bourgeois revolution in the middle of the seventeenth century.

INDEX

Abingdon Abbey, 105
Acle, Norfolk, 59n, 61, 165, 166
aid, *auxilium*, 54, 166, 176
Akyni, J. de, 148
Alconbury, Hunts., 147, 266
Allington, Wilts., 343
Almer, Dorset, 57n
ancient demesne of the crown, 123,
    150, 337, 339–44
anelepemen, 79
Armingford Hundred, Cambs., 8
* Arundel, John, 14
Ashley, Hants, 54n
Ashley, W., 292n
Aspernil, Margaret, 72, 78
assarts, 36, 72, 184, 203
Atteasse, John le Moyne, 77
Attewater, John, 340
Augustinian Order, estates of, 116, 150
Aungevin, William, 261
Avenel, John, 77
    Richard, 80n
    W., 80n
Aynho, Northants, 188

Baldon St. Laurence, Oxon., 85
Baldwinho, Hunts., 118
Ball, John, 318
Ballard, A., 31, 32, 167, 231
Bampton, Oxon., 17n, 78n
Bampton Hundred, Oxon., 8, 104, 114,
    127, 159, 161, 168, 259, 291n
Bampton Pogeys, Oxon., 75n, 76, 344
Bampton Regis, Oxon., 75n
Banbury, Oxon., 8n
    Castle, 263
Banbury Hundred, Oxon., 8, 104, 114,
    127, 159, 259, 263, 291n
Bardfield, Essex, 190n
Barg, M. A., 149, 311n
Barnwell, Cambs., 8
    Priory, 80n, 82, 105, 106
Barons' Wars, 13
Barrow, Leics., 52n
Barton, Cambs., 82
    Walter, lord of, 82

Bassingbourne, Nicholas of, 14
    Richard of, 81
Battle Abbey, 209n
Beachampstead, Hunts., 261
    Thomas of, 261
Beauchamp, William, 102, 351
Beaufuy, Geoffrey, 261
Bec, Abbot of, 342, 343
Bedford, St. John's Hospital, 114
Bedfordshire, 7, 21, 25, 38, 70, 73, 79,
    81, 84, 93, 99, 102, 113, 114, 117,
    123, 124, 132, 158–9, 181, 186,
    189, 193, 195, 217, 222, 246, 248,
    291, 294
Beetham, Westmorland, 53n, 182
Below, von, G., 74n
Benedictine estates, 112, 116, 129, 147,
    171
Beneit, J. de, 78n
Bennett, H. S., 200n, 230, 236, 298, 299
Bentley, Essex, 52n, 190n
Bereford, Humphrey de, 80n
Berkshire, 128, 129, 181, 186
*Bernewelle, Liber Memorandorum Ecclesie
    de*, 15n, 19, 28, 32, 80n, 82n
Bewmis, Roger, 84
Bicester, Oxon., 107
    Priory, 105
Biddenham, Beds., 83, 114
Binfield Hundred, Oxon., 8
Bircham, Norfolk, 190n
Birling, Kent, 52n
Bishop, T. A. M., 83n, 137
Bishops Itchington, War., 102, 129n,
    130, 161, 170
Bishops Tachbrook, War., 171
Bittlesden, Bucks., 125
    Abbey, 106, 113, 125, 343
Bladon, Oxon., 252
Bletsoe, Beds., 148
Blewbury, Berks., 342
Bliburgh, Suffolk, 289
Bloxham Hundred, Oxon., 8, 127n
Bluntesdene, W., 78
bocland, 279–80
Bonde, Walter, 225–6
boon works, *precariae*, 60, 156